T0333511

ROBERT ICKE: WORKS ONE

Robert Icke

WORKS ONE

methuen | drama

LONDON • NEW YORK • OXFORD • NEW DELHI • SYDNEY

METHUEN DRAMA
Bloomsbury Publishing Plc
50 Bedford Square, London, WC1B 3DP, UK
1385 Broadway, New York, NY 10018, USA
29 Earlsfort Terrace, Dublin 2, Ireland

BLOOMSBURY, METHUEN DRAMA and the Methuen Drama logo are
trademarks of Bloomsbury Publishing Plc

First published by Oberon Books Ltd 2020
This edition published 2023 by Methuen Drama

A catalogue record for this book is available from the British Library.

A catalog record for this book is available from the Library of Congress.

ISBN: PB: 978-1-350-40729-9
ePDF: 978-1-350-40732-9
eBook: 978-1-350-40730-5

Series: Methuen Drama Play Collections

Printed and bound in Great Britain

To find out more about our authors and books visit www.bloomsbury.com and sign up
for our newsletters.

Contents

Introduction

Helen Lewis

Thirty-Three False Starts
after Janet Malcolm

Author's note: in 1994, the journalist and critic Janet Malcolm profiled the collage artist David Salle for the New Yorker. *She delivered a piece comprising 'forty-one false starts', arguing that it was the best way to write about 'his melancholy art of fragments'.*

1.
'You should interview Robert Icke,' my editor said to me. 'He's a genius.'

It was the winter of 2016, and the 30-year-old director had only a handful of professional credits to his name. However, these included an adaptation of Chekhov's *Uncle Vanya* which had bewitched my boss with its heady, drowsy depiction of the sorrows of middle age. Icke was the youngest ever winner of the Olivier Award for best director, which he had earned the previous year by turning the Oresteia trilogy into a single three-hour epic. Now, he was updating Friedrich Schiller's *Mary Stuart*, offering Juliet Stevenson and Lia Williams the chance to alternate playing the murdered queen and the queen who murdered her, with each night's casting dependent on the spin of a coin.

At that point, I liked theatre a reasonable amount. I was wary of punishingly earnest leftwing bromides, and pretentiousness made my teeth itch. Icke apparently shared some of these views, which caught my interest. He had given an interview where he confessed to walking out at the interval 'all the time' – something I had always been too cowardly to do – and decried the tendency of theatre to be politely dull. 'So much of great drama was profoundly troubling when it was first done,' he told the *Evening Standard*. 'The word radical actually means to go back to the root. They rioted at Ibsen's *A Doll's House*, for goodness sake. Audiences shouldn't be allowed to feel nothing.'

Instantly, I was intrigued.

2.

I first met the director Robert Icke in a backroom off the Union Chapel in Islington, north London. It was a Friday afternoon in the early summer of 2017 and he was recalibrating his production of *Hamlet* ahead of its transfer to the West End.

The move meant subtle tweaks to entrances and exits. Exchanging the intimacy of the Almeida for a proscenium arch required the performances to be recalibrated. Another actress would replace Juliet Stevenson as Gertrude halfway through the run. A new Horatio, Marcellus and Guildenstern were needed from the start.

It was an early introduction to the essential fluidity of theatre. There comes a point where the writer, and later the director, has to cede control: to the demands of the space, to the preconceptions of the audience, to the vagaries of missed cues and misplaced props, to sick actors and the tinny insistence of a left-on mobile phone. Theatre is the most human form of drama. It lacks the magic of special effects or the precision of a second take; instead we get to see it develop in real time, like a Polaroid. If a human being can't do it, live and in front of us, it can't be done.

3.

Before reworking the Oresteia, Robert Icke was just another promising unknown. *The Guardian*'s Lyn Gardner had given a warm review to his version of *Romeo and Juliet* for Headlong, and his co-written adaptation of *1984* had received a nationwide tour, helped by the Orwell brand. (Cutely, on a good night the production ran for precisely 101 minutes.)

What stunned the critics about his *Oresteia* was its unapologetic ambition. Reading the reviews now, the common subtext is astonishment at how fully-formed the play was, as if its creator were a grizzled veteran, not some random Cambridge graduate still in his twenties. Under this lay the unspoken assumption that the classics were an old man's game, while anyone that young – particularly if they had been to a (gasp) state school – should be writing angry plays about flatshares, avocados and The Snapchat. At minimum, their work should be 'promising' but dismissable as naive, or overly didactic, or 'unpolished but energetic'. A rising star, yes – but still with a lot to learn. This guy, however, seemed to have hatched from an egg straight into a mature playwright.

4.

In Robert Icke's *Uncle Vanya*, there is no Uncle Vanya. To a Russian-speaking audience, the familiar overtones of a character called Ivan (John) being addressed instead as Vanya (Johnny) would be obvious. To the rest of us, it's meaningless. And so in the Almeida's 2016 production, Paul Rhys's character became . . . Uncle Johnny. 'I had a good fight with an American academic who told me your audience must be morons if they don't realise it's a nickname,' Icke told *The Guardian* at the time. 'Well, I didn't [realise]. So we've changed it.'

Other holy relics ruthlessly discarded from Icke productions include five hours of Schiller's original *Mary Stuart*; rafts of extraneous characters from the first scene of *The Wild Duck* (goodbye, 'pale and fat gentleman'; farewell, 'short-sighted gentleman'); and the samovars and parasols traditionally associated with Chekhov.

These are offset by additions. *The Wild Duck* had a real duck, a gorgeous glossy brown thing which prompted an involuntary 'ahhh' from the audience when it appeared from Hedwig's box, like a magic trick. Icke's version also had a whole meta-narrative, which caused harrumphs about the excesses of 'director's theatre'. *Hamlet* gained video cameras and screens, overseen by Tal Yarden, silently reminding us that royal families have always been surveilled and scrutinised (then: courtiers checking for blood stains on the wedding sheets; now, tabloids taking long lens shots of princesses in swimwear). In the productions where Icke has strayed furthest from his source texts, the additions extend to entire new storylines: Arthur Schnitzler did not give *Professor Bernhardi*'s protagonist a dying partner, nor a teenage protégé(e), as *The Doctor* did to Ruth Wolff.

The effect is of an Old Master being restored: the bad varnish of received wisdom is chipped away, and the original artwork allowed to shine. Or maybe it's more like a reconditioned classic car, with a new engine under the bonnet. Everything down to the fundamentals can be replaced if the essence survives.

5.
Every performance is an adaptation. At the start of the Robert Icke version of *The Wild Duck*, the writer and director has Gregory – Gregers in the Ibsen – tell the audience: 'People say they want to see the real version, true to Ibsen, but that version is in Norwegian – actually, a sort of outdated Danish-Norwegian, so even if we could do it, you very likely wouldn't understand it.'

6.
Here's a thought experiment: imagine you've never seen *Hamlet* before. What would surprise you about it? Perhaps that there are two Hamlets: the old king and his young son. What about Macbeth? Perhaps you'd wonder how Birnam Wood could come to Dunsinane, before the final act solved the riddle. What about *Romeo and Juliet*? Perhaps you would gasp as Mercutio, the charismatic storyteller, dies unexpectedly in Act 3.

Robert Icke uses these examples to explain his theory of adaptation. The point is to strip away both assumed knowledge and the accumulated dust of performance history. He tries to put himself in the place of the original audience. Imagine an episode of *Friends* where Joey dies halfway through, he says—that's how surprising Mercutio's death would have been.

To work like this requires intellectual self-confidence. After all, everyone knows the plots in Shakespeare, don't they? Except... they don't. And Shakespeare belongs to them just as much as the people mentally measuring up this Hamlet against Jonathan Pryce and Kenneth Branagh. To successfully adapt a classic play, you have to forget that it is a classic, and think instead about why it became a classic. Forget the reverence: every performance is an adaptation.

7.

'You should interview Robert Icke,' my editor said to me. 'He's a genius.'

I did a cursory Google: he was the youngest ever winner of the Olivier Award for best director. He was 30. He had been to Cambridge. Everyone agreed with my boss: he really was a genius.

Instantly, I hated him.

8.

In the works of the writer and director Robert Icke, language often runs ahead of conscious thought. In *The Wild Duck,* James – who will later be driven to distraction by the possibility that his wife has cheated on him – starts off by laughing at her malapropisms. 'Cuckoo! cocoon! cuckold! my wife, and the perils of language!'

The idea finds its fullest expression in *The Doctor,* which is studded with clues to its final destination. 'It's not over until there's a body,' Dr Ruth Wolff says early on, laying out her medical philosophy. She's right: except this time the body will be hers. She will have to 'swallow some pills', says the careerist politician who lets her down, meaning 'eat some humble pie'.

Ruth takes that advice rather more literally. In a play about a witch hunt, the very first word is 'which?'.

Sometimes, though, the words are chosen for their musicality as much as their meaning. In *Oresteia*, Menelaus tries to reconcile Agamemnon to killing his own daughter. Left alive, Iphigenia would 'just become an adult. Like me. Flawed and sweaty and fundamentally sad.' In *Mary Stuart*, the doomed queen is consoled over her fatal obsession with Darnley, in a sentence that ends with thumping, definitive monosyllables: 'Falling in love's a madness with no cure but time.'

The aim is heightened naturalism, poetry which doesn't draw attention to itself. The first time I saw Mary Stuart, I didn't realise that it was written in blank verse – iambic pentameter, Shakespeare's favourite. I don't feel bad about my obliviousness, because Icke would undoubtedly take it as a compliment.

9.

Robert Icke has many strong opinions. You can change a lot of things in Chekhov's *Three Sisters*, but Andrei should be fat, he insists: his first appearance then offsets the heroic picture painted by Olga, Maria and Irina. The writer and director has little respect for the cherished theatrical attachment to 'projection', preferring the naturalism of mics to the 'Gielgud boom'. Dialogue does not have to be colloquial, but it should be spoken as though it is. (When rehearsing *Hamlet*, the company had a bell to ring if anyone started doing their Important Shakespeare Voice.)

All of these questions go to the heart of what adaptation means, and what liberties it can take. Deciding, instance by instance, whether theatrical tradition provides useful handrails – or prison bars.

10.

'The Deadly Theatre approaches the classics from the viewpoint that somewhere, someone has found out and defined how the play should be done,' writes the director Peter Brook in *The Empty Space*. 'Living theatre . . . is always a self-destructive art, and it is always written on the wind.' From the day a production is finished, Brook believed, 'something invisible is beginning to die... in the theatre, every form once born is mortal, every form must be reconceived, and its new conception will bear the marks of all the influences which surround it.'

11.

To this day, it bothers me that I never got the introduction right when I wrote my profile of the director Robert Icke. With most articles, I would forget and move on, but Icke – Rob – and I stayed in touch, alternating between intense discussions of dramaturgy and arguing over period drama and Jordan Peterson. As our relationship changed, I decided I couldn't review his plays anymore. I glumly resigned myself to one day being asked to edit *The Cambridge Companion to Robert Icke*.

Our friendship has given me something most critics would kill for: direct access to the process of creation. (Janet Malcolm had to resort to looking for traces of Chekhov in modern Russia; if only she'd been able to ping him a WhatsApp.) Here is why *The Doctor* has an interval (he tried it without, didn't work). Here is why a new storyline involving a teenager called Sami was added (Rob saw Ria Zmitrowicz in *Three Sisters*, and wanted to write a part just for her). Here is why the play exists at all (he wanted to work with Juliet Stevenson again, and the canon has pitifully few star roles for women over 50). I have seen what few critics, reviewing the glossy shell of the finished product, get to see. I've seen the creative exchange between writer and performer, and how the right person can create meaning far beyond the words on the page. I've learned that underneath the polished surface is layer upon layer of finely balanced decisions, compacted by time and pressure.

12.

Robert Icke's theatrical career began at school. As a geeky teenager in a comprehensive in the north-east of England, pranking the teachers was the best way to avoid being gaffer-taped to a tree. He would instruct his fellow pupils to move their desks forward imperceptibly, millimetre by millimetre. They would ask questions which made no sense. At the end of one term, he staged a brutal parody of the headmaster.

If it sounds cruel, it was. The 33-year-old's code of ethics comes not from Confucius or Christianity, but Roald Dahl. It distinguishes him in the sometimes cloying world of London theatre – where the jealousy, competitiveness and schadenfreude which flourish in any tight-knit community are often smothered under thick layers of syrup. He is an instinctive contrarian, a writer who needs something to be against: reverence, hypocrisy, mediocrity, authority figures. Traces of the teenager who looked at all his classmates drinking cider and vowed never to touch alcohol are still discernible in everything he does. 'The reasonable man adapts himself to the world: the unreasonable one persists in trying to adapt the world to himself,' wrote George Bernard Shaw in *Man and Superman*. 'Therefore all progress depends on the unreasonable man.'

13.

The productions of the director Robert Icke have a distinct visual style, thanks to his repeated collaboration with the designer Hildegard Bechtler. She once told me, with German frankness, that work for small theatres 'doesn't pay'; what kept her coming back was the quality of the texts.

Bechtler's aesthetic is cool and clinical. It is full of right angles, free from clutter. For *Hamlet*, *Oresteia* and *Oedipus*, she used a material I call 'Hildeglass', which flicks from transparent to opaque in a split second. This gives stage productions a filmic quality, allowing something close to a jump cut, as action behind the glass is suddenly revealed. It can create cross-cuts, too, as action happens simultaneously on two planes, with the emphasis alternating between them. And it gives Icke's productions one of their most consistent emotional notes, of lead characters trapped outside a party, condemned to think while everyone else just lives.

14.

'I had to do an interview a while back,' the director Robert Icke said during a talk with the actor Andrew Scott, one summer evening at the Harold Pinter Theatre in London. 'Andrew read it and said that he could get more out of me in ten short-answer questions than the interviewer had got out of me in, what, like, six pages.'

They were talking about me; about the profile I had written. It made me feel–

15.

adaptation (n)

A film, television drama, or stage play that has been adapted from a written work.

A form or structure modified to fit a changed environment.

The process of change by which an organism or species becomes better suited to its environment.

16.

If there is anything I have learned from the writer and director Robert Icke, it's that the medium is the message. A play about identity should play with identity. A play about the truth should question whether what we are seeing is the truth. A play about justice should ask us to judge.

Form and content are two sides of the same coin, just like the two queens in his adaptation of Schiller's *Mary Stuart*. The play begins with the company walking on stage, and Juliet Stevenson and Lia Williams dressed identically, in black trousers and white shirts. A courtier spins a coin, with its slow revolutions captured on an overhead camera. (In the West End, the coin-toss was projected not just into the theatre, but the foyer outside. Icke had wanted anyone walking past to be able to see the outcome, in a small, democratising gesture.) Whoever calls the coin toss right is Elizabeth I, all-powerful Gloriana: the company turns and bows to her. The loser becomes Mary, Queen of Scots, destined for capture, imprisonment and death.

That opening highlighted the arbitrary nature of fate, and the kinship between two women in a man's world. It also had a purely theatrical element, turning the play into a demonstration of virtuosity. Both Lia Williams and Juliet Stevenson had to learn two lead roles in a ferociously verbal drama. (They had more lines than Hamlet.) The rest of the company, meanwhile, rehearsed each scene twice, and never knew which reactions would be needed. The high-wire uncertainty removed the deadening hand of perfection from the performance – the sense that you're getting a theatrical McDonalds, made to a fixed recipe designed for scale. Here, instead, was a complicated meal being cooked in front of you.

Icke also foregrounded the act of theatre in *The Wild Duck*, which started with an empty stage. Gregory (Gregers in the Ibsen) walked on, wearing rehearsal clothes, and told the audience to switch off their phones. Icke's version is full of these addresses, delivered through a microphone, constantly undercutting what we see on stage: Ibsen himself had an illegitimate child, we are told, but unlike Charles Woods, he did the absolute minimum he could to support him. Once the boy was old enough – Hedwig's age – the playwright cut her off. Ibsen's text can be read as an excuse, or a confession, or a cover-up.

The Wild Duck is a play obsessed with truth. Is James (Hjalmar) better off not knowing about Hedwig's parentage? Are all of us happier, as Relling suggests, with a 'life-lie' to make our existence bearable? And so Icke put storytelling itself on trial. The handheld microphones and direct address forced the audience to confront the fact that theatre bends the truth, adapting messy reality to something neater, cleaner.

That suspicion of storytelling is a motif of Icke's work. In the words of Orestes: 'There isn't one true version. There isn't. There isn't one story—a line of truth that stretches start to end. That doesn't happen any more, maybe it never happened, but even as I say this now, as I say this now, in each of your minds you create your own versions, different lenses pointing at the same thing at the same time and seeing that thing differently…'

17.

In the loo queue at the Almeida on press night of Robert Icke's play *The Doctor*, I heard a famous actor say: 'It's a lot, isn't it?' Well, why wouldn't it be? Who writes a play hoping it will only be a little?

18.

'I find period dress as an aesthetic choice to be like a political choice – lazy and safe,' the director Robert Icke told me the first time we met. He believed that corsets and codpieces encouraged a nostalgic vision of the past: 'You know, it was safer then and there were no brown people to fuck things up'. His Agamemnon dressed like a modern politician, as did his Claudius, with the austere figure of Angus Wright playing both in dark suits and white shirts.

His frequent collaborator Hildegard Bechtler favours an aggressively neutral palette – grey, navy, khaki, beige – and the company's clothes are often almost interchangeable. That minimalism has the unexpected effect of creating more capacity for meaning, not less. The occasional deviations, the small details, stand out. *The Doctor* begins with the company putting on their identities: stethoscopes, clipboards, lanyards.

In *Oresteia*, Agamemnon, Klytemnestra and Orestes – three killers – wear flashes of red against the monochrome palette. The couple's young daughter Iphigenia, who is sacrificed to win the war, wears a yellow dress. That colour becomes her signifier, as she wanders ghost-like through later scenes. The tortured, prophetic Cassandra, whom the stage directions tell us should be 'reminiscent somehow of Iphigenia', wears yellow too. The echo highlights the full horror of Agamemnon's decision to bring his sex-slave home from the war, and sit her at the family dinner table. He is haunted by girls in yellow dresses.

Bechtler also clothed the Tudor court of *Mary Stuart* in business-casual. The queens looked alike throughout, until their fates (and costumes) diverged in the final act. Mary was stripped to a plain white shift, surrounded by her waiting women, renouncing the world, at peace: her death was also a kind of liberation. Elizabeth's burden got heavier. She stood still while attendants loaded on a farthingale, corset and white face paint – a rig which snuffs out any chance of spontaneity or intimacy. The powerful, flirtatious queen was revealed as a fundamentally lonely figure, an icon from whom everyone else had to keep their distance. Elizabeth the Queen was a more powerful image because it was withheld from us for so long.

19.
Robert Icke has never watched a whole episode of *Friends*. He has never seen *Star Wars*. He has never seen *Back to The Future*. It sometimes feels like he has read every play ever written. I suppose this is how he had the time.

20.
When *Mary Stuart* first played at the Almeida theatre in north London, the contest for the Conservative leadership had recently narrowed to an all-female final round. Andrea Leadsom, a mother – she was proud of this – was pitted against the childless

Theresa May. It gave an extra resonance to the play's mirror-monarchs, Mary and Elizabeth.

It took that production nearly a year to make it to the West End, by which time Leadsom was a pub quiz answer and May a rusted Iron Lady. Instead, the audience brought into the theatre their frustrations with Brexit, sighing over the lines which evoked a divided nation – and how a single moment could send a country down two different paths. Then again, what else would we expect? Every performance is an adaptation.

21.

Here is a short list of the places I have waited for the director Robert Icke. On Upper Street, after rehearsals for *Mary Stuart*. Outside the theatre, after a preview performance of the same. In a cake shop. In a branch of Côte restaurant, nursing a Diet Coke while receiving increasingly apologetic text messages from a stationary taxi. At a steakhouse in Borough Market, receiving increasingly apologetic text messages from a stationary Tube carriage. Last summer, he finally entered a restaurant seconds before me, and turned round at the counter, flushed with triumph. 'I saw you outside, so I knew I could beat you for once,' he said.

No wonder his plays are so long, I always find myself thinking. The man has no concept of time.

22.

Men have a way of becoming women in the plays of Robert Icke. In *Hamlet*, his Guildenstern was female (adding further depth, she was the prince's former girlfriend and Rosencrantz's current one). In *Mary Stuart*, the Catholic priest who takes Mary's confession is, heretically, a woman. Arthur Schnitzler's Professor Bernhardi becomes Icke's Dr Ruth Wolff. The play's career-oriented politician is a woman, and Ruth's partner might be too. We are never told.

For anyone adapting the theatrical canon, its missing women present an unavoidable challenge. Leaving the text untouched would privilege male voices, male relationships, male perspectives – and opportunities for male actors. Instead, in Icke's work, women always have a chance to hold the stage, from Lia Williams's howl of anguish as Klytemnestra to Jessica Brown Findlay's Sonya, revealed as the crux of Uncle Vanya (he is her uncle, after all, suggesting the action should be seen from her point of view). Adding more women to the mix seems natural.

Klytemnestra comes closest to voicing the politics behind this, when she challenges the punishment for killing her husband. 'Allow me to ask the house: why does the murder of the mother count for less than that of the father? Because the woman is less important. Why is the mother's motive for revenge lesser than the son's? She avenged a daughter; he a father. Because the woman is less important. This woman has paid the price. But this house cannot be a place where the woman is less important.'

That's why the canon needs adaptation. The theatre – this house – cannot be a place where the woman is less important.

23.

Here's one thing you'll never hear in a play by Robert Icke: a brand name. The 33-year-old is allergic to them, reasoning that nothing dates as fast as the present. His characters do not visit Nando's, get an Uber, or watch *Game of Thrones*. In *The Doctor*, a play which deals with the mobbing effect of social media, the words 'Facebook' and 'Twitter' – never mind 'Snapchat' or 'TikTok' – do not appear. The closest we get is Ruth Wolff's observation that she is 'trending'.

It is partly a rejection of easy laughs: the ironic distance between Shakespeare's time and the world of peri-peri chicken can furnish a solid joke, but it comes at the expense of the play-world's integrity. Many of Icke's productions have a dreamlike quality, where very little feels fixed and substantial. The lack of proper nouns encourages this mood, lending his adaptations a kind of timeless modernity; a review once described them as poised 'between yesterday and today'.

24.

There's a guy on the internet who makes playlists of the music from Robert Icke's adaptations. You can see why. In *Oresteia*, Agamemnon sacrifices his daughter Iphigenia to the Beach Boys' 'God Only Knows', one of the most passive-aggressive love songs ever written. In *The Wild Duck*, the Ekdals happily lip-sync to the Brazilian pop song 'Aguas Di Marco', about the rains marking the end of summer. (It sounds joyful but it's secretly an elegy, and the Ekdals will need one of those quite soon.) *Hamlet* is stuffed full of Bob Dylan songs, in homage to the Belgian director Ivo Van Hove's own Shakespeare megamix, *Roman Tragedies*. Icke also has a longstanding collaboration with the singer-songwriter Laura Marling (who suggested 'Aguas Di Marco' to him). She wrote a song for the end of *Mary Stuart*, as the queens are dressed and undressed, ready for death or glory, and came up with original compositions for Ophelia in *Hamlet*. The music is deliberately . . . not unfashionable, but not fashionable either. Nothing too modern, nothing too old, like the plays themselves.

25.

'I'm wondering if I should cast everyone else AGAINST identity type,' the writer and director Robert Icke messaged me in March 2019. He had been mulling over his final production at the Almeida in the summer, and had settled on a 'weird old Schnitzler play' called *Professor Bernhardi*. I couldn't imagine what he saw in it. The premise of a girl dying of a septic abortion interested me, having covered Ireland's Repeal the Eighth referendum the previous year, but the rest seemed to be interchangeable doctors having tedious Shavian discussions in early twentieth century Austria. Rob, as usual, had found the kernel of the drama; what he called the 'identity politics explosion' which follows the Jewish doctor's sacking for not allowing a Catholic priest to visit the dying girl.

The original version asked if the witch-hunt against the doctor was driven by anti-semitism, and showed how the Catholic establishment closed ranks against Bernhardi. The new version stacks up identity questions into a Jenga tower: what if the priest is black and the doctor calls him 'uppity'? What if the doctor were a woman? What forms does anti-semitism take in the twenty-first century, given the existence of the Holocaust?

The political left has developed a theory of oppression where 'punching up' is forgivable, even praiseworthy – where you can 'milkshake' Nigel Farage, as a white straight male rightwing politician, even while telling your children that physical violence is reprehensible. It has shades of Marxism (everything is about power relations), shades of postmodernism (language creates reality), and shades of the Inquisition (self-righteousness allows you to revel in sadism). Casting against identity type short-circuits the easy arbitration of right and wrong. It forces the audience to replay what they've seen once they realise – oh, that white actor is playing a black man; wait, if she's not Jewish, can she say that? The effect is a sharp rebuke to those who blithely claim they 'don't see race' and even a sharper one to those who judge everything through the prism of identity.

The update also asked: who is the establishment these days, anyway? A government can fear a mob, even when that mob is a few hundred anonymous Twitter accounts and the viewers of a manipulative television show. Identity is diffuse. Power is diffuse. Sometimes punching is just punching. The old certainties have mutated into something much more multifaceted. In *The Doctor*, Arthur Schnitzler's stark binary – Catholic vs Jew – becomes shattered, prismatic. The world of yesterday speaks to the world of today.

26.

'I suggested he change some of my speech,' the actor Ria Zmitrowicz told me in the bar of the Almeida theatre in north London in August 2019. In the course of researching her character in *The Doctor*, the transgender teenager Sami, she had found a blog by a young non-binary person, which expressed their absolute need to be accepted for who they were. She had duly relayed this information to *The Doctor*'s writer and director, Robert Icke.

During the show's preview period, there were whispers on Twitter and theatre blogs that it was being 'heavily rewritten', as if this suggested some deficiency. The opposite was true. The text on the page, beautiful but inert, was crawling into the light, gasping for its first breaths, drawing on the bodies and minds of its actors to give it life, becoming *this* version for *this* moment in *these* mouths, to be spoken aloud and then vanish into air.

27.

'We have a really weird attitude to the word adaptation in this country and this theatre culture, which I find quite funny,' the writer Robert Icke told an audience after a performance of his version of Schiller's *Mary Stuart*. 'We always cut and change Shakespeare, and yet we pretend that there's such a thing as authentic, 'full text' Shakespeare. So many of the plays that we think of as single-authored plays are adaptations: all of Shakespeare, all of the Greek tragedies, are adaptations by our modern definition.'

28.

After watching the second preview performance of *The Doctor*, I was quietly alarmed. There was something . . . wrong. Perhaps it was the loudness of the persistent drumbeat which underlay the scenes. Perhaps it was the clumsy pauses and overtalk of a cast still settling into the fast rhythm of the dialogue. Perhaps it was the way in which the three interlacing storylines felt jagged and disconnected.

Two vital scenes – where Ruth Wolff physically bars the priest from the dying girl's room, and where the dead girl's raging, grieving father later assaults her – felt too overt. The audience could see exactly what happened, so there was no dispute; the characters might tell us they remembered it differently, but the evidence of our own eyes provided a definitive version. The play lacked the fluidity it needed to keep all possibilities open, to deny us easy heroes and villains. The text could not provide the answers; it was the staging which needed to adapt. By press night, both incidents had changed. They were rendered in freeze-frame, with flickering lights: we saw the moment before, and the one after, with the gap left to be filled in our own minds, by competing truths.

How Rob found the way to stage those moments I will never know; it left me feeling that what a great director does is indistinguishable from magic. Anyone could have identified the problem with those scenes. But I still don't understand how anyone could have found the solution.

29.

> '*Writing about music is like dancing about architecture.*'
> –attribution disputed

Writing about theatre is clumsy. You are trying to capture something shifting, mutating from night to night, a unique encounter between actors and audience. Every performance is an adaptation.

It bothers me how little of that texture I can capture in a review. The teenagers who sat next to me at *Hamlet*, vibrating with excitement at the prospect of four hours of Shakespeare. The moment in *The Wild Duck* where the audience thought, just for a minute, that it was one of them audibly scoffing – *Ha!* –

at James mispronouncing the name of the fancy French wine (what a *prick*). Their relief at the realisation it was the character Charles, planted in the crowd before they arrived, when the actor picked up his chair and walked on stage. The time when 'God Only Knows', deconstructed into parts by sound designer Tom Gibbons for *Oresteia*, is finally heard in full, feeling as inevitable as tragedy itself. The tableau of Juliet Stevenson's Ruth Wolff, bathed in a shaft of cathedral light, alone on stage during the interval of *The Doctor*, like a sentry, or a penitent. The actor who stumbled on press night, which went unmentioned in any reviews, because – well, these things happen. (I later discovered that the stumble was an accident in previews that became a deliberate part of the staging; it is a play about forgetting, after all. *Goddammit*, I thought. *How long has it been and I still think I can trust the evidence of my eyes when watching a play?*)

What the texts in this book can't capture are the perfect, serendipitous moments that come from performance. They are only blueprints. At least one, *Oresteia*, is now being regularly performed around the world, from Japan to Israel. New directors, new actors and audiences are creating their own versions, the same but different.

30.

After watching the second preview performance of *The Doctor*, I was quietly alarmed. If it flopped – or even failed to reach the full five stars – then Rob's own story would change. All artists are stalked by a parallel version of themselves, woven out of gossip and reputation and 'critical consensus'. Rob had attracted a set of nouns – iconoclast, *enfant terrible*, boy wonder – which are impossible to sustain. A certain weariness had crept into some of the reviews for *Hamlet* and *The Wild Duck*: yes, he's done it again. After all that praise, an absolute howler, a humbling flop, seemed in order. The narrative arc demanded it.

I expressed this anxiety to him. Wasn't it slightly mad to adapt a weird old play, use it to say provocative things about race and gender, and cast it so that it deliberately confused the audience? He was, as ever, unmoved. The play was the play. It could only be what it was.

The reviews came in. Five stars. Five stars. Five stars. It was another lesson about the nature of adaptation: you can't astonish people by giving them what they think they want.

31.

'I had to do an interview a while back,' the director Robert Icke said during a talk with the actor Andrew Scott, one summer evening at the Harold Pinter Theatre in London. 'Andrew read it and said that he could get more out of me in ten short-answer questions than the interviewer had got out of me in, what, like, six pages.'

They were talking about me. No reviewer expects to be reviewed in turn, and the verdict landed on me like a punch. 'Every journalist who is not too stupid or too full of himself to notice what is going on knows that what he does is morally indefensible,' writes Janet Malcolm in *The Journalist and The Murderer*. 'He is a kind of confidence man, preying on people's vanity, ignorance, or loneliness, gaining their trust and betraying them without remorse.'

An interview is an adaptation, just as much as any new version of Chekhov. Journalists and artists take the messy stuff of life, the infinite chaos of a real human mind, and flatten it into the finite world of words. We both try to cling to the essence of the truth – the animating spark that motivates the story, makes it worth telling – and we resist, to different degrees, the subtle manipulations that hammer down existence into prose. Why should Rob have liked the portrait I drew of him after a single meeting? It was no more him than his footprint, or his favourite song, or his most embarrassing memory. It was a story. We are not our worst impulses, our deepest desires, our moments of hubris, and yet these are the slices of humanity captured by journalism and drama.

Perhaps there is a more honest way to write – by admitting my artifice, my ambivalence, my adaptations.

32.

In September 2019, twenty-five months after meeting Robert Icke, he sent me a series of messages.

> Oh btw my publisher is going to do collected
> adaptations to coincide with Dr West End and I've said
> I want you to do intro
> It's Oresteia, Vanya, Mary S, Wild Duck, Doctor
> all in one big selection box
> like a multi cereal pack

How the hell can I do that, I wondered. I'll have to call him 'Robert Icke', and that will just sound unnatural and constipated. Can I mention how weird it is that he's never watched *Friends*? Can I talk about how I was predisposed to hate him? Can I do justice to him? Can I capture how much richer my life has been because I've spent years watching his work – and watching him work?

God, though. It really is odd that he hasn't watched *Friends*.

33.

Sometimes I feel as though I know a dozen Robert Ickes. It is hard to reconcile the man who can write pitch-perfect blank verse with the one who plays *The Witcher* and bakes a show-stopping pavlova. The perfectionist who pores over texts with the man who can forget what time I booked lunch. The genius and the geek. As Copley says in *The Doctor*, all attempts to categorise people – to reduce them to this or this – are doomed to failure, because 'there is no human being on this earth that does not defy that sort of simplistic bullshit with their technicolour, thousandfold complexity'.

All the best plays have this quality, too. Shakespeare's genius is his ambiguity, his possibility, his depth. Gertrude slept with Claudius before her husband died. No, she didn't. The ghost is real. No, it's not. Hamlet is really mad. No, he's pretending. OK, now he's really mad. Is he?

The best dramatists give us plays where all of these things are true, and none of them are. Works that can bear this galaxy of interpretations, that can adapt – those are the works which survive. Like a living, breathing person, they contain multitudes.

Helen Lewis is a staff writer at *The Atlantic* and the author of *Difficult Women: A History of Feminism in 11 Fights*.

ORESTEIA

Acknowledgements

I am indebted to a whole host of generous people
who read drafts, watched run-throughs, commented,
interrogated, supported, and generally suggested ways
to make things better. First and foremost: the company
of the first production; the actors who participated in
various development readings; and, in alphabetical
order, Anthony Almeida, Liz Eddy, Simon Goldhill,
Rupert Goold, Robin Grey, Rebecca Hill, Dan Hutton,
Zoe Johnson, Duncan Macmillan, Ben Power,
Duška Radosavljević, Daniel Raggett, Moses Rose,
Zara Tempest-Walters and Anne Washburn.
Thank you all.

Introduction

What was Greek tragedy for? What was its function in the society in which it first developed?

One fundamental answer to these questions is that tragedy rewrote the inherited myths of ancient Athens for the new democratic city – and performed them before the assembled citizens. Tragic drama produced a new and challenging repertoire of stories for the city to explore what civic life now meant.

By the fifth century B.C.E., the era when all our surviving tragedies were written and produced in Athens, the poems of Homer had been sung for three hundred years across all of Greece. The Iliad, the Odyssey and the other tales of the sack of Troy and the return of the Greek heroes, provided the foundation of the history of Greece and, above all, the images and stories by which people made sense of the world. It was Homer that was taught throughout schools, Homer that was sung at festivals, Homer that was learnt off by heart by keen culture buffs as well as by professional performers, Homer who was quoted as The Authority. Homer made up the furniture of the Greek mind.

The first word of Homer's Odyssey is 'andra', 'man', and since antiquity this great epic has been seen not just as the adventures of one tricky man, Odysseus on his way home from Troy, but also as an exploration of what it is to be a male adult in society. It offers a vivid and engaging story of what it means to care for a family, to struggle for a home, to find a place as a man among other men. In this epic, the story of Orestes is told more than eleven times. Again and again, it repeats the tale of how Agamemnon came home and was murdered by the usurper, Aegisthus, and how Agamemnon's son, Orestes, then killed Aegisthus and took back control of his household. Each time the story is told, it is offered as an example of how things can go wrong in a house – adultery, murder, disorder – and how things can be put right by a young man doing his duty. Telemachus, the son of Odysseus, is told by princes, kings and gods to 'be like Orestes'. Orestes is the exemplary hero for the young man trying to find out what it means to be a man.

Aeschylus' great trilogy, the *Oresteia*, retells this story. It stages the return of Agamemnon, his murder, and the revenge Orestes takes on his murderers. But it tells the story in a new and profoundly troubling way.

First of all, it takes a great silence in Homer and makes it scream. In Homer, Orestes can be a great and exemplary hero for young men to learn about masculine values, because he takes charge of his own house – and because the death of Klytemnestra is barely mentioned. He comes back and kills the usurper, Aegisthus. Klytemnestra in Homer disappears without any description of how she died. In Aeschylus, in the central play of the trilogy, centre stage, mother and son come face to face. Klytemnestra bares her breast and demands pity; Orestes stops dead, and, in the archetypal tragic question, asks in anguish: 'What should I do? Should I respect my mother and not kill her?' What was repressed in Homer, becomes the dramatic turning point of Aeschylus' drama. In the same way, the sacrifice of Iphigenia by her father, Agamemnon, a story not mentioned in Homer but well-known to its fifth-century audience, becomes the trilogy's foundational act of violence. In the *Oresteia,* the exemplary hero has become the exemplary matricide. After Aeschylus, no-one ever again could simply say 'Be like Orestes, my son….'. The paradigm has become a problem.

The new problem, however, also needs a new solution. In Homer the solution to the problems was simple enough: if the household is properly organized with the right man firmly in control everything in society will function smoothly. In Aeschylus' world, this is no longer adequate. The family needs the state. There can be no answer for Orestes until he goes to Athens itself and inaugurates the legal system. Now the democratic city is the framework which makes sense of what it is to be a man.

So the *Oresteia* is a perfect instance of how tragedy rewrites the stories of the past as a story for and as a challenge to the democratic city and its values. What should the city do with a man who has killed his mother or a man who has killed his daughter? What is the place of violence and revenge in society? Can law provide the answer? What does justify violence in a community? How does one family's strife relate to social order? It is no surprise that this masterpiece of theatre has been produced again and again across the world at time of intense social disquiet as a way of publicly exploring the most pressing questions of justice in society.

The fact that Aeschylus himself was redrafting the old and privileged stories to talk directly to new and insistent politics demands that each new version of his masterpiece speaks to its own modern condition, if it is be true to the spirit of Aeschylus. This translation and performance does just that – with immense verve and intellectual brilliance. Take the transition from the second to the third play of the trilogy. At the end of the *Libation Bearers*, Orestes who has killed his mother goes mad and the symptom of his madness is that he – and he alone – can see the Furies of his mother pursuing him. He rushes offstage in despair pursued by these imagined horrors. At the beginning of the third play, however, the Furies not only come onstage and are visible to everyone, but make up the chorus of the drama and speak in the courtroom against Apollo. How can we deal – dramatically or conceptually – with this shift of perceived actuality, where the signs of madness become the real on stage? In this version, the shift itself becomes fully part of the psychological deformations of violence, revenge and remorse. This version recognizes the dynamic of the Aeschylean model and restages it in a powerfully contemporary form.

So, too, the recognition scene where Electra decides Orestes has finally returned home by comparing her foot to a footprint he has left, and her hair to a lock of his hair left on the tomb of their father, has troubled literal minded critics since antiquity – and the great tragic playwright Euripides was already the first to parody it on stage. Here it becomes part of a complex web of feelings, imaginary projections, memories and interfamilial distortions between brother and sister in a profoundly dysfunctional family.

It is central to Aeschylus' play first that Athene establishes the court to decide about his responsibility because it is too great a decision for one person alone to make – an icon of democratic principle – and, second, that the court itself produces a tied vote. Orestes only gets off because of the goddess' casting vote. In Athens, if a trial jury was tied, the defendant was given the benefit of the doubt, and this was known as 'the vote of Athene'. So Aeschylus' play stages the origin of this institution. But it also insists that Orestes' case remains as difficult and as balanced as possible. It resists easy answers. This continuing anguish of difficulty is integral to Aeschylus' dramatic vision. There are very few actions – in the Hollywood sense of action – in the trilogy: Agamemnon comes home and is killed; Orestes takes revenge; the court acquits him. Each play centres around an intensely dramatic moment of staged choice: should Agamemnon step on the carpet or not? Should Orestes kill his mother or not? How will the court vote? Each of these stark choices, however, is surrounded by an ever expanding network of images of imagined consequences and causes, by a swirl of doubts, reading of ambiguous signs, and worries about how communication works too well or fails too dangerously. Aeschylus' world is a very frightening one, where humans are necessarily ignorant, suffering, confused and desperate for elusive clarity. This human condition is tempered but not assuaged by the possibility of living in a democratic city. The trilogy offers at best a cautious collective optimism, mired by the inevitability of individual downfall and despair, seeded by familial transgressions. It is impressive that this version of the trilogy faces this dynamic squarely, and allows the uncertainties and black undertow of Aeschylus' drama to echo through even its celebratory trajectory.

The danger for any work when it becomes a classic is that it remains under aspic, an out-of-date dish admired out of duty. Aeschylus' *Oresteia* is undoubtedly one of the greatest works of western culture, but it needs continual and active re-engagement with its immense potential to make it speak with its true insistence and power. All translators are traitors, but some traitors turn out to be liberators who let us recalibrate what matters, and see the world from a startlingly new perspective.

Professor Simon Goldhill

Simon Goldhill is Professor of Greek at Cambridge University where he is also Director of the Centre of Arts, Social Sciences and Humanities (CRASSH). He has written for many years on Greek tragedy including *Reading Greek Tragedy*, now in its twentieth re-printing, and *Sophocles and the Language of Tragedy* which won the Runciman Prize in 2013. He is a regular broadcaster on radio and television, and has lectured on tragedy all over the world. He was the Consultant Academic on the original production of this adaptation.

A note on the text

A forward slash (/) marks the point of interruption of overlapping dialogue.

A comma on a separate line (,) indicates a pause, a rest, a silence, an upbeat or a lift. Length and intensity are context dependent.

An ellipsis (…) indicates a trailing off.

Two lines printed without space between them and marked as (chorus) should be spoken simultaneously:

> AGAMEMNON: *(Chorus.)* You're getting big!
> IPHIGENIA: *(Chorus.)* You're getting big!

Square brackets [like this] indicates words which are part of the intention of the line but which are **not** spoken aloud.

Double square brackets [[like this]] indicate text which should be updated to reflect the precise date and time of the events in each performance.

A note on productions

This adaptation was written to be staged with a bare minimum of props (other than exhibits: essential to the story) and to be performed on a bare stage. As with any good court case or family occasion, the feeling of ritual is essential. The text assumes that what will be staged is for the most part not the literal action.

In the original production, exhibits and Times of Death were displayed on an LED ticker – and video was used to live relay public-facing scenes. Iphigenia's song was the Beach Boys' *God Only Knows.*

This adaptation needs simply

A CHORUS OF ACTORS

who move fluidly between roles
with a minimum of costume changes.

In the original production ten actors
played the major roles like this:

CALCHAS
AGAMEMNON / AEGISTHUS
DOCTOR
ORESTES
KLYTEMNESTRA
ELECTRA
MENELAUS
TALTHYBIUS
CASSANDRA / ATHENE
CILISSA

and two child actors played

IPHIGENIA
YOUNG ORESTES

But there are also other ways.

This adaptation was commissioned by and originally produced at the Almeida Theatre, London, where it had its first performance on Friday 29th May, 2015.

The Company

Lorna Brown
Jessica Brown Findlay
Rudi Dharmalingam
Annie Firbank
Joshua Higgott
John Mackay
Luke Thompson
Lia Williams
Angus Wright
Hara Yannas

Amelia Baldock
Eve Benioff Salama
Ilan Galkoff
Cameron Lane
Clara Read
Bobby Smalldridge

Creative Team

Director Robert Icke
Design Hildegard Bechtler
Lighting Natasha Chivers
Sound Tom Gibbons
Video Tim Reid
Casting Julia Horan CDG
Consultant Academic Simon Goldhill
Dramaturg Duška Radosavljević
Assistant Director Anthony Almeida

This adaptation transferred to the Trafalgar Studios, London, where it had its first performance on Saturday 22nd August, 2015. Produced in the West End by The Almeida Theatre, Ambassador Theatre Group, Sonia Freedman Productions, Tulchin Bartner Productions, 1001 Night, Scott M. Delman, Brian Zeilinger / Matt Kidd.

The Company

Lorna Brown
Jessica Brown Findlay
Annie Firbank
Joshua Higgott
Jonathan McGuinness
Oliver Ryan
Luke Thompson
Lia Williams
Angus Wright
Hara Yannas

Children:
Ilan Galkoff
Matt Goldberg
Cameron Lane
Cleopatra Dickens
Dixie Egerickx
Ophelia Standen

Creative Team

Direction/Adaptor Robert Icke
Design Hildegard Bechtler
Lighting Natasha Chivers
Sound Tom Gibbons
Video Tim Reid
Casting Julie Horan CDG
Casting Associate Lotte Hines
Associate Direction Anthony Almeida
Consultant Academic Simon Goldhill

Dramaturg Duška Radosavljević
Costume Supervision Laura Hunt
Sound Associates Sean Ephgrave & Pete Malkin
Lighting Associate Peter Harrison

This adaptation made its North American premiere at Park Avenue Armory, where it played its first preview on July 13th, 2022.

The Company

Michael Abubakar
Tia Bannon
Marty Cruikshank
Calum Finlay
Joshua Higgott
Anastasia Hille
Gilbert Kyem Jr
Kirsty Rider
Luke Treadaway
Ross Waiton
Peter Wight
Angus Wright
Hara Yannas

Bartley Booz
Lise Bruneau
Alexis Rae Forlenza
Wesley Holloway
Jacqueline Jarrold
Andrew Long
Hudson Paul
Elyana Faith Randolph
Harry Smith

This appointment occurs in the past

(Outlook calendar error message)

ACT ONE

First, the chorus of actors.

Then, AGAMEMNON *and* CALCHAS.

CALCHAS   Theous

Zeus. Allah. El.
Jehovah. Janus. Jupiter. Jove.
Elah. 'ilah. Elohim. Ishvara. Ra. Raven.
Dagda. Anguta. Yahweh. Apollo. Olorun.
Chronus. Osiris. Brahman. Buddah. Odin.
The Mountain. The Godhead. The Way.
The Door. The Truth. The Life. The Light.
The Lamb. The Creator. The Maker. The
Supreme Being. The Holy Name. The One.
The King. The Lord. The Judge. The Father.
The All-Knowing, who can never be known.

God. The word was there in the beginning.
And now we're at the end. Or not quite.

It's a buyers' market now. A thousand words
looking at the same thing. And more words,
I'm afraid, than meaning. Not that there
isn't meaning, there is, of course, it's just
extremely hard to come by – with any sort of
certainty.

But you pay your money, you make your
choice.

AGAMEMNON   Sorry, yes, the money – here it is –

CALCHAS   Thank you.

I meant to apologise about the steps, by the
way, it's storey after storey, and it's, uh / hot

AGAMEMNON   hot, yes, no. It's fine.

CALCHAS   This has all happened before. And more
than once. You're desperate that it isn't this,

not now, not to you, it doesn't make sense.
But you're thinking about diagnosis when
your mind should be on cure.

There is a communication and to the best
of my ability it seems reasonably, not
unusually, clear. But you already know that.

CALCHAS closes his eyes. And sneezes.

AGAMEMNON   Bless you.

Opens his eyes.

CALCHAS   That really won't be necessary –

Closes his eyes again. Sneezes again.

It reads as follows:

By his hand alone. The child is the price. Fair
winds.

Opens his eyes.

Which you also knew. But it's your money.
Perhaps there's part of it that isn't clear?

AGAMEMNON   No. Fair winds is / winning the war

CALCHAS   Winning, yes, very likely. Winds, wins:
similar in sound. That's characteristic

AGAMEMNON   Is it reliable?

CALCHAS   You know there's a message. A story. Maybe
that proves it was created, maybe it's just a
story.

AGAMEMNON   It's not [a story], it's a prophecy

CALCHAS   It's a fact. At least, it's going to be a fact.
What you're being told is that the road is
about to split, that an action is coming which
you either perform – or you don't. Make that
judgement.

Forewarned is forearmed. Not forestalled.
There's no armour that protects you from the
future. It comes. You suffer: you learn.

CALCHAS moves to the side of the stage. He'll stay here for the duration of the evening, sometimes involved, sometimes observing. When an exhibit is required, he will with careful deliberation hand it to the necessary person – delivering it into the onstage action.

Two people are talking. We don't know who the man is yet, but we'll find out eventually that his name is ORESTES. Now, he is holding a piece of paper. We're not ever sure who the woman is, but for now, she'll speak after the prefix DOCTOR, which is how she seems initially.

DOCTOR   Just try and tell the truth. Tell me where it started.

ORESTES   I don't remember. I don't remember.

DOCTOR   You will remember something. We just have to begin. Travel back along the road, all the way back to where it began.

In the house, IPHIGENIA enters, wearing a saffron dress, carrying a doll. She takes her shoes off. She whispers to the doll.

What's this? What are you holding?

ORESTES holds out the drawing and we can see it. Two eagles and a hare.

EXHIBIT: DRAWING OF A HARE KILLED BY TWO EAGLES

DOCTOR   What is it?

ORESTES   The hare. The mother hare. She's pregnant with two babies.

DOCTOR   Go on.

ORESTES   Beating in the sky. The eagles. Two eagles cutting down through the air and their wings flapping on top of her and they rip her stomach open. Their claws are hard and her stomach is soft – and she didn't have a chance really. All her inside came out.

17

DOCTOR	That's good: remember those words. It's a story. The pregnant hare killed by two eagles. And this story is one you keep returning to, again and again, not exactly the same, but – versions of the same thing. I wonder – what does it *mean*?

ORESTES holds his hands out. He doesn't remember.

ORESTES	I don't think I believe in this. In your – practice.
DOCTOR	What is my practice?

They smile at each other.

	Let's see if I can understand. The mother and her unborn children are the victims of an attack, an attack from above. Is the mother your mother?
ORESTES	No. Are you my mother?
DOCTOR	No. Any further questions? I'm just trying to understand you.
ORESTES	To *simplify* me. To pack me down into one easy diagnosis. A judgement. He's *this one thing*. Finished.
DOCTOR	I don't think it's ever finished. And I don't think we're one thing. Any of us.
ORESTES	No?
DOCTOR	No. You are yourself. But you are also a part of a family and a country. And a world. And a religion, if that's what you [believe]. You could be a brother and a son and a father all at once. I think we're all several things, even just within our family.

IPHIGENIA sings a few lines of her song.

ORESTES	It's always families, isn't it? Distant fathers and inscrutable mothers and
DOCTOR	And?

ORESTES   Sisters.

                 ,

DOCTOR   Tell me about your family.

IPHIGENIA   Mum! Mum! MUM MUM MUM MUM

                 *ORESTES (YOUNG) enters – played by a child. He's followed by
                 his mother, KLYTEMNESTRA. We're in the family home.*

                 This was by the door. We found this by the
                 door.

                 EXHIBIT: HANDWRITTEN NOTE, WITH ENVELOPE

ORESTES (Y)   It's addressed to Dad.

IPHIGENIA   Last night we had a dream about a snake that
                 killed a bird.

KLYTEMNESTRA   Right. Was she an evil bird?

IPHIGENIA   I think so.

KLYTEMNESTRA   Then there's nothing to worry about, is there,
                 honey?

IPHIGENIA   This house is too hot. This was by the door.

                 *AGAMEMNON is prepared for his interview. CALCHAS reads the
                 facts; KLYTEMNESTRA hears it like a weather forecast.*

CALCHAS   This is the longest period of calm since
                 records began. With no wind at all recorded
                 anywhere: the stillness is becoming palpably
                 uneasy, the atmosphere / staying very, very
                 still.

KLYTEMNESTRA   But how do you *know* tomorrow's weather?
                 You don't.

                 I don't want to miss the beginning.

                 AGAMEMNON is interviewed. The family watch from the house.

AGAMEMNON   I'm in at the very end. Turning up to find it's
                 all over.

QUESTION   So your starting point is ending the war?

AGAMEMNON	Well, I think that's all that's left. It's been a long time, a lot of blood. A lot of men.
KLYTEMNESTRA	Can we CUT the offstage noise please and remember that we are all part of the same family and that to be supportive / might not be entirely
IPHIGENIA	What's going on?
QUESTION	Do you look to history? Do you study other conflicts?
AGAMEMNON	I'm not here to repeat something that happened years ago. I'm not here to follow a pre-ordained plan. I can only make the decisions I can make: regardless of what I say, I can only do, fundamentally, what is in me to do. And that's / bringing this conflict to the right end
QUESTION	And do you blame your predecessors for where we are now?
AGAMEMNON	I try and look forward rather than backward. And we can get so consumed by the local detail, by the right here right now – it's essential to ask the bigger questions. Why are we doing this? What are we trying to do? And what I want to say is this: it's ending. It is ending.
QUESTION	But not yet. You were a controversial choice. An unpopular choice.
AGAMEMNON	Well, look, I'm on trial until such a time as I prove myself. I'm not here for popular. No one votes for what's *popular*: they vote for what they think is right, and what's popular, the thing in the middle, is what they end up with. And it's probably pleasing nobody. Or displeasing them all equally.
KLYTEMNESTRA	Yes. Good. / Yes.

QUESTION	So you know that people disagree –
AGAMEMNON	I respect that. I get the letters from the people who think I'm, uh, evil. And that's fine. They're entitled to think that. But it can't change the way that you lead / and that's
QUESTION	How can that possibly be democratic?
AGAMEMNON	I think that's precisely democratic. I'm not a puppet for the majority view; it's how you persuade the people in the room that your idea is right.
QUESTION	You're not frightened of being direct.
AGAMEMNON	*Everything* is recorded now, written down, dug up, so if you say it, you say it with full awareness it might – it likely will be – taken down as evidence. And we are alive in a time that has mountains of dead words but not enough action. That's a difficult truth, perhaps, but it is a truth.
QUESTION	It's been a difficult year for you, hasn't it? In your personal life?
AGAMEMNON	You're referring to my father, yes? Who died. Of course, that's difficult. Grieving. An easy word. Harder, as we will all find out – harder to do, harder to actually *live* it, to *react* to a, uh, death. But we do.
QUESTION	Your father was also a military man –
AGAMEMNON	Many of our men fought alongside him.
QUESTION	That must be a pressure.
	,
AGAMEMNON	It is and it isn't.
	Look, there are always things we *feel*, that if we allow them to, would threaten to, uh, upset the balance. But you hold that down.

	It's – it's a state of – the mind is a *civilization* and there's always some army trying to invade. Keeping the guard watchful, that's a *daily* thing, that's a *routine,* for everyone, being aware of the chance of attack –
	I'm sorry, do you mind if I take this off?
QUESTION	It's hot, isn't it?
	You mentioned your father's death. You're famously a religious man. How does your faith help you day to day?
IPHIGENIA	Today we learned a song for Daddy.
KLYTEMNESTRA	Iphigenia, honey, please
AGAMEMNON	That's a leading question.
IPHIGENIA	Do you want something to eat, mum?
	,
	Mum?
KLYTEMNESTRA	PLEASE.
AGAMEMNON	I won't discuss my family, that should have been / made clear
QUESTION	I didn't ask you about your family.
AGAMEMNON	No. Famously religious. Honestly? I think most people are still religious in the same way I am.
QUESTION	And what way is that?
AGAMEMNON	I don't *subscribe* to a – I just believe that there's something – bigger than us. An order. A whole other storey above us. And that belief [in a higher system] isn't a *doctrine*, isn't – a structure of temples and churches – it's – look: I deal in violence: my life is a violent life. Countries run on wars. I'm not a pacifist. But some things are just *right*. The bigger questions, like I said. From there, you make

	your judgement: from above. It's a way of thinking.
QUESTION	Some would argue it's nothing more than that.
AGAMEMNON	They would. And they can. How do we make difficult decisions? We look above us – in all sorts of ways: to wiser people – to knowledge, to counsel, to conscience. Now perhaps when I pray, when I look *above* myself, people might say, well, I'm only seeking deeper *inside* myself, asking my, uh, subconscious sense of justice – and perhaps I am. But that process of humbling oneself to the idea of a greater wisdom, that questioning process, the faith that there is a *right* – well, any success I've had at anything – is thanks to that.
KLYTEMNESTRA	I don't think I can watch any more. It's done.

The interview is over. In the house, a moment of pause, of reflection, the house during the day. It's hot. The family's old nurse, CILISSA, cleans.

IPHIGENIA	Why do you wear make-up?
KLYTEMNESTRA	Why do you think?
IPHIGENIA	So the bits of your face seem bigger. Like more people can see it.
KLYTEMNESTRA	Sometimes. Sometimes to hide behind.
IPHIGENIA	Like a mask?
KLYTEMNESTRA	Sort of like a mask.
ORESTES (Y)	Where's Electra?
KLYTEMNESTRA	What? – I don't [know] –
IPHIGENIA	When I dance the world gets hotter.

IPHIGENIA sings a few lines of her song.

| KLYTEMNESTRA | Could you stop singing for a – ? |

'

23

AGAMEMNON arrives home.

He's here

AGAMEMNON   I'm HOME!

The family are together, high-spirited, a welcome home, a family wrestling match, them all falling all over each other.

KLYTEMNESTRA   Someone will get hurt one of these days. And it will be me, innocently looking on –

AGAMEMNON   Iph-i-gen-i-a!

IPHIGENIA runs into the arms of AGAMEMNON who lifts her up, she gives it to AGAMEMNON, they share a little ritual. The dinner bell is rung. CILISSA is there, standing beside the table.

AGAMEMNON   *(Chorus.)* You're getting big!
IPHIGENIA   *(Chorus.)* You're getting big!

The table is set, a family ritual: a white tablecloth is spread, a decanter, glasses. A moment of tenderness between KLYTEMNESTRA and AGAMEMNON.

KLYTEMNESTRA   Hello. You look terrible. Absolutely terrible.

Sit down, sit down, sit down. Everybody's *here* / this is lovely

ORESTES (Y)   Where's Electra?

AGAMEMNON   If she isn't here, she doesn't eat.

KLYTEMNESTRA   Nothing'll spoil if we just / wait a moment

AGAMEMNON   We are not going to wait. We're *hungry*, / aren't we?

KLYTEMNESTRA   God, this thing [tablecloth] is filthy.

AGAMEMNON   Less god, please.

Whose turn is it?

IPHIGENIA raises her hand, another ritual, thanksgiving:

IPHIGENIA   For the food we are about to enjoy, for this day and for the safety of this house, we give thanks.

AGAMEMNON	We give thanks. And what have we got in front of us?
KLYTEMNESTRA	Well, we really shouldn't, but I just thought we might all appreciate something old-fashioned, something comforting. There is also a cake.
AGAMEMNON	Thank you. Something to look forward to.
ORESTES (Y)	So why is it on the table now?
KLYTEMNESTRA	Because the person responsible / doesn't listen to instructions
AGAMEMNON	So we can look forward to having it later
IPHIGENIA	We learned a song / today.
ORESTES (Y)	I love cake.
IPHIGENIA	Dad we learned a / song for you today.
ORESTES (Y)	It's too hot. My head hurts. Why does my head / hurt?

Enter ELECTRA, *late.* YOUNG ORESTES *sneezes.*

AGAMEMNON	*(Chorus.)* Bless you
KLYTEMNESTRA	*(Chorus.)* You and your questions.
ORESTES (Y)	Electra's here.
AGAMEMNON	Good evening. What time is it?
ELECTRA	Sorry
	Dad. Sorry. Lost track. Forgot to remember.

YOUNG ORESTES *is amused.*

KLYTEMNESTRA	Are you a part of this family or not?
ELECTRA	This looks delicious.
KLYTEMNESTRA	In this house, on this day, dinner / is served at
ELECTRA	is served at, yes, I know. I was late. I have apologized. Let's all just move forward.

KLYTEMNESTRA	That is not the way, at this table, *we don't talk like that here.*
AGAMEMNON	This is a time for the whole family to be together, to enjoy the meal that your mother has prepared // and for us to
KLYTEMNESTRA	Thank you, dear
ELECTRA	Dad, it was two minutes late, it was two minutes it's not like the first dinner we've had, it's not important / – God – that / everyone's sitting in position ready for the bell to ring
KLYTEMNESTRA	It is important. It is important.
AGAMEMNON	I don't like that language at this table, I do not like you saying that
ELECTRA	I know that you like everyone to be together. I'm sorry that I ruined that.
ORESTES (Y)	She's sorry that she ruined that.
AGAMEMNON	And you're missing a very nice meal
KLYTEMNESTRA	*(Chorus.)* Thank you
ORESTES (Y)	*(Chorus.)* It is, the meat's delicious
IPHIGENIA	What is it?
AGAMEMNON	So how was our day today?
IPHIGENIA	What is it?
KLYTEMNESTRA	What?
IPHIGENIA	The meat. What is it?
KLYTEMNESTRA	It's venison.
ORESTES (Y)	*(Chorus.)* It's deer.
ELECTRA	*(Chorus.)* It's deer.
IPHIGENIA	Deer?

AGAMEMNON	Right. What I want to know is – who at the table is going to tell this family the story of / their day?
ORESTES (Y)	*(Chorus.)* Dad
ELECTRA	*(Chorus.)* Dad
IPHIGENIA	*(Chorus.)* Dad
ELECTRA	Not this again.
AGAMEMNON	What have we done?
ELECTRA	*(Chorus.)* Dad, you don't need to know
AGAMEMNON	*(Chorus.)* Dad, you don't need to know
AGAMEMNON	But I'm your father
ELECTRA	*(Chorus.)* You don't need to know
AGAMEMNON	*(Chorus.)* You don't need to know
AGAMEMNON	I know *everything.*
IPHIGENIA	It's not real, is it?
	,
AGAMEMNON	What, sweetie?
IPHIGENIA	The deer. It's not a *real* deer.
AGAMEMNON	*(Chorus.)* What do you mean?
KLYTEMNESTRA	*(Chorus.)* No, no, it's not
ELECTRA	It's a real deer.
KLYTEMNESTRA	Orestes, enough.
IPHIGENIA	Like it's a real live deer?
ELECTRA	*(Chorus.)* Yes – well, it's a dead deer
KLYTEMNESTRA	*(Chorus.)* No
KLYTEMNESTRA	Enough.
ORESTES (Y)	It is a dead deer –
KLYTEMNESTRA	It's part of a deer but now it's meat. It's not the same as eating it when it was alive, that would be different.
IPHIGENIA	But it was alive once?

KLYTEMNESTRA	Yes.
IPHIGENIA	Why did it die?
ELECTRA	Natural causes
KLYTEMNESTRA	So we could eat it
IPHIGENIA	You mean we *killed* it?
ELECTRA	*(Chorus.)* Yes.
KLYTEMNESTRA	*(Chorus.)* No, no we didn't kill it, someone else killed it

This doesn't make it better.

Look it's perfectly normal, you've eaten it before

IPHIGENIA	But if we eat animals, animals die.
KLYTEMNESTRA	Yes, honey, but it's – the animal died in order that we all got to live, to eat. If you could ask the animal it'd be glad that its life keeps all of us alive, by feeding us, happy that / we can keep going, and we can eat.
IPHIGENIA	But we could eat something else. I don't like it that they die.
ELECTRA	And you can't ask the animal.
ORESTES (Y)	Don't eat the / meat then
KLYTEMNESTRA	Not eating it won't bring it back to life
AGAMEMNON	And your sister is not old enough to be confronted with the realities of death.
IPHIGENIA	*(Chorus.)* I *am.*
ELECTRA	*(Chorus.)* She is – there's no time / like the present.
KLYTEMNESTRA	In this family we eat what's on our plate. No matter whether we like it. We eat it. We're grateful.
AGAMEMNON	Which is why we say thank you. Each meal.

IPHIGENIA	I didn't think of it as that.
AGAMEMNON	What did you think we were doing?
IPHIGENIA	I / dunno.
ELECTRA	Can I have wine?
KLYTEMNESTRA	I don't approve of children having wine
ELECTRA	Is that a no or a grudging yes?
IPHIGENIA	I don't want to eat the deer.
AGAMEMNON	*(Chorus.)* Iphigenia
KLYTEMNESTRA	*(Chorus.)* Stop. It's *just deer.*
IPHIGENIA	I'm not. I'm not eating it. Animals are people. It's really *sad.*

'

KLYTEMNESTRA motions to IPHIGENIA to stop.

ELECTRA	Dad? What's going on? It's just grapes.
KLYTEMNESTRA	I think it's too early for you to have wine. It's not appropriate.
ELECTRA	It's dinner time
KLYTEMNESTRA	That's not what I meant as you perfectly well know.
ORESTES (Y)	Why is it not appropriate? Dad?

ELECTRA has tried to uncork the wine – her father rescues it.

AGAMEMNON	If you're going to do that, you could at least do it / properly
IPHIGENIA	It's a *sacrifice*
KLYTEMNESTRA	It's a not / up to you
IPHIGENIA	*(Repeats.)* It's a little dead body, it's a little dead body –
ORESTES (Y)	If it's basically just grapes. How can there be a right and a wrong?

AGAMEMNON suddenly loses his temper.

AGAMEMNON   *Dinner is a family thing.* Orestes, [before you
              start,] enough of the questions. Iphigenia
              I'm not having you dictate what happens to
              everyone. Animals and plants and – have
              died to feed the members of this family since
              long before you were around. So. You eat
              what you can.

ORESTES (Y)   I didn't say / anything.

AGAMEMNON   Orestes, just *take* some *responsibility.*

              ,

              *AGAMEMNON knocks over the wine bottle, wine pours onto the
              tablecloth. KLYTEMNESTRA rescues it.*

ORESTES (Y)   Why do we pour it into there anyway?

KLYTEMNESTRA It's just *nicer.*

ORESTES (Y)   Why?

KLYTEMNESTRA It – matters what things are inside.

AGAMEMNON   We are going to change the subject.

KLYTEMNESTRA How was today otherwise?

              *His mind is elsewhere. AGAMEMNON and KLYTEMNESTRA talk
              in code. The children sense it, nervously; another atmosphere
              blooms, silent.*

              I thought you spoke very well.

AGAMEMNON   Sorry. Thank you. Today otherwise was
              tense.

KLYTEMNESTRA Any sense of when – when it'll start? When
              you might have to –

AGAMEMNON   No

KLYTEMNESTRA And we don't know which way the wind is
              blowing?

AGAMEMNON   What? No – no. Could be at any time.

KLYTEMNESTRA	Well. If it stays like this, and you're with us for longer, that's fine by me. If things stayed like this forever, I'd be happy.
AGAMEMNON	Well, yes, me too, but things won't stay like this – I mean, the feeling is that we need to move as soon – we have to get there first. And you heard what I said today, but the big picture really is we're sitting targets, life as usual, just waiting for them to really surprise us. And if we don't, we'll pay / the price
KLYTEMNESTRA	Is that actually / what they're saying now
AGAMEMNON	Anyway. Enough of that. My children, now how has today been?
	,
KLYTEMNESTRA	My day has been busy but perfectly pleasant
	,
AGAMEMNON	Come on. I can't be there for your whole lives. I was there for the whole of the first / part
KLYTEMNESTRA	Some of the first / part
AGAMEMNON	And as you grow up, and this country needs me more and my days get longer, our little family is going to be put under pressure. And I can't always be here, not as much as I'd like to be, not any more – and I miss you, sweethearts, even if you do drive me mad. So tell me the story of everything I'm missing, bring it back to life, help me to feel like I'm a part of your lives, that you'll – you'll remember me when I'm dead and buried
IPHIGENIA	Don't say that
AGAMEMNON	You're *all growing up* and it stabs you from behind, time, – you don't even feel it happen. And when it ends, you will look back on this, this table, our meals, on your

31

> strange old parents and our moments all
> together – and these times –

AGAMEMNON suddenly emotional, choked –

> it's it's it's – these times –

He can't speak. His family look at him aghast. ELECTRA goes to him. Hugs him.

ORESTES again.

ORESTES	There's a dead girl
DOCTOR	Where? Did you dream her?
ORESTES	No, she's real, she was real. I don't sleep. But it's like a dream: it's hazy – in the middle, falling between.
DOCTOR	That's true of most things now. Not quite order, but not chaos – not tyranny, not anarchy, but somewhere between. It's complex but perhaps it's – good. To see both sides. A balance. Why does it have to be only one thing?
ORESTES	It's not a balance. It's a battle. It *can't* ever be a balance. Something has to win.
DOCTOR	And what does she do? The girl? What does she / say?
ORESTES	I'm – this, it's this –

ORESTES holds his hands out, palms turned upward. AGAMEMNON murmurs:

AGAMEMNON	The child is the price.

AGAMEMNON wakes up. KLYTEMNESTRA with him.

KLYTEMNESTRA	You were dreaming. I let you sleep. Sorry.
AGAMEMNON	The water?
KLYTEMNESTRA	Just the bath. Are you alright?

,

He's still disturbed.

32

AGAMEMNON	Yes. How are you feeling?
KLYTEMNESTRA	Fine.
	What is the child the price for, dare I ask?
AGAMEMNON	It doesn't matter. Dream. What are you thinking?
KLYTEMNESTRA	Nothing.
AGAMEMNON	Was there / crying before?
KLYTEMNESTRA	Crying? Just / Orestes.
AGAMEMNON	Orestes.
KLYTEMNESTRA	He stops. He's asleep now, I think. Come here. Your eyes look tired. Pale. I know there must be things going on. But don't lose faith.
AGAMEMNON	No. I think I'm going to take a bath. Try and – you know
KLYTEMNESTRA	All right. You're in love with that bath.

AGAMEMNON moves to the bathroom, puts on his red dressing gown. KLYTEMNESTRA goes elsewhere in the house.

	Oh. Orestes. Are you eating that cake?
ELECTRA	For gods' sake / you wanted us to eat it
KLYTEMNESTRA	I wasn't berating you, I was pleased – I was pleased. And you know how your father feels about that word.
ELECTRA	Oh. Will you have some?
KLYTEMNESTRA	I will not. Anything I eat in any quantity that tastes of anything and my body just wreaks revenge. We have to hope you don't end up like me.
IPHIGENIA	Is Dad angry with me?
KLYTEMNESTRA	Don't be silly.

,

Iphigenia? Go and see him. He's just hot and
bothered, I expect.

IPHIGENIA remembers the letter. AGAMEMNON prays.

AGAMEMNON   I have always believed in you. I have always
              loved you and revered you. I have raised
              my family in reverence and awe of the world
              you have created. I honour you and praise
              your might and your name and your works.
              I know I've failed sometimes, I know I could
              have been better, but I was always trying and
              I will keep trying. And I ask you tonight: just
              let me understand for certain what you want.
              Give me wisdom. I don't – I'm not asking for
              mercy, I don't want – I trust that you set the
              course of the ship. A sign. That's all. I love
              my family –

IPHIGENIA runs in with the letter (the first exhibit).

IPHIGENIA   DADDADDADDADDAD

AGAMEMNON   The door is SHUT DO YOU NOT
              UNDERSTAND THAT

              ,

IPHIGENIA   Sorry. Sorry. Sorry – I was just bringing – this
              came –

She's upset, drops the envelope, runs.

AGAMEMNON   Iphigenia. Come back. I'm sorry. I didn't
              mean –

              ,

*AGAMEMNON opens the envelope, unfolds the message. He looks
at it dumbly. He sneezes. And then he's violently, suddenly
sick. The note says in red letters: CHILD KILLER.*

*Elsewhere, ORESTES and ELECTRA and KLYTEMNESTRA. CILISSA
cleans.*

ELECTRA   There's going to be a war, isn't there?

34

KLYTEMNESTRA	There's already a war.
ELECTRA	Do you ever worry he'll – not come back?
	,
KLYTEMNESTRA	I do, actually. But there's no point worrying about the future.
ELECTRA	No. It's scary though.
KLYTEMNESTRA	Things don't happen. We make things happen. Your father was told – long before you, before me, even, before we were [married] – that he would die in water. And when he told me that story, do you know what I said to him? It's nonsense. And it is.

In the bathroom, AGAMEMNON turns off the bath taps.

ORESTES (Y)	Will I ever be a mum?
KLYTEMNESTRA	Dad. Will you ever be a dad.
ORESTES (Y)	Dads love girls the most. They do.
ELECTRA	Who tells you how? to be a dad?
KLYTEMNESTRA	You tell yourself. And you ask people bigger than you.
ORESTES (Y)	How does it feel though to be a dad?
KLYTEMNESTRA	Well, I don't [know] – it's a change. When you and your sister were born, I suddenly felt this burning need to stay alive. I am alive, I thought, and now I *can't* die: he needs me to keep living, small soft helpless little thing. And I still feel like that, even when the whole old place is falling apart, and it's too hot, and the systems don't work, and no one knows what to do.
ORESTES (Y)	How do wars end?
KLYTEMNESTRA	I don't know, darling. Someone breaks. Someone wins.

ELECTRA	You don't agree with it. With what he thinks about – going there? About the war?
KLYTEMNESTRA	Not about everything, no.
ELECTRA	Do you love him?
KLYTEMNESTRA	Yes. I really do.

,

ELECTRA	You look nice. By the way.
KLYTEMNESTRA	Thank you, dear.
	The light's going, melting, kind of. Butterscotch. What an evening.

The bathroom. AGAMEMNON has got IPHIGENIA back. There should be a sense throughout the below that he is about to kill her.

IPHIGENIA	Did you lock the door?
AGAMEMNON	Force of habit. Sorry. You can unlock it. Unlock it.
IPHIGENIA	Why are you angry with me?
AGAMEMNON	I'm not angry with you. It's nothing to do with you. Honestly. Come on. Chat to me.
IPHIGENIA	I'm glad that I don't have to go to work. What do you do at work when there isn't a war?
AGAMEMNON	There is a war.
IPHIGENIA	Yes, but you aren't at it.
AGAMEMNON	In one way, I am. I'm – between there and here.
IPHIGENIA	We learned a song today for you. Mum said it was one you liked.
AGAMEMNON	Did you?
IPHIGENIA	Sometimes I worry that maybe one day you'll die. And we'll be sad.

AGAMEMNON	I will, sweetheart.
IPHIGENIA	Not soon, though?
AGAMEMNON	Well, I hope not.
IPHIGENIA	But your job means that's it's more likely, doesn't it?
AGAMEMNON	Not really.
	Are you going to sing this song for me?
IPHIGENIA	I don't want to do it now. Actually no I do but my body's saying no. You know that feeling.
AGAMEMNON	I know that feeling.
IPHIGENIA	When there's something you have to do – but you can't?

AGAMEMNON looks at her. He winds the dressing gown cord around his hands, ready to strangle her.

I should just do it. Get on with it. NOW. DO IT. DO IT. DO IT.

She has her eyes shut.

,

All right.

IPHIGENIA sings the first verse of her song, and one line of the chorus and then stops. Looks at him.

This is everyone. For everyone.

AGAMEMNON	What?
IPHIGENIA	There's a word for it. The everyone – Can't remember it. We know it, but …
	You don't like it.

,

| AGAMEMNON | I love it. It's brilliant. You're brilliant, sweetheart. Well done. |

AGAMEMNON hugs his daughter.

IPHIGENIA	Chorus. That's the word. I knew I knew it.
	You don't wash yourself in the bath, anyway, you just sit there. Don't blame me if you never get clean.

She leaves. AGAMEMNON reels, inhales. Elsewhere:

KLYTEMNESTRA	My little warrior
ORESTES (Y)	I wasn't
KLYTEMNESTRA	What?
ORESTES (Y)	Worrying.
KLYTEMNESTRA	Warrior, I said, silly, *warrior*. You're not worried, are you, darling?
ORESTES (Y)	No. It's strange how words sound so much like each other.
KLYTEMNESTRA	You never stop thinking, do you? Bathtime.

KLYTEMNESTRA and AGAMEMNON meet as he leaves the bathroom – and he catches sight of MENELAUS and TALTHYBIUS standing in the house. MENELAUS is a little younger than AGAMEMNON; TALTHYBIUS younger than both of them. KLYTEMNESTRA takes ORESTES and IPHIGENIA into the bathroom and the children are bathed.

AGAMEMNON	I didn't know you'd all be standing in the hall. It's bathtime. Sorry / about the
MENELAUS	I'm sorry to do this so late, but there's been a development, it / was something you needed to hear
AGAMEMNON	That's fine, what's happening? I'm sorry it's so hot in here.
TALTHYBIUS	There is a communication, and it seems reasonably, not unusually, clear: the submission is that the enemy is mobilising – a huge movement of troops into positions

	which suggest we are extremely close to an / attack
AGAMEMNON	So we need to strike first
MENELAUS	Yes.
AGAMEMNON	And that's what you're here to advise me to do?
MENELAUS	Weather conditions are far from ideal / but [no other options now]
AGAMEMNON	Is it – reliable?
TALTHYBIUS	The / message
AGAMEMNON	Prophecy. Communication. Call it what you want, is it reliable as an indication of what is going to happen?
MENELAUS	Agamemnon –
TALTHYBIUS	Yes / we think it is.
AGAMEMNON	So where's your document? What is your recommendation?
TALTHYBIUS	It's a complex / situation.
AGAMEMNON	That is not, that is *not* an answer, I'm sorry but I am so sick of being offered complexity like it's in any way useful as an endpoint. This conflict is now *my* prerogative: the buck has stopped. I long for something I can do. Give me *options*. We run the better part of the *world*. Great men have sat in your chairs. Honour their memories.
	It seems pretty *simple* to me.
	,
MENELAUS	Agamemnon, he knows. He knows the – full extent of the situation
	,
AGAMEMNON	You gave your word. He knows about –

39

MENELAUS	Your daughter. Yes.
AGAMEMNON	You gave your *word* – so what's the counsel, then? Why have you come? Because what has been suggested is an unthinkable course of action. I'm not going to do it. So we will need to look at it some other way.
MENELAUS	We're here to try and help / and I gave my word to
AGAMEMNON	And you take it at face value, this – prophecy? You're prepared to have me make a judgement entirely based on faith?
TALTHYBIUS	Are you asking me?
AGAMEMNON	*Yes*
TALTHYBIUS	I think, well, I think you were elected for you to use *your* judgement.
AGAMEMNON	And if it got out – if the public found / out
MENELAUS	Then there could be nothing more fundamental, no greater / sacrifice
AGAMEMNON	They don't all believe what I believe: if it got out, they'd think a fanatic did what fanatics do
MENELAUS	Not when they see the consequences, not when the war is / won
AGAMEMNON	It's acting on *faith, killing* in the hope that there'll be a certain / outcome
MENELAUS	All acting is acting on / faith
AGAMEMNON	But nothing is this certain, not to them. I'd be a fanatic –
MENELAUS	You would be putting this country before your family *in real terms.* Your fear of them is totally absurd. And out of date. This *is* public. This is absolutely about them, about everyone. You'd hold their kids up higher than your own, and – if *that* got out, you

40

would be – idolised. That is by anybody's standards an act of heroism worthy of the highest conceivable honour.

,

AGAMEMNON   So you've come to persuade me to do it.

Say it isn't true. Let's say I did this, we went ahead, my daughter dies by my hand alone, the child is the price, but then the fair winds just do not blow. Silence. And it turns out we *read it wrong*, that there was some kind of flaw in the plan – and we are still at war

MENELAUS   Then the men know what their sacrifice / is worth

AGAMEMNON   This is not a public / thing

TALTHYBIUS   It would be preferable to – doing nothing, if the prophecy is real

AGAMEMNON   *If* the prophecy is real

MENELAUS   You have had the second opinions, checked and re-checked and it's always exactly the same. I'm saying: I believe the thing and so do you.

,

We brought these. I thought it might help.

EXHIBIT: SEVERAL PORTRAITS OF SOLDIERS

TALTHYBIUS   This is the commanding officer of each unit of / the defence staff, there are over [two hundred men]

AGAMEMNON   I know the men, I know their ranks and their / faces

TALTHYBIUS   But you don't know their families. These faces are brothers and fathers and sons. Almost every one of these is dad. And no one thinks this thing is close to the end. It's

	cut in deep, it's gone too far for that. And our enemy is prepared, planning *years* beyond – so there's no road to the end of this / that's swift
AGAMEMNON	I know. I know
TALTHYBIUS	But if we won. If it was ended, could be ended: no more deaths. No broken families following after coffins. No urns packed smooth with ashes. The thousands of lives that we'd save if it ended even a year early. *These* lives for these families in this army, in this *country,* never mind the people in the other camp on the other side of the ocean, the pure number of lives you would save –
AGAMEMNON	I understand the point. But what I'm being asked to do – I can't – my brain can't hold it as an *argument*
MENELAUS	What more could you give than your child? This sacrifice / would be a monument.
AGAMEMNON	Murder. At least talk to me like a man, don't give me sacrifice when what you mean / is [murder]
MENELAUS	It's never been murder before. When the men die, you never used that word. Their deaths are in service of a greater cause – they're heroes, not victims. They made a sacrifice. An active thing, a decision *they* made.
AGAMEMNON	But they are ugly deaths, unpeaceful deaths, and she has not made that choice, she is not a soldier
MENELAUS	But you are.
AGAMEMNON	In no code or system or law – no social law, even the law of nature, is this considered to – and I know that there is a higher power and a bigger picture – but she is not a soldier, for her to die / like that

42

MENELAUS	She wouldn't die like that.
AGAMEMNON	It said 'by his hand alone', the prophecy; I think that's pretty clear –
MENELAUS	It is, but – if – if you go ahead
AGAMEMNON	What if I don't? What happens then? If I refuse to 'go ahead'?
MENELAUS	*(Chorus.)* Then they'll [take other measures to insist that you do]
TALTHYBIUS	*(Chorus.)* Then we remain at your command.

,

MENELAUS	But if you go ahead, the means, we'd submit, it's a gentle process. Humane. Preparations have been made / to move forward
AGAMEMNON	Preparations
MENELAUS	Yes. I don't know what you think you gain by hearing me say the words. I know you know we would prepare in case that was the decision you made. And there are plans for both roads forward. You don't need to hear / the details
AGAMEMNON	'By his hand alone'. I *can't* just close my eyes. Go on.
MENELAUS	She wouldn't feel anything.
AGAMEMNON	*Go on.*

CALCHAS *reads the facts.*

CALCHAS	Administering first orally an ultra-short action compound, active ingredient metoclopramide, at a dose of 70mg, which acts as an antiemetic in order to prevent later vomiting. Then following the removal of any clothing likely to impede blood flow around the chest or upper arms, checks are undertaken to ensure that the procedure is fully understood by the parties before

it begins. Following the success of these, administering a single tablet with active ingredients sodium pentobarbital at 75mg and phenytoin sodium at 30mg. This solution has a particularly bitter taste, so a sweet drink is normally offered thereafter for comfort. Sleep would follow, then unconsciousness. The central nervous system is almost immediately depressed, inhibiting the stimulation of any muscles, followed eventually by respiratory arrest and circulatory collapse, cerebral death and cardiac arrest. No discomfort would be experienced.

AGAMEMNON   And the [body] – she would be unmarked?

CALCHAS   Entirely unmarked.

AGAMEMNON   I wouldn't want her body to be harmed. If we –

CALCHAS   *(Chorus.)* Yes

MENELAUS   *(Chorus.)* Yes, obviously it's not [a given that we go ahead]

TALTHYBIUS   *(Chorus.)* Yes.

AGAMEMNON   Thank you.

    And the recommendation is unanimous?

TALTHYBIUS   Yes.

AGAMEMNON   You're not her father.

    I didn't ask to be here. / I didn't ask to be in the middle of this complete and utter –

TALTHYBIUS   No.

AGAMEMNON   I should resign.

    I am in no way fit to make this judgement. I cannot – I cannot in good conscience make this decision

MENELAUS   Agamemnon –

AGAMEMNON	I've been dreaming, the last nights – the colours inside my mind, it's – like I'm living in a cartoon, a nightmare or something, but I've been wondering if I might be unwell. Mentally.
	I should resign. No: the life I should take is my own.
MENELAUS	And if you did, this decision would come in front of council, we'd meet, we'd talk, we'd put it to a vote. And in that room, the room that runs the better part of the world, there's not a man would vote *against* her death. Not him. Not even me. The price of her life, the *cost* is too high. One life to end / the whole sorry
AGAMEMNON	It's just wrong
MENELAUS	But if *she* doesn't feel pain, and it is a civilised procedure, and it is the clear and greater good then / who are the victims
AGAMEMNON	It's just WRONG
MENELAUS	Wrong in the sight of whom?
AGAMEMNON	In the sight of [god] –
	,
	Give us the room.
	And hey – I know, I'm – that's a good night's service.
TALTHYBIUS	I'll wait / outside
AGAMEMNON	It's fine. It's late. Go home.

TALTHYBIUS leaves.

I want to pray. I want to pray.

AGAMEMNON prays.

Father. I ask a second time. I will do what you want. I am your humble servant, we, my

brother and I, we bow before your might,
and will obey. But let me understand the
justice that will follow, let me – let me want
what you want. Let me understand.

,

MENELAUS   It isn't death you're afraid to [inflict] – it's
suffering. You don't want her to suffer – and
she won't. She won't *know* her death, she
can't, who does, it's just *absence.*

AGAMEMNON   But what she would *lose*: growing up, her hair
longer, her *mind,* her first – love – first taste of
wine, we're taking all of that away, her future

MENELAUS   But that's not, we know that's not the world,
I know you know that that's *not true*, it's just
a story you're telling yourself to make this
harder than it / is

AGAMEMNON   Harder than it is

MENELAUS   Why are you alive? Why do you stay alive?
What do you hope will happen? What
makes it worth another day, the next day,
continuing? What do you want from it?
Because the life you want for her, the quality
of [life] – all of the things you just [said], is not
an option, is not going to happen. We have
not made that world. If she's alive, it does
not look like that. It just doesn't. It wouldn't
look like *this*. We lose the war. We're defeated.
Dominated. Enslaved, and imprisoned – and
worse. She's a beautiful girl. Imagine her.
In that world. And if you think that, of all
people, your family would have any chance,
any chance at all, of staying in this house –
that *she* would have any chance of *anything* –

Even to us. Our people. She would be alive,
the fact of *her being alive*, would be instead of
their daughters and their brothers, pits full of

46

corpses that didn't need to die. The weight of
that brought down on them because of her.
They'd curse her name. That's not a world
in which she'd want to live. She *only* suffers if
she stays alive.

AGAMEMNON   She is a child. Just / a child.

MENELAUS   But you can see her future. And unlike
every other parent, you're not pushing
her forwards into a world you've failed to
guarantee. You *know* there's nothing good to
come. She only suffers if she stays alive.

,

AGAMEMNON   I worshipped them when I was young – the
generals, their ranks, their battles, their
medals, you know? They moved the borders
of the world. They were *huge*. And then
somehow, their names became our names –
those bronze-edged portraits were *of us* – and
you realise that you're now sitting in their
seats, the holder of their offices – and it's
so *disappointing*. It's not heroic, you're not
making history: just compromising, problem-
solving, hoping against hope that something
can at some point be achieved – day to day
to day. It's just *people*.

MENELAUS   And that wouldn't be different for her. She'd
just become an adult. Like me. Flawed and
sweaty and fundamentally sad.

But it is different for you. You're my brother,
Agamemnon but – it is different for you –
because I think you're about to do something
that will unlock every thing else, something
that makes you a thousand times any of the
people who came before you. You – and her.
An act of sacrifice that will – actually make

things better. And god knows, god knows
that on a thousand fronts we need that now.

,

AGAMEMNON   I don't want it to be public. We cover it up.
We bury it down so deep that no one ever
finds out.

AGAMEMNON   *(Chorus.)* All right?
MENELAUS   *(Chorus.)* All right.

AGAMEMNON sort of laughs.

AGAMEMNON   Look at us. Given the man Dad was, given
what happened, you have to think that we
managed to drag the family line forward
a certain distance. Considering how it was
in this house, how we could have just been
eaten up by all of it. And if we manage to do
one thing that's good, in its own way that's
astonishing.

MENELAUS laughs too.

I don't know why I'm laughing. It's just sort
of coming out.

It's important that she – she doesn't *speak,*
can't – during

MENELAUS   Yes. She won't feel anything. I promise you
that. And we'll give you all, the whole family
something to ensure you sleep. During.

AGAMEMNON   And in the morning, we wake up, she finds
her daughter in bed

MENELAUS   Natural causes. You won't see anything.

AGAMEMNON   That isn't what it says. It's 'by my hand',
not 'by my order': it has to be me. It's my
judgement – it's right I should be there.

MENELAUS   I'll be right next to you. I'll – come back later
to – but I need to go, to arrange [everything]
– I want to say I'm proud / of you

48

AGAMEMNON   I just don't understand what this is *for*.

MENELAUS   It's the right thing. It is an impossible
             decision

AGAMEMNON hears this afresh.

AGAMEMNON   It is not a decision, she is my daughter.
             Can you just. She is your niece, she is my
             daughter, and as her *family*, we – for crying
             out *loud* it's not something I am doing *lightly*
             SHE IS MY FUCKING DAUGHTER.

             I'm sorry, I'm – can you stay for –

But MENELAUS is gone.

             ,

KLYTEMNESTRA and AGAMEMNON.

             Oh. Hello. I didn't think you'd be up

KLYTEMNESTRA You didn't think I'd be up

             What you said to me before. I just … this is
             going to sound silly, 'The child is the price.'
             I know it's [secret], you can't discuss it, but I
             just – I'm just saying, be careful. If people's
             children are involved. I know your tracks are
             covered and it's in service of the country, but
             it comes back to you if it's your decision, and
             if someone found out – the cost to us, to all
             of us

AGAMEMNON   You're all well protected

KLYTEMNESTRA What's wrong? What's wrong?

AGAMEMNON   I'm just – too hot. There's – no, I'm – just

*He suddenly, forcefully tries to kiss her. She, surprised, stops
him – then:*

KLYTEMNESTRA Promise me – I'm saying, if I've read it right,
             'the child is the price' – promise me you
             won't get hurt

AGAMEMNON   I won't. / We won't

KLYTEMNESTRA	Agamemnon / I worry
AGAMEMNON	No revenge. No chance of that.
KLYTEMNESTRA	How can you be sure?
AGAMEMNON	I'm sure. *I'm sure.* I really don't want to keep talking about this, Klytemnestra, I really don't.
	,
KLYTEMNESTRA	It was a dream. Why are you – ?
	,
	'The child is the price'. It's. It's our child.
	That's what it meant.
	You can't think that you're going to [do it]. I don't believe that there's even a world in which you could consider – I can't – believe this, I can't believe / you
AGAMEMNON	I was going to tell you, Klytemnestra, listen –
KLYTEMNESTRA	It was a dream. A *dream.*
AGAMEMNON	It's more than that. I need you to listen to me. I'll tell you the truth, but I need you to understand. Please. *Everything* is telling me that something *more* is happening here, there have been signs / and I have tried to
KLYTEMNESTRA	And signs are scientific proof
AGAMEMNON	I know you're not behind me in my faith / we both know that, but
KLYTEMNESTRA	That's simplistic, that's a simplistic / version of what I think
AGAMEMNON	– but everything is pointing the same way
KLYTEMNESTRA	To kill our child. You're ill. You're mad. To kill our child?
AGAMEMNON	I wouldn't consider her / death – this is *why* I didn't say anything – I have looked for a way

	out, I *have* looked and looked and looked and looked –
KLYTEMNESTRA	'Her'! I am behind you, I have always been behind you, but Agamemnon, I don't *understand* how you could even think –
	All right. Stop. Tell me what you think is happening.
AGAMEMNON	I take her life by my own hand and then – we win the war.

,

KLYTEMNESTRA	So why has she not fallen ill? Why can't the god just take her life himself?
AGAMEMNON	I don't *know* – but the signs are clear. I've asked again and again and the signs *are clear.*
KLYTEMNESTRA	I'm going to tell the truth. The signs aren't *real* – Agamemnon, it has to be the whole truth now before you [go ahead] – yes, you have a difficult life, a difficult job, and your father did – bad things *happened* to you, but life is hard, it is always hard, it is hard for everyone and your faith helps – I understand – I really do, but it's in your *head,* there isn't any evidence
AGAMEMNON	The whole world is evidence
KLYTEMNESTRA	The world in which you have to kill your child? But let's call god by his real name, tell the truth, call him the way we *actually* live our lives, the things you actually serve – call him money, call him power, call him wars against the weak –
AGAMEMNON	I'm trying to be honest and you *know* this war is a necessary evil, we are fighting an enemy that can't be / left unfought

KLYTEMNESTRA	Yes but the end result is people die. You kill people and people die. Put whatever words on it you like but it's killing people in order to take their things or prove them wrong or 'cause you don't like the people they are – but let's be clear, those people die.

Look, it's good that we're here, it's good, it's clearly what was meant to happen. There'll be another way, another route, and we will find it. This isn't right. Look at me. It's me. Tell me this feels right.

, |
AGAMEMNON	When did we, when did we when did we decide that the right thing always *feels* right, it doesn't, it's hard, it's it's destructive and it's a sacrifice it's – putting yourself last, far faraway last, cold at the back, in the service of *other lives*, in the service of the greater good
KLYTEMNESTRA	The death of our child is not the greater good
AGAMEMNON	Their people, our people, the soldiers, you'd have *them* die and all so she can live. But we lose this war, and *my* daughter, she'll be lucky if all she is is dead. And – what if she dies and the wind comes?
KLYTEMNESTRA	You don't *know that will happen*
AGAMEMNON	I know that someone has to win this war. I didn't ask for this. You think I want to thrash inside this net? I tried to think. I sought advice. And now there's no more time. So what do I do? What do you want me to do?

, |
| KLYTEMNESTRA | I'm going to be sick. Your eyes are open – and you choose your war. Your men. The expression of the anger and the safety in |

	numbers, throwing ornate chairs through thick glass windows, the women all begging for mercy, and all signed off by the people above you, you're men / you've *overcome*
AGAMEMNON	well, that is all just myth and actually there is no one above me
KLYTEMNESTRA	And this is about you, the leader, inhumanly committed –
AGAMEMNON	It isn't. It isn't that / at all.
KLYTEMNESTRA	Mr Noble. Mr Resolute. The hero, the *man* that does the *thing*
AGAMEMNON	It won't be made public – it's / not about us
KLYTEMNESTRA	Some part of you must recognize that, if it has to be a secret, then it's probably [a crime]
AGAMEMNON	I know how it sounds – but you cannot think one child – that *any* one child – is worth the loss of this war and this country and troops and / troops and troops
KLYTEMNESTRA	This is *my child.* She was a part of my body. I don't *feel* the people whose lives will be saved, this is our bright-eyed little daughter who wants to sing you her song or tell you her story or just – chatter. Remember when she was born? Remember that? I am not crying and – remember when they came to us and they said they weren't *sure* if she would *make it* and I – and just ignore this I'm I'm I'm / not crying
AGAMEMNON	This isn't about us
KLYTEMNESTRA	This is about you and me, this is about the state of our – I don't even know the word because it's not marriage, it's not union, not united – because the last thing we are, the last thing we are now is on the same side / but this *is* about us, this is about a person

who came *from us*, who would never have *lived* if we hadn't loved each other, what you are / destroying is us, doing something that will overwhelm our history, a single action which if you bring it down on us will obliterate the whole story which precedes it

AGAMEMNON   Klytemnestra I need you to listen –
AGAMEMNON   Klytemnestra

KLYTEMNESTRA   She was a part of my body

AGAMEMNON   I don't want to do it

KLYTEMNESTRA   Then don't do it

As her mother, I am begging you. I am begging you: find another way. There will [be] – there is another way. I know that you won't do this to your home.

AGAMEMNON   You're not the only mother

AGAMEMNON sneezes.

I asked for wisdom. And it came. It came from you. The child is the price of the war, and we don't see the price of the war, we don't see it, and this this will insist that I do, that my judgement is clear, the whole truth of it, that – we are a hurricane like the force of gods' own fury, ripping buildings into dust. We kill *their* children, their mothers are begging for mercy and – he said, 'you suffer, you learn'. And the child is the price of the war. It's knowing fully what our action *means*. The sacrifice of life begins at home.

,

KLYTEMNESTRA   Sacrifice? This is slaughter, this is butchery – at this point, call it what you want but – smash a *bowl,* the bowl is smashed; she dies, your daughter dies, *Iphigenia* dies

I'm waking her up. I'll tell the house – I'll
WAKE THE HOUSE and / get her out of
bed and run

CILISSA is visible, awake, hearing this.

AGAMEMNON	Stop it, Klytemnestra, *stop,* you haven't got a chance

KLYTEMNESTRA   You're *killing* her. She won't *be here.* You're
taking what's hers and it looks like *this,*
this is destruction if you really want 'your
judgement to be clear', we can just take what
she loves and see what we learn from ripping
it to pieces with our hands

*KLYTEMNESTRA destroys IPHIGENIA'S doll. He tries to stop her,
get the toy back, she wrestles free. She physically pushes him.*

AGAMEMNON   Stop it Klytemnestra / stop it, this isn't fair –
give it *back*

KLYTEMNESTRA   Man resents child. He looks elsewhere. And
you have made a fool of me for years. Of our
marriage. For years. Don't think for a second
that I didn't / know

AGAMEMNON   And what is that supposed to mean? [You
stupid woman] has it been *a struggle* to live
your life from the fruits of my success?

KLYTEMNESTRA   Are you going to *hit* me now? Do it – do it
DO IT

*KLYTEMNESTRA pushes his chest again – and he tries to restrain
her and they fight – and it's ugly and it takes some time
and she beats his back and eventually they fall apart from
each other, breathing heavily. Both surprised by what has
happened, by the speed at which their marriage has fractured.*

,

Violence is how you've put food on our
table. And that, I have allowed. What are
you and I going to say to each other? How

will you hug your son? How are you going to look at us once you come back home –

We hear crying. In this calm, KLYTEMNESTRA and AGAMEMNON have never felt so far apart.

It's / Orestes

AGAMEMNON   Orestes, I know.

I'm sorry.

,

I wouldn't hurt you

KLYTEMNESTRA   In this conversation. That's an absurd thing to say.

,

God, it's so *hot* in here.

ORESTES is visible. He might have been listening.

ORESTES (Y)   I had a bad dream. Snakes.

What's happening?

AGAMEMNON   Come here. Nothing's happening. You're not in trouble. It's over now.

KLYTEMNESTRA   It's over now? Orestes, honey, let me tell you what your daddy thinks, he thinks your bad dreams / are just the beginning, that they don't go away when you wake up, they swell inside

AGAMEMNON   *Don't.* They don't need to be involved –

ORESTES is caught between his parents.

KLYTEMNESTRA   You were always going to do it. You liked to push back against it – it's a good feeling, surrender, actually – but you knew, you knew from the first moment you heard – even before you heard the question – you knew what your answer would be. This was always going to happen.

She's been dead since the beginning.

KLYTEMNESTRA'S gone.

IPHIGENIA walks forward, looks at AGAMEMNON. A camera is set up, and AGAMEMNON notices.

AGAMEMNON   Is that / necessary?

MENELAUS   Yes. Yes. It's procedure, it's controlled,
I'm – don't worry.

ORESTES and the DOCTOR.

ORESTES   I don't remember it. I was too young.

DOCTOR   That's all right. What are you holding?

ORESTES   A silver tray on which are three small,
pleated paper cups.

EXHIBIT: SILVER TRAY WITH THREE PAPER CUPS

AGAMEMNON has IPHIGENIA on his knee. MENELAUS and another woman also present. The camera is switched on.

WOMAN   Iphigenia. What a beautiful name.

MENELAUS   Are we ready?

,

WOMAN   I need you to confirm as Iphigenia's guardian
that you fully understand the course of action
in front of her today, and that you consent.
I need you to / clearly conf

AGAMEMNON   Yes. Yes. Yes. Yes.

MENELAUS   She has to – ask the questions. It has to be
done.

WOMAN   I need you to clearly confirm that you
understand the procedure.

AGAMEMNON   I understand.

WOMAN   And I need you to confirm that you know
what will happen as a result of the procedure.

AGAMEMNON   I know.

WOMAN	Thank you. OK.

,

Right, Iphigenia. You're doing very well.
I need you to drink this.

IPHIGENIA sits on AGAMEMNON's knee. Looks at him for confirmation. He nods. If he could say something, he probably would. He can't.

ORESTES	One of them contains a small amount of translucent liquid.

AGAMEMNON gives her, and IPHIGENIA drinks, the contents of the first cup.

WOMAN	And now just swallow this one. Try and make it just one swallow, straight down. It's not a nice taste, so you might need this one afterwards.
ORESTES	The second one contains a small orange tablet. The third one a sweet-flavoured liquid. Inside that tablet somewhere, one atom – makes it too much, tips the balance.

AGAMEMNON takes the tablet from the second cup and puts it on IPHIGENIA's tongue. She swallows it. It's bitter, and she crumples the cup. She's given the third one.

WOMAN	Very good. Well done. You're a very brave girl.

,

There's a long, long, long, long sharp pause. Total stillness and silence. We're waiting for the child to die.

AGAMEMNON	I love / you
IPHIGENIA	I think now I want to lie down.

She stretches out across AGAMEMNON. Eyes closed. Another long pause.

He suddenly lifts her up and he holds her tight, protective, impossible to believe he's here. As he resettles with her, she's drowsy, incoherent, but looks right at him and says something that's clearly discernable as

water, Daddy … water.

AGAMEMNON makes to get it for her –

MENELAUS   No, we can't, that's not –

– and AGAMEMNON would get it, except her eyes have already closed. There's another long pause. Then:

IPHIGENIA. TIME OF DEATH: [[TODAY'S DATE, THE TIME]].

WOMAN   She's gone.

Do you feel / alright?

AGAMEMNON   I feel like I've done something so wrong that my whole life, my family, nothing will be able to – the worst mistake. The worst mistake. I got it wrong. It was wrong. It was wrong.

But the last bit of this is drowned out the sound of the wind, real wind. Doors and windows rattle and fly open and the still, heavy heat is ruptured by cold wind flooding like a tide through the theatre.

KLYTEMNESTRA steps forward in front of this, she's heard the wind, realizing something. In a moment, she will scream.

IPHIGENIA'S body is carried away.

The wind rages now. Paper, fabric, lamps go flying, anything not fixed down, blows all over the set. KLYTEMNESTRA stands in full blast of it.

CALCHAS reads the facts.

CALCHAS   Areas of very high pressure circling down onto us, and extraordinary winds are picking up across the whole of the West now, so there's quite a time ahead for us, I'm afraid, it looks like this sudden onset is likely to remain with us, and even in the weeks to come, these systems seem reluctant to fade away so we'll be living with them for some time. Good night.

Wind rumbles underneath, distant, restless.

DOCTOR   Orestes. Do you remember the words you
           used – before?

ORESTES   Beating in the sky. The wind.

DOCTOR   The mother hare, it's Klytemnestra, the
           eagles are the men and the dead child inside
           the womb – It was *this story*. Her story.
           Iphigenia.

The stage is a mess. AGAMEMNON enters, sees KLYTEMNESTRA.

AGAMEMNON   There is a statement. Natural causes, deep /
                shock, asking for privacy –

KLYTEMNESTRA   I heard. And the wind.

           ,

He makes to leave, when:

           I'm really quite tired, but I want you to know
           that I – I won't say this tomorrow or again,
           perhaps. But

*Perhaps KLYTEMNESTRA stands behind him, puts her arms
around his waist.*

           I admire it. Somewhere. The decision.

           It's so mercilessly brave.

AGAMEMNON   Don't – [make a fuss]

KLYTEMNESTRA   I'm not, I won't. I mean: I mean it.

AGAMEMNON   It's hard not to interpret that as –

KLYTEMNESTRA   Let's just hold off the interpretation tonight.

                I know you feel it. I know it was hard. I do
                know that.

                And I do love you

                ,

                You're not going to come back, are you?

If it doesn't claim you – once you've won this war, once we've played the happy couple, you're going to leave. It's all right. I would prefer the truth.

You're not intending to come home, not to us. Not now.

AGAMEMNON   I don't know, there's no need to be [rash], it could be years before –

KLYTEMNESTRA   But –

AGAMEMNON   No.

KLYTEMNESTRA   Thank you.

,

AGAMEMNON   I don't want that to imply any criticism / of you or the way

KLYTEMNESTRA   Don't. Don't.

Go to sleep. I won't come up tonight. Please. Tomorrow this will all be fresh history. You will be setting out across the water. And I will get up at the very first sign of morning, and I will make a plan.

He kisses her gently, no reaction, he leaves. She sits for a while entirely alone on the stage. Maybe quite a while.

CALCHAS   Please be upstanding. We pause there for the first time. Thank you.

The act is over.

ACT TWO

ORESTES I watch it again, happening for the first time but – too late, too late to stop it. It pours out of me. But what if what's next is – ? What if it's better left sealed up, undisturbed?

DOCTOR We have to understand the truth.

ORESTES What if it's a dream? What if it's a lie?

DOCTOR Then those lies reveal something about you. 'Our self' isn't an absolute thing. It's handfuls of memories and moments and people – and we form them into who we think we are. For most of us, it's only partly true: one version of truth. / A story.

ORESTES A story. A story I've been through before. As a child. But I don't know where it ends –

DOCTOR To be a child is not to know what went before you. And we know where this started, Orestes, we stopped at what happened to your sister.

ORESTES She died. Iphigenia.

KLYTEMNESTRA still in position as at the end of the first act. IPHIGENIA stands where KLYTEMNESTRA can see her. She's dead, but she looks exactly as she did in the first act.

KLYTEMNESTRA This whole thing, this whole thing is about you.

IPHIGENIA is gone.

DOCTOR You look tired.

ORESTES Thank you. I try to sleep. I have bad dreams. Why is that? Which cell is that carved into? Some people just sleep.

CALCHAS reads the facts.

CALCHAS	… for several years – and that is what foreign stations are suggesting, though at this stage there is no official news or any formal statement. Good morning. Details are still coming in, but early reports are suggesting significant news concerning our troops and what may mark a significant watershed in this conflict …

There are sudden loud fireworks.

ORESTES	The war takes years. Much longer than they'd thought. And – we don't know what to believe –
ELECTRA	So how do you decide?
ORESTES	Electra. Electra would know what to do.

More fireworks. ORESTES *steps into the action, taking over from* YOUNG ORESTES.

ELECTRA	Wake up. Wake *up.* It's true.
ORESTES	What's happening?
ELECTRA	Wake up. It's happened. Last night. It happened. I don't know whether to believe it or not but it's what everyone's saying.
ORESTES	Don't kiss / me.
ELECTRA	I can kiss you if it's good news
ORESTES	What's happened?
ELECTRA	We won.
ORESTES	We – what? How do you know?
ELECTRA	Mum said. The war, we've won. It means Dad's coming home.

Suddenly the atmosphere of preparation, distant bands play, smoke in the air, we're outside, people rushing everywhere preparing for a major public event. ORESTES *sees his mother, being prepared for interview.*

ORESTES	Mum … say hello … say hello … wave …

KLYTEMNESTRA	I want you to remember today. This is one of the good days. This is an important day.
ORESTES	When did we win? How did you know?
KLYTEMNESTRA	I know. We won. They're all on their way home. And your father.
ORESTES	Are you pleased?
KLYTEMNESTRA	I'm delighted, Orestes. I'm ecstatic. Are you pleased?
ORESTES	Yes.
	But how do you know that we won? I don't want to believe it until I *know* it's true, because if it / isn't, then I –
KLYTEMNESTRA	I'm sure. You don't need to / doubt
ORESTES	But is there evidence? Was there any sign? Did you dream it?
	,
KLYTEMNESTRA	Dream? I'm not a child. Are you going to question your father like this? And there are always signs. You just have to know how to read them.
ORESTES	How?
KLYTEMNESTRA	Why do we call that thing a 'chair'? It's just sounds in the air, strange black symbols on white paper. Chair. But you and I both know the code – that word – 'chair' – points to that thing. *This* means *that*.
	I have come to realise that everything, my darling, is about the connections between things, between – word and deed, inside and outside. One person and another.
	Once it was signal fires. Lit in one place, the light seen miles away. Then that became

	'if it's a yes, go to the window and light the lamp' – like in the story, you remember?
ORESTES	Yes
KLYTEMNESTRA	And it's still light. Light inside your brain, impulses, burning, firing forwards, carrying signs – continuous light – but smaller even than we can see it, fired up inside the hollow of the walls, sweeping under the floors and up over the roofs, bouncing distantly unbroken in the sky, and so *fast,* so inconceivably impossibly fast, splitting a second into a thousand parts. And, this moment, now, there are so many infinitesimal points on the globe ablaze, so many rapid lines of light, connecting 1 to 2 to 3, lines shimmering and intertwining and reweaving themselves, that we have wrought a net which holds the world, illuminating like another sun.

And the moment that war ends, the final
occupation is complete, on the ground,
there – one signal is sent, then another
signal screaming through the lines of this
massive invisible structure, like runners in
a relay race, cutting across the deep buzz of
civilisation – to this house and this room and
this hand – and:

The sign. And you read. And you judge. And
you know. Just like that 'chair'.

I know where the bases were, what roads
they took, what weapons they used, that
it was too hot for the most part to wear a
uniform. And I know for a fact that we've
won.

| DOCTOR | Why have you stopped? |

ORESTES	There's a way of reading the signs – gathering little things up into big slabs of meaning – but it just slips. There's things missing.
DOCTOR	Are you talking about your sister?
ORESTES	No. I don't – no. It's what came next –

KLYTEMNESTRA is interviewed. She is more open in public than in private.

QUESTION	I will understand if there are things you don't want to say.
KLYTEMNESTRA	I'm happy to talk about my family, I'm not ashamed at all. I love my husband. I love my husband. And I can't tell you what it means to welcome him home. I've been the man of the house, keeping the home fires burning. And now. HE'S COMING HOME. God, I'm not ashamed to shout that from the rooftops – it's the, time really doesn't do wonders for modesty.
QUESTION	But it hasn't been an easy time for you?
KLYTEMNESTRA	How could it ever be easy?
QUESTION	Your husband left only days after the tragic passing of your daughter, of Iphi*gen*ia.
KLYTEMNESTRA	Iphigen*i*-a. Yes.
QUESTION	She died of natural causes. But that must have been hard.
KLYTEMNESTRA	Just – look at my face. I'm an old woman now. You cry. You pull yourself together. You see her clothes in the wardrobe. You see *his* clothes. You cry. You try to sleep, but, the tiniest sound, a fly beats its wings and your eyes crack back open.

Which is to say, you live alone in the house, yes, but where you're really alone is inside |

66

your head. You dream the worst. It's not helped by the age we live in – there are the rumours, of course, and if he had been wounded every time it was reported, there'd be more holes than flesh, like a net (!) or something – you can't trust what's being said – [but] you can't ignore it either. It worms its way in. Relentlessly imagining his death. You walk the halls, you wait for it to come. An arrival, the bell rings – some stranger, formal – and you know what he's here for as soon as the door swings open. But the stories, the endless cacophony of judgement – even today when the news first came, the voices, people saying 'don't rejoice too early, typical woman, jumping to conclusions' – it doesn't help anything.

QUESTION   Of course. And that has affected your health.

KLYTEMNESTRA   Yes, it has.

,

QUESTION   Which is something you've been very brave in discussing.

KLYTEMNESTRA   Thank you. I thought it was important – important to speak about the pressure at home. You're being very, well, dignified in not saying it, but, for those who haven't read between the lines, I attempted suicide. I tried to hang myself.

,

QUESTION   Yes. But you're doing better now. Your mental / health

KLYTEMNESTRA   I'm not sure that's – well, I'm not sure it's really a *medical* thing, I mean it's not an *irrational* response, given the position in which I found myself. Who knows?

	But yes. I am in full command now. You protect your children.
QUESTION	Your husband has been fighting for several years now, and under his command our forces have, as you know, suffered substantial losses. I wondered whether you thought he might feel in some way / responsible
KLYTEMNESTRA	I wouldn't know about that. I'm his wife, not his conscience.
QUESTION	You wouldn't know?
KLYTEMNESTRA	I've been in this house. I haven't seen him.
	,
QUESTION	But as a woman, you must have an opinion? These are people's / children
KLYTEMNESTRA	'As a woman'. I find that a disquieting phrase. I mean, I don't have sets of opinions depending on the mask I'm wearing, it's not as if I think one thing when I'm – breastfeeding and then change entirely when I'm doing something – I mean, I can't answer you *as a woman*. I contain multitudes. I'm not sure how much being a woman means to me. I've never been a man. My gender isn't something I selected for myself; it doesn't surprise me when I look in the mirror.
QUESTION	Yes – I'm sure you are aware of the reports: alleged incidents abroad, the violations of civilian homes and places of worship in the / final stages
KLYTEMNESTRA	I've heard reports, like everyone else. What none of us know yet is the truth – and so what we say is merely speculation. I'll wait for clearer information before I assume to judge.

QUESTION	Finally, what does today mean?
KLYTEMNESTRA	Who wrote your questions? Well, it means something different to each of us. The war is finished, that's the – fact – if you like, but we all look at that fact through our own lens, our own families, our own dreams and sadnesses. To me? What does it mean? Too much. Let's just say that it's an extraordinary *relief* that today is here, finally here.
QUESTION	Thank you. I know you'll need to prepare – we're expecting them to reach us at any moment –
KLYTEMNESTRA	Thank *you*.
ORESTES	You watch yourself like in a dream, it's like watching someone else, you're walking back along the road, but the trap is still a shock the second time, you have to fall into the trap – the trap is yours. That's stupid, isn't it?
DOCTOR	No. I'm here to help you. I'm not here to judge you.
ORESTES	It was solid, then. And now it crumbles – it breaks into memory – and I force the pieces back but they're all in different places and it doesn't work, there's holes. The thing won't *hold*. There's something *wrong*.
DOCTOR	Just tell me what happens. One step at a time.
ORESTES	He comes home.

AGAMEMNON enters. He looks older, greyer. He's been through a lot.

KLYTEMNESTRA looks at him. She moves swiftly to him, hugs him. It takes some time for her to let go. They move to a podium and address the crowds.

KLYTEMNESTRA	Before we begin our lives again, before we take the time for this family to heal, I just

have a few things to say. God, you're so used
to hearing these speeches, so well-trodden,
but it's different when you're here.

This is a happy day, but it cannot be a day
entirely without sadness. As we celebrate, we
think of those who will not be at home today,
and we think of those families who are not
welcoming home their hero, and we think
of the empty chair at their table tonight. To
them, I say this: we are all, every one of
us, all your families. Around the world. We
stretch our hands out to hold yours. We share
your loss. We mourn your loss. We honour
their sacrifice.

And as for those who come back to us today,
we are truly lucky, but their trials are not
yet over. They have made it to the opposite
bank, but now they have to turn around,
swim back home, to climb back out where
they first dived in. As these soldiers once
more become accustomed to the way they
used to live, keep them well. Allow them
to fall backward into the embrace of their
homes.

And this house too has missed the head
of its table. Whatever he is to you, inside,
he's just another husband, another father.
Another man. The best of men. My hero. My
husband.

AGAMEMNON   Well. Your speech, like my, uh, absence,
went on for longer than perhaps –

(He laughs.) – I'm happy to be home, though
I think, my wife is perhaps not best placed to
praise me, for –

,

I'm not going to cry or anything.

70

We won. We got them. It happened.

And we are all thankful to be home. It's in the lap of the gods – and we've been *lucky*, to win, to return, to – look, it came down on our side and we are *thankful* for that. The city god didn't favour – well, she's not a city any more.

It's a hard place to be. The heat, especially and the sand, the lice. You miss a cold tap that's actually cold. Even in the winter it's not cold but the birds die, somehow – couldn't figure out why that happened but they're everywhere, strange feathered lumps all over the roads. But we have remained *unified*: it's a hard thing to do to look on other people's success and be happy for them, no jealousy, no bitterness – and that's the sort of company I am lucky to have had. That's the truth. There are some of us who haven't come back, as she [said] – including my brother, who sadly, uh, as I'm sure you know. So.

MENELAUS. TIME OF DEATH: [[TODAY'S DATE, THE TIME]].

There's a lot of work to do to put our house in order. There are many things that will need our intervention – we'll be asking where things have gone wrong, and taking whatever action necessary to put things right. Which will include the healing of the sick.

I was also, uh, moved, by some of the civilians, the ordinary people over there, after – one of whom I've brought home, at my own expense. She's only a girl, her family were sadly, uh, [casualties], and she's – she was hidden in a church when we found her, knees bleeding on the stonefloor, underneath the altar, shaking – and I wanted to save her, Cassandra, she's [called] – she's not yet ready to speak in public but she will, in time, and I think her story will be important for all of us to hear. Because I understand – it's important to remember – that victory was dearly bought – is, always.

All right. Thank you. To all of you. For your support and prayers. To my family. And bringing us safely home was gods' work and for that I say – thank you.

KLYTEMNESTRA   Thank you for coming back. In so many ways, it's been a long journey – and now there are only a few steps left. We all wanted those steps to be soft – for you to walk in on a river of scarlet – we wanted to do justice to you – to give you a just welcome home.

A carpet is spread out for AGAMEMNON to walk in on.

AGAMEMNON   It's not right

KLYTEMNESTRA   It's your right – and no one would deny it

AGAMEMNON   It's a red carpet – I'm not a priest – it's wrong

KLYTEMNESTRA   It's a welcome home – and those times over there when you longed to be here, it's something that you'd have *sworn* to do. It's what the enemy would be doing / if he was in your shoes

AGAMEMNON   It's extravagance – expensive cloth – I don't like how it looks

KLYTEMNESTRA   It's not for you to be led by jealousy

AGAMEMNON   This shouldn't be a fight

KLYTEMNESTRA   Then surrender: you don't need to win

AGAMEMNON   Does it really mean that much?

AGAMEMNON smiles, tired.

	Let the record show that she made me do it. I'll take my shoes off. I'm not sure I can walk on this. It's about as extravagant as I am ashamed. I – I don't like taking curtain calls.
KLYTEMNESTRA	I'm sorry. Don't prepare to come inside. You don't get to come inside the house.
AGAMEMNON	Thank you.

AGAMEMNON takes a single step onto the red carpet.

,

ORESTES	My breath smells of fear. I feel like there's a bird inside me beating to get out. I *know* I know what's coming – but I don't.
DOCTOR	What are you scared of?
ORESTES	What *happens* when I dream? What is knotting together with what – what is being made? Fear and wishes and – and if it's me, if it's just inside me with no meaning elsewhere, can't I create something *better* than this, can't I choose imagined hope rather than imagined fear?
DOCTOR	Perhaps the fear is real.
ORESTES	Is it? Is it illusion? How do I know?
	I feel like everything is *full*, interwoven, *significant* – and it goes so fast, a white sea of eyes and every single person there, every single person now alive will be dead in – what in historical terms is no time at all. And what does it *mean*?
DOCTOR	Just – tell me what happens
ORESTES	I look up and it's like my heart is pumping out the blue of the clouds hot onto my face

AGAMEMNON first one inside, same position as before, same words:

AGAMEMNON	I'm home.

He touches the table. Looks back around the house. It's familiar, though years and years have passed. And then KLYTEMNESTRA *is inside. It's difficult to tell what their relationship is now.*

What was that supposed to mean?

,

KLYTEMNESTRA *goes up to him, almost aggressive. She takes his head, rests it against her forehead. Then she kisses him, hungrily. He kisses her back. Maybe they'll have sex. But then they don't. And he says:*

There's so much to say, I –

CILISSA *is there. She has* AGAMEMNON'S *dressing gown. He puts it on.*

ORESTES	It's like a net of animals hoisted above you and it's going to split and they'll fall onto [you] – but it's too high for you to see what animals are in there now, you can just hear them and (you think) smell them but you're not sure whether it's snakes or birds or fish or what – and you just – you think – I want one to slip through, to drop down into my hands – and then at least I'd know –
DOCTOR	What would you know?
ORESTES	Or a sea of fluid slapping against the weakest wall of a room, trickles running down the cracks, tiny shudders, any moment it smashes through –
DOCTOR	Are you scared of your father?
ORESTES	I can't get it. I can't get it.
DOCTOR	I need you tell me the truth. What happens?
KLYTEMNESTRA	And it's a simple task: it shouldn't take hours.
CILISSA	And what shall I do with his clothes?

KLYTEMNESTRA	Anything stained, just – actually, throw them all out.

CILISSA and ELECTRA try and bring in CASSANDRA. She wears a saffron dress, and is reminiscient somehow of IPHIGENIA.

CILISSA	It all comes home. She's a prisoner of war – she'll fit right in. Come on.
ELECTRA	You can come in. You can come into the house now.
CILISSA	Your mother doesn't want her seen.
ELECTRA	Hello? Speak? Come. In. DO. YOU. SPEAK?
CILISSA	Like a wild animal.
ELECTRA	She won't speak the same language as us.
CILISSA	Oh, I think she understands us. I think she's angry. Angry to be away from home, angry to be trapped.
	I feel sorry for her.
	Make a sign. If you understand. Make a sign.

ORESTES and DOCTOR.

DOCTOR	We have to accept that our parents are people. No greater or better than us. Just people, at the end.
ORESTES	But they *created* you. They made you, they're – they're more than human if they – they're creators. Your creators. Mythic.
DOCTOR	That's true for all of us.
ORESTES	Dinner. The family.

KLYTEMNESTRA rings the dinner bell. The family assemble. The table is set again: a version of the same ritual. CASSANDRA sits in IPHIGENIA's seat, takes her place. Deep unease with this stranger at the table. Everyone looking at her.

KLYTEMNESTRA	What's your name?

ELECTRA	She doesn't speak.
KLYTEMNESTRA	I can't blame her for that.
AGAMEMNON	Be kind to her. She won't be here for long.

,

ELECTRA	Dad. What's going on?
KLYTEMNESTRA	That's an interesting question.
AGAMEMNON	I have had *enough* of being questioned, everyone.
ORESTES	Dinner in silence. Wine.

ELECTRA uncorks and pours wine.

ELECTRA	It's better at least than the old tell the story of your day thing, do you / remember
ORESTES	Electra.
	It's like the ghost of how we used to be, the family, years earlier, that ghost is fluid up to our [waists] and we're moving around in it … it's all new but the feeling is just behind our heads
DOCTOR	That's good. Old feelings. Strong feelings.
ORESTES	I want to stop.
DOCTOR	We can't stop. What happens?
ORESTES	It ends. Dinner ends.

As they rise from the table, AGAMEMNON speaks to KLYTEMNESTRA.

AGAMEMNON	I miss her. It's strange without her here. You can feel the … the – I don't have the word.
ORESTES	More must have happened, it's all rushing, I can't – it's rushing forward in my head. More was said. We're here too soon.
AGAMEMNON	We will talk later. About everything. I'm going to take a bath.

CILISSA has started the bath running. ELECTRA knocks on the table. CASSANDRA becomes gradually more frenzied.

ELECTRA Why do you keep swallowing?

     What happened to you?

     Did you even want to come here?

     ,

     Is my dad fucking you? Are you in love?

ORESTES Can you ever know you're going to do something *before* it happens – there are too many little things that can throw it all off course, everything has an effect –

ELECTRA *Can you actually speak?*

Then: CASSANDRA suddenly speaks in Ancient Greek from the original Aeschylus – passionate, furious, tearful. It's terrifying to listen to.

CASSANDRA οτοτοτοO ϖόϖοι δO

ORESTES and ELECTRA jump.

ORESTES She speaks, but I don't understand her, it's another / world

CASSANDRA now continues to speak in Ancient Greek underneath the below.

ELECTRA *(Ad lib.)* I don't understand you – I don't know what you're saying.

ORESTES It's too much – like the blood rushing to my heart. I'm pale, I can feel myself feeling dizzy – I don't remember specifically what – I don't have *access* –

     Is this what I felt then or what I'm feeling now?

DOCTOR I don't know what you think the difference is

ORESTES Why do we do things?

DOCTOR What do you mean?

ORESTES	Is it because we – can you predict based on our parents and our actions and our – every single day is another another – can you know, can you ever know, what someone is going to do until it's done?

AGAMEMNON has a thought. He's remembering IPHIGENIA.

AGAMEMNON	I'd like to hear some / music.
ORESTES	Music.

We hear IPHIGENIA's song in its original recording. It plays underneath the below action – an accumulation of sounds now, fighting for dominance.

As AGAMEMNON reaches the bathroom, IPHIGENIA is sitting at the end of the bath. The little girl in the yellow dress. Their eyes meet. He shakes his head, eyes full of tears.

CASSANDRA suddenly speaks in English:

CASSANDRA	catched in trap. same story. it's same story doesn't stop doesn't cease it's same same story my story is your story is – family extinct – only survivor – father after father the blood runs down, seeps thick through the generations, hangs over house like a blanket, house beats like heart hearth it all burns turns blisters the blood the line the word a net a web a trap and fury is already here inside, screaming children / already inside
ELECTRA	You're mad. You're seeing things. There's nothing / there
CASSANDRA	the house breathes slaughter. he dies. murder. he dies now. no good gods here. not in this story. these are his final moments. these ones. he dies now.
ELECTRA	WHO dies? Who's died? I don't / understand
CASSANDRA	can you hear the singing? they are all singing in this house, always in the house, in every

room, smells of the grave, sweet, salty, thick, the open ground. thick, warm blood sweeps through the house, splashes up the walls, like oil across the floor, there's no way out, no way back

Elsewhere, KLYTEMNESTRA *addresses* CILISSA.

KLYTEMNESTRA   I wonder at what point you'll actually wake up.

CASSANDRA   i try to tell you – i *know.* i know you. you're in the same place as i am – taste the iron in the air. and look. the child outstretches handsfull of flesh.

please don't forget me. it is written, written in clear black – everywhere dead girls. dead girls.

CASSANDRA   / the sadness washes all the rest away

ORESTES   the sadness washes all the rest away: I remember –

The playback speed of the music gets sickeningly faster and faster.

DOCTOR   What are you holding?

ORESTES   It's a knife, a knife – that – it's silver, long-bladed, it has the name of its maker, 'lábrys', engraved on the [handle] –

EXHIBIT: SILVER LÁBRYS KNIFE

AGAMEMNON *gets into the bath – the sense of something finally completed.*

I – I know what happens.

KLYTEMNESTRA *whips the tablecloth off the table. Walks to the bathroom.*

AGAMEMNON *sees her, conciliatory. She enters and calmly throws the cloth over his head and stabs him. We don't see it, but he falls hard against the bath. She stabs him again and again and again.*

ORESTES   The girl is dead. I don't – remember how she
            died

*CASSANDRA lies to one side. Blood runs from the corner of
her mouth.*

CASSANDRA. TIME OF DEATH: [[TODAY'S DATE, THE TIME]].

            I stand right there and my first thought is
            I should call Dad, I should ask God, I –
            where's Electra? – Electra would know what
            to do – and things congeal, the moments
            thicken – I don't know where to cast my
            vote – not sure enough to judge or know
            what to do – and though it's slower now, I
            do nothing – and it's already done. It's her.
            It's *her.*

It's suddenly silent. The music stops.

AGAMEMNON. TIME OF DEATH: [[TODAY'S DATE, THE TIME]].

*Then, KLYTEMNESTRA comes very precisely out of the bathroom,
dragging the body of AGAMEMNON into view covered in
bathwater and blood. AGAMEMNON's body continues to bleed.*

KLYTEMNESTRA   There … there … there … there … there
               … there are some things to say now, some
               things to –

KLYTEMNESTRA is entirely rational, quiet, collected, forceful.

            Everything I have said until this point – all of
            it – was lies. To myself, to my family, to the
            public, to *him,* it was all, all untrue but as I
            speak this, in this moment, this *is* true – from
            now.

            'Killed by his *wife.*' Not a person. Not a
            murderer. A woman. Because we love a
            female criminal, that *strength* a transgression,
            carnal, sexier or some[thing], the stronger-
            weaker vessel or [whatever] – but this is
            not the world. Not now. The lights are on.
            Your houses have drawers full of knives. It's

80

not biology, not destiny, it's just – *balance,*
the law of *moral appetite,* the inevitable act
that follows when when when – he killed
our daughter. He killed our daughter, my
daughter that I carried in my body. And so
this right hand had the right to strike – and it
struck. It struck his foreign bitch and it struck
him down.

The war came home. This is what he *did*: this
is the war that put food on our table. This is
how it *looks.* What did you think was inside
that word? You know this is what happens,
what it looks like, this is the human animal
panicking as the cord is cut – and you can
look away but he did this thing, in your
name, to our enemies, and he did it to our
daughter, did this to her, set the thing in
motion, and now *just* is the *balance* of his act.

– and when the life, struggling out of him,
sprayed by lumps of blood, blood hitting
blood on my neck and down my arms
and soaking up my clothes but god it was
something it did not disgust me not even for
a second – the rhythm of it – the way it slid
into him – god it was so fucking *easy* – even
just thinking it I want to do it again, I want
another *ride,* I want it always – *now* – I want
the *(Scream.)* of it all – and I open my mouth
like a plant in the rain in the red and I feel so
awake, it's like liquid *rightness* pumping into
arteries, he's *dead,* I am alive – and I'm free –
and from this point, from now, this house is
set in order ONCE AND FOR ALL

CALCHAS   Please be upstanding. We will now take a
pause. Thank you.

The act is over. The body is removed.

ACT THREE

The sound of wind. The feel: grey morning. CILISSA is cleaning.

KLYTEMNESTRA lifts the dinner bell, doesn't ring it.

ELECTRA   We don't have to do that any more. We
               could just break the habit. We could just stop.

KLYTEMNESTRA   It's a tradition, not a habit.

ELECTRA   What's the difference?

KLYTEMNESTRA   Whether or not it means anything.

*KLYTEMNESTRA rings the dinner bell. KLYTEMNESTRA and
ELECTRA sit down. The tablecloth has holes in it and the
bloodstains are now dried.*

ORESTES   He died. She killed him.

DOCTOR   And you survived that trauma. We're barely
               there in the moment it blossoms – we hardly
               feel it as it hollows us out – what hurts is the
               next second; awakening into what's *left* –

               And I don't think you've woken up. I'm not
               sure you want to wake up.

ORESTES   Why would / I

DOCTOR   Fear. Of where you might be. Where you
               might really be.

IPHIGENIA stands on the table, dancing.

KLYTEMNESTRA   There are a certain few people in a life that
               you *absorb*, they stay alive in you, even after
               they've [gone], ideas, what they would *think,*
               their way of laughing – and by my age you
               have them in place. And your connection
               with them is so strong, that splitting, when it
               comes, will be violent. It can't not be violent.
               They made you.

82

And losing them, you lose a part of yourself.
We are so horribly tied to each other,
so bound up together. And as you [lose
someone], as they fall over the edge some
invisible cord pulls tight, and rips a huge
lump out from under your skin.

Which is to say, I miss him. I know you think
I don't feel anything, that I'm ... but the
person who knew you when you were young
and beautiful, loved you when you were.
Well, you only get one of those.

My brain still thinks she's here. Even now. I
thought it would stop. This house so silent. I
keep thinking I can smell her hair –

Are you wearing her dress?

Are you?

ELECTRA   Why shouldn't I?

KLYTEMNESTRA   Because it's wrong. It isn't – civilised. Take
               her clothes off. Take them *off*. It isn't right.

ELECTRA   They're there. There's no one to wear them
               now.

Enter AEGISTHUS, *late. He takes his place at the table. He is
played by the same actor who played* AGAMEMNON.

AEGISTHUS   Sorry, sorry for lateness.

ELECTRA   If you're not here, you don't eat

ELECTRA opens wine, easily now.

CILISSA is staring sort of intensely at AEGISTHUS.

KLYTEMNESTRA   She doesn't remember *anything*. Your brain is
               holed below the water line –

She gives up. What's the point.

               (Slow, loud.) This is Aegisthus. You've seen
               him before. And now you can go and look
               for dust again.

CILISSA	The man of the house. My lady, I am having a bit of trouble with the house, the stains won't / wash away
KLYTEMNESTRA	I am sick of you telling me this. Really, really sick.

CILISSA leaves.

	I don't like the way she looks at people. I've never liked it.
ELECTRA	At what point is the house going to be unlocked? And why are we not talking about Orestes? Why are you not worried? He's *gone*. He's been gone for –
	,
AEGISTHUS	It's nice to eat all together like this.
	And it's a delicious meal.
ELECTRA	What is it?
KLYTEMNESTRA	'It' is *not up for cross-examination.*
DOCTOR	Were you afraid of him? When did Aegisthus arrive?
ORESTES	I don't know.
DOCTOR	Was it before your father's passing? Did Aegisthus play a part in your father's / death?
ORESTES	I don't *know.*
DOCTOR	And he was your mother's lover? He was in the house?
ORESTES	Yes.

Though only a few moments earlier the actor was playing AEGISTHUS, he now becomes AGAMEMNON and ELECTRA talks to him.

ELECTRA	Dad. You used to sit right there.

AGAMEMNON	I did. Family meals. Your mother's custom. Still going.
ELECTRA	We're not the model family of the modern major general. But then we weren't that when you were here either.
	It's strange that you aren't here.
AGAMEMNON	You'll get used to it.
ELECTRA	I haven't yet.
AGAMEMNON	You will.
ELECTRA	It feels like minutes. I know it's been longer than that.
AGAMEMNON	This is it now. This is doing things fatherless.
ELECTRA	I just thought that.
AGAMEMNON	Like father [like son].
ELECTRA	I sharpen my pencil fatherless. I pour a glass of wine fatherless. I don't drink it fatherless. I hear a song fatherless that I used to [like] –
	I feel absolutely nothing at all.
	I imagine a conversation with my father fatherless. The colour of it stains my head. It echoes. It stays with me. Whether or not any of the words were ever spoken, it's the realest thing that happens all day.
AGAMEMNON	It isn't easy. But it will be worth it.
ELECTRA	Ah, you're not really there.
AGAMEMNON	Neither are you, most of the time.
ELECTRA	Now what does *that* mean?

AGAMEMNON smiles.

| AGAMEMNON | In some ways it's better like this than it was before. We're better like this. |

ELECTRA	At least we talk now. Before you were like a god or something. As in, I asked for things and you ignored me.
	What do you miss the most being dead?
AGAMEMNON	Red wine, probably.
ELECTRA	I miss *you*.
	,
AGAMEMNON	You don't need me. It's all ahead of you. Old age. Before that, children. Before that, marriage. Before that, falling in love for the first time.
ELECTRA	I think that happened. Did you fall in love with mum?
AGAMEMNON	Yes.
ELECTRA	And the others?
AGAMEMNON	Yes.
ELECTRA	I don't understand.
AGAMEMNON	Why does it have to be only one thing? Can it not be more?
	,
ELECTRA	Did you believe in god – the storey above – did you believe all that because you were scared? Or because you really believed?
AGAMEMNON	What's the difference?
ELECTRA	You see, I think there is one.
	I don't drink any more. I did for a while. But the pain sort of soaks through the wine and it doesn't really taste like anything.
AGAMEMNON	You got used to wine.
ELECTRA	I did.
	I wonder a lot about what it's all for. What it all means.

AGAMEMNON slowly gets up, leaves.

	And this doesn't really work because you're not really there. And the second I'm conscious of that, properly conscious, you're not there at all. You're just a guest in my imagination – some diluted performance of you replaying and replaying and replaying
ORESTES	I want to *stop*.
DOCTOR	That isn't possible: we are trying to understand the truth
ORESTES	This is *my life* – and I do not want to talk about the truth, there isn't one, there are just versions of versions, twisting variations, seething over each other like bees, and one of them actually happened, there's one that is actually *right*
DOCTOR	Orestes, / that's not
ORESTES	All we have is *this.* Just people and their outsides like shells, hard and shiny and beautiful and *hollow* – and the truth is swimming dark underneath and if you prise it out, prise truth out into the light, it evaporates as it comes to the surface.

I don't want to answer your questions. I don't. I don't even know who you *are*.

I want this all to stop. Just *end*. This is finished.

The DOCTOR leaves ORESTES.

The grave appears, ELECTRA by it; elsewhere, KLYTEMNESTRA and AEGISTHUS are in the house.

ELECTRA	The day peels open slowly. I can't sleep but I wake – and for a moment it holds – but like a wound you forgot in the night, you move and it hits – and he's gone.

And all I can feel is that gap. The place where he should be. It doesn't close up. It's real – a solid hole engraved into the world. It feels like feeling scared.

I wish it would rain. Something at least – what's the opposite to indifferent? Different. Not the same. But it is the same. The world kept going. White clay sky. Flat land.

'In loving memory' 'In a better place' 'Sleep well' – *sleep well?* 'We will remember you'. We. There really is no 'we'. You can't be 'we' if you're written by a single person – and it's just words. Words are defined by – words. Words chasing each other round in circles until they quietly just stop existing.

And why flowers? Once it was *personal,* someone who loved flowers and this was for them – and now it's repetition, one size fits all, bled dry of all the things it used to hold, *things we do* for a reason that no one remembers.

And the flowers are dead and the language is dead and the stars are dead and the light is dead and everything reminds me of the loss, everything points to the fact that he isn't *here,* he isn't here, he isn't *here.* He survived a war. And he came home. And she –

,

The sum total of someone you knew – and it's this

Old meat buried in the earth

KLYTEMNESTRA and AEGISTHUS.

KLYTEMNESTRA   You were so much more interesting the way I imagined you.

I couldn't stop thinking about you. I couldn't stop. Your face was everywhere and it was all the clichés, it hurt but it was a pleasure, it stretched from my throat down into my stomach and I made another person inside you.

And it wasn't you at all.

Was it? Was it? *Aegisthus*.

AEGISTHUS   I don't know. I can't see inside your head.

KLYTEMNESTRA   *Exactly*.

,

AEGISTHUS   I wish we could leave the house. It's been long enough now, surely, that we can assume / that nothing …

KLYTEMNESTRA   Don't say it. Don't *say* it. Have you been drinking?

It's the chase isn't it. That first time. You knew I was married. You knew who he was. You wanted it to happen and you didn't think it could happen so you wanted it more. And I wanted it to happen and I thought be brave I'll do it I'll cut the cord and just run

AEGISTHUS   I still / want it …

KLYTEMNESTRA   I feel like I'm just waiting to die. I feel a thousand years old.

Fuck me or something.

KLYTEMNESTRA screams.

ELECTRA   *Dad* I don't know what to *do*

How do you mourn? There's nothing to say. *No response.*

I suppose this will at least mix in with you, somewhere. And you liked wine.

ELECTRA uncorks a bottle of red wine very easily, kisses it, pours it into the grave. Simultaneously, AEGISTHUS turns on the bath taps – and elsewhere, KLYTEMNESTRA pours herself wine. The sound of water.

KLYTEMNESTRA   I felt so alive once I'd killed him, *conscious* that perhaps holding death in your hands is as alive as you can ever feel – I was *free*, it was finished. And then it slowly ran into the ground.

CILISSA arrives to ELECTRA.

ELECTRA   Don't feel like you have to sit there in silence. I'm not my mum.

CILISSA   I can see how angry you are, Orestes.

ELECTRA   I'm not Orestes either. And anger is a natural response to an unnatural fucking act.

CILISSA   She sent these flowers. Orestes, your mother / sent

ELECTRA   I'm not even going to [answer] – and my mother wouldn't send flowers – oh. You're right. That's her – her writing –

EXHIBIT: SMALL MESSAGE CARD, SEALED

ELECTRA reads the card. Doesn't read it out.

Guilty. Maybe she'll kill herself now rather than just talking about it. I don't know why you stay with her.

CILISSA   I'm too old to leave now. Have you thought about god?

ELECTRA   I have thought about why he's not preparing a flood of vengeance to burn them both away.

CILISSA   Maybe he is.

ELECTRA   *Maybe* he's doing all sorts of things.

Some ghost or man or judge or gods.
To put things right.

Come on then. Now. Strike her down.

,

| CILISSA | There's something – on the grave. There. |

EXHIBIT: LOCK OF BROWN HAIR

ELECTRA	This? Oh. That's strange.
CILISSA	What is it?
ELECTRA	It's – someone's cut a lock of their hair and put it here
CILISSA	I don't understand. Why would you / do that?
ELECTRA	It looks like … it's exactly like …

,

Oh my stomach just turned to ice

CILISSA	What?
ELECTRA	My hair. It's exactly like my hair.
CILISSA	Is it your mother's?
ELECTRA	She's never been here. It's *my hair*. Is my hair falling out? And those footprints – I haven't – they're my footprints. I can even see the tendons. A perfect fit with mine. I'm mad. I haven't slept.
CILISSA	Orestes, / I think we should [go home]
ELECTRA	Orestes – yes. Of course. Orestes. It's his hair, his footprints – but then that means he's come back. He's been / here

ORESTES is next to ELECTRA.

| ORESTES | I am here, next to you. Don't be scared, it's all right. |
| ELECTRA | Is this a trap? |

ORESTES	If it was, the net would catch me too.
	You look –
ELECTRA	I know. I look different now. People keep saying I look like you. Including her, but she's – it doesn't matter. Are you all right? I'm glad you're back. You left traces. The footprints. Same as mine. The hair. Same as mine.-
ORESTES	Electra, why are you here?
ELECTRA	She's moved him in. Aegisthus. Our new father.
ORESTES	I know. I know.
ELECTRA	I miss him. It's *strange* without him here. I smelled his clothes for a while but that stopped working. They're there, she hasn't burned them or anything.
ORESTES	She's in there, now.
ELECTRA	The house is locked. She watches.
ORESTES	Then we go by night. When she's asleep.
ELECTRA	She doesn't sleep.

KLYTEMNESTRA wakes up suddenly.

ELECTRA	Bad dreams.
AEGISTHUS	You were dreaming. I let you sleep. Sorry.
KLYTEMNESTRA	The water?
AEGISTHUS	It's just the bath.
KLYTEMNESTRA	Agamemnon?
AEGISTHUS	You're cold.
KLYTEMNESTRA	Aegisthus. Don't [touch me] –
	I was I was giving birth. Nurses, starch, warm water – it didn't – it didn't hurt, but then the baby, its head smelled right – and I looked and it was a snake. But I – I loved it. And

I wrapped it in a cloth, a warm, comfy old
cloth, full of holes, tighter, and it was hungry
so I gave it my breast – and it was biting
through the cloth, but then feeding happily
and I was *laughing* but then it started to tear
the flesh, its teeth, bitter little teeth, they cut
in and the blood mixed with the milk and
it's hot, fluid running down me, it doesn't let
go, it doesn't let go – and it *hurts*, the pain
through the soft skin was – god, I want to
nurse it, but I can't make it / stop –

ELECTRA   Stop. Her dream. Tell me you / see

ORESTES   See the meaning - yes

ELECTRA   It's you: the snake.

ORESTES   Or you.

ELECTRA   Same thing. It's a sign. The thing we have to
            do.

            For me, you're all that's left now. Father,
            sister – mother - and what she did to him – I
            don't understand the point of anything if we
            don't do something against that act, against
            her, because mourning just slides off the back
            of it. Orestes. You know what has to happen.
            What we have to do.

ELECTRA   *(Chorus.)* You don't need me to tell you
ORESTES   *(Chorus.)* I don't need you to tell me.

            We end it. We finish it.

ELECTRA   And we burn the house to ash. We wipe
            out its history. And we cut off its future. No
            weddings for us. No children to sit at that
            table. No more of it. No more of us, of any of
            us.

ORESTES   We kill her. We kill our mother.

ELECTRA   Orestes. Thank you for coming back. We're
            the same, you and me. We're like corks –

93

keeping the net afloat – holding it from
sinking to the depths

ELECTRA kisses ORESTES.

ORESTES   Don't kiss me

ELECTRA   I can kiss you if it's good news. Don't you
                 want to know how it would have felt?

ELECTRA and ORESTES kiss.

ELECTRA   DAD. Hold my hand.

                 Dad. We hold hands.

ORESTES   Agamemnon. Dad. God or father or dad or
                 whichever word you'd prefer us to say – if
                 you can hear us. Even if you can't.

                 We burn this moment into the timeline.

                 We bear witness together that she deserves
                 to die, that she *has* to die, and by this hand,
                 this right hand – justice will shatter through
                 the doors and tear into her body like rotten
                 meat, pull her apart for what she did to you -
                 she has to *die,* suffer and die, she has to suffer
                 and learn that what she did was *wrong*

ELECTRA   We kill her like she killed you. In secret. No
                 sign. She has to die – or none of it makes
                 sense

*KLYTEMNESTRA in the bathroom. IPHIGENIA present singing
her song.*

KLYTEMNESTRA   STOP IT - STOP

                 She regains herself.

                 I am a person. I am *alive.* I could live another
                 fifty years.

                 The sound of wind. The feel of evening.

ORESTES   It's cold. Does the disguise work?

ELECTRA   She won't recognize you.

94

ORESTES	Does the disguise work?
ELECTRA	Yes.
ORESTES	This house. My entire life was here. All the time bottled up inside these walls.
ELECTRA	I'm still here too -
	Orestes, do you love me?
ORESTES	I think I need you outside.
KLYTEMNESTRA	I'd like to hear some music.
	,
ORESTES	Hello? Hello?
CILISSA	Who is it?
ORESTES	I'm not a threat. We're travelling alone. I've got something to say to the lady of the house.
CILISSA	To say? Who are you?
ORESTES	Look can you either let me in or send a man out or something because I haven't got *time*. Send me a man and at least I can have a straightforward conversation.

ORESTES enters the house. Same position as AGAMEMNON was twice before.

I'm home.

KLYTEMNESTRA enters, surprised anyone is present in the house.

KLYTEMNESTRA	Good evening.
ORESTES	Good evening.
	You might want to sit down

She works it out fast.

KLYTEMNESTRA	Oh – I dreamed this once. Orestes. He's dead. Isn't he? Dead.
ORESTES	I'm not the official [message, but] – yes. Orestes is dead. I'm sorry, I don't know more than that, but I know that's [right]

KLYTEMNESTRA	right. Yes. Well, thank you for, uh –
	,
	I hate this house. There's no escape.
	I thought he was finally gone, I hoped he'd
	– but hope is a lie, you realise, it's the feeling
	you can ever really win.
	He's dead, you're *sure* he's dead?
	Sorry, yes, I'm in shock, probably.
	You must have come a long way. Please stay
	here, rest tonight –
CILISSA	I nursed him at my breast. He drank my
	milk.
KLYTEMNESTRA	yes
CILISSA	Sickly baby, he was. He screamed and
	screamed at night. Never a good sleeper.
KLYTEMNESTRA	yes
CILISSA	Babies are little animals; never can tell
	whether they're hungry or thirsty or what –
	their insides are a law unto themselves.
	I used to always read him wrong, you'd wind
	him and then he'd mess himself, '*that's* what
	you were crying at', constantly washing his
	clothes – nurse, cleaner, and – I just can't
	believe it. I wore away my life for him.
	How old was he? It's really no age at all.
	There's no justice.
KLYTEMNESTRA	She'll find you somewhere clean to sleep.
ORESTES	Yes. Thank you. I really am sorry.
KLYTEMNESTRA	There's several storeys of rooms. There are
	clean towels and please just help yourself to
	anything you need. Or want. There's wine. If
	you'd like a hot bath or anything. That's fine.
	I think I'll go to sleep.

KLYTEMNESTRA exits.

CILISSA   Excuse me, I wouldn't trust her. Her eyes are
             always hiding something. I don't trust them.
             I'm just saying, I don't know you, but be
             careful what you say in this house. There's
             always been unhappiness here. He was a
             good little boy. Quiet. Thoughtful. There's
             no justice.

             Thank you for coming back.

*ORESTES moves to the bathroom. His father's dressing gown
is there, the red one. He puts it on. It's too big. He puts his
hand in the pocket and there's a crumpled up note. He reads
it: the text reads* CHILD KILLER. *He sneezes. He turns and*
AGAMEMNON *is watching him. Their eyes meet.*

KLYTEMNESTRA   Aegisthus? Darling?

ORESTES   Agamemnon. It's a sign, isn't it? An
             instruction. Received. Thank you.

*ORESTES runs to him, hugs him. As they separate from the
hug, blood everywhere, all over both of them.*

KLYTEMNESTRA   Aegisthus? Aegisthus, what's going on?

AEGISTHUS. TIME OF DEATH: [[TODAY'S DATE, THE TIME]].

CILISSA rushes in panicked.

CILISSA   He's alive, he's – the dead are killing the
             living –

KLYTEMNESTRA   He?

She works it out.

             That story wasn't a – it was a plot. OK, you
             need to move now and get me a weapon –

             MOVE woman, don't just –

*Enter ORESTES. He makes for her and she moves swiftly,
talking all the time: her words are the only weapon she has.*

ORESTES   Mum. I'm here to make things right.

KLYTEMNESTRA	Orestes. Thank you for coming back. Thank you.
	I know why you've come. But it's more complicated than you think, and you need to listen –
	,
	Your father was a killer, and it's my fault, it's my fault who I chose to mate with but you do not want to become your father
ORESTES	I am him. I'm half him. Look at – he's me, he's / *me*

AEGISTHUS is covered in blood. He sits down at the table and becomes AGAMEMNON.

KLYTEMNESTRA	And *so am I.* He killed your sister, he killed my daughter, and she isn't here any more. She isn't here any more. I know you think this this comes from your instinct, or from – some – I don't know – heroic idea of what a son does but your father has a hook sunk into your soul, and, without you even knowing it, is pulling you back towards him. I know you grew up with it – I'm not saying it's your fault, it's not your fault, but you don't want to *be him, you do not want blood on your hands.* That's just not you – and this isn't how it ends for us, there's so much more – we grow old together, Orestes, me and you. I'm your mum.

ORESTES runs to his mother and hugs her.

	It's all right. Nothing has happened. Let's go back.
ORESTES	Yes.
KLYTEMNESTRA	Orestes. Orestes. Orestes.

He relaxes. Things slightly clear. Then she rings the dinner bell. She laughs from exhaustion. For the final time, dinner is laid. It's slow. There's just two of them now. Occasional bangings from outside, wind blowing. Suspended. Held. Uncertain.

KLYTEMNESTRA   Eat something. You must be hungry. It should be meat really, I'm sorry, but I can't seem to face it these days –

ORESTES opens the wine. KLYTEMNESTRA laughs – notices.

ORESTES   Where's Electra?

KLYTEMNESTRA   What, darling?

ORESTES looks at his mother. He realises:

ORESTES   *(Chorus.)* Something's wrong
KLYTEMNESTRA   *(Chorus.)* Something's wrong

Enter ELECTRA, suddenly, late

ELECTRA   If you're not here, you don't eat

Blackout of only a few seconds. When the lights come up, ELECTRA is struggling with KLYTEMNESTRA – both over the top of each other, screaming:

ELECTRA   You destroyed our home – you killed my dad. You're not my home, no mother would / be able to – How could you do it to us – he was the only thing that held it together – and you sacrificed all of that and us and him, and now you're here, sitting in everything he created, with some man in his bed, wearing his clothes, and god I want you to DIE I HATE YOU

KLYTEMNESTRA   I did the *right thing*

Blackout of another few seconds. When the lights come up, ORESTES is exactly where ELECTRA was – and ELECTRA has vanished.

KLYTEMNESTRA   If you kill me, you kill yourself / Orestes

ORESTES   You did wrong. Now you suffer wrong.

KLYTEMNESTRA	I know what's right for you. I am your *mother*.

KLYTEMNESTRA unexpectedly bares her breast

I fed both of you from this breast, inside me, Iphigenia – and you. You were given *life*

,

ORESTES	This is / your dream.
KLYTEMNESTRA	That dream. The snake was you.
DOCTOR	Orestes. What happened?
ORESTES	My sister with me – she kills my – mother –

IPHIGENIA on stage somehow.

DOCTOR	Orestes. Listen. Your sister died. Your sister died. Orestes? Let's please just try and reconnect with that.

ORESTES' nose is bleeding.

ORESTES	No, that's not her – that's – it was Electra, she kills her –
DOCTOR	Electra?
ORESTES	Yes
DOCTOR	Where was Electra?
ORESTES	She was outside – no, inside, at the table, in the house ...
DOCTOR	And where were you?

The DOCTOR becomes more insistent, firmer.

Whose hair did you find at the grave?

ORESTES	Mine. No. *She* found it. The lock of – that's how she knew it was me –
DOCTOR	Your hair was the same? And your footprints and hers were the same? A girl? That doesn't make sense. Listen to me. Orestes.

ORESTES	No: Electra was there: we were there together –
DOCTOR	I think we have to consider the possibility that those were *your* footprints, that that was *your* hair –
ORESTES	I feel like my head has split in two, it keeps *shifting* but Electra
DOCTOR	Orestes. I don't know who that is.
	You've survived a trauma. Your sister died, Orestes: your sister, Iphigenia. She died. You survived. We have no record of another sister. You had *one* sister.
	What are you holding?

ORESTES looks at his hands. There's a sudden blackout. Then lights up and KLYTEMNESTRA's dead, sprawled across the table. ORESTES holds his hands out – they're bloodied. Perhaps he wears a saffron dress. A sense of dawning calm.

ORESTES	This was always going to happen.
	She's been dead since the beginning.

KLYTEMNESTRA. TIME OF DEATH: [[TODAY'S DATE, THE TIME]].

DOCTOR	So you're alone?
ORESTES	yes
DOCTOR	And you killed her? What are you holding?

CILISSA has entered, stands, looking at the pool of blood. Somehow she's in the shade. Something is slightly different about her.

ORESTES	I feel like we're travelling fast, I've gone off road and I don't know where I'm heading and I'm – my heart is racing – but I ended it, it's – look at this, this cloth, destroyed, destroyed like the family, the house destroyed by her, I don't know what to call it, a tablecloth, a flag, a net, a trap, a curtain for a bath, a snare – a shroud – it was a

perfect thing and she threw it across my father's eyes and stabbed it full of holes – to this. There's *nothing* good here but – she had to *die,* suffer and *learn* and die. And now it's done.

EXHIBIT: TORN AND BLOODSTAINED CLOTH

He throws the thing over his mother like a shroud. The DOCTOR is wearing court robes, she seems different, suddenly:

DOCTOR   Could we have the next exhibit? Thank you.

ORESTES   What did you say? I don't –

DOCTOR   We need to reconstruct your act. We need to be sure.

DOCTOR   *(Chorus.)* What are you holding?
FURY   *(Chorus.)* What are you holding?

FURY   It won't wash away. It stains. This is who you are now.

DOCTOR   Orestes. Answer the question. What are you holding?

The actor who played CILISSA has become the Fury. She is terrifying, inhuman. Perhaps she holds a real snake.

Other people start to enter – ORESTES feels he is going mad. He could be right; or we could be, for the first time, seeing things as they really are.

FURY   Your father killed the girl. So your mother killed *him.* And you killed *her.* Now she must be avenged. There is a death outstanding. The child is the price.

ORESTES   Who are you?

DOCTOR   Who? Orestes – who?

FURY   There is a death outstanding.

ORESTES   The – *fury,* her – there's something wrong. Is this a dream?

DOCTOR	Orestes, if you're seeing things that is concomitant with serious mental illness. Madness. I understand that this is difficult but I need you to answer the question. What are you holding?

To his surprise, ORESTES' hands are suddenly handcuffed.

Something big happens to the feel of the space, something formal, huge: electric, shadowy, smooth. The light on ORESTES gets whiter and whiter.

FURY	I am only what you feel. And the water breaks through the walls, the blood breaks out of the vein, and the runner slips with a relentless doom. You cannot know you fall – and a mist descends over the house, white foam sprouting out, cursed, infected
ORESTES	I need you to help me. You're here to help me
DOCTOR	No. We're here to try and understand the truth. What are you holding?

Trolleys of papers. Each of the exhibits is displayed somewhere, behind glass. Everyone wears robes oddly reminiscent of Agamemnon's dressing gown. The flavour of a court, wooden tables, microphones. ATHENE sits as judge – she is played by the actor who played Cassandra. A crest of two eagles killing a hare. The doctor now seems to be a lawyer (but we'll call her DOCTOR still, simply for ease of playing). CALCHAS takes an official role in proceedings, a kind of clerk of court.

The stage is now a dream-like version of a court – at once familiar and strange. Everyone is waiting for ORESTES to speak.

ATHENE	The respondent must *answer the question.*
AGAMEMNON	My lady, could we request that the question is repeated?
DOCTOR	What are you holding?

ORESTES   It's right – bright – silver – a knife – a knife

                   CALCHAS puts it finally in his hand.

                   EXHIBIT: SILVER KNIFE, BLOODSTAINED

DOCTOR   And you confess that you killed your
                   mother?

                   ,

ORESTES   Yes

DOCTOR   Thank you, my lady. No further questions.

AGAMEMNON   Can I therefore request a break, my lady /
                   given that

ATHENE   Granted.

CALCHAS   Please be upstanding.

                   Everyone stands. ATHENE leaves.

                   We pause there. Thank you.

                   The act is over.

ACT FOUR

Throughout the pause, the company reassemble. They wear court robes. They are simultaneously the characters they have already played this evening, and representatives in the court case. The FURY is present.

ORESTES   Where are we?

CALCHAS   What do you mean?

KLYTEMNESTRA enters.

ORESTES   Is that / my mother?

CALCHAS   Your mother's representative.

ORESTES   Who are all the people?

CALCHAS   They're here for you.

ORESTES notices that one of the walls has partly fallen in. In fact, the room itself is crumbling, as if the set itself has aged in the course of the evening.

ORESTES   It feels familiar. It feels like I've always been here.

DOCTOR   That's hardly surprising.

Something crumbles above and a little dust falls.

ORESTES   It's falling apart.

AGAMEMNON   We don't talk like that here.

CALCHAS   Please be upstanding.

ATHENE enters.

ATHENE   Thank you for coming back. Thank you.

People sit down.

I would remind this house that it must consider every step of the evidence presented, as it bears witness to each story, each committed act and makes its judgment. It must consider what it does not know:

	the gaps in the available evidence. It is incumbent on this house as a collective that the care taken in this case is no less than if you yourself were the respondent.
ORESTES	Is this a dream? Am I / mad?
CALCHAS	The respondent should please observe the times to speak and to be silent.
ATHENE	We have now witnessed completed re-enactments at – could we clarify – [amass the evidence]?

Folders, boxes are brought in, piled on tables.

CALCHAS	Each actor of each respective action here is guilty of murder – though only the respondent lives to undergo examination. The first act the killing of the child, Iphigenia, at [[TIME OF DEATH]], the second act the killing of the husband Agamemnon by his wife at [[TIME OF DEATH]], and the examination and enactment of the third act concluded before the break - the killing of the mother Klytemnestra at the hands of the respondent at [[TIME OF DEATH]]. The respondent has confessed to the third act.
ATHENE	Are there immediate objections arising from any of the prior exhibits? Anything further to submit?

AGAMEMNON and KLYTEMNESTRA both shake their heads.

	Then: we present conclusions and we move to closing arguments
CALCHAS	Please be upstanding. This house now comes to an end.
ATHENE	As the embodiment of both heaven and earth, state and god, male and female, I announce myself the higher power of

right, and I inaugurate this house once again for our purpose as a house of *justice* with mandate to establish, enforce and engender what is right.

Everyone acknowledges.

CALCHAS	Please raise your hands and answer the questions.
ATHENE	Do you submit to the practice of this house?
ORESTES	I don't think I believe / in
CALCHAS	This is not a religious house.
ORESTES	And – why swear if it isn't a / religious
AGAMEMNON	We don't talk like that here.
CALCHAS	The respondent should observe the times to speak and to be silent.
ATHENE	My role here is to *represent* the gods.

ORESTES raises his hands.

	Do you submit to the practice of this house?
ORESTES	– the practice of this house? What / is this?

The FURY laughs.

FURY	There is a death outstanding. The child is the price.
ORESTES	What is the practice of this house? What are you going to do?

Some conferring.

CALCHAS	The respondent has a right to make the request.
ATHENE	Very well. Orestes, you killed your mother. This house will proceed to consider your act. We hear both sides. We make a judgement.
ORESTES	Judgement?

ATHENE	In the absence of a living family member to avenge your victim, this house and its systems inherit your judgement collectively.
	Do you submit to the / practice of –
ORESTES	The penalty is death. The judgement. If I'm not set free, you're going to kill me. At the end. That's what happens, isn't it?
ATHENE	Yes. Your life for your mother's.
CALCHAS	Could we please keep to procedure?
ATHENE	Do you submit to the practice of this house?
ORESTES	I do
CALCHAS	Please read the lines in front of you.
ORESTES	I swear to tell the truth – the whole truth – a true and binding version of events –
	'
	in the sight of – ?
CALCHAS	Theous.
	Zeus. Allah. El.
	Jehovah. Janus. Jupiter. Jove.
	Elah. 'ilah. Elohim. Ishvara. Ra. Raven. Dagda. Anguta. Yahweh. Apollo. Olorun. Chronus. Osiris. Brahman. Buddah. Odin. The Mountain. The Godhead. The Way. The Door. The Truth. The Life. The Light. The Lamb. The Creator. The Maker. The Supreme Being. The Holy Name. The One. The King. The Lord. The Judge. The Father. The All-Knowing, who can never be known.
	God. Gods. Instinct.
ORESTES	I swear to tell the truth – I can't swear. I don't / know

AGAMEMNON	Forgive me, my lady – Orestes. We are trying to reconstruct your story, the events, what happ/ened
ORESTES	But some things *happen*. How can / I swear to tell the truth?
ATHENE	Could we *please* keep to procedure?
AGAMEMNON	Orestes, as best you can, you swear to give the true version / of what you did
ORESTES	There *isn't* one true version. There isn't. There isn't one story – a line of truth that stretches start to end. That doesn't happen any more, maybe it never happened, but even as I say this now, as I say *this* now, in each of your minds you create your own versions, different lenses pointing at the same thing at the same time and *seeing that thing differently* – it depends on too much – the day you've had, what you feel about *your* mother, the thought you thought before this one – it all floods in, this thing this whole thing is *helpless* because your brain creates stories in which it is *right*
ATHENE	Do you refuse to swear to tell the truth?
DOCTOR	My lady / this is unacceptable
TALTHYBIUS	My lady, one moment. Orestes, do you believe you were wrong to kill your mother? The story your brain told you, was it
ORESTES	I –
TALTHYBIUS	Was it the right thing?
ORESTES	Yes
TALTHYBIUS	Then will you undertake to persuade this house of that? This house exists to enact justice and justice will be done

Something else happens to the house: something crumbles somewhere.

ORESTES   How long have I been here? How long has /
                this been

ATHENE   You undertake to tell the truth, to tell here
                today a true and binding version of events?

                '

ORESTES   Yes.

                To KLYTEMNESTRA:

ATHENE   The representative may continue

                The FURY laughs, low and slow.

KLYTEMNESTRA   Thank you, my lady. Resuming with
                some final questions before proceeding to
                conclusion.

ATHENE   Thank you.

DOCTOR   We heard before that you killed your mother.
                Is that correct? / Try to be clear.

AGAMEMNON   This has already been established, my lady.

ORESTES   Yes

DOCTOR   How did you kill her?

ORESTES   A knife.

DOCTOR   I couldn't hear / that, I'm afraid.

ORESTES   With a knife.

DOCTOR   Why?

MENELAUS   In vengeance for his father. On instruction of
                the gods, my lady.

ATHENE   For the last time, let the respondent answer
                the questions.

DOCTOR   Thank you, my lady. Orestes, the gods spoke
                to you?

ORESTES   Yes.

DOCTOR	Directly?
ORESTES	There were signs
DOCTOR	So not directly. Were there not similar signs endorsing the first act, read by your father as sanctioning his murder of your sister, his daughter?
AGAMEMNON	The respondent does not remember, he was too young, we have been through this / already, my lady
ATHENE	The respondent must answer the question.
ORESTES	There were signs then, I think. And he read them correctly.
KLYTEMNESTRA	I'm sorry – how do you know?
ORESTES	The wind came. They won the war.
KLYTEMNESTRA	Can we prove that Iphigenia's death caused those events? Do we *know* it would not have happened anyway?
	,
ORESTES	No.
DOCTOR	Could you tell us what the signs were that night, the night of your mother's / murder?
AGAMEMNON	My lady, we have already witnessed / this reconstructed in its –
ATHENE	Continue.
ORESTES	I went back to his house in disguise, I was, in the room in which my father died, and in his pocket, I found a note, it said 'CHILD KILLER'.
CALCHAS	Submitting to the house the exhibit.

EXHIBIT: HANDWRITTEN NOTE, WITH ENVELOPE

ORESTES	It was a sign from him, beyond the grave – or from god. I was his child, I was to be his avenger, the killer / on the –
KLYTEMNESTRA	I'm sorry – why does it have to be only one thing? Can it not be more?

Could it not have been a note sent to your father by one of the many people who disagreed, passionately disagreed, with military action which resulted in the deaths of countless innocent children? Was he too – in several senses – not a *child killer*? Might the note have been penned by his wife? |
MENELAUS	It is some coincidence for this not to be meaningful: the will of the gods / is clear –
KLYTEMNESTRA	My lady, could we clarify – how the gods / might
ATHENE	Gods speak in signs. Signs are interpretable. Open.

Something else crumbles, gently sets alight. Only ORESTES registers.

DOCTOR	If we might travel back along the road, all the way back to where things began – the exhibit, thank you –

The drawing from the very beginning is put into ORESTES' hands.

EXHIBIT: DRAWING OF HARE KILLED BY TWO EAGLES

A pregnant mother hare, killed by two eagles.

ORESTES	It's the death of Iphigenia. The eagles are my father and his brother, the mother hare is my mother – and Iphigenia dies in the womb. She didn't know.
DOCTOR	But – I'm sorry – the mother also dies. Could we not submit that the death of the mother hare is the death of your mother

ORESTES	And the eagles are me and – yes. It could be that.
DOCTOR	She's been dead since the beginning.
MENELAUS	My lady, what point / is being made here?
KLYTEMNESTRA	Or could we offer this interpretation: the eagles are simply the symbol of this house. The eagles represent justice, and the pregnant hare is the respondent.
AGAMEMNON	My lady, this is / just not appropriate
KLYTEMNESTRA	The pregnant hare is the respondent – and the children are his children set free from having ever to be born – when he is executed by this house
AGAMEMNON	My lady, this is / unacceptable
ATHENE	State your case
KLYTEMNESTRA	We read the signs like mirrors, my lady. They show us what we want and nothing more.
FURY	There is a death outstanding.
KLYTEMNESTRA	What injuries did your mother suffer at your hands?
	,
ORESTES	I killed her, I don't remember / what her injuries were
AGAMEMNON	My lady, this is unacceptable
KLYTEMNESTRA	Perhaps if we travel further backwards. How did you gain access to your mother's house?
ORESTES	In disguise.
KLYTEMNESTRA	In disguise. So you had already decided on your course of action? You knew what you were there to do.
ORESTES	Yes.

KLYTEMNESTRA	Some part of you must recognize that, if you had to keep it secret, then *maybe* it was wrong?
ORESTES	Yes. I recognize [that] – but she killed my / father.
KLYTEMNESTRA	What did your mother say as you raised your knife?
AGAMEMNON	She *was a murderer herself.* My lady, we have already witnessed / what happened
KLYTEMNESTRA	What did your mother / say?
MENELAUS	My lady, there is no need to make him say the words / he has confessed –
ATHENE	This house must hear all of the evidence, all of the competing versions, and make its judgement then. Continue.
KLYTEMNESTRA	What did your mother say?
	What did *she say?*
	Then let us witness it again. Could you? And – thank you – [read it –]
CALCHAS	'I know what's right for you. I am your *mother.* I fed both of you from this breast, inside me, Iphigenia and you, you were given *life.*' There is then a silence of several seconds.
ORESTES	This is / your dream.
KLYTEMNESTRA	That dream. The snake was you.
	'
	And you hesitated?
ORESTES	Yes.
KLYTEMNESTRA	Why?
	'

	You looked into your mother's eyes and hesitated – I imagine she was scared. She knew. And part of you was unsure what to do. That's right, isn't it?
ORESTES	How can we ever be sure. Of any decision about any thing.
	,
KLYTEMNESTRA	Of course you couldn't be sure. Of course. This was your mother. Your hesitation is a recorded fact. And what that hesitation represents is a screaming acknowledgement that murder is wrong, that the murder of a mother is a crime which even then, at that moment, you knew was wrong, acceptable in no code or system or law – no social law, even the law of nature. Against the fact of your birth. Your blood. She was your mother. You knew it was wrong.
ORESTES	Yes. Yes. You're right. That's right. I did love / her.
KLYTEMNESTRA	Thank you
ORESTES	I'm sorry – I'm sorry
FURY	There is a death outstanding.
AGAMEMNON	My lady, if I may – Orestes, where were you?
ORESTES	Here. Right here.
AGAMEMNON	And when did you take that step forward – towards her? Where were you when you killed her?
ORESTES	I … I don't remember
AGAMEMNON	Could you repeat that, please?
ORESTES	I don't remember

AGAMEMNON	My lady, the last memory the respondent has is of the hesitation – and all that hesitation represents is a gap in the evidence we have. The respondent has suffered the loss of his father, of his sister, we saw, even in this house, how deeply those traumas have affected him, how the balance of his mind / was under constant attack
DOCTOR	This was a pre-meditated attack carried out in disguise: hardly the actions of a madman, hardly someone in mental distress –
AGAMEMNON	He has spoken about his deceased sister in / this house
KLYTEMNESTRA	His madness is still his, it is still *him*. We cannot discount *parts* of the respondent's personality, either he is responsible for his actions, or he is not.
AGAMEMNON	There is a history here: his mother had herself attempted suicide
ORESTES	That wasn't / true, she said things –
DOCTOR	We can *not* admit *your* story and not the story of your victim.
MENELAUS	What part of the victim's story do we in fact possess?
ATHENE	Could we please keep to procedure?

The FURY is banging on the table.

ORESTES	She paid NO PRICE. Nothing *happened* to her, she didn't suffer for what she'd done / she *meant* it, she was *sure*
TALTHYBIUS	*(Chorus.)* My lady, the respondent is under extreme pressure and a line of questioning which is frankly irrelevant
DOCTOR	*(Chorus.)* How could you possibly know that?
ATHENE	Could we please keep to procedure?

DOCTOR	Moreover, her act was not like yours. Agamemnon did not lift her from her crib. He did not breastfeed her.
ORESTES	But that's *different* / it's not a –
KLYTEMNESTRA	Everything always is. All families are different, my lady, and yet somehow exactly the same. We are hurt, so we hurt back. Agamemnon had murdered his daughter. And for that first act / Klytemnestra *rightly* sought revenge
AGAMEMNON	His act served the greatest possible good – he sacrificed his family for the state. My lady, he had fought and won a war: he was safe, he thought, from death. He was *in his bath* – can we see the [evidence] – when she *struck*, covered his eyes with this cloth, blinded him and cut him to pieces

EXHIBIT: TORN AND BLOODSTAINED CLOTH

MENELAUS	He only killed his daughter for our good. And his murder was an act that tore at the fabric of this country's security, it hurt us / all
KLYTEMNESTRA	And she *paid* for that act with her life. Once the blood has soaked into the carpet it can't flow back into the body: that woman who killed him is dead.
FURY	The child is the price.
ATHENE	Could we please keep to procedure? Are we any closer to conclusion?
KLYTEMNESTRA	Thank you, my lady. What injuries did your mother suffer at your hands?
AGAMEMNON	The respondent has been clear that he / does not remember
KLYTEMNESTRA	We have not witnessed what he did. We might at least exhibit how *she* died. Could we please [read the report]?

AGAMEMNON	This is / completely unnecessary
KLYTEMNESTRA	THIS IS THE STORY. THESE ARE THE FACTS. Thank you.
CALCHAS	'Time of death [[22:12]]. The body is that of a [[well-developed, well-nourished Caucasian]] female which weighs [[129 pounds]] and measures [[65 inches]] from crown to sole. Both upper and lower teeth are natural, without evidence of injury to the cheeks, lips or gums.'
KLYTEMNESTRA	You can take a step forward here –
AGAMEMNON	These facts are not material to the decision before this house
KLYTEMNESTRA	My lady, my equivalent seems not to have understood that we have only one unquestionable fact. That fact is Klytemnestra's corpse. Cold and hard. And real. Her carcass is the *only* fact. It proves two things: the existence of her killer, and the way in which she died. These are then the material facts before we move to conclude. Continue. Please / continue
CALCHAS	'At the time of autopsy examination, rigor mortis has set in. The body is not embalmed. Bruising of the limbs, especially of the hands and feet, strongly suggests struggle. There are very numerous incised and stab wounds of the neck, torso and genitals, which will below be itemised. These sharp force injuries ultimately led to transection of the left and right common carotid arteries, as well as incisions of the left and right internal jugular veins which in turn caused fatal exsanguinating haemorrhage'
ORESTES	Each thing leading to the next thing

ORESTES is sobbing

MENELAUS	My lady the respondent is becoming extremely distressed / this is distressing in the extreme
KLYTEMNESTRA	As he himself best knows, this is what happened / to her.
MENELAUS	My lady, there is no need for / this to continue
KLYTEMNESTRA	*This is what he did*, these are the consequences OF HIS OWN ACTIONS my lady
ATHENE	Continue
CALCHAS	'The primary deep incised wound of the neck is gaping and exposes the larynx and cervical vertebral column. It measures four and a half by three inches in length and is found diagonally oriented at the level of the superior border of the larynx. On the ...' some text has been lost here ... 'upwardly angulated toward the right earlobe. On the left side it is transversely oriented and extends three inches to the anterior border of the left sternocleidomastoid muscle.' There are gaps in the text here too, my lady, picking up ... 'edges of the wound are smooth ... ' the text here is corrupted, continuing 'intramuscular haemorrhage, fresh, dark-red purple, evident'
TALTHYBIUS	My lady –
DOCTOR	There is more / my lady
TALTHYBIUS	This evidence is full of holes, my lady, we have not borne witness to the event itself
DOCTOR	My lady, we submit that it is impossible for this house to witness the event itself, what really happened. None of us know. None of

	us *can* know. We can only reconstruct the way she died.
ATHENE	To which this house has already borne witness.
TALTHYBIUS	Thank you, my lady.
KLYTEMNESTRA	My lady, we now move to conclude.
CALCHAS	Please be upstanding. The house now moves to conclusion.
ATHENE	Thank you.
KLYTEMNESTRA	Thank you. A sister, a father, a mother – are dead. There has to come an end. But allow me to ask the house: why does the murder of the mother count for less than that of the father? Because the woman is less important. Why is the mother's motive for revenge *lesser* than the son's? She avenged a daughter; he a father. Because the *woman* is less important. This woman has paid the price. But this house cannot be a place where the woman is less important.
FURY	There is a death outstanding. The child is the price.
KLYTEMNESTRA	How are we to resolve the respondent's double role? He is both the surviving son of the victim – and the victim's murderer. He by right should argue both for his innocence and his guilt. He is bound to both sides of this house. My lady, our conclusion is clear: the respondent must avenge the murder of his mother – by taking his own life.
FURY	By his hand alone. The child is the price.
	,
KLYTEMNESTRA	In doing so, we submit that he will eliminate the last member of a family which has almost eliminated itself.

AGAMEMNON	My lady, we cannot *kill* the respondent *symbolically* – he is a *person* not a fact, this *house* is people, not symbols: he will still die. This house / must find
ORESTES	STOP STOP STOP / STOP
CALCHAS	The respondent must observe the times to speak and to be silent.
ATHENE	The system of this house is clear. The / representatives act on behalf of
ORESTES	You can't use some system from centuries ago to explain – there is no explaining why, she'd done what she did because of my sister, but she also had a *lover* – there are *too many things* here, what use is the system, what *use* is the system, what *justice* can it possibly perform – you can't just *decide* what I felt or why – there is no explaining *why*
ATHENE	The *representative* may continue
ORESTES	She stabbed him so hard they couldn't get the bits of cloth out of his skin / cloth hardened like a net
AGAMEMNON	The respondent has undergone a trauma and clearly presents *no further danger* to / any living person
KLYTEMNESTRA	He presented no danger before. But this house / exists for justice –

ORESTES is exhausted but this comes from somewhere deep.

ORESTES	This house is falling apart. And what *does* this *mean?* How can you punish a *natural impulse*? Who is that *for*? Who benefits? How are things BETTER? It won't stop revenge, it won't stop murder. It is still going to happen it was *always going to happen.*
ATHENE	This house is all of us. Its beliefs / are the

ORESTES	It doesn't believe. Once upon a time, someone just made it up. And in here you forget that moment before it existed. *It's just people.* That's all there *is.* And what I feel, what I felt, what I did – it could have been any of you –
ATHENE	This house is *all* of us.
	You made this happen. It came from you.

ORESTES looks at the people. His nose is bleeding.

ATHENE	Is that the conclusion complete?
KLYTEMNESTRA	It is, my lady.
ATHENE	I accept the submission. The respondent dies by his own hand if the house returns a guilty verdict. We will now proceed to judgement.
AGAMEMNON	My lady, could we take a moment before – ?
	,
ATHENE	One minute.
CALCHAS	Please be upstanding. We pause there for one minute. One minute. Thank you.

Like a pause but not one – the staging language should match each of the act breaks used in the production.

AGAMEMNON	Orestes. You need to prepare for the vote.
ORESTES	A vote
AGAMEMNON	It can't be just a single person. The decision is too complex for one. It has to be more.
ORESTES	But what if someone hates me or misheard the / evidence or
AGAMEMNON	That could happen if one person decided.
	,
ORESTES	But what if they do the wrong thing?

TALTHYBIUS	Then – they're all implicated in the consequences.
ORESTES	But it's madness – it doesn't change anything. I mean, because they say I'm guilty that doesn't make me *guilty*. It's not like the atoms in my body change into guilty atoms, it it – it's arbitrary. It's wrong.
AGAMEMNON	I know it's not perfect. It's an old idea, that if we all sit together in the same space and listen and consider the problem, suspend our doubt, trust that meaning will come, and we do it for long enough and we look hard enough – in the end, somehow, something will come of that.
ORESTES	It's – it's fragile.
MENELAUS	It's been like that for a long time.

MENELAUS and TALTHYBIUS leave.

ORESTES	Dad? *What's going on?*
	,
AGAMEMNON	Orestes –
ORESTES	I –
AGAMEMNON	There's no more time

The pause ends.

	Thank you, my lady
ATHENE	This house has witnessed the entire story. The respondent's mother and father were both murderers – he himself is the last of his house. It is undeniably complex. But the judgement before us is simple. Innocence or guilt.

The FURY laughs at ORESTES.

Let me remind you to think not of this one instance but of the instances to come, people thousands of years from today. Your judgement will judge them; the justice we serve will be their justice too.

CALCHAS addresses the audience.

CALCHAS   The respondent's life is forfeit if he is found guilty of the murder of his mother. He is freed if he is found innocent. We have borne witness to the evidence. And now this house must vote.

Think clearly of one word and hold it in your mind – either 'INNOCENT' or 'GUILTY'. Make that judgement. In 3. 2. 1.

Thank you.

ORESTES is brought forward. CALCHAS puts a tray into his hands.

What are you holding?

ORESTES   A silver tray on which are three small, pleated paper cups. One of them contains a small amount of translucent liquid. The second one contains a small orange tablet. The third one a sweet-flavoured liquid.

The child is the price.

KLYTEMNESTRA   Orestes. You won't suffer. It won't hurt.

AGAMEMNON   Home. It'll feel like coming home.

ORESTES   And the family is waiting for me.
Everybody's there. I'm the last one, in at the very end.

A bell rings.

It could have been me at the start.

ATHENE   Do we have a verdict?

CALCHAS   We do.

My lady, I present the decision of this house in relation to the case of the respondent,

Orestes, the charge of murder, his story as presented, and his act of matricide, to which he has confessed.

The judgement of the house is binding.

On [[DAY, the DATE[th] of MONTH]] at precisely [[TODAY'S TIME]] this house found that

Found that –

He reads the result. For the first time, he seems not to know what to do.

The vote is tied.

My lady, there are equal votes for both sides.

,

ATHENE	In the case of a tied ballot I believe it falls to me to conclude the judgement.
ORESTES	That's – that's just one person
ATHENE	Is that correct? That it is my deciding vote?
CALCHAS	I believe that is the procedure, my lady, yes
ATHENE	If there are no objections? In the practice of our lives, we favour men in all things – in our society, in our religion, and in our law – and as the just representative of our society, our religion and our law, it is appropriate that on behalf of this house of justice it is emphasised that men are favoured.
	Judgement is as follows, which constitutes my vote, and which is based upon the presumption of innocence: on the charge of murder, this house finds the respondent not guilty – and he is therefore acquitted with immediate effect.

,

ORESTES can't speak, he's overcome.

Justice is done and the house is adjourned.

The FURY is putting on court robes. Everyone else starts to leave.

CALCHAS	The house is adjourned.
ORESTES	My lady – I don't know whether – what is *real*, whether –
	Does she belong here?
CALCHAS	We need her here. A murderer should fear the retribution of this house. A murder cannot just be wiped away. She is essential: the terror she holds keeps us from collapse. It keeps the house of justice standing. She is a part of us. And we of her.
ORESTES	But – what is she?
AGAMEMNON	What do you think she is?
ORESTES	She's – pure – *fury* …
KLYTEMNESTRA	No, she's just like us. She's *kind*.
ORESTES	It's not about the word we use –
KLYTEMNESTRA	You see, I think it is.
ORESTES	One vote and I'm dead. It's – I mean. One person. The bias. I wasn't *sure*. Yes, I am [relieved] it's just – so – *small*.
	Excuse me – my mother, my father, my family, they're dead. They all die.
	What happened?
CALCHAS	They find you innocent. But you already knew that.
	You're free.
ORESTES	But I still killed her.
	Where does it end?

,

Perhaps I always *feel* guilty

,

What do I do?
What do I do?
What do I do?
What do I do?

The act is over.

UNCLE VANYA
SCENES FROM COUNTRY LIFE

In real life, people don't spend every single minute shooting each other, hanging themselves, and confessing love. They don't always say clever things. They are occupied with eating, drinking, flirting, and saying stupid things – which is what should be shown on the stage. A play should be written in which people arrive, go away, have dinner, talk about the weather, and play cards.

Life must be exactly as it is, and people as they are. Not on stilts. Let everything on the stage be just as complicated – and at the same time just as simple – as it is in life. People eat their dinner, just eat their dinner, and all the while their happiness is being established – or their lives are being broken up.

Anton Chekhov

The doctor looks at human beings as insects. When he's drunk. Once a month, he gets this drunk. Once a month he lets himself get lost in his maps, which show how humans have destroyed their own habitats. Michael tries to humanise the maps for Elena, but they remain inaccessible, forensic: bacterial slides. But then, outside the window, bereft of the forests that the maps eulogise, wild life is dying.

The play is neither sentimental nor judgmental. It's real life. It's people eating, drinking and sleeping. It's theatre. Dramatic tension. Soliloquies. It knows that sometimes we get sad and we don't know why, it knows that we often give others the advice we need ourselves; it knows that it sometimes takes several failed attempts to articulate what we mean – and that sometimes, there are no words for the job. It knows that in life, you can't see the future. Everything every character says might be true. (When John claims that, under different circumstances, he could have been a Schopenhauer or Dostoyevsky, he is both true and false, comic and tragic.)

Elena has a weakness for talented people, just as Michael has one for beautiful people. Sonya thinks Sonya's not beautiful. Alexander thinks Alexander's ill. Elena thinks that Elena's a good person. She tries to help Sonya by asking Michael whether or not he loves her. He eventually thinks Elena's manipulating him. Out of such misunderstandings is comedy born – but also tragedy. (Is the play a comedy? Is your life one?)

Michael and Sonya know how to talk to each other, and seem to get on. John and Elena are 'good friends', and John loves her, he says (though she can't seem to respond). These relationships might be budding. It's hard to tell. There's a storm, later. And at the end, they say goodbye. It might be forever. The cows have got to the young trees, after all. It might not be forever. But then delicate ecosystems sometimes don't survive the winter.

People go by nicknames, French names. People go by titles: Professor, Doctor, mother, wife, stepdaughter, daughter, father, godfather, Nanny – and Uncle. Sonya has two fathers: her real one, and her uncle. Two mothers live in the house, Nanny and Maria (the nurturer and the immaculate conceiver). Michael and Sonya love forests. Elena and Michael both think the world holds no happiness for them. John and Elena are both 'just incredibly boring'.

A series of failures. Might have beens. Cartwright's marriage. John's achievements. Elena's music. Alexander's career, perhaps. Connections. Romances. An emergency surgery a few months ago. John's gunshots are two more failures, perhaps, but then failure too can be redeeming. If a bullet hit Alexander, the play would be very different.

Time washes gently under foot. Twenty-five years John has worked on this estate. Six years Sonya's been in love with Michael. Nanny's known Michael for eleven years. She calculates that by working out how long it's been since Faith's death (there was the time before, and now the time after): nine years. Maybe more. Time stretches out before us like a yawn – open, intimidating – the potential to leave the world better than we found it.

Faith is gone. She cried and wasted away. People aren't happy. The forests are almost all destroyed. Michael thinks we might not leave any lasting legacy to the people of the future; John thinks John might not make it until tomorrow; Sonya thinks we should keep going. It's sometimes the right advice. And then it's sometimes time for bed.

Acknowledgements

I am indebted to a whole host of generous people who read drafts, watched run-throughs, and generally suggested ways to make things better. First and foremost: the actors and creative team of the first production; and then, in alphabetical order, Jocelyn Cox, Rupert Goold, Daniel Raggett, Helen Rappaport and Laurence Senelick.

Robert Icke
January 2016

A note on the play

This version was written to be produced in contemporary or timeless costume, but short of a few cuts and gentle updates, is faithful to Chekhov's play and intentions. That is, the time is now.

Some small characters have been trimmed: a workman and particularly, a watchman, who, for Chekhov's audience, would have functioned as little more than a familiar sound: the Russian night watchman, a familiar fixture of country estates, patrolled the grounds at night knocking with a long wooden rattle, which discouraged intruders and reassured those living there. In modern terms, he's simply the regular beep of a security alarm.

The translation of the Russian names (at the time of writing, unusual in British productions) is simply to preserve their carefully-chosen meanings for an Anglophone audience. To leave them in Russian in an English-speaking production is to make strange that which Chekhov intended ordinary. Most are simple translations of the Russian: Ivan, for example, becomes John (his mother calls him 'Jean' in French in the Russian too) and his reductive nickname, Vanya, is Johnny. The exception is Telegin, whose name derives from the Russian *telega*, a two-wheeled cart: he becomes Cartwright. Most revealing of all is the literal translation of the Russian name Vera (Petrovna, Sonya's mother), the character dead before the play begins: Faith.

Characters

JOHN (UNCLE JOHNNY), 47

MARIA
his mother, and the widow of a government official

SONYA
his niece

ALEXANDER
her father, a retired Professor of Aesthetics

ELENA
the professor's second wife, 27

CARTWRIGHT
who lives on the estate

NANNY
who has worked for the family for a long time

MICHAEL
a doctor

FAITH
Sonya's mother and John's sister – the Professor's first wife.
(deceased before the play begins, but still very much in the
house)

This adaptation was commissioned by and originally produced at the Almeida, where it had its first performance on 5 February, 2016.

Cast (in alphabetical order)

Sonya	Jessica Brown Findlay
Elena	Vanessa Kirby
Cartwright	Richard Lumsden
Alexander	Hilton McRae
Michael	Tobias Menzies
Nanny	Ann Queensberry
John	Paul Rhys
Maria	Susan Wooldridge

Creative Team

Direction	Robert Icke
Set	Hildegard Bechtler
Costume	Jessica Curtis
Light	Jackie Shemesh
Sound	Ian Dickinson for Autograph
Casting	Julia Horan CDG
Assistant Direction	Jocelyn Cox
Fight Direction	Kevin McCurdy
Original Composition	Richard Lumsden

Production Team

Production Manager	Aggi Agostino
Company Stage Manager	Sarah Alford-Smith
Deputy Stage Manager	Lorna Seymour
Assistant Stage Manager	Erin McCulloch
Production and rehearsal photos by	Manuel Harlan

A forward slash (/) marks the point of interruption of overlapping dialogue.

A comma on a separate line (,) indicates a pause, a rest, a silence, an upbeat or a lift. Length and intensity are context dependent.

An ellipsis (…) indicates a trailing off.

Square brackets [like this] indicates words which are part of the intention of the line but which are *not* spoken aloud.

This text went to press before the production opened
and so may differ slightly from what was performed.

ONE

A farmhouse, a long way from the city. It's quiet. A distant burglar alarm somewhere.

Outside. Things are set for a tea party.

MICHAEL has recently arrived. He has something of the woods about him. This is his third visit since the PROFESSOR arrived. NANNY, imperturbable, old, pours some tea, is handing it to MICHAEL –

NANNY   Have something to eat, my love.

MICHAEL   What's this?

NANNY   Tea.

MICHAEL   Oh. I don't really feel like it.

NANNY   Maybe a glass of something stronger, then?

MICHAEL   No

               I don't drink every day, you know –

               It *is* close, isn't it?

               Nanny, how long have we known each
               other?

NANNY   *(Thinking.)* How long? Christ, my memory.
               You moved here … moved to these parts
               … when was it? Well, Sonya's mother was
               still alive when you first came to us and
               you were calling here for – what was it,
               two winters before she [died] – which is –
               what? Eleven years?

               Maybe more.

MICHAEL   Have I changed, do you think?

NANNY   Oh, yes. You were young and handsome
            then – a young man – and you've aged.
            We all have. You've lost your looks. And
            you like a drink now – more than you did,
            anyway –

MICHAEL   Yes. Ten years and I'm a different person.
            And you know why? Work. Overwork.
            Morning 'til night without a moment's
            peace – not a second to switch off – lying
            awake in bed at night just waiting for
            some patient to scream for my attention.
            All those years we've known each other, I
            haven't had a single day off.

NANNY   The doctor's life

MICHAEL   'I've aged.' Of course I've aged. Life is
            boring, isn't it? Stupid and sordid and
            squalid. Surrounded by people who are just
            – *strange*. All of them. Hard little closed-off
            eccentrics. Surrounded by strange people,
            living among strange people and before
            you know it you turn into one yourself.
            Bound to happen.

            I mean, look at me. Look at *this*. Stupid.

            I've got strange, haven't I, Nanny? I mean,
            I can still *think*, my mind's still in some
            semblance of order, it's just my feelings
            – my feelings have all gone a bit blunted.
            Don't want anything. Don't need anything.
            Don't love anyone.

            Except just – you – maybe.

Kisses her.

I had a nanny just like you when I was a kid.

NANNY   Can I feed you something?

MICHAEL   No. Will you just [let me talk to you] –?

Few weeks before Easter, I went out to that epidemic, you remember? Trying to lend a hand, horrible conditions: people packed into tiny huts, animals sleeping alongside the sick – I was on the go all day, barely sat down, no bite to eat – and I finally got back home but even there, they don't let me sleep – because I'm called in for a patient, rushed in, an emergency, some man working on the railways, so I get there and he's laid on the table to operate and as I put him under the anaesthetic he goes and dies on me.

And at that moment, my feelings are suddenly there – hello! – and – it slices into my conscience, all this feeling – as if I'd done it on purpose, as if I'd *murdered* him –

,

And I sat down – and I closed my eyes – like this –

And I thought about the future, the people two or three hundred years after us, the people we're clearing the way for, and – will they remember us?

You know, I don't think they will.

NANNY	People won't – but God will.
MICHAEL	Yes. Well said. As ever. Thank you.

JOHN has awoken. He looks a little dishevelled. Attempts to smarten himself.

JOHN	Yes.
	,
	Yes.
MICHAEL	Good sleep?
JOHN	Yes. Very. It's since the Professor and his wife got here: my life has just fallen off its tracks. I'm sleeping at the wrong time, eating all this spicy food, drinking wine – it's not good for me. We used to never have a spare minute, Sonya and me, working, working, working – but now she's doing all of it while I sleep and eat and drink. It's not right.
NANNY	I don't know. This Professor. Has to be fresh tea constantly ready for him, all morning – but he doesn't get up 'til midday. That gets poured away. We have lunch so late that it's practically night-time. Only the night-times he's up, reading and writing – until past one in the morning that bell's ringing and what is it? He wants tea. Everyone up, out of bed. I don't know.
MICHAEL	Will they be staying much longer?
JOHN	A hundred years. He's decided he's going to live here.

NANNY	Like now. That tea's been there for two hours and they've gone off for a walk.
JOHN	They're coming. They're coming. Don't worry.

Enter ALEXANDER, ELENA, SONYA, and CARTWRIGHT. The other three try to look like they haven't been talking about them.

ALEXANDER	Splendid, splendid. What wonderful views. Horizons. Sheer horizons.
CARTWRIGHT	They are, Professor, they are indeed.
SONYA	Daddy, tomorrow we were going to go the forest, if you wanted to come?
JOHN	All right, ladies gentlemen, tea is served! And we also have / some cakes –
ALEXANDER	My friends, would someone send my tea into the study? I have a little more work to get done today.
SONYA	I really think you'll like it there –

ALEXANDER exits, followed by SONYA and ELENA. JOHN's attempt to apologise has been abruptly derailed.

JOHN	A punishingly hot day and yet our great scholar is kitted out with his coat, his gloves, an umbrella – and galoshes.
MICHAEL	Clearly a man that looks after himself.
JOHN	– but she is beautiful. So beautiful. She's still the most beautiful thing I've ever seen / in my entire life –

CARTWRIGHT   Whatever I get up to today – drive in the
               country, stroll in the garden, or just sit and
               look at this *table* – I just have this feeling
               of – *bliss*. I can't explain it. The incredible
               weather, the singing of the birdies, we
               live, all of us, in a time of peace – and in
               harmony with each other – what more
               could we possibly want?

               NANNY gives CARTWRIGHT tea.

               Tea! Thank you, Nanny, thank you.

MICHAEL   So, John. Tell us something.

JOHN   Tell you what?

MICHAEL   What's new?

JOHN   Nothing's new. Nothing to tell you. All
               old stuff. I'm just the same. Or worse,
               actually, because now I'm lazy and do
               absolutely nothing. Except moan. And my
               mother, that old crow, still picking through
               the latest in feminist literature, one eye
               searching for the dawn of the new world
               and the other on her imminent grave.

MICHAEL   And the Professor?

JOHN   And the Professor as usual sits in his
               study from morning 'til night, writing.
               Writing. It's the paper I feel sorry for.
               He'd be better off embarking on his
               tell-all autobiography. Title: The Retired
               Professor. Chapter one: Gout. Chapter
               two: Rheumatism. And his migraines.
               And his gallstones. So it might be a very
               long book. And the desiccated old roach

has decided he's going to live here, in his *first* wife's house, not that he *wants* to, but because he can't afford to live anywhere else now. So unfortunate that he complains about it all the time – when in fact, in actual fact, he's really been just incredibly lucky. From a poor unprivileged background he sprang to the world's attention, took all his degrees, a university chair, joined civilised society, and then married the daughter of a diplomat [Elena] – and so on and so forth –

But actually, no, here's the thing, listen to this: the man spends twenty-five years lecturing and writing and reading about *art,* when he understands *nothing at all about it.* For *twenty-five years*, he chews over other people's ideas of realism and naturalism and the precise meaning of the representative arts – twenty-five years on things that intelligent people already know and that no one else cares about anyway. Twenty-five years of *wasted time.* And the pretension! The arrogance! So he reaches the end of his magnificent career, settles down to his glorious retirement, and *nobody knows who he is.* He's totally obscure. So for twenty-five years he's been keeping someone better out of a job. And yet there he is, walking the earth like he's Jesus of fucking Nazareth.

MICHAEL   I think we might have a case of jealousy –

JOHN   Yes, of course I'm jealous! Look at him with women! The Don Juan of college

	dons. My sister, Faith – of course, you remember – his unfortunate first wife, a beautiful, tender, gentle woman, had more admirers than he had students, loved him like an *angel*. My mother, his mother-in-law? Still worships him, and looks at him with awe and reverence. His second wife, a woman with looks, brains – you saw her just now – married him when he was already ancient, and handed over to him her youth and her beauty and her freedom and her radiance. And what *for*? Why?
MICHAEL	She's faithful to him?
JOHN	Unfortunately she is.
MICHAEL	Why 'unfortunately'?
JOHN	Because it's false, that faithfulness. It's a *lie*. It sounds transcendent but it doesn't make sense. To be unfaithful to your hated, fossilised husband is immoral – but to crush down the feelings that tell you you're alive, to smother your youth – that's not, that's moral, that's *exactly* the right thing to do.
CARTWRIGHT	John – I do not like that at all. A man who deceives his wife, or a woman who betrays her husband, that's *trust*, that's the problem with the country we live in today, an / important thing to preserve
JOHN	Oh can you shut up, please just / shut up
CARTWRIGHT	Excuse me, I was deceived. I was deceived. I'm allowed to say something on this subject: my wife left me, the day after

the wedding, probably my looks to blame
–

But I have kept my vows. I still love her.
I am faithful to her. I help her when I
can, and I've paid for the education of the
children she had by the man she loved. I
have never had happiness, but I have had
my pride. And what about her? She's not
young any more, her beauty – as the law of
nature dictates it will – has faded – and the
man she loved is dead. So what has she got
left?

*MARIA enters, settles herself, reads. She's given a cup of tea,
drinks it without looking up.*

*A bell rings somewhere. And keeps ringing. Eventually,
SONYA, grumpy.*

SONYA   Nanny. Nanny. *Nanny.*

There's someone trying to [call]. Could
you [go and see] – ? I'll look after this [the
tea].

*NANNY heads off. MICHAEL, somewhat stranded in a strange
atmosphere, attempts to provoke some action.*

MICHAEL   I came to treat your husband. Your
message said he was very ill – rheumatism,
and something else? But he seems fine –

ELENA   Last night he was moping, pains in his legs,
he said. Today: nothing.

               ,

MICHAEL   And I drove miles to get here.

               Ah well, not the first time.

151

	I might cut my losses and stay here tonight, then. A decent night's sleep is just what the doctor ordered.
SONYA	Yes! It's so rare that you stay here now. And I bet you haven't had dinner?
MICHAEL	No, I haven't.
SONYA	Then you can have dinner here too. We have it at seven now.

SONYA drinks her tea.

And this is cold.

CARTWRIGHT   Well, it won't be cold, I don't think. It'll be tepid. Room temperature. Ambient. Not quite hot enough for enjoyment.

ELENA   Just drink it cold, Mr –

ELENA can't remember CARTWRIGHT's name.

CARTWRIGHT   *Cartwright.* It's Cartwright. Mr. Cartwright. I'm Sonya's godfather and the Professor, your wedded husband, knows me extremely well. I *live* here, on the same estate as you now. You might have noticed me having dinner with you every day.

SONYA   And he's our help and our strength and our right-hand man. *(Affectionately, re: tea.)* I'll get you some more, Godfather.

MARIA   Oh!

SONYA   What? Grandma, what?

MARIA	I forgot to tell Alexander – my mind's going – this new essay came today, in today's post.
MICHAEL	Anything interesting?
MARIA	Interesting but odd. She's attacking the very thing she was defending seven years ago. It's terrible.
JOHN	Nothing's terrible. Drink your tea.
MARIA	But I want to *talk!*
JOHN	We've had fifty years of talking and talking and notes in the margin – and now's the time to *stop*.
MARIA	So you've taken against the sound of my voice for some reason. Forgive me, *Jean,* but I barely recognise you. This last year, you've changed beyond recognition – you used to have such conviction, an enlightened man / and I was –
JOHN	Oh yes! An enlightened man but completely in the dark. An 'enlightened man'. There's salt in the wounds. I'm forty-seven years old. Until last year, I had my head buried in a book, like mother like son, hidden from life and reality, *blind* – and – God – I thought I was doing all right. But now – I can't sleep at night, I'm anxious, I'm just so *angry*: I've wasted so much time – the time when I could have gone and got all of the things that I can't get now because I'm just too old –
SONYA	Uncle Johnny, stop it – it's boring –

MARIA	It's almost as if you're blaming your ideals for whatever it is that's wrong – but it's not their fault. It's yours. Ideals are nothing, darling, just words – you should have got up and *done* something.
JOHN	Done something? Writing, perhaps? The search for the holy grail – or just keeping my hands generally busy like your beloved Professor Alexander?
MARIA	And what do you mean by that, exactly?
SONYA	Grandma – Uncle Johnny – *please!*
JOHN	I am silent. Silent.

,

I'm sorry –

,

ELENA	Nice weather today. Not too hot.
JOHN	Nice weather for hanging yourself –

CARTWRIGHT fiddles with the instrument, tunes it.

CARTWRIGHT plays something.

NANNY enters, with a chicken in her arms. Nobody notices.

,

NANNY	Chuck chuck chuck chuck
SONYA	Nanny – what are you doing?
NANNY	Here she is! Keeps wandering off – but the chicks are left unprotected – well *(Lowered voice.)* I don't want the ravens to get them.

SONYA	Who was it? Before?
NANNY	Oh. Someone for the doctor. It's urgent, they said – he's needed –
MICHAEL	Thanks. In that case, I have to go. Bloody annoying.
SONYA	It is – but you could come back afterwards, for dinner, if you [liked] – ?
MICHAEL	It'll be too late. Where's my [item of clothing]? Where could I have [put it]? Nanny, I might have that glass of vodka now, would you [bring it]? Where could I [have put it]? Where on earth – ?

NANNY takes the chicken out. MICHAEL finds the item of clothing he's misplaced, puts it on.

All costume, no content. That's me. Anyway, goodbye all.

(To ELENA.) Look, if you ever want to – come and look in on me at some point – you could come with Sonya – I've got eighty acres, not a big estate, but if you're interested there's a model garden and a nursery, nothing like it for miles, so – and there's a forest right next to me, state-owned, though the old guy who's supposed to be in charge of it, his health's not what it was, so I pretty much run the whole operation.

ELENA	Yes, I've heard you like your forests. Not to say it isn't valuable, but doesn't it get in the way of your real work? After all, you're a doctor.

MICHAEL	God only knows what our real work is.
ELENA	And is it interesting?
MICHAEL	Yes, it's interesting
JOHN	Hugely interesting.
ELENA	*(To MICHAEL.)* You still look youngish. Thirty-six? Thirty-seven? I mean, it can't be *that* interesting. Trees. And trees. Isn't it – monotonous?
SONYA	No, it's interesting. Really interesting. Michael plants a new forest every year and they've already honoured him for it – he's saving forests from destruction. And if you'd listen to him, you'd agree with him. A hundred percent. He says that trees are what makes the earth beautiful, forests teach us to appreciate beauty, they inspire us with a sense of – majesty. And forests soften the harshness of the climate, and in countries where the climate is gentle, human beings don't struggle as much – they become gentle too – people are beautiful and flexible and sensitive in those countries, they speak well and they move well and the arts and the sciences flourish – they're *happy* – and the way they think about women is decent / and noble and

JOHN applauds.

JOHN	*(To SONYA.)* Bravo! Bravo! Beautiful words [but] *(To MICHAEL.)* terrible argument – so don't mind me if I throw another log on the fire and build myself a big wooden barn.

MICHAEL	Throw something else on the fire – and build your barn from stone. Look, I don't mind cutting down trees if we need to cut down trees – but that's different from mindless destruction. Thousands of millions of trees are perishing, wrecking the homes of animals and birds, river levels are drying up and the landscapes, the most beautiful landscapes on the planet are vanishing, and that's all because of humans – too lazy to throw something else on the fire.

(To ELENA.) That is true, though, isn't it? You have to be genuinely mindless to take beauty and then burn it – to destroy what we cannot create. Humans have the gift of reason, we have the ability to increase the gifts we've been given – but so far, we've created nothing and inflicted only destruction. Forests are shrinking, rivers dry up, wild life is becoming extinct, the climate is *ruined,* and with every new day the earth is a little poorer – a little uglier.

(To JOHN.) And you can give me that ironic look – you don't take it seriously – and maybe I'm just strange – but when I walk past a woodland I've protected, or hear the whisper of a young forest I planted myself, with these hands, I know that some little part of the climate is under my control, and if in a thousand years people are happy then that will be a little part my fault too. When I plant a birch tree – and later it's this delicate green – shimmering

in the breeze, I feel – proud – my heart fills
up and I – I –

NANNY has arrived with a glass of vodka. Caught somewhere almost visionary, MICHAEL loses the next idea, loses his train of thought altogether, and gets self-conscious.

Anyway – *(He drinks the vodka.)* – time's
up.

JOHN   *(To ELENA.)* He doesn't eat meat either.

MICHAEL   No, I don't like to murder living creatures.

                  Though I'm not sure any of it adds up to
                  much. Anyway. Goodbye, all.

As MICHAEL makes to exit:

SONYA   But when are you coming back?

MICHAEL   I – don't know.

MICHAEL exits, followed by SONYA and NANNY. JOHN looks at ELENA.

ELENA   Well, you did it again.

JOHN   Did what again?

ELENA   Unnecessarily upset your mother. And
                  today at lunch, arguing with Alexander?
                  Unnecessary.

JOHN   Unnecessary? With the Professor?

ELENA   You're impossible.

JOHN   I hate him.

ELENA   He's just like everyone else, I don't know
                  why you'd hate him. He's no worse than
                  you.

JOHN	I wish you could see your face. And the way you move now. It's like everything is just a bit too much effort – it's just so lazy –
ELENA	Lazy *and* boring. Everyone attacks Alexander, everyone feels sorry for me – at least, they look at me like – 'God, the poor girl is married to the old Professor'. But what that's really about is what that doctor was just saying: you recklessly destroy the forests until soon there'll be nothing left, and you do the same with humans. You destroy them. And soon, thanks to you, there'll be nothing left – no loyalty or – integrity or self-sacrifice left. You just can't be indifferent to a woman who isn't yours. Because there's a dark, demon thing – desperate to destroy – lurking in all of you. Nothing is spared. Not trees, not birds, not women, not each other …
JOHN	I hate all this philosophising.
	,
ELENA	He looks tired, that doctor. You could see the fatigue in his face. An interesting face. Sonya likes him. She's in love with him. obviously – and I can see why. He's been here three times since we arrived but I'm so *shy* – can't talk to him properly or even be nice to him. He thinks I'm evil.
	John. You know why we make such good friends? Because we are both just incredibly dull. Boring. Both of us.

	Stop it. Looking at me like that. I don't like it.
JOHN	I can't help it – I love you.
	,
ELENA	What?
JOHN	I love you. You're my happiness – you're my *life,* my hope – you make me feel young again and I know my chances are impossibly small – I know there is *no* chance – but I'm not asking you for anything, I just want to look at you, to listen to you, hear your / voice

ELENA makes to leave, JOHN follows.

ELENA	People can *hear*
JOHN	Let me speak – I have to tell you I love you – I love you – you're all that I need to be happy / – don't push me away
ELENA	John, this is painful –

CARTWRIGHT plays the instrument. MARIA makes a note in the margin.

ACT ONE ends.

TWO

The dining room in the house. It's close: about to be stormy. Wind bangs at a window, whistles in at the cracks. Heating pipes clunk and grumble; the old house murmurs.

ALEXANDER is asleep in a chair, dozing. He seems older than he did before, less confident. ELENA in the room too, also asleep.

ALEXANDER wakes up, perhaps from a nightmare.

ALEXANDER	Who's there? Sonya, is it?
ELENA	It's me.
ALEXANDER	Oh. You. Elena. I'm in agony.
ELENA	Your rug's fallen on the floor. Alexander. Alexander. I'm going to shut the window.
ALEXANDER	No. I'm already suffocating. I was asleep then and I dreamed my left leg wasn't really mine. And then woke up in agony. And no, Elena, it isn't gout, it's more like rheumatism. What time is it now?
ELENA	Twenty past twelve.
	,
ALEXANDER	There are some books I need you to track down for me in the morning. They're in the house somewhere, I think.
ELENA	Mm?
ALEXANDER	Books. Poetry books, I need you to – God, why can't I breathe?

161

ELENA	You're exhausted. That's two nights you haven't slept.
ALEXANDER	I've read about cases where gout gets into the heart, angina –
	I'm afraid that's what's happening to me.
	Fuck. Revolting, disgusting old age. I'm so horribly old it disgusts even me – I bet none of you can stand the sight of me.
ELENA	You talk like it's our fault you're old.
ALEXANDER	And who finds me most disgusting? You.

ELENA moves away.

	And you're right. Of course you are. I'm not stupid – I understand. You're young, you're healthy, you're beautiful – you want to live – and I am almost dead. That's it, yes? Have I got it right? And it's ridiculous that I'm still alive. But hey – give it a little longer – and I shall set you free. Not much further to go.
ELENA	I'm exhausted – for God's sake, be quiet –
ALEXANDER	Yes – exhausted – everyone's exhausted – my fault – and everyone's bored and wasting their youth while I have a wonderful time – that's *exactly* it! / Of course it is!
ELENA	Stop it – stop it – you're torturing me –
ALEXANDER	I torture *everyone*. Exactly right.

ELENA	I can't take this – just tell me what you want me to do – tell me what it is that you want me to do –
ALEXANDER	Nothing.
ELENA	Then stop it. Please.
ALEXANDER	It's a curious thing: John says something, or his idiot of a mother, it's fine, everyone listens, but if I so much as open my mouth, everyone's immediately depressed. Even the sound of my voice disgusts you. Well, let's say it: I'm disgusting, I'm selfish, I'm a tyrant – but consider the following: might I have the right to a bit of ego in my old age? Haven't I earned that? Haven't I earned some peace? Some attention? I'm asking you, haven't I got the right / to that?
ELENA	No one's disputing your rights –

The window bangs in the wind.

The wind's up. I'm closing the window.

Any moment now it's going to rain.

No one's disputing your rights.

,

Noise heard outside.

| ALEXANDER | You give your life to learning, you're at home in your office, writing and lecturing and teaching, and then suddenly – for no reason – you find yourself in this crypt, looking at the faces of the stupid and listening to their banal conversation. I want to *live*. I want success, and recognition, and |

to make a bit of a stir – but here? This is the desert, this is *Siberia*.

I'm not ready to stop. This yearning for the past, *reading* about other people's successes, terrified of death – I can't do it. I haven't got the strength.

And then people can't forgive you for the fact that you've got old.

ELENA   Wait five or six years and I'll be old as well.

Enter SONYA. It's started to rain. The roof, here or elsewhere in the house, leaks.

SONYA   Daddy, you specifically told us to send for the doctor, you wouldn't let him see you when he got here – and it's just thoughtless – it's not fair to trouble / him for no reason –

ALEXANDER   He knows as much about medicine as I know about astronomy.

SONYA   The whole of medical science can't come running to attend to your gout.

ALEXANDER   He's an idiot. I'm not seeing him.

SONYA   Do what you want. *(Sits.)* I don't care.

ALEXANDER   What time is it?

ELENA   Gone midnight.

ALEXANDER   It's suffocating. Sonya, give me those tablets – over there –

There are a whole range of tablets.

SONYA	Right away.
ALEXANDER	Not *those.* Jesus, you can't ask anyone for anything!
SONYA	Please stop being so volatile. Some people might like it: I don't. And I have to be up early tomorrow. There's so much work to do.

Enter JOHN, in his dressing gown.

JOHN	There's a storm coming.

Thunder. And then lightning. The room sudden white. Perhaps the lights go out and JOHN lights candles.

	And there it is. Elena, Sonya, go to bed. I've come for the 1am shift.
ALEXANDER	No – no! Don't leave me with him. He'll talk me to death.
JOHN	They need some peace. They didn't sleep last night either.
ALEXANDER	They can go to bed then, but you go too! Please. I'm begging you. We used to be friends – please, don't argue. We'll talk another time.
JOHN	'We used to be friends' – 'used to be' –
SONYA	Shut up, Uncle Johnny –
ALEXANDER	Please don't leave me with him. He will, he'll talk me to death –
JOHN	This is a joke.

Enter NANNY, with more candles.

SONYA	Oh, Nanny, it's late – you should be in bed.
NANNY	Fat chance of that. The tea things haven't been cleared.
ALEXANDER	None of you sleeping, all of you worn out – but I'm blissfully happy!
NANNY	*(To ALEXANDER.)* What's the matter, my love? Have you got a pain? I've got aches in my legs too, something rotten. You've had that trouble a long time now. Sonya, your mother could never sleep at night, wasting away – *(To ALEXANDER.)* She loved you, that woman –

,

Old people are like kids, wanting a bit of pity, but who feels sorry for them now? *(Kisses ALEXANDER's shoulder.)* Come on then, you. Come on up to bed, my love. Come on. We'll give you some lime-flower tea, and we'll warm up your feet – and we'll say a prayer for you –

ALEXANDER	Off we go, then –
NANNY	My legs have got their aches, that is for certain.

NANNY, ALEXANDER and SONYA start to leave, but then:

Yes, she wasted away did Faith, never stopped it, always crying. You were just a child then, Sonya, innocent of all of it. Come on then, you.

They've gone.

ELENA	I'm exhausted with him. I can hardly stand.
JOHN	He's exhausted you; I've exhausted myself. I haven't slept for three nights.
ELENA	Something is seriously wrong in this house. Your mother hates everything except reading, and the Professor – well – the Professor is constantly irritated, doesn't trust me, terrified of you, Sonya's angry with her father, more angry with me – hasn't spoken to me in two weeks now. You hate my husband and openly despise your mother. And I'm just tearful all the time. I can't stop – god, something is seriously wrong.
JOHN	Philosophy again –
ELENA	John, you're educated. You're clever. You must know that it isn't – I don't know – fire and violence that's wrecking the world, but all of this *hatred,* all of this petty cruelty for no *reason at all.* You should be trying to make it peaceful, not just complaining –
JOHN	Then let me be at peace with myself – you are so *beautiful*

Impulsively tries to kiss her hand or something. Outside, the rain hammers at the windows.

ELENA	*Stop* it. Get off.

,

JOHN	Look, the rain will stop, and nature will be *refreshed,* it will be able to *breathe,* but I will stay the same – strangled by the

knowledge that I've had no life. My life, the best part of it, the biggest part of it, has *gone,* and it is never coming back. My past – I have no past, that was *wasted* on nothings, and my present is so completely fucking absurd I find it terrifying.

My life. My love. What do I do with them? My better feelings are just pouring out of me and going nowhere – clear, pure *water* bursting out of me and running straight into the drain – they're dying, and – I'm dying with them – Elena / please listen – listen

ELENA   When you talk about love, I don't know what to say. It makes me go numb. I'm sorry. I can't – I can't tell you anything. Sleep well.

She makes to leave.

JOHN   Wait! Do I really have to tell you – what hurts is knowing that my life is not the only life rotting away to nothing in this house, knowing that you are wasting too, knowing we're *exactly the same.*

I mean, what are you WAITING FOR? What *ideology* could possibly hold *you* back?' You're wasting *time* / seize the day –

ELENA   You're drunk, then.

JOHN   Possibly. It is possible that that's what this is.

,

ELENA   Where's the doctor?

168

JOHN	In there. Staying the night, now.
	It is possible. Anything's possible.
ELENA	And you've been drinking today? Why?
JOHN	It feeds the illusion I'm alive. Don't tell me to stop.
ELENA	You never used to drink. And you never used to talk. Not like this. Go to bed. It's – to be honest, it's just boring
JOHN	Oh God, my wonderful, beautiful woman –
ELENA	Stop it. STOP it. Get off. It's *disgusting* –

ELENA leaves.

JOHN	Gone.

I met her at my sister's. Ten years ago. She was seventeen, I was thirty-seven. Why didn't I love her then? Why didn't I ask her to marry me then?

I could have done that. It could have been that. My life. My wife.

Tonight, we'd be woken by the thunder. She's frightened, I hold her, I whisper, 'Don't be afraid. I'm here.' Even the thought of it is heaven, it's so *beautiful*, but – God – the thoughts roaring in my head –

Why am I old?

Why doesn't she – see me? Why doesn't she understand? That talking of hers, that facile moralising, some hand-wringing,

cardigan-wearing apocalypse of the felling
of the trees. Sickening.

Oh, I have been deceived. I worshipped
him, that pathetic gout-rotted Professor,
worked like an animal for him. Sonya
and I squeezed every last drop out
of this estate, selling oil and peas and
cheese, haggled over the smallest thing
like peasants, skimping on food to save
tiny amounts so that he could be sent
the riches. I was so proud of him and his
learning. I lived and breathed for him. And
now? Retired. And what does it all add up
to? The sum total of that life? Nothing. A
soap bubble. Not one page of his work will
endure. I've been conned. And I do see
that. Gullibly, wilfully conned –

*Enter MICHAEL with CARTWRIGHT. MICHAEL in a state
of undress.*

MICHAEL   Play!

CARTWRIGHT   They're all sleeping.

MICHAEL   Play!

CARTWRIGHT plays the instrument, some song we recognise.

You on your own in here? No ladies?

CARTWRIGHT stops playing, tunes the instrument.

Storm woke me up. Some rain, no? Time is
it?

JOHN   God knows.

MICHAEL   Thought I heard the Professor's wife.

JOHN	She was just in here.
MICHAEL	One hell of a woman.

MICHAEL inspects ALEXANDER's medicines.

	God, he has the whole set, doesn't he? Prescriptions from all over the country. That gout's better travelled than I am. Now is he really ill – or pretending?
JOHN	He's ill.

,

MICHAEL	Why are you so miserable? Feeling sorry for him?
JOHN	Leave me alone.
MICHAEL	Or are you in love with his wife?
JOHN	She's my friend.
MICHAEL	That *was* quick.
JOHN	What was?
MICHAEL	There's only one way a woman can become a man's friend. Three-step process. First, acquaintance – then mistress – then friend.
JOHN	That's impressively vulgar.
MICHAEL	Really? I suppose it is. I'm becoming vulgar. Coarse. Of course. I am drunk. Look. I get this drunk once a month. And I get so fucking *arrogant* I think I can do anything. I take on the most difficult operations, and I perform them easily. I don't even think I'm strange any more

                    – I am an important part of mankind, I think, I have a service to offer that is of tremendous benefit! Will you *play that thing*! I have my own philosophical system – and the rest of human life, all of you, my friends, appear to me as tiny as insects – as microscopic microbacterial lifeforms. *Play the fucking [instrument]!*

CARTWRIGHT   I'd be very glad to play for you – but people are asleep.

MICHAEL   I said, *play*. Tell him to play.

JOHN   Play.

MICHAEL   I need a drink. As soon as it's light, we'll head over to my place. Right? Right? Right. I think there's still some cognac in here *(Perhaps his medicine bag.)* – more-on that, if you please – there's this man I know, doctor, actually, he's always saying 'more on' instead of 'more of', 'we need moron the medicines', but it's never –

SONYA enters.

                    Sorry – let me get dressed –

MICHAEL exits. CARTWRIGHT follows him out. The wind blows outside.

SONYA   So. Uncle Johnny. Drinking with the doctor again. He's always been like that, but you – why do you have to be? At your age.

JOHN   Age is nothing to do with it. When there isn't real life, people live on illusions. It's better than nothing.

SONYA	Real life? The hay lying mown in the field, the rain pouring down every day, everything *rotting* and you're just obsessed with illusions. You've done nothing on the farm for [weeks] – I'm on my own. I'm worn out with it –
	(Scared.) There's tears in your eyes.
JOHN	Tears? There isn't. I haven't. Nonsense.
	You looked at me then just like your mother.
	,
	Oh, sweetheart – *(Kisses her, greedily.)* my sister, my poor sweet sister. Faith. Where is she now? If she only knew. God, if she only *knew* –
SONYA	Knew what? Uncle, if she only knew what?
JOHN	It's so hard to bear – it doesn't matter – *later* – don't worry about it. Don't worry about it. I'm going.

JOHN goes.

SONYA alone on stage. Eventually:

SONYA	Michael, are you [there?] – you're not asleep are you? Can you come in here?
MICHAEL	Coming.

Enter MICHAEL, a bit smarter – more dressed.

	Are you all right? What is it?
SONYA	Drink if you want to, but don't let Uncle drink. It's bad for him.

MICHAEL	All right. We won't drink any more.
	,
	I'm heading home, anyway, so that's that. Dawn by the time I get back.
SONYA	It's still raining. Wait until morning.
MICHAEL	Storm's passing, I'll just catch the edge of it. I'm going. And please, no more invitations to visit your father. I tell him he has gout, he tells me he has rheumatism, I tell him to stay lying down, he sits up. And tonight I didn't even have the pleasure of his conversation.
SONYA	He's a spoiled brat.
	Could you eat something?

SONYA gets food from somewhere in the room.

MICHAEL	Yes. Why not?
SONYA	I love a midnight feast. He had a major way with the ladies, apparently – when he was younger, and it spoilt him. That's why he's [like that]. Have some cheese.

They both eat.

| MICHAEL | I haven't eaten anything today. Just drank. Difficult man, your father. |

Pours a drink for himself.

Do you mind if I [drink] – ? It's just us, so can I be honest? I wouldn't last a month living here, I'd suffocate. This atmosphere. Your father's obsessed with his illness, your

	Uncle Johnny's obsessed with his misery, your *grandmother* – and Christ, your *step-mother* –
SONYA	What about her?
MICHAEL	The totality of a person should be beautiful: face, clothes, yes – but soul and ideas. She *is* the fairest of them all, look, she's obviously beautiful, but she just eats and sleeps, goes for a walk, enchants us all with her beauty, and – well, that's it. No responsibilities. She doesn't *do* anything. No work. You know? Hardly a life well-lived.
	Maybe that's harsh of me. Life is just so – so – *unsatisfying*. Me and your uncle, the pair of us, stamping out joy.
SONYA	You're not satisfied with life, then?
MICHAEL	Life in general – yes. This life, our life, day to day, constricted, narrow, *provincial* fucking life – no, can't stand it, hate it from the bottom of my soul. And as for my personal life, honest to God, there's absolutely nothing good about it. I mean, if you're travelling through a deep green forest on a dark night and you see a glimmer of light, golden in the distance, then you don't even notice how tired your calves are, or how dark it is, or the branches scratching at your face like fingers, you're [heading towards it].
	I mean, I work – and I know you know this – I work harder than *anyone* – but fate

175

just slams you back down, it beats you down, and it's unbearable sometimes, life – without that light in the distance.

It's not there.

I don't hope for anything – for me, I mean. I don't love people. You know, they say, love your neighbour, well, I don't love people. I don't. Haven't for a long time.

SONYA   You don't love anyone?

MICHAEL   Well, the one person – actually – your Nanny.

There's real affection there. Old times.

Normal people, you know, *most* people, are just completely fucking backward, and then the special ones, *cultured* people, God, it just makes you *tired,* our good friends, their petty thoughts and their petty feelings and the fact they can't see past the end of their noses – and even if they're a bit more intelligent, a bit less *pathetic,* it's all analysis and introspection, whining and carrying out evil little vendettas, bad-mouthing whoever for whatever reason, looking at you sideways from the corner of their eyes, and then, 'Oh, he's a psychopath' or 'he's all talk, that one' – or if they don't quite know which label to slap on my forehead, they just say, 'He's a strange man, that doctor' – strange! I love forests – and that's strange. I don't eat meat. Strange. A direct, open, pure relationship with nature – or

with people – it's strange, by which we
mean: it's gone. It doesn't *exist* anymore.

He goes to drink.

SONYA	Please don't.
MICHAEL	What?
SONYA	Drink. Don't drink any more. Please.
MICHAEL	Why not?
SONYA	You're just – so much greater than that. You're so advanced, your voice is so gentle, and it's not that – it's out of all of the people I've met – you're the best one, I mean, you're different to everyone else, so why be like everyone else and – drink? People don't create, they destroy, you always say, so why – why are you destroying yourself? Don't do it.
	Please. Don't do it.
	I'm begging you.
MICHAEL	I won't drink any more.
SONYA	Promise me.
MICHAEL	Word of honour.
SONYA	Thank you.
	,
MICHAEL	Enough! Right. I've sobered up. I am completely sober and shall remain so 'til the end of my days.

He looks at his watch.

	Shall we keep talking? Shall we? What I'm saying is, I suppose: my time has crumbled away, it's run out, I'm old and burned out and I got coarse in my old age. My feelings are blunted. I don't think I'll be connected with anyone again. I don't *love* anyone, I mean. I don't think I ever will, now. Fall in love. But you know what does get to me?
SONYA	What?
MICHAEL	Beauty. It's just so – *exciting*. I can't be indifferent to it. That there Elena – your wicked stepmother – could get my attention in less than a day. If she so desired.
	But then that's not *love,* that's not connection.

He closes his eyes. Shudders, almost: an odd reaction. SONYA, of course, sees it.

SONYA	What's the matter?
MICHAEL	No, nothing.
	So. Just before Easter, a patient of mine, he was under anaesthetic – and he died – / he he
SONYA	It's time to forget about that.
	,
	Michael. Tell me this. If I had a girlfriend. Or a sister, a younger sister. And you found out that she – well let's say that she

178

	loves you – what would your [reaction be] – how would you respond?
MICHAEL	*(Shrugs.)* I've no idea. I wouldn't [respond], probably. I'd make it clear: I can't love her and there are too many other things to think about.
	Anyway, time to go if it's time to go. I'll bid you farewell, or we'll still be here when the sun comes up. *(Touches her hand.)* I'll go the other way out, avoid your uncle detaining me!

MICHAEL exits.

SONYA	He said nothing to me, I don't know what's really in his heart, but – why do I *feel so happy*?

SONYA laughs – screams – overjoyed.

'You're so advanced', I said, 'your voice is so gentle'! Did that sound bad? The vibrations of his voice are still in the air and they're – like a hug or something – 'you know what does get to me? Beauty' – then when I said the thing about the younger sister he just didn't understand – he didn't even notice –

SONYA hits herself.

Why am I so ugly? It's the worst thing. And I know I'm not beautiful, I know that, I know that – someone the other day I overheard saying 'she's a nice girl, her heart's in the right place, but it's a pity she's plain.' Plain.

ELENA enters.

ELENA	The storm's passed. That *air*. Wonderful.
	Where's the doctor?
SONYA	Gone.
	,
ELENA	Sonya –
SONYA	What?
ELENA	How long is this going to go on? Can we really not be friends? We haven't hurt each other. Surely enough is enough, now …
SONYA	I wanted to say it too –

SONYA embraces ELENA.

| | No more anger. |
| ELENA | Thank God – |

They are both moved.

SONYA	Daddy in bed?
ELENA	No, he's in the other room. We don't speak to each other for weeks – I don't even know why that [is] – what's this?
SONYA	Michael was having some supper.
ELENA	There's wine! Let's drink to being friends.
SONYA	Yes
ELENA	Out of the same glass. Much nicer. So. Friends?
SONYA	Friends. I've wanted to make it up with you for a long time, but I just felt ashamed –

ELENA	Why are you crying?
SONYA	It's nothing, it's just the way I am –
ELENA	Hey – it's all right, you're all right. You strange little thing, you've set me off now!
	,
	You're angry with me because – because you think I married your father for the wrong reasons. But I'd swear to you on anything, if that means anything to you: I married him for love. Really. I was so fascinated by him because he was famous and he *knew* so much. It wasn't real love, it was [artificial], but at the time I thought it was real – it's not my fault. But since the day of the wedding, you've never stopped punishing me with those eyes – suspicious, clever eyes.
SONYA	We're at peace now. Just forget all of that.
ELENA	You shouldn't look at people like that. It doesn't suit you. You have to trust people or life is just impossible.
	,
SONYA	Tell me this. Be honest. We're friends. Are you happy?
ELENA	No.
SONYA	I knew it – one more question. Honestly … would you like to have a young husband?
ELENA	You're a child.

	Yes. Yes. Of *course* I would. Ask me something else. Ask me.
SONYA	The doctor. Do you like him?
ELENA	Yes.
SONYA	A lot?
ELENA	Yes.
SONYA	Sorry, I'm pulling a stupid face, aren't I? *(Laughs.)* I mean, I know he's gone but I still think I'm hearing his voice and his steps and his hand on the door and – looking at the dark of the glass of the window and thinking I'm seeing his face – wait, let me finish, let me [say I LOVE HIM I LOVE HIM I LOVE HIM] –
	,
	I can't say it. I can feel my cheeks red. Argh. OK, let's go to my room and we can talk there. No? I'm an *idiot*. Admit it. Tell me a fact about him.
ELENA	Such as?
SONYA	Anything. He's intelligent. He can do anything. He's a doctor. He makes people better. He plants trees.
ELENA	But it's not just that, not just trees and – tablets, he's – listen – he's got *talent*. And that's magic – that means he's free, his spirit is free, he's brave and his horizons are endless. He puts a seed in the ground and he knows what it will become in a thousand years, he can see all the way to

the next millennium. There aren't many people like that. Like him. He's special. Rare. And those people, you can't help but love them. He drinks, and he can be … common, but does that really matter? He travels miles to heal people, to cure disease, to tend to the poor, and – I don't know how you could do his job, see the things he's seen –and reach forty innocent and sober.

ELENA kisses SONYA.

I really truly hope you end up happy. You deserve it.

I'm just boring. Insignificant. Just passing through. In music, in my husband's house, in every drama of my life, everywhere, actually – forgettable – a walk-on part. Actually, Sonya, you know what, thinking about it, I'm actually really, really unhappy. There's no happiness for me. Not in this world. None.

Why are you laughing?

SONYA laughs, covering her face.

SONYA   I'm so happy. So happy.

ELENA   You know what? I want to play the piano. I'll play something now.

SONYA   Yes! Play!

SONYA embraces ELENA.

I can't sleep. Go on! Play!

ELENA   In a minute. Your father's awake. And
               music irritates him if he isn't well. Go and
               ask him if he minds me playing. And then
               we'll play. Go on.

SONYA   I'm going!

SONYA exits. ELENA alone.

The noise of something outside, distant. Security alarms.

ELENA   I haven't played in ages. I'll play and I will
               cry and I'll sob like a child.

               ,

SONYA comes back.

SONYA   He said no.

End of ACT TWO.

THREE

Some time later. A room in the house. 12:45.

JOHN and SONYA. ELENA walks around, thinking.

JOHN	His eminence the Professor has deigned to express his sincere desire that we are all assembled in this particular room at precisely one o' clock. Which is in fifteen minutes. He will speak and the world will listen.
ELENA	Business, probably.
JOHN	He doesn't *have* any business outside writing, whining, being jealous – that's *it*.
SONYA	Uncle
JOHN	All right, [I'm] sorry – *(About ELENA.)* – hobbies include walking around being bored, and *being bored*. Charming. She's charming.
ELENA	I'm bored with the sound of your voice. It never stops.
	It's killing me, the boredom. I don't know what to do.
SONYA	There are plenty of things to do.
ELENA	Such as?
SONYA	Work. It's a farm. The crops. The animals. The fields. Teaching. Making people better. Isn't that enough? Before you and Daddy were here, Uncle Johnny and I used to sell the produce at the market ourselves.

ELENA	Yeah, I don't know how to do that. It wouldn't be interesting, anyway. Sounds like something from a fairy story. Teaching the poor. Healing the sick. Anyway, you can't just wake up one day and start teaching.
SONYA	You can – I don't understand how you aren't doing it already! Just try it and with a bit of time, you'll get used to it. Don't be bored. It's contagious.
ELENA	Contagious?
SONYA	Look: Uncle Johnny does nothing. Well, he follows you round like a shadow, and I've left my work and I'm standing here talking to you. Doing nothing – and there's so much to do! Doctor Michael used to visit us once a month, it was hard to get him to come at all, and now he comes here every day and he's abandoned medicine and forests and everything. You're a witch.
JOHN	*(To ELENA.)* What's wrong with you, anyway? Come on, *think* about it – you're a *mermaid,* with mermaid's blood rushing through your veins – let yourself go for once in your life, fall headfirst in love, dive deep down into the water and leave the Professor and the rest of us standing on the shore –
ELENA	Leave me alone – it's just *cruel*

ELENA tries to leave, JOHN prevents it.

JOHN	I'm sorry, I'm sorry, come on, I didn't mean [to upset you] – forgive me

JOHN kisses her hand.

	Peace perfect peace?
ELENA	It's getting close to the limit, John. It really is.
JOHN	As an olive branch, to engender harmony, I'll bring you an armful of roses – picked them this morning – autumn roses, beautiful, mournful roses –

JOHN goes.

SONYA	Autumn roses, beautiful, mournful roses –
	,
ELENA	That's September already. And being here in winter, God, it'll be [horrible] –
	,
	Where's the doctor?
SONYA	In Uncle Johnny's room. Writing something. I'm glad he's gone – because I need to talk to you.
ELENA	What about?
SONYA	What about?
ELENA	All right. All right, all right.
SONYA	I know I'm not beautiful
ELENA	Your hair is beautiful.
SONYA	No.
	No. It's what you say to an ugly woman: 'Your hair is so beautiful, you have beautiful eyes' – *Six years* I've been in love with him.

I love him more than I loved my mum – I hear him everywhere, I imagine the feel of his hands, and I look at the door and I wait – I'm *desperate* – it's like he's always about to walk in – and I just want to talk about him, and look! – I come to you – and – and he's here every day, every day now, but he doesn't look at me. He doesn't see me. FUCK. This is completely *hopeless*. Give me strength – give me *strength*. Pathetic. I keep trotting up to him, starting to talk to him, looking in his eyes, it's pathetic. I can't control myself. It's embarrassing. And I told Uncle Johnny I love him. Yesterday. And they all know I love him. Everyone knows.

ELENA   And him? Does he?

SONYA   No. He doesn't notice me.

ELENA   He's a strange man. You know what? Let me talk to him. I'll hint – gently.

,

Honestly, you can't go any longer without knowing. Let me ask.

SONYA nods yes.

Beautiful. He either loves you or he doesn't: it's a simple thing to find out. Don't be embarrassed, sweetheart, don't worry – I'll ask him so subtly, he won't even notice. Yes or no. That's it.

,

If it's a no, he shouldn't come here any more. Right?

SONYA nods yes.

	It'll be easier if you don't have to see him. We'll do it right now, question him now. He was going to show me some drawings or something. Will you tell him I want to see him?
SONYA	You'll tell me the truth?
ELENA	Of course. Not knowing is worse; whatever the truth is. I think. It's all right, you can trust me.
SONYA	Yes. OK. I'll say you want to see the drawings –

SONYA makes to leave, and then stops.

	Wait
	No, not knowing is better – at least then there's *hope* –
ELENA	What are you [saying]?
SONYA	Nothing.

SONYA exits.

ELENA	There's nothing worse than knowing someone's secret and not being able to help.
	He's not in love with her – it's obvious – but why shouldn't he [marry her]? She's no great beauty, but for him – a doctor – at his age? She'd be a perfect wife. Clever, so kind, good – but no, it's not that. It's not that.

,

I understand her. Living in the middle
of all this desperate boredom, no real
people, just grey things roaming around,
hearing nothing but banalities, no one
does anything beyond eating and drinking
and sleeping – then he appears. And he's
different from all of them. Handsome,
intelligent, compelling, like a bright moon
rising in the darkness. And you forget
yourself – and fall under his spell.

I think I might have done too. I'm bored
when he's not here – and now, look, I'm
smiling thinking about him – mermaid's
blood racing through my veins – 'Let
yourself go for once in your life' – maybe
I should – maybe I should – soar off like
a bird from all of you and your work and
your talk and your tired faces and forget
that you ever existed –

But I'm such a *coward*. I'm so shy. I feel
so guilty. He comes here every day now
– and I guess that it's [because of me] – I
think it might be because [of me] and God
I already feel guilty – I want to cry – and
beg Sonya to forgive me –

Enter MICHAEL with three home-made maps.

MICHAEL   Hello. You wanted to see these?

ELENA   Is it a good moment?

MICHAEL   Sure.

MICHAEL sets out the maps.

	You weren't born in the country, were you?
ELENA	Child of the city. And then studied there too.
MICHAEL	Did you? Where did you [study]?
ELENA	At the music conservatoire.
MICHAEL	Oh – Then this may not be very interesting.
ELENA	Why not? I don't know much about country life, but I've read a lot –
MICHAEL	I've got my own table here. In John's room. When I'm exhausted with everything, completely wrecked, sometimes I come here and I settle down and amuse myself for an hour or two with this. Sonya sits and goes through their accounts, her and John – and I sit here fiddling, working on the tiny details – and it's warm and it's quiet. It's fun. Though I only allow myself that pleasure – now and again – once a month.

So: this is the district as it was fifty years ago. Dark and light green is forest – so basically – half of all of it, the whole area, is forest. Where the green is cross-hatched with red – that was wild animals, wild goats – and this lake here, there were swans, geese and ducks – people remember huge clouds of birds flying overhead. Villages. Hamlets. Small farms. An old monastery, water mills. There were a lot of cattle and horses too, that's the light blue – here, for example, very heavy blue, so there were lots of horses here.

Next. This is how it was twenty-five years ago. The dark green now only a third – so only a third of it is forest now. The goats have gone. The green and blue are paler.

And so on and so forth.

Let's look at exhibit number three. Today. Now. Tiny patches of green but scattered, no large areas. Birds and animals gone. All the little settlements gone. It's a gradual but undeniable decline, a slow disintegration, which looks good to be a complete disintegration in ten, fifteen more years.

Now perhaps that's just civilisation, that's progress, the old giving way to the new. Which I would understand, if in place of the forests we had brand new roads and railways and hospitals and schools – if people were healthier, richer, smarter – but that's not really what's happening. All the health problems, the social problems, the problems with the environment – are staying exactly the same.

So the trees are destroyed and we are standing still. We're stagnating. But this first map – this was a richer world – a richer habitat – for the animals, yes, but for the people too – and what I can't mark on the maps is the sensation of life in the wild, the purer air and gentler climate and its effect on the body, the human animal free

to stretch its muscles and breathe – and
that has all been lost as well – as a result
of our lack of self-awareness – we've lost
ourselves – and so everything is destroyed
and tomorrow is entirely forgotten –

It is almost all destroyed. Wrecked. And
nothing is created to replace it

I see from your face that you're bored.

ELENA   But I know so little [about it] –

MICHAEL   There's nothing to know – you're just not
               interested. It's all right.

ELENA   To be honest, my mind was – I was
               thinking about something else. Sorry. I
               need to, uh, interrogate you about a thing,
               and it's a bit awkward, I don't know how to
               start, really –

MICHAEL   An interrogation?

ELENA   An innocent interrogation. It's fine. Sit
               down.

They sit down.

               The case concerns a young lady.

               Shall we just be straightforward? Honesty,
               no games. Is that [all right]?

MICHAEL   Yes

ELENA   It's my stepdaughter. Sonya. Do you like
               her?

MICHAEL   Yes, of course –

ELENA   Do you like her – as a woman?

193

His reply, not immediately:

MICHAEL   No

ELENA   Two or three words and it's over. Did you really not notice?

MICHAEL   Notice? No. Notice what?

ELENA   You don't love her – I can see that in your eyes – but *she* is suffering – understand that and – stop coming here.

The penny drops for MICHAEL.

MICHAEL   Oh

                      I've had my time – that's [fine] – and yes – besides, there's no time

He shrugs.

                      When could I – ?

He is very embarrassed.

ELENA   Oof! That was a horrible conversation, I've been so worried it's been like dragging a weight around – but thank God it's over. Forget it. Let's not even talk about it. But you can't come here any more. You're a smart man and you understand.

                      God, it even made me blush – am I [blushing]?

MICHAEL   If you'd said this a month or two ago, I probably would have thought about it, but now –

He shrugs.

But if she's suffering, then – of course.
The only thing I don't understand is why
you carried out the interrogation –

MICHAEL looks at ELENA. He wags his finger.

You. Clever.

ELENA   What do you mean?

MICHAEL   Crafty. I believe you that Sonya is
suffering, yes, accepted, but why the
interrogation? Why you? *(Stopping her from
talking, excitedly.)* Hang on, don't do the
surprised face, you know exactly why I
come here every day. The reason why –
and the reason *who* – you know. I know
you know. Predator. I'm old meat, darling,
I've been there –

ELENA is genuinely bewildered.

ELENA   Predator? I don't understand?

MICHAEL   Beautiful, sleek animal – and you need
a *victim*. I've done nothing for a whole
month, thrown over everything looking
for you – and you *love* that – stop *pretending*
you don't know, you don't need to
interrogate that –

I surrender. I'm yours. Eat.

ELENA   Are you mad?

MICHAEL   So you're shy now.

ELENA   I am *so much better* than you think. I *swear* –
I

She makes to leave, he stops her.

195

MICHAEL   I'm leaving today. I won't come back. But
                 –

                 He takes her hand.

                 Where will we see each other? Quickly.
                 Where?

                 Someone might come in. Speak to me.

                 You're wonderful. Luxurious.

                 One kiss. Your hair.

                 I want to inhale you –

ELENA   I swear –

                 He stops her from speaking.

MICHAEL   What? Don't swear, no need to swear, no
                 need for words: you're so beautiful: your
                 hands – your hands.

ELENA   No. Enough – go – you've gone mad –

MICHAEL   Speak. Speak. Tomorrow. Where?

                 The two are very close now.

                 It's inevitable. We *have* to see each other,
                 you and I –

                 *They kiss. At that JOHN enters, bouquet of roses in hand,
                 freezes – they haven't seen him, he stands, stricken in the
                 doorway –*

ELENA   Please. Please have – pity.

                 ELENA gives in to it – moves in again –

                 No

MICHAEL   The forest. Tomorrow. At two. Yes? Yes?
                 Will you?

ELENA sees JOHN.

ELENA   Let me *go*.

ELENA, embarrassed, moves away.

                      ,

                 Horrible. It's horrible.

JOHN   Nothing – yes – no, it's nothing –

MICHAEL   Today, it isn't bad weather, my friend –
                 cloudy in the morning, threatening rain,
                 and now – sunshine. It's the beginnings of
                 a beautiful autumn, you really do have to
                 say – and the winter wheat is coming along
                 –

He collects his things and heads for the door.

                 The days are getting shorter, is the only
                 thing –

MICHAEL exits. ELENA makes for JOHN.

ELENA   You try, you use your influence, to get us
                 out of here – my husband and me – we
                 need to leave this place *today.* Are you
                 listening? TODAY.

JOHN is wiping his face.

JOHN   What? Well, yes – well –

                 I saw everything, Elena. Everything.

ELENA   *Listen* to me: I have to get out of this house
                 – today

Enter ALEXANDER, CARTWRIGHT, NANNY. It's time for the one o' clock meeting.

CARTWRIGHT   I'm not actually feeling well myself,
              Professor, which is two days now I've not
              quite been right, something in my head,
              I think, / that

ALEXANDER   Where are the others? I hate this house.
              Like a maze. Twenty-six enormous rooms,
              everyone scatters and you can't find a soul.
              Can you invite Maria and Elena to join us
              in here, please?

ELENA   I'm here.

ALEXANDER   Please have a seat, everyone –

SONYA enters impatiently to ELENA.

SONYA   What did he say?

ELENA   Later.

SONYA   You're shaking. Are you upset?

SONYA looks into ELENA's eyes.

              I understand.

              He isn't going to come here any more.

              That's right, isn't it?

              ,

              Yes?

              Just *tell* me – am I right?

ELENA nods yes.

ALEXANDER	I can put up with ill health, just about, but life in the bloody countryside – the *tone* of life – it's like I landed on an alien planet. Sit down, everyone, please. Sonya!

But SONYA doesn't hear him. Head down.

SONYA

	Doesn't even hear me. Sit down, Nanny, thank you –

NANNY sits and begins to knit.

	Very good. Now please all hang up your ears, as they say, on the coathook of attention. That was a joke.
JOHN	I don't need to be here. Can I go?
ALEXANDER	No, no, I need you here most. The most / needed.
JOHN	Oh, what do you *want*?
ALEXANDER	What are you angry about?
	,
	If I've done something wrong, then I sincerely apologise, / John
JOHN	Drop the tone. Get on with it. What is this?

MARIA enters. A frisson between her and the Professor.

ALEXANDER	And here is the matriarch. Then ladies and gentlemen, I shall begin.
	,
	I have brought everyone together to inform you that a Government Inspector is on

his way here. That was a joke as well, but joking aside, I'm, I am here to – this is serious. I have brought you all here to ask for your help and your advice, with which I'm sure you will oblige me. Look, I'm an academic, my head is most usually in a book and not in the real world – not in practical life. So I need the guidance of people with experience – John, that's you of course, and you, Cartwright, and you too, dear mother –

Look, what I'm saying is – *manet omnes una nox,* we all are all mortal under God, and I am – old. And ill. And it's time for me to have my affairs set in order in so far as they relate to my family. My life is over now, this isn't about me, but I have a young wife and an unmarried daughter.

,

To continue living in the countryside is impossible for me. We're just not made for this place. And this place just doesn't generate the funds to enable us to live in the city. We could, say, sell our forest [or at least, what's left of it] – an extraordinary measure – we can only do it the once. However: we are now in need of measures which will guarantee us a permanent and more or less definite level of income. I have come up with one such measure, and I shall offer it to you now for discussion.

Omitting the details, explaining it in general terms: this old house, our farm, gives an average return of no more than two per cent per annum. I propose to sell it. If we put the proceeds of that liquidation into interest-bearing securities, it will yield four to five percent, and I believe, a surplus that might allow us to invest in a small cottage, a little nearer the city –

JOHN   Wait – my hearing isn't right – say that again –

ALEXANDER   The money would be converted into interest-bearing securities and a small surplus, which would buy us a modest / cottage

JOHN   Not the cottage – not that – you said something else

ALEXANDER   I propose to sell the estate.

JOHN   That's it. Yes. You sell the estate. Excellent. Great idea.

And where do you propose I go with this old woman – and your daughter, Sonya?

ALEXANDER   We will discuss all of this in time, but not everything / at once –

JOHN   Wait a minute. Clearly I've been a complete and total idiot up until this point. A moron. Because until now, I have been stupid enough to think that the estate belonged to Sonya. That my late father bought this estate as an investment for my sister, and that, when she died, given that we do not live under *sharia law*, it was Sonya who inherited it from her –

ALEXANDER	Yes, it belongs to Sonya, nobody has suggested otherwise – and without Sonya's consent, I'm not going to sell it – and this proposal is for Sonya's benefit.
JOHN	It's incomprehensible – I just cannot *understand* it – or am I mad – or – or
MARIA	Jean, will you *please* stop contradicting Alexander. Believe me: he knows better than we do what's right and what's wrong –
JOHN	No, give me some [water] –

JOHN drinks water. He's getting seriously worked up. Feeling now that the civility of proceedings comes off the rails, starts to spin out of control.

Say whatever the hell you like. What do you want?

ALEXANDER	I don't understand why you're so worked up – I'm not saying my proposal is ideal – if everyone thinks it's unfeasible, we'll abandon it, of course –

,

JOHN is silent. ALEXANDER uncertain. No one in charge now. CARTWRIGHT, embarrassed, tries to take the wheel.

CARTWRIGHT	I, sir, Professor – have a profound respect for academics, but it does also run in the family. My brother – well, his wife's brother, perhaps you know him, actually / was something of a master

JOHN	Can you WAIT – can you wait – there's something to deal with here, leave it 'til later.

JOHN suddenly remembers something, hauls CARTWRIGHT round in front of ALEXANDER.

	Here. Ask him. This estate was bought from his uncle –
ALEXANDER	Oh, ask him *what?*
JOHN	This estate was bought then for about ninety-five thousand. My father paid seventy and left a debt of twenty-five thousand. Now *listen* – this estate would never have been bought if I hadn't given up *my* inheritance in favour of my sister, my sister that I *loved* – more than you will ever understand – and, actually, that debt would never have been paid at all had I not worked like an ox for a decade to pay the fucking thing off –
ALEXANDER	I'm sorry I started this.
JOHN	The reason she owns this estate, the reason the debt was paid, the reason this house is still standing is *me* – and now I've got old, you're just going to throw me out like a dead dog –
ALEXANDER	I don't understand what you're driving at –
JOHN	Twenty-five years I worked, I managed this estate, I sent you all the money, the most meticulous accountant – and when did you once say 'thank you'? And in all that time – starting from when I was a very

	young man indeed – I have received the same salary, exactly the same, tiny salary, a *nothing* – and you never once thought to raise it, to give me a little *more* –
ALEXANDER	But John, how would I know? I'm not here, I'm not practical: you could have given yourself as much of a raise as you wanted –
JOHN	Why didn't I *steal?* So you all hate me for not stealing? It would have been justice, true – and I wouldn't be a fucking beggar –
MARIA	*John*
CARTWRIGHT	John, don't – please – I'm shaking – let's not spoil a friendship – don't do this. Don't do / this
JOHN	For *twenty-five years* I have been imprisoned between these walls like a – *mole* – with my mother – and all our thoughts and feelings belonged to you: every day, talking about you, about your work, proud of you, praising your name, every night, reading your books and your articles and – now, my God, I feel such profound contempt for the whole fucking lot of it –

CARTWRIGHT severely panicked. ALEXANDER angry.

CARTWRIGHT	No, John, don't – I CAN'T –
ALEXANDER	I don't understand – what do you *want?*
JOHN	You were a higher power – the embodiment of an ideal order – and we knew all your writing by heart – but now my eyes are *open*. I see everything.

	You *write* about art – but art is completely beyond you. Nothing of your work, not one piece of your work that I *loved*, is worth anything at all – you *fooled* us all –
ALEXANDER	Enough – that's enough. I'm *leaving* –
ELENA	John, stop it – I want you to be quiet – can you / hear me?
JOHN	I will not stop talking –

Stops ALEXANDER from leaving.

	STOP. I haven't finished. You ruined my life. I haven't *lived*, I never got to *live*. Thanks to you I have destroyed the best years of my life. You're my worst enemy.
CARTWRIGHT	I can't – I can't – I can't – I can't –

Greatly agitated, CARTWRIGHT exits.

ALEXANDER	Oh what do you *want* from me? And what right do you have to speak to me like that, you insignificant little no one? WHO ARE YOU?
ELENA	I have to get out of this *hell* –
	(Screams.) I CAN'T TAKE THIS ANY MORE
ALEXANDER	The estate is yours, is it? *Have* it! Take it! I don't need it!
JOHN	My life is wasted. I'm talented, I have a brain, I'm brave – and if I'd led a normal life, I could have been a Schopenhauer, could have been a Dostoyevsky – God –

	I'm mad, I'm going mad – I don't know what I'm saying – mummy, I'm desperate – mummy – help me –
MARIA	*(Stern.)* Listen to Alexander.
JOHN	Mummy – *help me* – Tell me what to do! Tell me what to do!
	No – actually. No. Don't tell me. I know what to do.
	You're all going to remember me.

JOHN exits. MARIA goes off after him.

ALEXANDER	Keep that *insane madman* away from me. I cannot live under the same roof as him.
ELENA	We're leaving today – we have to get out of here now –
ALEXANDER	Nonentity. He's a worthless little no one.
SONYA	Daddy, please have mercy – *please* – Uncle Johnny and I are so unhappy. Remember when when when you were younger, Uncle Johnny and grandma – they translated your books for you, copied things, papers – the whole night – and Uncle Johnny and I have worked every day, every day, scared to spend money on anything but we sent it to you – no – I'm not saying it right, it's all coming out wrong – but you have to understand what we feel – we have to have mercy –
ELENA	Alexander, for God's sake, you have to talk to him, I'm begging you –

ALEXANDER	All right. I'll try and reason with him. I'm not blaming him, I'm not angry, but his behaviour is a little bit out of the ordinary, we must concede –
	I'll go and talk to him.
ELENA	Be gentle. Calm him down.

ALEXANDER goes out, ELENA after him.

SONYA	Nanny, nanny
NANNY	Shush shush shush, child, the geese scream and then stop screaming – scream and then they stop –
SONYA	Nanny –
NANNY	Shivering like you've been in the snow. Right, little orphan, God have mercy on you, some tea, some raspberry drink maybe, and this will pass – don't cry, little orphan, this will pass –

NANNY looks to the door, angry.

These geese need to stop screaming for a while. Quieten down.

A gunshot.

SONYA looks up.

Christ Almighty, what are they – ?

ALEXANDER runs staggering in, frightened, followed by ELENA.

ALEXANDER	Stop him – stop him – he's *mad* –

JOHN enters, with a gun.

ELENA	John. John. John. Give me it – hand it over –

ELENA moves to JOHN, tries to take it from him, he throws her aside.

JOHN	Let me go. Let me go. Let me go. Where is he? Where *is he*?

JOHN sees ALEXANDER.

　　　There he is.

JOHN shoots at ALEXANDER.

　　　BANG.

　　　,

　　　Did I miss him?

　　　Another failure. Of course. Of course.

　　　,

JOHN laughs.

　　　Oh fuck – fuck – fuck – fuck –

A moment of exhausted calm. ALEXANDER stunned. ELENA leans against a wall.

ELENA	I don't want to be here. Get me out of here. Kill me – but I can't stay here, I can't –
JOHN	What am I doing? What am I doing?
SONYA	Nanny – Nanny –

End of ACT THREE.

FOUR

JOHN's room. This is where he sleeps and also the office from which the business of the estate is conducted. All sorts of papers and books. A writing desk, stacked with papers. On the wall, for no reason, a map of Africa. A huge sofa, sleeping things in evidence. A sense of confinement, stuff: a little overwhelming. A mat to prevent people from dragging mud in.

Autumn evening. Silence.

CARTWRIGHT and NANNY. She's got her knitting wool: winding it up.

CARTWRIGHT	Come on, Nanny, hurry it along – we're about to say goodbye.
NANNY	Not much left now.
CARTWRIGHT	Off to the city. They'll live there.
NANNY	All for the best.
CARTWRIGHT	They got frightened. Elena saying, 'I won't live in this house another hour – we have to go, we have to go – we'll find somewhere in the city and then send for our things.' Travelling light. So, Nanny, not their fate to live here after all. Not meant to be.
NANNY	Good riddance. That commotion they kicked up. And guns. They should all be ashamed of themselves.
CARTWRIGHT	Yes. A battle scene worthy of a painting.
NANNY	To have to see that at my age.

'

	It'll all go back to how it was before. The old ways. Breakfast in the morning at eight, lunch at one – and sitting down to supper, everyone together, in the evening, properly. Like other people do.
	It's a long time since I had dumplings.
CARTWRIGHT	It is a long time. It is indeed.
	,
	A long, long time.
	You know. This morning. I was in the village and the man in the shop shouts at me, 'Oy, you! You! *Scrounger*!'
	It was hurtful, if I'm honest.
NANNY	Don't dwell on it. We're all scroungers at the good Lord's feet. You and Sonya and John, not one of us sits idle, we work hard. We do, we all do. Every one of [us] –
	Where is Sonya?
CARTWRIGHT	Outside. With the doctor. Looking for John.
	They're afraid he might hurt himself.
NANNY	And where's the gun?
CARTWRIGHT	*(Shh.)* I hid it. In the cellar.
NANNY	*(Smiles.)* Terrible.

Enter JOHN and MICHAEL.

JOHN   Leave me alone. And you lot, out. Just give
                me an hour on my own. I really don't need
                to be watched.

CARTWRIGHT   Right away, John, right away.

                CARTWRIGHT tiptoes away.

NANNY   A goose. A right old goose, aren't you?

                *NANNY makes a goose screaming noise at JOHN, gathers up
                her wool, exits.*

JOHN   *(To MICHAEL.) Leave.*

MICHAEL   Happily – I should have left a while ago,
                but – again – I'm not going to leave until
                you return what you took.

JOHN   I didn't take anything from you.

MICHAEL   I'm serious, stop wasting time. I should
                have gone an age ago.

JOHN   I didn't take anything from you.

MICHAEL   Really? Well, fine, I'll wait a bit longer –
                and then I'll have to use force. We'll tie
                you up and search you. I'm serious.

JOHN   As you wish.

                '

                I'm a fool. Two shots – close range – two
                misses. I'll never forgive myself for that.

MICHAEL   If you wanted to put a bullet in something,
                why not your head?

                JOHN shrugs.

JOHN	Strange. I attempted murder – and they don't arrest me or put me on trial. Must mean they all think I'm insane.
	I'm insane. But people who hide their – lack of talent or their stupidity or their palpable cruelty under the guise of being professors or scholars or friends, they're not insane at all. And nor are people who marry old men, and then publicly lie to them – I saw. I saw you holding her, and –
MICHAEL	Yes, all right, I kissed her. I kissed her. And John?

MICHAEL makes an obscene gesture at JOHN.

JOHN	It's an insane world that lets *you* stay alive.
MICHAEL	Well. That's a stupid thing to say.
JOHN	Well. I'm insane, aren't I? I'm not a responsible adult. I say stupid things.
MICHAEL	It's getting old, this: you're not insane. Just strange. You know, I used to think being strange was the exception, and now I think it's the basic human condition. You're strange – and so you're completely normal.

JOHN covers his face with his hands.

JOHN	I feel so ashamed. If you only knew how ashamed I feel. It's this very acute, sharp feeling of shame – and it's not like any other pain I've ever felt. It's –
	It's unbearable.

JOHN bends his head low.

	What can I do? What can I do?
MICHAEL	Nothing.
JOHN	Give me something to take. Oh God. I've lived for forty-seven years. Say I live to sixty, I still have thirteen years left. And that is such a long time. Thirteen years left. How can I live for thirteen years? What will I do to fill up that gap of time? Oh, you know, though, you know, if I could start it all again, live the rest of my life in a different way – in a completely new way. To wake up one clear, calm morning and feel yourself starting to *live* again – and the whole of your past is forgotten, drifted away like smoke –

He weeps.

	A new life. To start again.
	Tell me where to start.
	Where do I start?
MICHAEL	Oh, come on. A new life? Our position, yours and mine, it's the same. It's hopeless.
JOHN	Is it?
MICHAEL	Absolutely. I'm convinced of it.
JOHN	Give me something to take – for *here (His heart.)* It hurts. It burns.
MICHAEL	*(Shouts.) STOP IT*

He softens.

In a hundred, or two hundred years, the people who come after us, people who will hate us because we lived such stupid, graceless lives, those people will perhaps find a way to be happy – but for us? There's just one hope – that the dreams we dream in our coffins will not be entirely unpleasant.

Yes, my boy. Across the whole, wide place there were only two decent, intelligent men – and here we are. But ten years of philistine life poisoned our blood, until nothing was left – and we were finally as common as everyone else.

But this is distraction. Give it back.

JOHN   I didn't take anything.

MICHAEL   You took a bottle of morphine out of my bag.

,

Listen, if you want to kill yourself, walk to the forest and take the gun with you. The leaves'll make a soft landing. But give me the morphine back, because people will talk – and jump to conclusions – and think I got it for you. And there'll be inquests – and I'm already the person who'll have to do your post-mortem. Interesting job, that'll be –

SONYA comes in.

JOHN   Will you *leave* me *alone*

MICHAEL	Sonya, your uncle has taken a bottle of morphine and won't give it back. Tell him it's – it's – idiotic. And I don't have time. I've got to go.
SONYA	Uncle Johnny, did you take the bottle of morphine?

,

MICHAEL	He took it. I'm sure.
SONYA	Give it back.

Why are you doing this to us? It's frightening.

(Tenderly.) Give it back, Uncle Johnny. I'm sad too – as sad as you are probably – but I don't give in to despair. I endure it, and I will endure it until the last breath leaves my body. Naturally. You endure as well – and give it back.

SONYA kisses JOHN's hands.

My dear, sweet, kind, special Uncle Johnny, give it back –

SONYA is crying.

You are a good man. You're kind. Take pity on us and give it back. You can do it. You can keep going.

JOHN gets the bottle and gives it to MICHAEL.

JOHN	Here. Have it.

(To SONYA.) But we have to work now, have to do something, or I can't – I can't –

SONYA   Yes, yes, work – as soon as we've seen
                   them off, we will sit down and we will
                   work –

                   *SONYA nervously runs her hand through some papers. There's
                   a lot of work.*

                   We've let everything go.

                   MICHAEL puts the bottle back in his bag, tightens the strap.

MICHAEL   And now I can get *moving*.

                   Enter ELENA.

ELENA   John, are you [in here]? We're leaving.
                   And Alexander has something he needs to
                   say to you.

SONYA   *(To JOHN.)* Come on, Uncle Johnny, let's
                   go. You and Daddy have to make up. It's
                   important.

                   SONYA and JOHN exit. ELENA and MICHAEL left alone.

ELENA   I'm leaving.

                   ELENA gives MICHAEL her hand.

                   Goodbye.

MICHAEL   Already?

ELENA   They're waiting for me.

MICHAEL   Goodbye.

ELENA   You said you wouldn't come here any
                   more. Earlier. You promised.

MICHAEL   I remember. I am. I'm leaving now.

                   ,

	You're terrified. Is it really so frightening?
ELENA	Yes
MICHAEL	Then it's not an unthinkable thing –
	Stay.
	Come to the forest tomorrow …
ELENA	No. The decision is made. Which is why I can look at you like this – because we're leaving.
	All I ask of you is this –
	Think better of me. Respect me.
MICHAEL	Stay. Please.
	Admit it. There's nothing for you to *do* in the world, no *purpose,* nothing to distract your attention, and sooner or later those feelings will rise above your head and you will give in to them – it's the thing that's going to happen. And why do it in the city when you could do it right here, surrounded by nature? It's poetic, you have to give it that. Even the autumn is beautiful. All forests and crumbling mansions –
ELENA	You're hilarious. I'm angry with you, but still – I'll enjoy remembering you. You're an interesting, original person. We're not ever going to see each other again, so – why hide? I even felt something for you myself.
	Well, let's shake hands, and part friends.

Don't think badly of me.

MICHAEL   Yes. Leave.

On the surface, you seem so good and warm-hearted, but there's something strange about you. You came here with your husband and everyone who was working here, swarming around creating things, stopped – and spent the summer dealing with gout and your husband and you. The pair of you infected everyone. I got captivated by you, a month doing nothing, people got sick, the forests went untended, and the cows got to the young trees and … and so wherever you set foot, you and your husband, you bring destruction.

I'm joking, of course – but still, it's – strange – and I'm convinced that if you were staying, then there'd be tremendous devastation. It'd be the end of me – and you – you wouldn't do too well either.

So. On your way.

The comedy is over. Curtain down.

ELENA quickly takes a pencil. Conceals it.

ELENA   This pencil – I'm taking it to remember you by.

MICHAEL   God, it's all so strange – to understand each other so well, and then never to see each other again. Such is life. Such the world.

218

As long as nobody's here, before Uncle
Johnny appears wielding a bouquet of
roses, let me – kiss you –

Our final thing. Yes?

He kisses her on the cheek.

Well. That was that. – and beautiful.

ELENA   I wish you the very best.

She looks round.

Fuck, all right, for once in my life –

*She violently embraces him, a deep kiss – and then they both
quickly move away.*

I have to go.

MICHAEL   Go, quickly. Go.

ELENA   I think someone's coming.

They both listen.

MICHAEL   Curtain down.

*Enter ALEXANDER, JOHN, MARIA with her book, CARTWRIGHT,
SONYA.*

ALEXANDER   Let's let bygones be bygones, John. So
much has happened – and I've rethought
so many things – in just a few hours,
that I think there might be a book in it.
Something for future generations – on how
to live. The art of living.

I accept your apology, and in turn I
apologise to you. Goodbye.

He kisses JOHN three times.

JOHN	You'll get exactly the same amount as before. Everything will go back to how it was.

ELENA hugs SONYA. ALEXANDER kisses MARIA's hands.

ALEXANDER	My matriarch –
MARIA	Alexander, have someone take your picture and send it to me. You know how much you mean to me.
CARTWRIGHT	Goodbye, Mr Professor, sir. Don't forget us!

ALEXANDER is hugging his daughter.

ALEXANDER	Goodbye. Goodbye – everyone!

ALEXANDER shakes MICHAEL's hand.

> Thank you for such pleasant company. I respect your views and your passions, and – impulsiveness – but allow the old man to make a parting observation: ladies and gentlemen, get on with it! One must get up, get on with it and get something *done*.
>
> My best to you all.

He exits, followed by MARIA, CARTWRIGHT and SONYA.

JOHN kisses ELENA's hand, hard. She's moved.

JOHN	Goodbye.
	Forgive me.
	We'll never see each other again.
ELENA	Goodbye, sweetheart –

ELENA kisses JOHN on the head and walks away. MICHAEL collects a few things.

MICHAEL You not going to wave them off?

JOHN Let them go, but I – I can't. It's so hard. We have to get on with it, quickly, get ourselves busy with something – work, work, work –

JOHN digs in the papers on the table. Finds a huge bundle of invoices, bills, receipts. The noises from outside.

,

MICHAEL They'll be underway. Gone now. The Professor'll be thrilled, I'd have said. There's nothing in the world would tempt him back here.

NANNY enters, sits herself down in a comfy chair, starts to knit.

NANNY They're gone.

SONYA They're gone. *(Wipes her eyes.)* God send them a safe journey.

Well, Uncle Johnny, let's do something.

JOHN To work, to work we go …

SONYA It's been a long, long time since we sat at this table together.

SONYA puts a light on. Tries a pen. It doesn't work.

No ink.

She goes to get another one.

And – I'm sad now that they've gone.

221

MARIA enters, slowly.

MARIA   They're gone.

MARIA sits down, starts to get herself absorbed in reading, same places as at the start of ACT ONE. SONYA starts to prepare the account book.

SONYA   Let's get the accounts written up, Uncle Johnny. We've let everything go. We've had second letters from some of them. Write. You do those, I'll do these.

JOHN   *(Writing.)* Account … Mister …

They both write, silently.

MARIA   *(Yawns.)* Time for bed, time for bed.

MICHAEL   Silence. Pens scratch. It's so warm and cosy.

                   I don't want to go.

A noise from outside.

                   But all that's left is goodbye. Goodbye to you, friend and friend and friend, goodbye table – let's get going.

NANNY   What's the hurry? You should stay a while –

MICHAEL   Can't be done.

JOHN   *(Writes.)* So the old debt hanging over is – *(Turns page.)* two-seventy-five –

MICHAEL   Well –

SONYA   When will we see you again?

222

MICHAEL	Not until summer, I should think. Not this winter. Obviously if anything happens, it goes without saying, just let me know – and I'll drop by.

MICHAEL holds SONYA's hand.

Thank you.

SONYA	For what?
MICHAEL	For your hospitality and your kindness. Well. For everything, in a word.

MICHAEL kisses NANNY on the head.

Goodbye, old woman.

NANNY	So you're going without any tea?
MICHAEL	I don't want any tea, Nanny, darling.
NANNY	A drop of vodka, maybe?
MICHAEL	*(Hesitantly.)* Maybe.

NANNY goes to get him vodka.

'

He moves to the map of Africa.

MICHAEL	It must be very hot in Africa. Now, I mean. It'd be unbearable.
JOHN	Suppose so.
NANNY	Here.

She's brought him vodka and a piece of bread. He drinks the vodka.

Good health, my love. Good health.

	Have the bread.
MICHAEL	I'm all right. All the best, everyone.

He hasn't had the bread.

Don't see me out, Nanny. No need.

After a beat, SONYA heads out after him. NANNY sits down in MICHAEL's chair.

JOHN	Second of February, twenty litres, sunflower oil. Sixteenth of February, sunflower oil. Twenty litres.

,

NANNY	He's gone.

,

SONYA enters, moves back to the receipts.

,

SONYA	He's gone
JOHN	So – when you count everything up: what did it all come to?
	Fifteen twenty-five.

,

The calculation is complete. JOHN looks at SONYA. SONYA writes it down in the book – and puts the pen down. JOHN strokes SONYA's hair.

NANNY	Ah, every one of us a sinner –
JOHN	Oh I am ruined, little one. Wrecked. Completely destroyed.

SONYA   But what can we *do*? What are we going to
do?

We have to just keep living. We'll keep
going. Uncle Johnny? You and me will
keep going – through the long procession
of days and the endless evenings, through
how much it hurts, through the *pain* that
we endure, and we will work every day to
make someone else rich and finally we'll
collapse into old age, and, when the time
comes, drop into our graves with the sad
knowledge we would always end up there

– and and whatever happens then, after
life, we will say – we'll say that we *suffered*
and we *cried* and we'll say that it was *hard*
and – and – and – God will listen, and
then we'll, Uncle Johnny, you and me,
my Uncle, we'll see pure light and we'll
see beauty shining and grace and we will
dance – and we'll look back on now, on this,
the present, and we'll smile – and we'll find
peace. We'll rest.

Uncle Johnny, I believe that with my
whole heart, I really do.

We'll rest.

CARTWRIGHT plays quietly.

We'll see the sky shimmer with diamonds.

We'll hear the music of the angels. And the
evil and the sufferings will all disappear as
mercy floods over the earth. And our life
will be peaceful and gentle and – strong

225

and clean and good – and beautiful, so
beautiful – it will be like being *hugged*.

I believe that

You're crying. Oh poor Uncle Johnny.
Here

*Wipes away his tears. Kisses his eyes, maybe. She's almost
crying herself.*

You've never been happy. In your whole
life. But you wait.

We'll be at peace. We'll breathe. We'll rest.

*Everyday life continues as normal elsewhere, a gentle rhythmic
underscore: the instrument, MARIA making a note, the click of
NANNY's needles, as SONYA and JOHN embrace –*

We'll rest.

Slowly, it becomes the end of the play.

MARY STUART

'Tell all the Truth but tell it slant'

Emily Dickinson

'The persona is a complicated system of relations between the individual consciousness and society, fittingly enough a kind of mask, designed on the one hand to make a definite impression upon others, and, on the other, to conceal the true nature of the individual… 'High rests on low' says Lao-tzu. An opposite forces its way up from inside.'

Carl Jung, *Two Essays on Analytical Psychology*

'It was Wilson; but now it was my own voice I heard, as he said: "I have lost. Yet from now on you are also dead… In me you lived – and in my death – see by this face, which is your own, how wholly, how completely, you have killed – yourself!"'

Edgar Allan Poe, *The Story of William Wilson*

'Women have one of the great acts of all time. The smart ones act very feminine and needy, but inside they are real killers… There's nothing I love more than women, but they're really a lot different than portrayed. They are far worse than men, far more aggressive, and boy, can they be smart.'

Donald Trump, *The Art of the Comeback*

Some thoughts on verse (and how it might be used)

Nothing terrifies actors like verse. Verse often means Shakespeare, and Shakespeare means rules. Right ways and wrong ways. But there aren't any rules – at least, none that Shakespeare himself ever thought worth setting down.

It's sometimes unclear quite what people mean when they comment on verse being 'well spoken' or on 'good verse speaking' – what they often mean is that the language is being spoken in a different kind of voice (posher and louder, usually) or explained (as if talking to a class of children, or to someone hard of hearing).

A century ago in England, verse-speaking meant speech as song: sonorous vocal effects drowning the nuance and detail of meaning. The next wave was an academic sharpness – meaning and sense – but with a pedantic focus on setting the rules of verse, and on the pointed underlining of literary terms (most of which were invented long after Shakespeare's death), iambic pentameter, caesura, antithesis and so on. The fallout from these ideas have badly damaged actors' relationship to Shakespeare in the English-speaking world – none more disastrously than the idea that every line of verse should finish with a pause.

In the meantime, American writers took the richer, organic, essential inheritance of Shakespeare: Kushner, Albee and Sorkin, to name but three, write words in music, in rhythm. Dialogue is musical.

Words are sound and sense – and not just sense. And sound and sense cannot be separated. Words built up into sentences have rhythm when spoken aloud. And verse (that is, a regular rhythmic structure underneath a sentence) can add pressure and petrol and poise to a thought. Verse is thought blossoming, bursting into words – in real time.

You should no more be aware of verse spoken than someone listening to music is aware of the beats of the bar. Or any more aware than you are of the number of vowels in this sentence. They're there, certainly, but they do not contain its deepest (or even shallowest) meanings. They are part of its meaning, part of its structure – but the number of them, the flow of them and their totality is difficult to describe. But you can kind of feel it. There's shape and architecture, swooping, soaring, sometimes hesitant *rhythm.*

Verse is a way of allowing energy into the sense of a line through its sound. It allows variety, and allows it in several ways: by allowing the first or last or middle word of a line to shake its rhythm, in the cumulative energy as the items in a list mount up on top of each other, or in the crisp, hard facts of monosyllables.

The heartbeat of an iamb closely echoes the human heartbeat. A continuing rhythm, like the bassline in a piece of jazz, and one that gives life. It gives no instruction to the actor. It is not to be counted or observed – though also not to be ignored. Hamlet warns us that – like all great art – it's a matter of balance: discretion and also wildness ('too tame' is deadly).

The verse is the structure of the pipe. The words are the water. The pressure of the jet of water is a combination of the two things. The sound and the sense are two sides of the same coin. Inseparable, neither could exist without the other; and mutually enriching.

The fact that there are five iambs in a line is a fact comparable to the fact that there are sixty seconds in a minute. It's not that the minute pauses after the sixtieth. It's not that we notice (or would want to notice) every time a second ticks from 'sixty' back round to 'one'. It's just an underlying structure, and one our lives sometimes observe (when, for example, the news begins exactly on the hour), sometimes not (at exactly what time did you go to bed last night?).

The seconds beat quickly through the minute. The minutes beat slower, deeper, through the hour. Your life plays out messily on top of that structure – is playing out right now across that structure, even as you read this – living through that structure and with it and despite it. The beat is everywhere. Each life finding its own way through it, its own form and speed and flow. There really aren't any rules.

RI
November 2016

Acknowledgements

I am indebted and grateful to all of the actors who read the play on the page, in a workshop reading, or in the rehearsal room for their time and their thoughts – and additionally to Rupert Goold, Josh Higgott, Julia Horan, Laura Marling, Lucy Pattison, Emma Pritchard, Ilinca Radulian, Daniel Raggett – and last (and most) Zara Tempest-Walters.

It's a play. It isn't history.

This adaptation of Friedrich Schiller's MARIA STUART (1800) was written to be produced in contemporary or timeless costume, not in the clothes of either Elizabethan England or Schiller's Germany. That is, the setting is 1587; the time is now.

Though Schiller consulted numerous historical sources, much of his play – including the character of Mortimer, and the queens' meeting – has no basis in historical fact. This version makes some cuts, partly for length, partly for leanness, and partly to enable a cast size of twelve. This text has four further handmaidens in the final act, but their lines are easy to cut, and Mary could certainly bequeath her belongings to absent handmaidens (via Melvil) should future productions so desire.

It is usually assumed that Schiller's first act takes place on one day, a month after Mary's trial, that the second, third and fourth act all occur on a second (the same) day, and then the fifth act on a third day. In this version, the action is compressed still further: to occur in a single (slightly more than) twenty-four hour period, beginning in the morning of one day and moving through to Mary's execution before dawn on a second. Elizabeth's final scene occurs at some point later on the second day.

Schiller either didn't know or didn't care that the travel between Fotheringay and London would take much longer than his play allowed – and almost certainly knew that this structure played fast and loose with historical events and their sequence. But then his design is symmetrical, not historical. The first and fifth acts are Mary in prison, the second and fourth Elizabeth at court, and in the third and central act, the two queens meet in the open air. The play's final scene sits outside of this mirrored structure – as if a new play is beginning now the old one's great rivalry has been ended.

Again: it isn't history.

The first production had two actors learn the roles of both queens, and, by spinning a coin live at the beginning of the evening, randomly determine which queen would be in power and which in prison – lending a play constructed around doubles, mirrors, equivalences, differences and mighty opposites a formal duality all of its own. It also allowed the first word of the evening to anticipate its ending: 'Heads'.

Characters

MARY STUART, the exiled Queen of Scotland

Hanna KENNEDY – her servant

MELVIL – her chief of staff

QUEEN ELIZABETH I, Queen of England

Sir Amias PAULET – Mary's current jailer

MORTIMER – his nephew

William Cecil, Lord BURLEIGH

Lord George TALBOT, Earl of Shrewsbury, Mary's former jailer

Robert Dudley, Earl of LEICESTER

Lord AUBESPINE, the French ambassador

William DAVISON, Elizabeth's secretary

Henry Grey, Earl of KENT

and Mary's ladies in waiting ALIX, GERTRUDE, MARGARET & ROSALIND

This adaptation was commissioned by and originally produced at the Almeida Theatre, where it had its first performance on 2 December 2016.

Cast (in alphabetical order)
Aubespine	Alexander Cobb
Mortimer	Rudi Dharmalingam
Burleigh	Vincent Franklin
Davison	David Jonsson
Leicester	John Light
Kennedy	Carmen Munroe
Melvil	Eileen Nicholas
Kent	Daniel Rabin
Paulet	Sule Rimi
Mary Stuart/Elizabeth I	Juliet Stevenson
Talbot	Alan Williams
Mary Stuart/Elizabeth I	Lia Williams

Creative Team
Direction	Robert Icke
Set and Costume Design	Hildegard Bechtler
Composition	Laura Marling
Lighting	Jackie Shemesh
Sound	Paul Arditti
Video	Tim Reid
Casting	Julia Horan CDG
Associate Director	Daniel Raggett
Resident Director	Ilinca Radulian

The show then transferred to the Duke of York's Theatre, West End, where it had its first performance on 13 January 2018, where it played with the following cast changes:

Cast
Talbot	Michael Byrne
Paulet	Christopher Colquhoun
Aubespine	Calum Finlay
Burleigh	Elliot Levey

A note on the text

A forward slash (/) marks the point of interruption of overlapping dialogue.

A comma on a separate line (,) indicates a pause, a rest, a silence, an upbeat or a lift. Length and intensity are context dependent.

Square brackets [like this] indicate words which are part of the intention of the line but which are *not* spoken aloud.

This text is written to be spoken fast.

ACT ONE

A room in a prison in the Castle of Fotheringay. HANNA KENNEDY (elderly, quietly ferocious, fiercely loyal) is mid-argument with SIR AMIAS PAULET. MORTIMER (young, intense, unflinching eyes) is searching the room.

PAULET   This is a jewel –

KENNEDY   It isn't yours to take

PAULET   A jewel – you can't deny it when it's in my hand

KENNEDY   Paulet, you've searched this place

PAULET   And found a *jewel*

KENNEDY   You found it in the grass, not up in here –

PAULET   – and jewels don't grow on trees. This thing was *thrown*
             Thrown from the window for someone to find –
             A bribe. A payment. Who knows what it means?
             I haven't slept, I've watched and watched and watched
             and *still* you lying women slip things through
             still some hidden dangers here to find –

             MORTIMER finds a hidden stash of letters. KENNEDY is incriminated, angered.

KENNEDY   LEAVE THOSE ALONE
             Her secrets are not yours

PAULET   Once they are found, they are

KENNEDY   She writes things down – it's just to pass the time
             They're drafts of letters to the Queen of England –

PAULET   Then I'll deliver them.

KENNEDY   Please – don't take those – you've stolen *everything*

PAULET   We'll store them with the other things we found.
             We'll keep them safe. In time, you'll get them back.

MORTIMER exits. PAULET looks at KENNEDY.

KENNEDY   What you are doing to us is outrageous.
           Who would look at these bare walls and say
           'A *Queen* lives here'? Where is the throne?
           Where are her golden canopies of state?
           There is no mirror here / for her

PAULET   it isn't safe

KENNEDY   You took her books –

PAULET   I said: it isn't safe

KENNEDY   Tell me when *music* became dangerous

           PAULET makes the case, spelling it out:

PAULET   While she owns things, the country isn't safe
           Look, it's a weapon if it's in her hands.

           ,

KENNEDY   A queen is not a common criminal

PAULET   A criminal is not commonly a queen.

KENNEDY   Your prisoner, Paulet – she was born a queen
           She was a queen when she was six days old,
           Raised in soft beds. She *is not used to this.*
           It should have been enough to take her power:
           But little things that keep someone *alive* –
           please – be kind – don't be the man who takes
           the last few things that decorate our life
           they're all that's left

PAULET   Distractions will not help her to repent
           or make atonement for the life she's led

KENNEDY   If in her younger years she made mistakes
           then she answers to God – and her own heart
           There is no judge in England over her

PAULET   She'll get her judgement where she broke the law

KENNEDY   How can she break the law from this bare cell?

PAULET   But yet – from a bare cell, her arm stretched out
into the world – a sequence of attacks
beat at the doors of our safety –
and strangely, every time it looked the same:
they'd kill the Queen,
and install Mary on the English throne
so first the Duke of Norfolk tried his luck
plotted to murder God's anointed Queen
he failed, then William Parry whet his knife
he was, I think, a friend of Mary's, he
attempted to assassinate the Queen –
then, somehow, from her cell, Lady Mary Stuart
got letters out to Babington, lit *his* flame,
(I don't know *how* she did it but she did)
incited *him* to regicide – which he tried
and failed – and died. Norfolk, William Parry, Babington
all dead – all lost their lives – for Mary's sake.
Three noble heads cut off in sacrifice
For her. But nothing – *nothing* – can deter
the jostling swarms of madmen, pushing forth
to jump into the abyss – to waste their lives – *for her.*
And every day the scaffolds heave to hang
the new – and newer – martyrs for her cause.
Black day that England ever welcomed her.

KENNEDY   Did England *welcome* her? Since that black day
when she, a queen, set foot on England's soil
to ask her cousin – fellow queen – for help –
despite her royal prerogative – she has
(against all international laws) been locked in here
in prison. She came here as a refugee –

PAULET   She came here as a murderer on the run
from her own people, exiled from a throne
that she'd contaminated with her sordid crimes
She came here to restore the Catholic faith
She came here to usurp the rightful Queen.

KENNEDY   That's just not true –

PAULET   Then why won't she renounce her claim?

            ,

            Why not just say – in public – that she has
            no claim, no hope of being England's queen?
            But she won't do it. She could sign her name
            on that one document – and she'd walk free.
            But no, she won't. And why won't she? Because
            she still intends – she still has hope – with sleight
            and skill and secret, violent plots
            to conquer England from her prison cell.

KENNEDY   You're joking – you have to be [joking] –
            these hopes you say she has – she's *in a cell,*
            no voice of comfort, no sight of her friends
            only these men who stare into her cage

PAULET   No cage protects us from her evil brain
            How do I know the bars have not been filed?
            or that these walls and floor aren't hollowed out
            for treachery to tunnel in at night?
            I wish your devil queen was somewhere else.
            I wish I'd never taken up this post –
            I just can't *sleep,* I check and check and check
            the locks, the doors, the walls – I wake up *cold*
            my dreams like needles – she's sneaked something through
            and a slip of my mind is a slip of the locks
            and all my men lie lifeless on the stone
            and Mary's next attack is hurtling forth –

            MARY enters.

KENNEDY   My lady, they are crushing us –

MARY   Be calm
            Tell me, Hanna – what has happened now?

KENNEDY   They took your letters – and your marriage jewels,
            the things we kept, the last few things we saved
            He's got them all. There's nothing royal left.

                            244

MARY	Compose yourself.
	These outward trappings do not make the queen.
	They have the power to treat us basely, but
	They cannot debase us. In England, I have learned
	to let things go. And this: just one more thing.
(To PAULET.)	You're holding something there I'd hoped to give you:
	among those papers, one is for your Queen,
	a letter to my royal sister – give me your word
	that you'll deliver it – place it in *her* hand
PAULET	I'll do what I think best.
MARY	Sir, all it says [is this] –
	the letter asks her for a great favour –
	I ask her for an audience in person –
	We've never met. I've never seen her face.
	The men that judged me – they were not my peers
	no man in England shares my royal birth
	I can't accept their judgement of my case
	My *only* equal is Elizabeth:
	my only equal breathing England's air.
	Your Queen alone is of my blood – my sex
	to her alone – as sister, queen and woman
	can I speak freely
PAULET	You've opened up your heart before to men
	who were less worthy of your royal trust
MARY	I ask her for a second favour, one
	inhuman to refuse: she took my crown
	my freedom and my life from me –
	perhaps my head is next – but not my soul
	she cannot want my soul, and for some time
	I have been asking for my basic right:
	I wish to practise *my* religion –
PAULET	Whenever you like, the Dean / of the prison
MARY	I have nothing to say to the Dean. A priest
	of my own church is what I'm asking for
	(as you well know). My days are numbered now.
	I'm waiting for my death –

PAULET	at least you know

MARY	– and I want to write a will.

PAULET	Go right ahead.
	The Queen desires no profit from your things.

MARY	And where are my women? I was separated
	from them – it's not that I need maids – it's just
	I want to know that they're alive and well

PAULET	They are. They're fine.

MARY	Are you leaving?

,

Before you do, you could at least release
my heart from its uncertainty. You see,
in prison, you have me confined. No news
gets through. This prison is my world.
It's been a month – and a long month – since I
was taken by surprise by forty men,
commissioners, who rushed into this prison
and set up court, completely unannounced,
I had no lawyer – but they made me answer
their formal charges – their words bristling with traps
I was in shock, could barely speak, but I
from memory replied as best I could –
then, like ghosts, they were gone. Since that day
nothing. Silence.
Now, I look into your eyes – is my fate there?
Who won the vote? My friends – or enemies?
And should I live in fear – or live in hope?

,

PAULET	Settle your account with heaven.

MARY	I pray to heaven for mercy – but on Earth
	I pray for justice.

PAULET	Oh, it's coming, don't worry –

MARY   Have they reached a verdict?

PAULET   I don't know.

MARY   Look: *is* my sentence death?

PAULET   I just don't know

MARY   Things happen fast in England. Like my trial.
              I'm sure my murder will be just the same:
              no warning.
              But then what's left that could surprise me now?
              That they think they can judge me! – but I know
              the depths to which your Queen's not scared to sink,
              the darker moves Elizabeth dares make –

PAULET   The Crown of England has no fear at all,
              outside its conscience and its Parliament.

              Enter MORTIMER, swiftly. He's young, seems strict.

              He pointedly (and entirely) ignores MARY.

MORTIMER Uncle, they're looking for you.

              Exit MORTIMER. MARY catches PAULET as he makes to follow.

MARY   Let me just say – you *do* have my respect
              I know this situation tests you too
              and anything *you* have to say to me, I'll listen
              But keep that boy away from me – your nephew:
              his arrogance is more than I will bear.

PAULET   And that's exactly why he's valuable.
              He travelled, went to Paris, and to Rheims,
              and came back just as English as he left.
              Your crocodile tears won't melt his heart.

              PAULET exits.

KENNEDY   That he *dares* speak like that – to you –
              and to your face – it's hard for me to hear

              MARY is lost in thought.

MARY	When we were in our former radiance
	we listened only to the flatterers;
	it's justice: now we only hear contempt
	it's a lesson, Hanna.
KENNEDY	hey – my sweetheart, we are not defeated
	Now – where's the girl who used to comfort me?
	It was your fickleness I had to tell you off for,
	Much more than gloom –
MARY	You've forgotten, Hanna,
	what today is. The anniversary of Darnley's death
	another black mark on the calendar.
	at night, his milky eyes still stare at me
	face dashed with blood – He'll never let me sleep.
KENNEDY	Forgiveness has been granted by the Church
MARY	No priest has ever laid that ghost to rest – or penance / either
KENNEDY	You *did not murder him* – your hands were clean
MARY	'My hands were clean' – my *conscience* isn't clean.
	Yes, Bothwell murdered Darnley, but *I knew.*
	and driven by my lust – a deadly sin –
	I married Darnley (sin) gave him a crown
	(another sin: defiling my own throne)
	then gave my heart to Bothwell – (sin sin sin)
	and pulled a world of guilt down on myself
KENNEDY	My sweetheart, why dig up your history?
	You were so young –
MARY	I hated Darnley, wanted a divorce
	wanted him gone so I could get to Bothwell
	but God in heaven knows how hard, how *far*
	I fell for *him* – I was his prisoner – anything he asked –
	and Darnley's life was nothing to me, then –
KENNEDY	Falling in love's a madness with no cure
	but time. Bothwell was evil to the bone.
MARY	It's my own weakness – weak before the men –

KENNEDY   Some shameless demon screamed inside you too:
            you wouldn't hear the warnings, you were *blind*
            possessed – I couldn't believe you were still you,
            parading Bothwell through the streets of Edinburgh
            (and not ashamed that people knew the truth:
            that a murderer was the lover of the queen)
            you made his judges clear him of his crime –
            and then – oh God

MARY   don't stop – I married him.

            ,

            I think back – I don't recognise myself.

KENNEDY   I know you. Who you are. You're gentle. Open.
            You won't be damned for that. You do feel shame.
            I nursed you, I should know – so be at peace.
            Everyone has history they'd rather forget.
            Whatever else you are, you're innocent *here*
            in *England* there's no sin you're guilty of –
            and England's Parliament is not your judge.
            The only thing that holds you here is force.

            *Enter MORTIMER, fast. The two women are shocked. Could this be
            the feared assassination? As MORTIMER produces a letter, MARY
            flinches as if it might be a knife – as he speaks urgently to KENNEDY.*

MORTIMER   Get out there. Guard the door.
            I need to speak with the Queen.

MARY   No, Hanna, stay –

MORTIMER   Don't be afraid.

            MORTIMER hands MARY the letter. She opens it, fearful –

MARY   And what is [this] – ?

            She's looked at it, stunned. MORTIMER turns to KENNEDY again.

MORTIMER   Wait outside. My uncle's coming. Please.
            We don't have long.

MARY   Go! Go! Do what he says –

KENNEDY, surprised, leaves.

It's from my uncle, the Cardinal of Lorraine

MORTIMER nods: she's understood something. She reads the letter:

'trust Mortimer, the bearer of this letter: there's
no friend more loyal to you in all the world'.

Can this be true?

MORTIMER Forgive the way I was – it was a mask,
the only way to get to you – the only way
to bring you help – and rescue

MARY   I'm in shock
I can't believe there's hope – so fast – I've been in prison
now for [so long] – sir, please explain yourself

MORTIMER Your Majesty, time is short. My uncle's coming back.
The man he's bringing with him hates you –
and once they're here, given that [sentence is passed] – but first
let me start by – I'm sorry. It's seeing you.
I don't – it's seeing you in person.

MARY   *Please* – explain

MORTIMER I have been raised a Protestant – as a child
they taught me to hate Catholicism
to see it as a dangerous ideology – a threat –
and I believed that fervently – until
at twenty, I set out into the world, in France
I was caught up in jostling crowds – pilgrims,
so many of them, as if the entire human race was
some boundless river, coursing swift to the kingdom of heaven
I was carried by that current to Rome,
and God showed me his Church – the Catholic Church –
and there – oh God, the things I saw
my heart beat harder – I could barely breathe
the pillars, arches, architecture, all lifting

our perception of this world into the sky.
The Protestant faith I'd followed hates the arts
deprives its world of colour – and of light –
and says the naked word should be enough
so I had never felt the power of art – but
now, the music of the heavens fell like spring rain
from the ceilings of the churches, and
I could see – and hear – and touch – pure holiness
in the world – I saw the Pope say mass – and bless / the people,

MARY   Stop. No more.
Your words unfurl a life in front of me
there's *hope,* a whole new path rolls out like silk
but I can't take a step – my feet are chained

MORTIMER   My mind had been in chains. But now – it's *free.*
The Protestant Church had been my cold, bare cell
but now, your majesty, I saw the light
I swore myself a Catholic – and I met
your relative / the Cardinal of Lorraine

MARY   the Cardinal of Lorraine – oh is he well? That man,
that beautiful man is a rock of the Church
he mentored me in France when I was young
and this letter is from him

MORTIMER   Yes – he spoke to me,
in his hands I confirmed my Catholic faith
and he, my holy teacher, sent me then
to Rheims, where I met your followers, Morgan,
and the Bishop of Ross, and in his home
My eyes were opened: windows to the soul
and God's wide world is there for us to *see* –
I saw your face – a picture – seeing you
my soul was shaken.

               ,

'The most beautiful woman', the Bishop said quietly,
'is also the most desperate, the martyr
of our faith.' My eyes filled up with tears.

251

                    'And it is England where she is in prison,
                    surrounded by our enemies, alone.'

MARY   There's hope – there's hope while that man is alive

MORTIMER   I didn't take his word for it – the books I read
                    the scholars that I spoke to – everything
                    confirms this single fact, this *primal* fact: that
                    your bloodline and your lineage prove you are
                    the rightful Queen of England. Not this illegal Queen
                    of tainted blood – born from adultery
                    a bastard called a bastard by the King
                    her own royal father cut her off at birth
                    tore down Elizabeth's claim to take his crown
                    The wrong you suffer is because they know
                    you are the rightful heir of England's throne.
                    The kingdom you should rule imprisons you.

MARY   That right has been the cause of endless wrong –

MORTIMER   And then news came the prisoner was transferred
                    they'd moved you – and my uncle was your jailer!
                    The hand of God had opened up a door
                    to help us get to you – we made a plan
                    The Cardinal and all our friends agreed
                    move fast: ten days ago, I landed here.

                    '

                    And then I saw you.

                    No light or beauty in these rooms you live in
                    but still – your light – holy, angelic light –
                    shines out. I think Elizabeth is wise
                    to keep you hidden – if your face was seen,
                    rebellion – if the people saw their Queen
                    a wave of blood would roll across the land
                    a violent revolution. But we don't have long
                    it's dangerous: and I must tell you the news –

MARY   Have I been sentenced? Tell me – I can take it –

                                        252

MORTIMER   Your sentence has been passed. The forty-two
           high judges reached their verdict: *guilty.*

                ,

           The Queen's advisers, and the House of Lords
           the House of Commons and the City of London
           all scream that sentence must be carried out –
           but the Queen still delays. Not for human reasons
           [but] political ones: it's tactics, not conscience:
           she knows they'll force her hand, eventually.

           MARY speaks with composure, but fear rises in her now like water.

MARY   I'm not surprised. I knew that this was coming.
           I know there's no way now they'll set me free –
           and so they'll keep me prisoner here forever –
           that way my claim dies with me / in my cell

MORTIMER   No – no – your majesty, they won't stop at prison.
           While you're alive, so is Elizabeth's fear –
           her only route to safety is your death –

MARY   You think the Queen would execute a queen?

MORTIMER   I do: she would. She will, make no mistake.

MARY   But France would declare war to get revenge –

MORTIMER   The rumour is she's going to give her hand
           in marriage to the heir to France's throne

MARY   The day she has my head down on the block
           she doubles every danger to her own:
           her power rolls with my head in the dust
           what would the word 'queen' mean after my death?

MORTIMER   Elizabeth's own mother, Anne Boleyn
           and Katherine Howard – and Lady Jane Grey
           were queens – of England – and they lost their heads

                ,

MARY   You're scared, I know. This terror's hard to think through.
                But it's not just the scaffold I'm afraid of:
                Elizabeth has subtler options open
                to wipe away my challenge to her throne
                A public execution is a risk
                but paying someone silently to do it?
                I cannot take a sip of water here
                without the thought that –

MORTIMER   Listen – don't be scared
                our plan is underway, it's happening now:
                just this morning – twelve young men – I'm one –
                have sworn to get you out of here by force.

                MARY really is afraid of that, angry –

MARY   What are you *thinking*? Don't you understand?
                Have you not seen the heads nailed up on bridges
                my friends' dead flesh pulled open as a warning
                to anyone who tries to fight for me?
                Just *GO – get out of here –* god knows that Burleigh
                already somehow will be on your trail –
                the friends of Mary Stuart end up dead.

MORTIMER Yes, I have seen the heads nailed up on bridges
                and dead men's flesh pulled open as a warning
                and no, in no way do they frighten me
                because they died and won eternal glory
                and death for what is right is *martyrdom*

MARY   Keep your voice down. As clever as you are,
                whatever force you use: *I can't be saved.*
                They're watching everywhere and everything
                it's not just Paulet, or the swarms of spies,
                it's all of England guards these prison gates.
                Elizabeth alone could open them

MORTIMER There is no chance

MARY   There is one man who could

MORTIMER Name him.

MARY	The Earl of Leicester.

MORTIMER   Leicester?
The Earl of Leicester, the favourite of the Queen?
The man who argues daily for your death?
I / hardly think

MARY   If anyone can save me, it's him.
Go to him. Speak to him: [include] everything. And –

KENNEDY runs in.

MARY suddenly produces a letter from her person –

and give him this. I've carried it for weeks –
in hope that somehow it could get to Leicester

MORTIMER Explain

MARY   Someone's coming – please: trust Leicester
And he will trust you – he'll explain the mystery

KENNEDY It's Paulet with another man – from court

MORTIMER That's Burleigh. Act surprised, your majesty.

MORTIMER exits.

PAULET and BURLEIGH enter. BURLEIGH is official, exacting, unforgiving.

This rush of possibility seems to have done something to MARY – she's brave.

PAULET You asked me earlier for certainty:
Lord Burleigh brings it. Listen patiently.

MARY – with all the dignity of innocence.

BURLEIGH I speak now with the voice of England's law.

MARY You constantly rewrite it – so it's right
it sounds like you.

BURLEIGH   It seems to me you know your sentence.

255

MARY	Your presence here, Lord Burleigh, makes it clear. Please carry on.

BURLEIGH
                              Lady Mary Stuart, you willingly
were subject to the court / of forty-two –

MARY
Lord Burleigh, I'm so sorry to interrupt
right at the start – just as you're setting off –
you say that I 'was subject to the court'.
A queen is not a subject – cannot be
a subject, unless I give away my right,
my royal prerogative – my rank
the honour of my people – and my son
(and actu'ally, the whole notion of the monarch)
At the foundation of the English law
is this precept: that any citizen
accused of crimes, is afforded the right
to trial before a jury of his peers.
Who is my peer among those forty-two?
Kings are my only peers.

BURLEIGH
                              You heard the charges

MARY
I heard the charges so I could reply
and demonstrate that I was innocent.

BURLEIGH   and you submitted to the questions of the court.

MARY
I answered questions only to respect
the noble lords – themselves – but *not* the court
which I reject.

BURLEIGH   Whether you reject the court or not,
it's just irrelevant formality:
you're breathing England's air. Its laws *apply*.

MARY
I breathe the air inside an English prison.
In what way do those laws help me in here?
I'm not from England – I don't know your laws
I'm not a citizen of this country
I'm queen of a completely different state

BURLEIGH   And so you think that the mere name of 'Queen'
            entitles you – in countries you don't rule –
            to stir up treasonous rebellion?

MARY   Of course I am accountable to justice
            It's just your *judges* are not fit to judge

            BURLEIGH is rattled now.

BURLEIGH   *Our judges* – in your eyes, apparently,
            are nobodies we've picked up off the streets
            just mouthpieces, we've bribed them, probably,
            they're just the tools of England's brute oppression.
            In fact, they've served us selflessly *for years*
            they are the *best men of this government*
            and what would *you* have done, 'Your Majesty',
            if *you* were Queen of England in this case?
            What better strategy could you recommend
            pray tell, than this: appoint the noblest men
            the *fairest* you could find, the best respected,
            and let those men serve justice in this case?
            Let's even say we hated you so much
            that some of them *were* bribed to vote against you
            (they weren't) – still: forty-two of them? Hard to control
            forty two – quite a large number to *corrupt*
            and looking at the verdict, that seems clear
            when *forty-one votes* sentence you to death.

            ,

MARY   I'm surprised. I'm an uneducated woman
            how can I match a speaker of such skill?
            You're right. Before the judges you describe
            I'd have no choice but to accept their sentence:
            their honour would make their judgement sacrosanct.
            But, problem is, in recent history,
            these men have not been pillars of the law
            it seems to me that they've been more like whores
            attending to the whims of my great-uncle
            Henry the Eighth (a man who loved his flatterers)
            it seems to me that, under him, the Lords

257

and your beloved House of Commons – would
enact a law, and then repeal that law
dissolve a marriage, now enforce that marriage
especially if *that marriage* is the key
to changing bastard daughters into queens
(I only call them bastards as they were
declared as such *in law* by – yes – those men)
and changing daughters into queens is not
the only changing they've been getting on with:
the *state religion* flip-flopped *four times over*
four religions under *four regimes*

BURLEIGH   You said before you don't know England's laws
you seem to know our miseries all right

MARY   Be fair with me – and I'll be fair with you.
They say you're honest, loyal, unbribable
They say you're driven by more than your own gain
We'll go with that. So. Please. You can't mistake
true justice for the politics of the state.
What is the logic of a 'trial by equals'?
It's this: we only trust people like us.
How can you judge someone who isn't you?
How could a Scotsman judge an Englishman
when they're *unlike*, in history and in culture?
Or zealous Catholic judge a Protestant?
Or commoner a queen – or man a woman?
There is deep custom in these differences
they hold their separate wisdoms, and we should
respect them – but there is a time for unity
and empathy. Do you not ever think
our countries are one island on the world
one circled space of ground for us to walk
one chalky rock, beaten about by green seas
and yes, two separate lands, but then, my Lord
those borders we created – in our minds –
imaginary lines – that cut the land in half
there's nothing in our geography to split
the top half from the bottom – yet, for years,
for centuries, we've only been at war

	we tear things up when we could come together
	nor will that (needless) conflict ever cease
	until these lands are *one* –

BURLEIGH   and [presumably] ruled by *you*?

MARY   Oh, why deny it now?
            It's true that once I thought I might bring peace
            and unity to these two lands – at last.

BURLEIGH   You set out to achieve that with *division*:
            by kindling civil war to get the throne

MARY   *(Ferocious.)* I did not – *did not* do that! Show me PROOF

BURLEIGH   I didn't come to argue. Anyway
            the time for making arguments is past.

            By forty-one votes out of forty-two
            the court decrees that Lady Mary Stuart
            deliberately violated last year's Act
            of Parliament, and thus incurs the sentence –
            'If any person makes Rebellion
            against the Queen, or claims Title to her Crown,
            they shall be prosecuted / by the law
            and / if found guilty, shall be put to death'

MARY   Sir – sir – Lord Burleigh.
            It's pretty likely I'll be guilty of a law
            conceived and passed expressly to convict me:
            the same few men, your judges, *wrote* that Act!
            And even *you* can't – please – try to deny
            that this Act was a trap designed for me –

BURLEIGH   It was a warning. *You* made it a trap
            when you conspired to kill the Queen of England
            with Babington and his accomplices
            the actors of a plot that you devised

MARY   And how could I have done that?

BURLEIGH   Well, you did –
            and from your cell you masterminded treason

MARY   So where's the evidence – the *proof* of that?

BURLEIGH   You saw the documents yourself in court

MARY   *(With irony.)* The *letters* that are so unlike my writing
            you had to claim that I dictated them

BURLEIGH   No, *Babington* said that you'd dictated them
            and sent them to him. Swore it, under oath,
            Then he was put to death. But on the record
            he testified the letters came from you

MARY   But he was not a witness at my trial.
            It would surely have been better to hear
            key evidence in person? No? Lord Burleigh,
            why *was* there such a rush to have him dead?

BURLEIGH   Your secretaries verified his story.
            They said they'd written down the words you spoke.

MARY   So now my *servants* are my judges too!

BURLEIGH   You said your Scottish staff could all be trusted

MARY   Yes – but history is written *at the end*
            after the fact. So what they *actually said*
            compared to what the court recorded – well
            [if] you torture people, they'll confess to things
            sometimes to things they'd never even *thought of.*
            Perhaps they knew it couldn't get much worse
            for *me*, and lied so *they* could stay alive

BURLEIGH   They gave their testimony under oath

MARY   But not in court. Hang on – they're still alive –
            why not just call my secretaries here
            and let them speak their evidence to my face?

BURLEIGH   I think that is –

MARY   – *that is* my legal right.
            My former keeper, Talbot, said himself
            the English law is clear on this: the defendant
            in any trial *must* hear the accusation,

	the criminal hears the evidence against him.
	Your predecessor said that, Paulet. No?
	Is that not right? You value honesty, I think –
	employ it now. That is the law? Yes? Speak!

PAULET   That is the law. I'm sorry – but it is!

MARY   So
The law's enforced whenever it does me harm
Ignored if it might prove my innocence.
So at my makeshift trial, where *was that* law?
And why was Babington not kept alive
until his evidence could be admitted?
And why not call my secretaries in?
they're still alive – why not bring them to court?

BURLEIGH This is a waste of time. Your plot with Babington
is not the only charge that stands against you

MARY   It is the only charge that breaks that law
the law you all designed to take my life

BURLEIGH You negotiated with the ambassador of Spain –

MARY   And now we change the subject!

BURLEIGH   – you made plans
to overthrow the religion of this state,
you instigated all the kings of Europe
to wage a war on England

MARY   If I did?
Would anyone be shocked or horrified?
I'm innocent of every charge against me –
but were I guilty, would you be surprised?
I came to England as a refugee
seeking asylum, I came here for *help*
to beg for mercy from my blood relation
Elizabeth – who, instead, had me *locked up*
which violates all international laws
and constitutes an act of warfare.
I don't believe – now look, sir, do you think

and let's be honest – do you *really* think
that I owe any moral debt to England?
Or that the English law is fair? Or just?
How can I possibly accept these chains
around my neck – having done nothing wrong? –
There's just so many questions – like how you
can justify detaining me in law?
and how are other nations, hearing this,
not forced to turn to force to match the force
with which Elizabeth holds me in here?
This is *war*. And in a war, some violence is just,
and reasonable – but even so – my conscience
would *never* sanction regicide.
Lord Burleigh, I could never kill Elizabeth:
the stain of murder would dishonour me –
dishonour – not 'make me subject to your laws'.
But regardless of your laws, this is not justice
this is a power struggle – this is force.

BURLEIGH Well, if it is: then she is on the throne
and you are not. You're powerless. You're here.

MARY hands the sentencing document back to BURLEIGH.

MARY So she is strong and I am weak –
So be it. Let your tyrant queen use force
and slaughter me to make her crown secure
A queen's head coming off like anyone's
is not a precedent I'd be keen to set
but if she murders me, the world will *know*
she used brute force 'cause she was scared of justice
and everything she hides behind her mask
will be exposed – and it won't look too good,
won't look like holiness or virginity or the law
but just like *tyranny* – which is what it *IS*.

MARY exits.

BURLEIGH She'll be defiant till her head is off.
She knew that sentence, somehow. Not a tear

	she didn't even blink. And she knows the Queen is wavering – and our panic makes her brave
PAULET	She's right, though, on Babington and the secretaries That trial cut corners. They should have been in court.
BURLEIGH	*(Fast.)* Too risky. Look – just now – the way she speaks her power over people's minds is clear – and when she *cries* – She'd get them to retract.
PAULET	But now there's rumours everywhere that we corrupted English law for our own ends.
BURLEIGH	And that's the thing that persecutes the Queen. Whichever way she moves, things fall apart – and Mary Stuart's really several things: she's Catholic, she's the heir (or so she thinks) and she's a female monarch. , I wish she'd died before she got to England.
PAULET	It would have saved us all a lot of trouble.
BURLEIGH	Or if she'd caught something – and died in prison. Though then no doubt they'd still say it was murder.
PAULET	Well, you can't stop people thinking
BURLEIGH	Still, there'd be no proof. And likely, fewer rumours.
PAULET	I wouldn't dwell on rumours.
BURLEIGH	The thing is, Paulet, the rumours come regardless of the facts attacking genuine justice just as much as – things we've done that we'd prefer to hide. The English public love an underdog, they always hate the person who's on top. And they prefer their justice from a man. so in this case, it's practically *unseemly* for a woman to kill a woman. Yes – I know –

but if the Queen were male? A different story.
The forty-two of us wasted our time –
the trial, the sentencing – a waste of time:
the consequences fall on the Queen's head.
if Mary dies, then God knows what comes next,
but it won't go unnoticed by the world.
The fact that she's alive in here's a *risk*
but execution could be even worse.
The Queen still has the right to grant her pardon –
and that's what she should do –

PAULET   And let her live?

BURLEIGH No – she cannot stay alive – she cannot live
[Be]cause every day she does, the danger grows:
alive, she breeds rebellion from this cell
but if she's killed, then untold retribution
the fear – the *fact* – her people will strike back
and that's the cage this case has locked the Queen in,
where every move available is wrong.
And sometimes you can see she wants to act –
but – no – the words can't pass her lips.
She's waiting for someone to take the hint.
Hoping someone saves her from this choice
of 'merciful but weak' or 'brutal tyrant'

PAULET   Well, that's the choice. It isn't going to change.

BURLEIGH I think the Queen thinks that it could. If she
just had some more attentive servants –

PAULET   attentive?

BURLEIGH Someone to hear her *un*spoken commands.

,

PAULET   I'll just remind you – what my duty is –
I guard whoever I've been asked to guard

BURLEIGH But if we'd said 'protect this poisonous snake'?
An enemy is different from a jewel

PAULET   A reputation is a jewel. I mean
         the Queen's good name must also be protected

BURLEIGH   Look, Paulet, when we moved the prisoner here –

PAULET   – you chose the most dependable pair of hands
         to keep this critical situation safe.
         If not, Lord Burleigh, then you got it wrong.

         ,

BURLEIGH   The news gets out: the Stuart queen is ill
         she worsens, week by week – and then she dies.
         That way, the people gradually forget her
         and you keep your hands clean

PAULET   But not my conscience

BURLEIGH   *(Angry.)* If you're refusing to co-operate
         I trust you won't object to someone / else [killing her] –

PAULET   *For God's sake* I will fight the man myself
         if someone tries to harm her in this prison
         No murderer will get beyond this door
         as long as my name's on the bloody warrant.
         Her life is in my hands – and honestly
         Elizabeth's life is no more sacred here
         than Mary's is. She's here under my guard.
         You bring me a signed warrant for her death,
         I'll happily let your men take her away.
         But until there's public process, under law
         she stays here and her hands stay tied, of course
         but she will stay alive. Keep your business above board.

ACT TWO

The palace of Westminster.

DAVISON   Excuse me, is it Kent? You're back sooner than we thought
Have the festivities all been and gone?

KENT   Were you not there? Did you not watch the games?

DAVISON   My duties held me here.

KENT   You missed quite the sight.
They put a play on – an expensive one:
The Virgin Fortress (it's a metaphor)
under siege from the troops of *Desire*. There were songs.
Desire's troops were French, of course, you know
the way these foreign visits work – but still
the cannons fired rich perfumes through the air
and silken petals rained down onto us
but, in the end, the troops were beaten back:
Desire had to retreat; the castle stood.

DAVISON   That's not an omen of good news to come
for this French marriage suit. Who set that up?

KENT   No, no; it was a joke – tell you the truth,
I think our Castle's planning to surrender –

DAVISON   I can't believe she'll actually give in –

KENT   The articles that were the sticking points
have been agreed – and France has given in.
The Prince can have his Catholic services
in secret, and behind closed doors at home
in public, though, he toes the party line
a practising, committed Protestant
who honours the religion of the state.
Don't look like that: the public mood is tense
and panicked – and their will is crystal clear: in fact
she knows a royal wedding's what they want

266

they know at some point she is going to die
and Virgin Queens cannot produce an heir
she dies without an heir – and chaos reigns
and (this is why the public's terrified)
Queen Mary Stuart claims the English throne
and England becomes Catholic again.

DAVISON   But Mary Stuart is an empty fear:
the day Elizabeth weds the Prince of France
the same day, Mary's head goes on the block

KENT   She's older than you think.

*Enter QUEEN ELIZABETH I, with AUBESPINE, the French
ambassador. The Earl of LEICESTER, Lord BURLEIGH, and Lord
TALBOT assemble.*

ELIZABETH   I'm sorry, sir, that you were sent to England
I'm sure you must miss France – the ladies there
are younger – lovelier – than here in England
at least, more lovely than we are ourselves
and yes, your views are better –

AUBESPINE   Well, though your country has but one royal lady
it's lucky she is the pinnacle of her sex
and quite delightful.

ELIZABETH   Flattering – *(She's forgotten his name.)*

BURLEIGH   – Lord Aubespine

AUBESPINE   Your majesty, I beg your leave to go
and take the joyful news back to the Prince
(His heart is so impatient that he couldn't
wait for us to get to Paris – so
he's in Amiens, waiting for the news)

ELIZABETH   Don't ask us to repeat ourselves, Lord Aubespine
We've said we cannot wear a wedding dress
when England's sky is ominous and black:
the threats against us rain down thick and fast
against us, and our courtiers – and my life

AUBESPINE Then just give us your *promise*, Your Majesty
the happy day can wait for happier days.

*Something gives in ELIZABETH. It could be a swing in honesty's
direction rather than anger's, but everyone except AUBESPINE is used
to the queen's volatility, and readies themselves.*

ELIZABETH A king is just a slave to being king.
The condition of a monarch is captivity,
hard labour: we may not follow our heart.
If it were my choice, I would live unmarried
and for my epitaph all I want is this:
'Here lies the Virgin Queen'.
My subjects, though, do not want that at all
and cast their minds *beyond* my funeral:
it's not enough that England prospers *now*
when there's a *future* I could help provide for.
I've given them my mind, my warlike arm
a whole lifetime of service – not enough
my virginity is now the thing they want
they'll take that too – and force me down the aisle.
I really thought I'd ruled them like a man
but what they're saying is 'No, you're just a woman.'
No, it's not enough to be a queen
relentlessly undaunted by the task
it's not enough to make the right decisions
time after time after time – it's not enough
that I don't dream the day away – but get things done –
you'd think that might exempt me from the law
the blind and meaningless – but natural – law
that takes one half of the entire human race
and beats it down, subservient to the other

,

AUBESPINE You've been – you are – an exemplary queen.
And there's no man alive worthy enough
that you should sacrifice your freedom for him.
But – if there were, for handsomeness, and birth
and virtue / not accounting for

268

ELIZABETH   A marriage with France would have advantages,
            I'm quite aware of that, Ambassador.
            Let me be honest – if that's what has to happen
            if public pressure forces me to yield
            (and their will is much stronger than my own)
            then there's no Prince in Europe that I would
            less reluctantly surrender to than France.
            Those words are all I have for you for now
            I'm sure you'll find some hope in there somewhere

AUBESPINE   It is a wonderful hope – but it's just a hope –
            the Prince of France wants something more

ELIZABETH   Like *what?*

            ,

            ELIZABETH might be about to lose her temper – but then changes
            her mind somehow. She takes off a ring from her finger. Looks at it.
            Tension mounts: is this going to be the wedding?

            A little ring. A little circled gold.
            This ring means different things in different places.
            It's duty – but it's also slavery:
            two rings can start a marriage – or a chain.
            You may take this – and give it to His Highness
            it's – well – non-binding. It's not yet a chain
            but it could grow – and bind me to a king.

            He kneels and accepts the ring.

AUBESPINE   In his name, I accept your gift, Great Queen.
            I kiss your hand to signify his thanks.
            Your mercy is an honour to behold.
            This is a day of joy. May God extend
            that joy to everyone in England –
            perhaps including that unhappy Queen
            whose fate concerns France and England alike / and

ELIZABETH   *Enough of that.* Ambassador, let's not mix
            two things that aren't compatible.
            Our future husband must share our concerns.
            and not be friendly with our enemy.

AUBESPINE   Your Majesty, forgive me, but you would
            doubt the nobility of France if we
            forgot the widow of our King – and fellow
            believer, in our Faith. Humanity
            and honour both demand –

ELIZABETH   I take that point
            above the line, as surely you intend.
            France may well choose to play the friend
            but I will act as queen.

She nods her head once. AUBESPINE bows and leaves.

ELIZABETH sits down. The Council is in session.

BURLEIGH   Your Highness, you have crowned your people's wishes.
            The future is assured. We can enjoy
            with confidence the peace you've given us.
            One thing alone remains. There is just one
            one last request your country begs you grant.

ELIZABETH   And what more do my people want?

BURLEIGH   Her head.
            The Stuart's head would set your people free.
            They want assurance that her threat to you
            is cauterised. There's rumours everywhere
            that Catholic cells are *here in our own country*
            cherishing their faith in secret – and – wait
            they want a war against the English throne
            and your annihilation is its aim
            there's Catholic networks operating *now*
            assassins sent out secretly from Rheims
            and landing on our shores – and this we know
            three times already we've intercepted them
            we've caught the traitors hiding in our court
            but why continue that? In Fotheringay
            we've *got* the goddess of their holy war
            the flame that gives them their fanatic hope
            and holds our national safety over the fire –
            there is no peace with them: their aims are clear:
            to break the Stuart from her prison cell

and set her firmly down upon your throne.
My lady, it is cut and dried – it's this:
if we won't pull the trigger, we get shot.
Her life is death to you – your death, her life.

ELIZABETH I know, Lord Burleigh, that your passion comes
from loyalty and wisdom. All the same
I hate it from the bottom of my soul.
I don't like wisdom when it's smeared in blood.
I want more moderate options –

TALBOT speaks from the heart – battered with time. He's older, somehow more direct, more sincere than his colleagues on the council.

TALBOT   In my heart
I feel the zeal Lord Burleigh feels, your Majesty,
and this Council must ensure that England's safe
and keep you on your throne for years to come
and keep our future bright. But security
sits side by side with reputation –
your glorious name, the respect that you command.
We must be careful to protect that too

ELIZABETH Of course we must, my lord. What are you saying?

TALBOT That there are other roads open to you
than beheading Mary Stuart. That her sentence
whether we like it or not – is illegal.
You cannot be her judge – or pass her sentence
when she is not your subject

ELIZABETH   In that case
this Council and my Parliament and the Law
have got it wrong. They say I *can* do that.

TALBOT A majority does not prove a thing is right.
England is not the world. Your Parliament
does not comprise the entire human race.
England today and England yesterday
are different things – and different from tomorrow's [England]
Things change – and world opinion changes too
it rises and it falls with England's tides

ELIZABETH   The opinion of my *people* does not change.

TALBOT   You say your people are your master here
            They're not. Let's test that. Exercise free will.
            Just say – you say – you don't want to shed blood
            say that in public – say you are for *peace*
            say that you *want* to save Queen Mary's life,
            shut down the people who would speak against it,
            and this deadlock will vanish – they'll accept: *you chose.*
            But *you* must make this judgement. You alone.
            Your *own* command is what you must obey
            advice like ours is insecure – at best

ELIZABETH   You put my enemy's case quite beautifully
            I must say I would rather hear *my own*

TALBOT   Her case has not been made by anyone!
            We've blocked her from her lawful right
            of legal council – and there's no man else
            will stick his neck out [by] putting Mary's side.
            I'm old, I'm close to death, so I don't spin
            my words to try and climb the ladder:
            but let it not be said, Your Majesty,
            that in your royal council, selfishness
            and pure self-interest hoarded all the votes
            made all the noise – while *mercy* just sat silent.
            The whole of England stands against that woman
            You've never seen her with your own two eyes
            And why would anyone pity a total stranger?
            Now I'm not saying she's a saint – she's not
            But she's just a woman locked in prison. Weak

ELIZABETH   Women are not weak. Some of us are strong.
            I will not have you say that in my presence

TALBOT   You're strong because your life was hard. No throne
            was promised you at birth, no flatterers
            told you each day how wonderful you were,
            you were locked in the Tower, you had your faith
            and that was all. But God did not save Mary.
            Raised a Catholic, raised in France and called

a queen when she could barely sign her name,
and brainwashed with it all – she never heard
the voice of truth: it was drowned out
in giddy whirling golden false frivolities
and she was the most beautiful young girl
and having royal blood [it's not surprising –]

ELIZABETH   Let me remind you that
this is a formal meeting of the council,
Lord Talbot. That might have slipped your mind
though I must say, her beauty must be something
to inspire such excitement in a pensioner.

             ,

The Earl of Leicester is extremely quiet.
Docs Mary Stuart not fire up your tongue?

LEICESTER I'm silent in astonishment, your Majesty,
to think that rumours from the common street
well, fairy tales, that scare the gullible
have risen to the level of this council.
I'm really quite surprised, I have to say
that Mary, Queen of Scots (though not a queen
in fact – she couldn't hold her tiny throne)
that Mary former Queen of Scots, an exile
an exile running scared from her own country
can suddenly breed such terror in a queen.
For God's sake – why are you so scared of her?
Because she claims your throne? Or do we think
a peaceful, Protestant England will – on a whim –
renounce its faith and turn back to the Pope?
There's nothing in me that can understand
this anguish on the question of succession
this push to get you married – I don't know
quite honestly why your councillors seem so panicked.
You're young. She's old. For years to come, you'll dance
over her grave: [there's] no need to push her in.

BURLEIGH It seems the Earl of Leicester's changed his mind

LEICESTER   I voted for her death sentence *in court*
             but in this private Council, my advice
             is *practical* – the best thing for the Queen
             Your Majesty, it seems a senseless time
             to murder her, when France has left her side
             and come to *yours, and* you look to *marry* France
             (renewing hope that you'll produce an heir)
             and she's in prison. She's *already dead.*
             being hated by the public *is* a death
             your mercy would just bring her back to life.

BURLEIGH   Is there a recommendation here, Lord Leicester?

LEICESTER   There is, my lord. We let her sentence stand
             and let her live, but living underneath
             a sharpened blade, held inches from her neck
             the second *any* uprising begins –
             it falls.

                     ,

ELIZABETH   My lords, I've heard your thoughts – and thank you for
             your passionate advice concerning this.
             With God's assistance, I will think it through
             and come to a decision.

        Enter PAULET, bringing with him MORTIMER.

                        Lord Paulet
             What have you got for us?

PAULET   My nephew, Mortimer.
             He has returned, your Majesty, from France
             from Rheims – and kneels now at your feet.
             I recommend him to your royal favour.

MORTIMER Long live Your Majesty. God save the Queen.

        MORTIMER kneels, ELIZABETH beckons him up.

ELIZABETH   Well, welcome back to England, Mortimer.
             You've been on quite the Catholic tour. So tell us
             how our enemies are getting on?

MORTIMER   I met the Scottish exiles who, at Rheims
are plotting violence against your throne:
I won their trust

PAULET   They gave him coded letters
to give to Mary: he brought them to *us*.

ELIZABETH   What are our enemies planning?

MORTIMER   They were shocked
when France abandoned them to come to you.
They're looking now to Spain.

ELIZABETH   Yes, so we hear.

MORTIMER   There is another thing

ELIZABETH   We are all ears

MORTIMER   The Pope has excommunicated you.
The Papal bill had just arrived from Rome
that sealed in law your banishment from their Faith
you're now an enemy of the Catholic Church.

LEICESTER   Such weapons don't hurt England any more

BURLEIGH   They could if they were in fanatic hands

ELIZABETH is looking at MORTIMER.

ELIZABETH   I've heard that you renounced our faith in Rheims.

,

MORTIMER   That was only my disguise, your majesty
deliberately – to better serve *your* cause

*PAULET has chosen this moment to put a letter into ELIZABETH's
hands.*

ELIZABETH   What is it?

PAULET   It's a letter from the Queen
of Scots

BURLEIGH   Give that to me

PAULET   You have no *right!*
              She charged me to deliver it to the Queen
              and not to you. A criminal still has rights.

*ELIZABETH looks at both of them. Then, opens the letter. As she
reads it, MORTIMER and LEICESTER secretly exchange a few words.
BURLEIGH is not happy with PAULET.*

BURLEIGH   What does it say, then?

PAULET   She made no secret of it
              She asks the Queen to meet her face to face.

BURLEIGH   *(Fast.)* Well that must never be allowed to happen!

TALBOT   Why not? What *possibly* could be the problem there?

BURLEIGH   You plot to kill the Lord's Anointed Queen [then]
              you lose the right to put your case to her!

TALBOT   So if your Queen *desires* to show her mercy
              then you're opposed to that?

BURLEIGH   She's *had her sentence!*
              She's going to lose her head – so what is gained
              by letting her Majesty see the corpse-to-be?
              If those two meet, then mercy is *implied*
              it makes a mockery of the court, the law –

ELIZABETH makes a noise. The letter has moved her to tears.

              ʼ

She dries her eyes.

ELIZABETH   Oh what *are* humans? What *happens* on earth?
              our happiness, our fragile, fragile lives?
              Nothing.
              You read this – and you think, she *was* a queen
              born to the oldest throne in Christendom
              who once had hopes to be the Queen of England
              and of Scotland and of France. This letter here –
              so different from the way she used to write,
              so changed. It's sad. And it hurts me to think

the ground beneath our feet is so unfirm,
that we might fall. How easily it comes.

TALBOT God speaks to you, Your Majesty, and puts
his mercy in your heart – listen to it!
She's guilty, she's been punished for her crime
and now this thing must end. Put out your hand
to her – let her *speak* to you

BURLEIGH   Your Majesty
be steadfast. Don't let emotion cloud your mind,
admirable sentiment though it is.
You have to do the thing that must be done:
She's sentenced – can't be pardoned, can't be saved
and if you meet her, none of that will change
and so it just looks cruel – you went to gloat
before she lost her head

LEICESTER   I think we might
remember where the boundaries are, my lords.
The Queen is wise, and she does not require
assistance in deciding what to do.
A private conference between the queens
would be quite separate from the course of law.
The *law* has passed its sentence, *not* the *crown.*
The Queen can do whatever her heart desires
and not affect the course of law at all.

ELIZABETH My lords, you are dismissed. We will find ways
to bring the two together – necessity
and mercy – and make them one.

Everyone leaves. At the door, she calls, noticed by PAULET –

            Mortimer –

She looks at him again. There's something sexual in this look, though
ELIZABETH hasn't yet decided whether she trusts MORTIMER. So
ELIZABETH and MORTIMER are dangerous to each other – and that's
erotic. He steps back towards her.

It's brave to live inside your enemy's camp
it takes great self control – a special thing
in a young man. It suggests a golden future.
And we can make that prophecy come true.

MORTIMER   My hand is yours, Your Majesty, my life
is dedicated to your service.

ELIZABETH   Well
You met my enemies – and England's, too
their hate for me is inexhaustible
and now they come to kill me. Thank the Lord
so far we have been saved – but for how long?
While she's alive, my crown shakes on my head.

MORTIMER   She dies whenever you give the command

ELIZABETH   A-ha! I thought we'd moved in that direction
but actually we've stood completely still.
Our thought was – let the legal system work
and then her blood comes nowhere near our hands.
The law has passed its sentence. Here we are.
What happens now? It must be *executed.*
And who must order execution? Me.
The bloody deed lands right back in my lap
but now – and worse – does so in public view

MORTIMER   Why do you care about how things appear?
You have just cause.

ELIZABETH   And you don't know the world.
The way that things appear is *what they are*
and people don't look deeper, don't dig down
into the complex, double-sided truth of things.
One glance – that's final judgement. As for me,
my people seem to want the Stuart dead
but there's no way that they'll think I'm in the right
when my signature's on the warrant for her head
and so we work to cloak her death in doubt
at least, my part in it. The deed has double form.
Confess a step one way – you pay the price

> and so the only safety is to cloud
> the water, mask the steps you take.

MORTIMER It would be for the best then if [someone else killed her] –

ELIZABETH   *(Fast.)* Exactly.
> My best angel speaks through you. Continue, please
> complete your thought. You're different from your uncle.

MORTIMER Has he been asked?

ELIZABETH   He has

MORTIMER   He's very strict.

> ,

ELIZABETH Are *you* reliable?

MORTIMER   I said, my hand is yours.
> And you can save your reputation.

ELIZABETH   Yes
> And perhaps one morning you can wake me up
> to tell me 'Mary Stuart died last night'.

MORTIMER I think I can

ELIZABETH   How long – how long before
> my sleep improves?

MORTIMER   Before the next new moon.

ELIZABETH Well. Farewell, sir.
> I know you'll understand if gratitude
> is forced to come in secret – and by night.
> Silence is the god of happy men.
> The closest bonds – the tenderest –
> are those that are not seen.

ELIZABETH leaves.

Whose side is MORTIMER on?

MORTIMER   Duplicitous, bloody, hypocrite woman!
                    As you lie to the world, I lie to you
                    dishonesty is purity in your court.
                    And every hour you wait for me to kill her
                    her rescue mission gathers speed – and force.
                    And what reward do you think you can offer?
                    Your body? I'd only touch it with a *knife*
                    There is a queen whose soul radiates *life*
                    she is the way to heaven – you're just earth.
                    You haven't been in love. You can't feel love.
                    You think that somehow you can see the truth
                    inside my eyes, but – no – that's your reflection
                    Elizabeth: you only see yourself.
                    You think I'll be your murderer? – I will
                    but in a second way: I'll murder you.

          Enter PAULET.

PAULET   What did the Queen say to you?

MORTIMER   Nothing, sir.
                    Nothing – of importance.

          PAULET looks at MORTIMER, honestly – fixed gaze.

PAULET   A shiny path you've started walking on
                    but slippery. You're young. And she's the Queen.
                    I understand – keep your ambition checked.

MORTIMER   You were the one who brought me to her court?

PAULET   I wish I hadn't, now. I'm only saying
                    your conscience is your ruler above all.
                    Hold fast to that. Don't pay too high a price.

MORTIMER   What are you scared of?

PAULET   That you'll trust her word.
                    She makes big promises – you take commands
                    you do your half of it – but she's the Queen
                    she saves her reputation, turns on you
                    and claims her vengeance for your bloody deed.

MORTIMER   I'm sorry, 'bloody deed' –

PAULET   STOP THE PRETENCE
           I *know* the thing the Queen's asked you to do
           You're young, she hopes that you're more pliable
           than your unbending uncle. Did you say yes?

MORTIMER   Uncle

PAULET   If you said yes to her, you're dead to me.

           Enter LEICESTER.

LEICESTER Excuse me, sir. A word with your nephew.
           The Queen is most impressed with him.
           She has transferred the care of Mary Stuart
           from you to him.

           PAULET looks at MORTIMER, and exits. LEICESTER is aware of it.

                              Your uncle seems upset.

MORTIMER   I don't know – the unexpected trust
           the Queen has placed in me –

           LEICESTER looks at MORTIMER.

LEICESTER *Can* you be trusted, sir?   .

MORTIMER   I ask the same of you.

LEICESTER You had something to say to me in secret.

MORTIMER   First reassure me that it's not a risk.

LEICESTER And who gives me that guarantee for you?
           Don't be offended, Mortimer, but you exist
           in court as two completely different people.
           And clearly one of them is false. But which?

MORTIMER   I see the same in you.

LEICESTER   So – who goes first?

MORTIMER   The person with the smaller risk to take
           and / that is you

LEICESTER   that is you. Well. I have influence here
                but one man's word can bring the whole thing down.
                You can speak first. Then I will follow suit.

MORTIMER produces the letter. Necessary to be very careful.

MORTIMER   This letter's from the Queen of Scotland

LEICESTER   What?

*LEICESTER reaches for it, looks around, hurriedly opens it. It's
obviously very sensitive. His eyes scan the paper: he's adrenalized.*

              I'm sure you know already what it says –

MORTIMER   No

LEICESTER   She must have told you

MORTIMER   Not a word
                just said that you'd explain the mystery.
                Though now, your eyes speak volumes

LEICESTER   I know that you have found the Catholic faith.
                Give me your hand. Forgive all the suspicion.
                There's no one in this court that you can trust.
                The times are violent, pressures are extreme
                the only kind of safety is disguise
                that's why I seemed to hate the Queen – Queen Mary
                though honestly the opposite is true –
                Mary and I were almost married once
                long before Darnley, long before all this
                and I had no idea what I was losing
                ambition swept me off, I couldn't see
                her youth or beauty, only that the hand
                I held in mine – her hand – was slight.
                I hoped to win the Queen of England's hand.

MORTIMER   And she loves you, it's said

LEICESTER   Well, so it seemed
                but ten years later, ten lost years of wooing
                of wooing someone so completely *vain*

of being chained to someone else's whims
and toyed with, screamed at, promised things – you're told
that you're the favourite, aren't you lucky?
isn't it great the Queen has chosen you?
but actually your life is hers for years to *play with*
and every day you face a different Queen:
tender – proud – or icy cold – who knows?
but now it's ending, there's a younger model
or actually, there's better politics
you heard, today, the young French prince will play
the leading role I gave ten years to learn
so my descent is coming fast – it's *days*
and as the water pours into my ship
and all my hopes get sodden, I remember
the beauty of Mary's eyes – and Mary's hand – and
then I see the jewel I threw away – that
young ambition is no match for love
that love can wait ten years without a scratch

MORTIMER What are you going to do?

LEICESTER   I'll set her free.

                    ,

This letter says she has forgiven me
and that she'll wed me if I rescue her.

MORTIMER Rescue her? You voted for her *death*
          You let her sentence pass without a word
          had I not come to bring her letter here
          a miracle sent by God – you'd never *know*

LEICESTER And you think that it doesn't torture me?
           But I would not have let her die. She won't die now.
           My acting will continue till I can
           find ways – and means – to somehow save her life

MORTIMER They're found. You trusted me: now it's my turn.
          I'm going to set her free. The plan is made
          and everything is ready. They're waiting.

LEICESTER	What?

MORTIMER There's more of us. We break her out with force.

LEICESTER There's more? You're frightening me. Wait. Do they know
the truth of my allegiance?

MORTIMER It's all right.
The plan was made entirely without you
without you it would still have been achieved
had she not dragged you in – but you *can* help

LEICESTER Can you assure me absolutely that
my name has not been mentioned in your plot?

MORTIMER Yes. I'm surprised that you're so cagey
you said you'd find the way to set her free
we found it – and we planned it – and you're scared?

LEICESTER This isn't how to do it. Shedding blood
is dangerous

MORTIMER Waiting's dangerous too

LEICESTER It's too much of a gamble

MORTIMER Yes – for you
because you only want her for your bed – but we
who want her on her rightful throne
` are far less apprehensive

LEICESTER With respect
you're young. You just don't understand the risk.

MORTIMER There isn't time to wait

LEICESTER The traps are laid
and you can't see them

MORTIMER I'm not scared of traps

LEICESTER This needs more thought. You'll ruin everything:
one night – and years of work are ripped away

MORTIMER Do you think there's time for waiting now?

LEICESTER   If we're discovered, they kill us and her

MORTIMER   Risk nothing and you don't deserve to marry her

LEICESTER   You're not *thinking* or *listening* – this is mad
             and stupid and impetuous. You'll kill her.

MORTIMER   And what have you been *thinking* all this time
             with all your influence? and you've done *nothing*?
             what if I was – as your Queen thinks I am –
             a murderer prepared to use the keys
             the keys that you came here to hand to me
             to walk into her cell, unlock the doors,
             and knife her while she sleeps – say I'd do that
             just as the Queen expects I will – so please tell me
             the steps you'd take, right now, to save her life.

LEICESTER   The Queen gave you that order?

MORTIMER   Yes.

LEICESTER   And you / agreed

MORTIMER   Agreed. While the task is mine, it's no one else's.

LEICESTER   All right. That wins us time.

MORTIMER   We're *losing time*

LEICESTER   Be quiet – let me think – the Queen believes
             that you will murder her illicitly
             so she can publicly be merciful
             Perhaps I can persuade her that she should
             as Talbot said, come face to face with her
             opponent – Burleigh's probably right that if
             she sees Mary's face, she'll see herself
             in the same situation – and that thought
             will stop her executing Mary's sentence
             if empathy can make Elizabeth weak –
             well, that's what I should try

MORTIMER   But won't she just
             find someone else to carry out the murder?
             And even if she doesn't, what will change?

285

                    Your Queen will *never* free the rightful Queen
                    she'll let her die in prison – and so then
                    to set her free, your only means is force
                    and then you're forced to end where I *begin:*
                    we break her out of there. Elizabeth
                    I've heard, has spent the night with you before
                    so take her to one of your castles, raise an army
                    imprison *her* – refuse to set her free
                    until Queen Mary takes her rightful place

        LEICESTER smiles.

LEICESTER   And now it's clear that you're entirely mad
                    you just have no idea how these things work
                    at least, not here in England. That woman
                    has every man and everything locked down
                    and not just in her court. Take my advice
                    you won't try anything wild or fast or rash

        ELIZABETH enters and they hear her.

                    Get out of here

MORTIMER   So what shall I tell Mary?

LEICESTER   Tell her I love her.

MORTIMER   Tell her that yourself.

        MORTIMER exits a split-second before ELIZABETH sees him.

ELIZABETH   And who have you been talking to, my Lord?

        LEICESTER is surprised –

LEICESTER   Oh – Mortimer

ELIZABETH   You're startled. What's the matter?

            ,

LEICESTER   I've never seen you look so beautiful.
                    And now – well, what I've lost –

ELIZABETH   What have you lost?

286

LEICESTER   You're playing games with me. I'm losing *you*
             your heart, your self – we know I'm not a king
             and so my marriage suit is crumpled up
             and so your new French husband takes your heart
             but I defy you – search across the world
             you'll never find a man whose love for you
             can equal mine. Your fiancé's never *seen* you
             so it's political love: he loves your *crown*
             but I love *you*. You – you – you – you – you – you

ELIZABETH   It's not my fault – it's not even my *choice*
             for God's sake if I could just ask my heart
             I'd get a different answer – but I *can't*.
             Oh why can't I just love the man I love?
             I'd lift you up – I'd have you wear a crown:
             I *can't*. But Mary Stuart could – she did –
             she put the crown just where she wanted it
             she let her femininity take the rein –
             followed her appetites – didn't hold back
             she filled the glass right to the brim – and drank it down

LEICESTER   But it didn't sustain her

ELIZABETH   Nonetheless
             she didn't care what people thought of her
             she wore life lightly – easily – with *joy*
             no chain of duty pulled tight round her neck
             just ecstasy and pleasure, full and deep
             I could have been like her – I am *like her*
             but I chose rigid monarchy – though *she*
             she won the heart of every single man
             simply by being a woman – while I
             I'm male and stern and like a king. She wins.
             That's men for you: if it smells like sex
             that's it: they're in, they're sold – and they forget
             everything that matters. Talbot today
             disarmed by Mary's charms – and at his age

LEICESTER   He was her jailer – saw her every day
             Perhaps she got him then

ELIZABETH   *Is* she so beautiful?

                   ,

                   I've heard so much about her face, her eyes
                   I often think – how much of it is true?
                   Don't look at me like that

LEICESTER   Sorry – I just –
                   I have a secret fantasy that I
                   could – once – in secret – see you next to her:
                   see you and Mary face to face – and then
                   see how completely you would *dominate*
                   and see her see your eyes – and see herself
                   a cruel reflection – then, of course, you'd know
                   just as in strategy you've beaten her
                   as well as virtue, power, politics
                   in beauty too – in luminosity
                   the victory is yours.

ELIZABETH   She's younger than me

LEICESTER   Well, she doesn't look it
                   It's suffering. She's old before her time.
                   If she saw you it would just torture her
                   her life behind her, you a future bride
                   and promised to the Prince of France – and she
                   once had a French husband herself

ELIZABETH   That's strange – the similarity. It is torture.

LEICESTER   She asked for it – that letter – just say yes
                   that favour will just feed her agony
                   by seeing you – your beauty, face to face
                   a perfect queen – a bride to be – and – *well*
                   if I were her, I'd rather lose my head:
                   we watch as what she asked for eats her up.
                   Your Majesty, your beauty's at its height.
                   Your radiance is armed to win this war.

ELIZABETH   Now would be – no – no – not now, Leicester
                   I have to think about it – talk to Burleigh

LEICESTER   What Burleigh understands is politics
            the court, the country – and so on – the state
            this isn't that: this is – woman to woman
            you'd do this for the state of your own heart
            and also mine – though on the side, no doubt
            to visit her plays well politically
            it makes you merciful – and makes her weak
            so visit her – and then dispose of her.

ELIZABETH   I hear she's not attended like a queen
            if I see that, then it becomes my fault –
            and she is my relation, after all –
            I shouldn't witness her reduced to that

LEICESTER   You won't – you wouldn't have to see her cell
            or even step inside the prison walls –
            the great hunt is today – let's say you ride
            your royal steed into the castle park
            and we let Mary take a walk outside
            you see her accidentally – total chance
            and if it doesn't suit you, just ride on
            don't say a word

ELIZABETH   If this is a mistake:
            your fault: not mine. I'm doing this for you
            because I know I'm hurting you – and so
            you see our heart – just think what they would *say*
            Leicester commands the Queen – and we obey.

289

ACT THREE

A park. Perhaps it's sunset. MARY running – fast –

KENNEDY   Come back – it's like you've got *wings* – I can't keep up

MARY   Oh I could drink the air – unfurl my voice
fling it across that huge gold disc, the *sky* –
I am a kid – a child – let out, set free to fly
to soar across the sheer unbroken space
to bound across the meadows – from my grave
I see the earth has crumbled open: I can see the sun
I'm climbing up and out and wide and *free*
I don't know how it's happened – but I'm free

KENNEDY   Your prison walls have just got slightly wider.
You can't see them behind the trees.

MARY   the trees
Oh thank you trees – thank you – you great wise histories
your paper's coarse and shiny, thick, deep, green
leaves block out the painful world – I'm dreaming
I'm held now by the heavens – held up, high
my eye is winging wide across the light
to where the border into Scotland lies
below, and that cloud there, he's sailing – sail to France
and say hello to all my memories
from me, down here, a captive – journey well
your road is yours – you're free in air
no queens you can be subject to up there

KENNEDY   My lady, sweetheart, please – look over there:
they're spies. We're being watched. I don't like it
they've cleared the park so that we're here alone

MARY   You're wrong – believe me – that's not it *at all*
that they've unlocked my prison is a sign
that better things are coming – I'm not wrong
it's Leicester – somehow – has a hand in this
and now my prison walls will widen out – and out

	and we will be more free with every inch
	until we see that face – and we're *released*

KENNEDY   It just doesn't make sense. First thing today
           they sentence you to death; and now you're free
           it gives me a strange feeling, something's wrong

MARY   Listen – the hunt is coming – that's the horn
           that mellow swelling golden sound – their hooves
           cast up the dust in clouds – and press the grass
           the memories – the memories – the joy

Enter PAULET.

PAULET   Now! Do I deserve a 'thank you'?

MARY   Was this *you*?

PAULET   I did just as you asked me. Happy now?

MARY   The letter? I'm here because she read the letter?

PAULET   It was delivered as per your request.

MARY   And now I'm free

PAULET   That's not the only thing

MARY   What do you mean?

PAULET   You must have heard those horns.
           The Queen is hunting in this park.

MARY   The Queen?

PAULET   And any moment now she stands before you.

MARY is shaking.

KENNEDY   What's wrong, my lady?

PAULET   This *was* your request
           your wish was granted faster than you thought
           well, now's the time: you're good with words
           this is your time to speak

MARY	You should have *warned me*

Now! I'm not prepared! I can't – not now
my best wish terrifies me now – Hanna,
I need to go inside – recover / there and

PAULET   Stand still
You wait here and you meet Her Majesty.
You must be frightened – on your terms, of course,
it's finally time for you to face a judge

Enter TALBOT, running.

MARY   It's not because of that – Talbot, help me
I cannot meet the Queen today – the sight
is more than I can bear

TALBOT   Control yourself
This meeting will determine everything

MARY   I hoped – I waited – years and years and years –
rehearsing what I'd say, and how I'd act
the words I'd use to cut right to her heart
and fill her full of empathy and pity:
forgotten – all of it – like *that* – and and and and
everything *lost* and nothing lives in me,
not now, *except* a white-hot hatred – swells
rearing up the kingdom of my soul
to *war* against the way she's treated me

TALBOT   Stop it
bottle your rage – when hate meets hate
the outcome's never good. Control yourself
obey the time – obey the situation
she has the power over you – *submit*

MARY   Submit – queen to a queen? I can't – I *can't*

TALBOT   *YOU HAVE NO CHOICE!* So, speak respectfully
submission is the only role you've got
so play it *well* – let her be generous

,

MARY   I've pulled my own destruction down
              heavy on my head – and neck – the two of us,
              Elizabeth and me – we should not meet
              we should not *ever* meet. And if we do
              it will be violent – what do you expect
              when flame meets water – [or] tiger meets a lamb
              I am too deeply hurt – so badly hurt
              and hurt *by her* – peace is impossible

TALBOT   I watched her while she read your letter – tears
              in her eyes – it shook her into pity
              The queen has human feelings – just be *brave*
              I ran ahead so I could say: be calm

              MARY takes TALBOT's hand.

MARY   Yes – oh you're a friend to me – I wish
              they hadn't transferred me from you
              and your kind, heartfelt care –

TALBOT   Forget that now
              and set your mind to pure subservience

MARY   Is Burleigh with her too, my evil angel?

TALBOT   It's only Leicester with her –

MARY   Leicester?

TALBOT   Yes
              but don't be scared – it's Leicester was the one
              who got the Queen to meet you face to face.

MARY   I knew he would

TALBOT   What do you mean?

PAULET   The Queen

              Everyone moves to the side. KENNEDY holds MARY to her.
              Then, ELIZABETH enters with LEICESTER – and as they approach:

ELIZABETH   What do they call this castle?

LEICESTER   Fotheringay

293

ELIZABETH looks at LEICESTER – and then at MARY.

The two of them are now on the same stage. It should feel as if something has completed: we're waiting for the two chemicals to react.

ELIZABETH   My people's love for me can be excessive
a god deserves such honour: not a man.

MARY for the first time turns her face to ELIZABETH. Their eyes meet – and hold.

Who is the Lady?

,

LEICESTER   My Queen, we are at Fotheringay –

MARY is shaking. ELIZABETH, darkly:

ELIZABETH   Who is responsible for this?

,

[SPEAK,] *Lord Leicester!*

LEICESTER   Well – it has happened, Majesty – and since
your God has led you here – be merciful
Your Majesty, let your compassion reign

TALBOT   Your Majesty, I beg you graciously to look
on the unlucky woman who stands before you

ELIZABETH   Well, everyone?

,

Who was it told me she was deeply humbled?
She's proud. Not beaten down by her misfortune.

MARY   Let that be.
I will forget now who I am – and what
I've suffered. I bow my self before you.

MARY kneels before ELIZABETH.

God fought on your side, sister. You have won.
Your crown – your victory – is at the height,
I honour you, Elizabeth, your highness
and honour most of all the highest King.
Now be my sister in compassion – offer
your hand and lift me up from where I've fallen.

ELIZABETH You are where you belong, Lady Mary.
It's God who makes you kneel to me, and God
decrees that I shall never kneel to you.

MARY's emotions are rising, but she keeps it together –

MARY Remember everything can change. Remember that.
And arrogance is punished by the gods
they cast me at your feet – to be *your test*,
not mine, in front of every person here,
honour your name and your royal blood, which runs
in both our veins – Oh God – *be merciful*
my all, my life, a woman's life now hangs
on what I say – my life is in my words
if I can make you see that I *am* you:
I am just as you are – let me *express* that,
but when you look at me like this, all ice
I'm choked – I'm terrified – no words can come

ELIZABETH is cold and severe.

ELIZABETH I thought you had something to say to me.
You asked us for this meeting – we put by
all of your crimes against us, our role as Queen
and came – to do the duty of a sister,
to bring you comfort in our presence here,
and grant your wish – but by stooping so low,
by yielding to our generous impulses,
we have exposed our crown to public shame
to meet someone who would have murdered us –

MARY I have something to say – but – I don't know
I don't know where to start. My words must pierce
your heart but never graze your skin – I mean

I mean you no offence – nothing in me
is trying to make you angry – but in my case – that is
to speak my case at all is to indict you. So
I ask God to give force to what I say – but
strip from my words the thorns of slight or harm
and let me tell the simple truth: you have
not treated me as I deserved – we are,
we are *both queens.* And you imprisoned me.
I came here as a suppliant and you
ignoring basic hospitality
throwing aside all international law
you locked me up, you tore my friends from me,
cruelly removed my servants, hauled me up in court,
that trial, that indefensible, illegal trial –
but no – *enough* – these things must be forgotten
Oblivion will shrink them into dust
I'll say that it was chance – that it was fate
not *your* fault – and not *my* fault, just the way
things happened. Let's let that be history.
We both know that this started long ago
and some black demon planted seeds of hate
when we were young – that swelled into *this* – now
and evil men have fed that, fanned its flames
until this *chasm* gapes between us now
and mad extremists push us to the brink –
but then the curse of every single king
is that our private feelings aren't our own
they magnify – and cleave the world in half
and in the gap between pure hate pours in
burning like ice – but no third parties now
no, now at last we're standing face to face
so speak to me – and name my crime
and I'll reply – I'll answer every charge
I'll satisfy you on the smallest point – my God
I wish you'd let me meet you years ago
I wish you'd let me look into your eyes
we never would have come to this today

ELIZABETH   My better angels saved me from the snake
             from bringing it so close to my own skin.
             You can't blame fate. Look at your own black heart
             the wild ambition of your poisonous house:
             between us, there was no hostility
             at all – but then your uncle declared war
             persuaded you to use my coat of arms
             and sign your name as England's Royal Queen
             you sought my death – enlisting godless priests
             and rabid frenzied cults to light their brands
             you goaded other nations' grudges, even *here*
             you tried to rip apart *this* nation's peace
             but God fights on my side – and He ensures
             your uncle's war is dead – and here we are:
             the blade you aimed at my neck swings back round
             and slashes into yours

MARY   I'm in God's hands
             you will not wield your power so bloodily

ELIZABETH   And who is going to stop me? Is it *you*?
             What is your 'international law' to me?
             And what is family? What is 'royal blood'?
             If we are so alike – then how about
             I follow the example of your Church
             that makes killing a queen a holy act
             and practise simply what your own priests preach?
             There's not a single promise you can make
             that I can trust – how can I set you free?
             On what book can you swear? 'Cause there's no lock
             that Catholic treachery won't unpick. *Speak up!*

             '

             Yes, as I thought. Our security is *force*.
             And we will not negotiate with *snakes*.

MARY   Oh that is your suspicious paranoia!
             You treated me as your enemy from the start
             and as the *other* – and ignored my claim,
             and how you look at something's what it *is*:

if you had simply named me as your heir
which I have every right to ask of you
I would have been your truest friend – and family

ELIZABETH Your family's over there in Catholic France!
The Pope's your friend! Name you my heir?
A trap – but telling: I'd sit there, alive
while you seduce my people – with your eyes
and throw your nets out for our younger men
so they all turn to the new-rising sun
while I –

MARY would rule in peace! Listen: here and now
all claims to England's throne I abdicate
I let them go – *ach* – my spirit's wings
are broken, lame – I do not feel the lure
of greatness. You've achieved it. I am –
I am only Mary Stuart's shadow.
You locked me up for years – my spirit's dead
you've done your worst – to catch me at my height
and crush me down to nothing – make it end
finish this – and say the thing you came
to say: I don't believe you came to taunt me:
just say the words – please say the words – you're free
Mary, you've felt my power until now – today
you feel my mercy' – say that and I will beg
my self, my life, my freedom and my crown
from your royal hand as gifts – just *say the words*
and none of this has happened – say the words
but please don't make me wait – say one word – sister
I fear for you if you can leave this park
not having blessed me. I don't *want* your power
I wouldn't take it for your entire kingdom – not
for all the earth and water on the globe

ELIZABETH So you confess – at last – you are defeated?
There's no more plots? And no more murderers
are on their way? no martyrs for your cause?
Yes – that's it, Lady Mary – you're old news.
There's no one left you can seduce – the world

has other things to think about – you're *done.*
No man is begging to be husband number four
though then that's not surprising – as we know,
your husbands – like your lovers – end up dead

MARY   Sister – oh God – let me control myself

ELIZABETH's eyes are bright and sharp, genuinely sexually triumphant:

ELIZABETH So this, Lord Leicester – *this* is the beauty
so dangerous that men fell with one glance
and earthly women just could not compete.
Really. It seems *that* reputation's cheap:
but then – it's true – the crowds *would* praise your charms
when you've had half of them between your sheets

MARY   *Too much* –

ELIZABETH   And now her mask slips, now we see
her face – her own true self

MARY glows with anger – but holds her dignity, just.

MARY   My sins were *human* ones
and I was young – I made mistakes – it's true
power seduced me, yes, I don't deny it:
instead of fabricating public lies
I chose the *honesty* that becomes a crown
I let the worst be known – and I can say
that I am greater than my reputation is.
But once they rip your ermine cloak away
once this façade of virtue falls apart
the world will see exactly what you are
the red hot fires of your secret lusts –
the Virgin Queen? just like your mother, then!
Control the way they write about it – fine! –
but that won't make it true – everyone *knows*
the reason Anne Boleyn was put to death

Something breaks in ELIZABETH.

TALBOT   No – it cannot come to this – control yourself

MARY   There comes a point where it is inhumane
              where any human would explode – would burst
              the walls – the anger rushes out like blood
              I wish my words could *kill* you – murder you
              slice out your *eyes*

              Things have reached the point of no return.

TALBOT   She is beside herself
              she's mad, your majesty – she needs your *help* /
              and not your condemnation

              *LEICESTER in huge anxiety tries to lead a speechless ELIZABETH
              away.*

LEICESTER Let's go – don't listen to her frenzy – come away

MARY   The Queen of England is a bastard Queen
              your throne's defiled, this honest country is
              the victim of a con – *you* [Elizabeth] are a fraud
              a thief – *imposter* – and if right prevailed
              you'd bow before me honouring my right
              you would be lying prostrate in the dust
              I AM YOUR KING

              ELIZABETH exits, swiftly – followed by the train.

KENNEDY   What are you doing?
              She's furious – [she's] leaving – our hopes are dead

MARY   'She's furious' – I hope her heart explodes
              I feel *well*, Hanna, finally – I can breathe
              after the years of shame – humiliation
              a single moment of pure victory
              A mountain's lifted off my chest – I stabbed
              a knife down deep into my enemy's stomach

KENNEDY   She's got the knife! You're mad! *She is the Queen*
              You slandered her – her lover heard it all

MARY   I humiliated her in front of Leicester
              He saw – he saw me win – my victory
              he gave me strength – he stood so near to me
              I climbed up and I beat her from her height

          MORTIMER runs in.

MORTIMER   *(To K.)* Make sure no one comes near
                  (To M.)   I heard it all

          *KENNEDY takes her place on guard. MORTIMER's whole being is
          suppressing a huge wave of ferocious, excited passion. Though he might
          first appear comic, there's something increasingly frightening about
          him – as this conversation progresses.*

              You've won. You *won* – you stamped them into dust
              They were the criminals – you were the Queen
              the *courage* of you – you are a *goddess*

MARY   Did you give him my letter – Leicester?

MORTIMER   Your anger *blazed* – it shone like holy light – you are
              the most beautiful woman in the world

MARY   Did you give him my letter? Is there *hope*?

MORTIMER   There is – but not from Leicester. He's a coward.

MARY   What?

MORTIMER   If he wants to rescue you – then first
              he'll have to fight me to the death

MARY   *LISTEN*
              Did Leicester get my letter?

MORTIMER   Leicester likes his life
              to save you now a man must love his *death*

MARY   Is Leicester going to save me?

MORTIMER   No, he's not.
              We don't need him. I'm saving you.

MARY   *(Sarcastic.)*   With *what*?

MORTIMER Stop lying to yourself. You're wasting time.
          Your case, this situation's crossed a line
          and how things were this morning? Dead and gone.
          Elizabeth left – and then – so did the chance
          of her showing you mercy – it's time to *act*
          we have to be audacious – and this fight
          is now. We break you out of here tonight.

MARY   Impossible

MORTIMER   No – it's happening – listen
          we came together secretly today
          we made confession to a Catholic priest
          who absolved us of our sins – and future sins
          (knowing your rescue will be dearly bought)
          but we took our last sacrament – and we
          are ready now to start on our last journey

MARY   I can't hear this

MORTIMER   You know I'm jailer now
          The Queen put me in charge of you – and so
          I have the keys. We blow open the walls
          we kill the guards and take you from your room
          tonight

MARY   You kill the guards?

MORTIMER   No other way
          we can't leave witnesses to your escape

MARY   And Paulet? And the guards? They're going to fight.

MORTIMER We kill them first.

MARY   Kill your own uncle?

MORTIMER   Yes

MARY   The crime of / murder's heavy

MORTIMER   murder's pardoned in advance
          Some things have to be done. And I am ready.
          I want it to come.

MARY   No – no –

MORTIMER   And if tonight
                  my knife must split the windpipe of the Queen
                  if that is what God wants – I swore on Jesus' blood
                  that I would do it

MARY   Too much blood for me –

MORTIMER   I'd give the world and everything for you
                  I love you – let the structure of the globe
                  dissolve and start a giant foaming wave
                  to flood the lungs of everything that breathes
                  There's *nothing* I respect – the end of days
                  will come before I let them put their hands
                  on you

MARY   You're frightening me

MORTIMER   Life is over quickly
                  so is death – let them restrain me, carry me to Tyburn
                  pull out my joints and flesh and burn my skin
                  let them bring red-hot knives – life does not *last*
                  I need to touch you now

MARY   Get away from me

MORTIMER   I want to taste your skin, your hands, your mouth
                  they're going to kill you – you're *already dead*
                  your white neck severed with a heavy axe
                  I'll hold them back – I'll kill a *thousand souls*
                  I'll rescue you – I will – and I will *have* you
                  God put you purposely into my hand – *you're mine*
                  I want to be inside you

MARY   Listen – *please*
                  respect me as a woman and a queen
                  my grief – my situation – and my crown

MORTIMER   There's no crown on your head. It's fallen off.
                  You have no power. You can't give commands.
                  Your body is the only thing that's left

you're you – your hair – your body – just a *girl*
but that's enough – for that I dare do *everything*
it drives me toward death

MORTIMER's eyes are wild – he is going to rape her if needs be.

MARY   I do not want this
I'll tell them all you're here to rescue me

MORTIMER COME ON – you're not like her – the frigid queen
I've heard the stories – Darnley and Bothwell

MARY   How dare you say his name

MORTIMER   Bothwell! I dare.
He was a bully – your love was soaked in fear
but maybe fear's the thing you understand

MARY   Let me go – *HELP*

KENNEDY runs back in, terrified, but not at this attempted rape –

Hanna, I –

*And suddenly PAULET and other men are running into the scene –
MARY is wrestled to the floor and gagged.*

PAULET   Where is the murderer? The gates are *shut*
Where is the Scottish queen? Don't move an inch –
Take hold of her – restrain her – now now now

MORTIMER Uncle? What's happening?

PAULET   Get the criminal
inside the prison – you do not leave her door
or even *blink* – without my saying so. Admit no one else

*PAULET looks at his nephew, wild-eyed – in shock, emotional, perhaps
tearful – voice trembling – something is very, very wrong…*

MORTIMER What's GOING ON?

PAULET   The Queen – oh God – the Queen

MORTIMER The Queen? Which Queen?

He can hardly believe he's saying the words.

PAULET   Elizabeth –
                   was murdered as she travelled back to London

    ,

Everyone exits, fast, different doors –

INTERVAL.

ACT FOUR

MORTIMER enters swiftly, pacing, thinking, then BURLEIGH and DAVISON enter – everyone adrenalized.

BURLEIGH   Draw up the execution warrant *now*.
Get on with it. The second it's complete
it goes before the Queen for her to sign.

MORTIMER   Sir, is the Queen alive?

BURLEIGH   Shocked – but alive

DAVISON   Lord Talbot saved her life – the madman's blade
glanced off the shoulder of the Queen – but missed
and then Lord Talbot [forced him to the ground]

BURLEIGH   Thank you, Davison
Your duty isn't journalism. Go.

DAVISON exits.

MORTIMER   Who attacked her?

BURLEIGH   A Catholic radical,
a priest – he's French – we're questioning him now.
The Pope had excommunicated her
so murder was fair game – and they moved fast
to liberate the Catholic church.

Enter LEICESTER. BURLEIGH ignores him.

LEICESTER   The park's locked down.

Enter AUBESPINE, out of breath –

AUBESPINE   Praise be to God that he has saved the Queen

BURLEIGH   Praise be to God that crushed her enemies

AUBESPINE   May God condemn whoever did this deed

BURLEIGH   The puppet and whoever pulled the strings

AUBESPINE turns to LEICESTER.

AUBESPINE My lord, please grant me access to the Queen
I wish to lay my lord the King's support,
and France's thoughts and prayers, down at her feet

BURLEIGH Don't waste your breath, Lord Aubespine

AUBESPINE, officially:

AUBESPINE Respect, Lord Burleigh, I have a duty here.

BURLEIGH Your duty is to go back home to France
as soon as possible.

AUBESPINE   I don't understand –

BURLEIGH The status of 'ambassador' keeps you safe
today – but not tomorrow

AUBESPINE   On what *grounds*?

BURLEIGH I'm sure you don't want me to name your crime

AUBESPINE My rights as France's royal ambassador / will –

BURLEIGH will not protect a traitor to our Queen.

LEICESTER Burleigh, what is this?

AUBESPINE   My lord, think carefully
before you –

BURLEIGH A passport with your signature on was found
on the assassin's person.

                    '

AUBESPINE I authorise many passports, sir. I don't read minds.

BURLEIGH The assassin made confession at your home.

AUBESPINE I am a Catholic and my home is open

BURLEIGH to every anti-English maniac?

AUBESPINE Lord Burleigh, I demand a full inquiry

BURLEIGH   Careful what you wish for

AUBESPINE   The French King will be furious
             to hear how you have treated him – through me.
             The marriage treaty will be reconsidered.

BURLEIGH   The Queen's already torn it up. For good.
             The English crown will not be marrying France.

             ,

             BURLEIGH has a piece of paper handed to him. Looks almost amused,
             quizzical.

             The people are incensed. They've stormed your house
             and found stockpiles of weapons hidden there.
             I'll grant you your immunity until
             you're off our soil – safe conduct and your life,
             that's more than you can reasonably ask.

AUBESPINE   To leave a country that ignores the laws
             that unite half the world – will be my pleasure.
             Your royal court's a playground – and the King
             will force your Queen to pay the price for this

BURLEIGH   Well, he can come and ask for it himself

             AUBESPINE leaves.

LEICESTER   The wedding suit with France is over, then.
             You built it up – and now you knock it down,
             Lord Burleigh. Keeping busy all the time.
             No benefits to England, though – a shame!
             you might as well have saved yourself the trouble.

BURLEIGH   I did what I thought best. God disagreed.
             If only every man could say the same.

LEICESTER   Be honest, you enjoy all this. Good time
             for you – you've got someone to hunt,
             a major incident – but the criminals' guilt
             wrapped up in secrecy – and so we need
             a court of inquisition! Weighing looks

and words – exhibiting private *thoughts*
to public view: and Burleigh reigns supreme!
the number one, the Atlas of our times
on his shoulders the safety of the state.

BURLEIGH   I've got a lot to learn from you, Lord Leicester:
your way with words won quite the victory

LEICESTER   What victory?

BURLEIGH   Your trip to Fotheringay.
The one you talked the Queen into behind
my back.

LEICESTER   Behind your back! And why would I
need to conceal something from you, my Lord?

BURLEIGH   You led the Queen to Fotheringay – I'm sorry
that's not quite right – the thing I meant to say
is that your Queen led *you* to Fotheringay.

LEICESTER is unsettled. What does BURLEIGH know?

BURLEIGH speaks with smooth, sharp confidence.

LEICESTER   If I were you, I would explain myself –

BURLEIGH   A very noble role you had her play,
the Queen – she trusts you, clearly – gullibly
and in return she's made a mockery of.
But that *was* why you came on merciful
before the council (quite the change of heart)
and quite the way with words: the Stuart *weak*
and insignificant – not to be feared
and barely worth the trouble of her death.
Good plan. Well, sharp. Well, sharpened to a point.
A shame the point snapped off.

LEICESTER   Say that again
say that again before the Queen.

BURLEIGH   I will
Let's see your way with words protect you then.

Exit BURLEIGH. LEICESTER alone.

LEICESTER He's onto me. Seen through me. If there's proof
I'm finished – if they know Mary and I
have understandings – God, there's no way out
she'll think I gave her dishonest advice
betrayed her to her oldest enemy
persuaded her to go to Fotheringay
it all looks like a *plan!* Oh Christ in heaven
she'll think that Mary's anger was an act
and even the assassin – no escape
from how they'll read events – no mercy then:
I'm finished.

MORTIMER enters, terrified, looks around apprehensively.

MORTIMER   Leicester – are we alone?

LEICESTER Look: go away.

MORTIMER   They're on my track
and they're on yours.

LEICESTER   GET OUT OF HERE

MORTIMER They know there was a secret meeting at
the French Ambassador's house –

LEICESTER   Why would I *care?*
I've had / enough

MORTIMER They know the assassin was there

LEICESTER   That was *your* plan
don't implicate me in your dirty crimes

MORTIMER Just *listen*

LEICESTER   Die in hell. I don't *know* you.

LEICESTER in violent anger is leaving, when –

MORTIMER I came to *warn* you. They know everything.

LEICESTER What?

MORTIMER   Lord Burleigh got to Fotheringay at once
            just minutes after everything had happened
            they searched her rooms – Queen Mary's rooms – they found
            a letter

LEICESTER   what?

MORTIMER   a letter that the Queen
            was writing to you

LEICESTER   no – *the STUPID WOMAN*

MORTIMER   in which she calls on you to keep your word – and
            renews the promise of her hand in marriage

LEICESTER   *God*

MORTIMER   Lord Burleigh has that letter

            '

LEICESTER   And *goodnight.*

            LEICESTER retches, perhaps. As MORTIMER speaks, LEICESTER thinks
            hard –

MORTIMER   Be brave – and seize the moment. Now. Before
            Lord Burleigh does – you can save her
            and save yourself – invent excuses, swear
            anything to get you out of this.
            Our men are scattered – nothing I can do
            the whole thing's blown wide open – I'll escape
            to Scotland, bring our cause to order there.
            But here, it's up to you. Be ruthless. Think.
            See what your influence can do. Good luck.
            Be *bold.*

            LEICESTER stops walking – totally still.

LEICESTER   You're right.

            He calls out of the door.

                            Hey – hey – HEY – GUARDS!

KENT enters.

This man's a traitor to the state.
He's just confessed his plot against the Queen
(To M.) In the Queen's name, you are under arrest.
(To K.) You guard the door. I'll call more men – and then
I'll take the news into the Queen myself.

LEICESTER exits, quickly. KENT stands at the doorway, preventing MORTIMER from getting away.

MORTIMER is astonished –

MORTIMER The bastard. But this is what I deserve
for trusting him. And he took my advice:
betraying me builds him a bridge – and he
walks free on top of it. And leaves me to
the wolves.

MORTIMER has the means of suicide on him: perhaps a tablet, taken from a small silver box. He's been prepared for this from the start.

But I won't do the same to him – my fall
won't try to bring him down: my lips are sealed.
This world is nothing – my eyes look to heaven
my freedom is my soul – and I ask God
to curse these men who turn from the true Queen
Queen Mary Stuart – and with my last breath
I love you – we two will be one in death

MORTIMER takes the tablet. And when KENT re-enters – MORTIMER is dead.

Enter ELIZABETH – her shirt is bloodied, partially ripped. There is a letter in her hand. BURLEIGH follows after her.

ELIZABETH To take me to that park – to laugh at me
make me perform in front of his vile whore
you *stupid woman*, tricked, betrayed and shamed!

BURLEIGH Your Majesty, I don't know what he did
to work his way around your royal wisdom –

ELIZABETH   He's laughing at me. I went to taunt *her*
              but she – and he – humiliated *me*.
              I'll swing the axe into her neck myself

BURLEIGH   You see now *my* advice was accurate

ELIZABETH   I should have listened: we wouldn't be *here*
              oh I trusted him – I shouldn't have trusted him
              and all his vows he loved me – they were traps?
              Who can I trust when even he betrayed me?
              I let him play the King within this court
              he wormed inside my heart, trussed up my soul

BURLEIGH   But all that time he was duplicitous:
              betraying you to Mary Queen of Scots.
              the letter in your hand confirms the truth.

ELIZABETH   They'll pay for this. In blood. Have you drawn up
              the death warrant?

BURLEIGH   They're doing it as we speak.

ELIZABETH   I want her dead. I want her DEAD. All right:
              She dies. He watches. Then he dies himself.
              (She roars.)
              I'll rip him from my heart, I'll spit him out
              and every fingerful of flesh that felt his love
              I'll slice it out and fill it with *revenge*
              You fall from high up – and you break. And he
              was high – enough! – drag him to the Tower
              I'll name the peers to sentence him, and he
              will face the full force of the law.

BURLEIGH   He'll try and talk to you –

ELIZABETH   What can he say?
              This letter casts its argument in stone.
              His crime is clear as day

BURLEIGH   You're merciful
              and seeing him, it's possible / you'll [think again]

313

ELIZABETH   I will not *ever* set eyes on him again.
            You gave the order barring him?

BURLEIGH   I did.

ELIZABETH   Wait here – and when he comes, arrest him.

            Enter KENT.

KENT   Your Majesty, Lord Leicester is outside

ELIZABETH   He can't come in. Get out and tell him that.

KENT   Your Majesty, I would not dare say that
            to Leicester – he won't accept that from me

ELIZABETH   My subjects fear his anger more than mine

BURLEIGH   Tell him the Queen denies him access

            *BURLEIGH gestures for KENT to go – ELIZABETH signals him to
            pause –*

ELIZABETH   This couldn't be – a trap that *Mary* set
            words on a page designed to draw me in
            and cut Lord Leicester down at the same time?

BURLEIGH   But think, Your Majesty / consider

            Enter LEICESTER, fast, sees BURLEIGH.

LEICESTER   I might have guessed that this was down to you
            if you'll see Burleigh, you can see me too

BURLEIGH   It's pretty brave to storm in here when you've
            explicitly been forbidden by the Queen

LEICESTER   It's brave of *you* to try and keep me out
            there's *no one* at this court who has the right
            to tell the Earl of Leicester where he can
            and cannot go. From my own Queen, I want / to hear

            He has approached ELIZABETH, who does not look at him.

ELIZABETH   Out of my sight

LEICESTER   Those aren't your words
           Lord Burleigh put them in your mouth, but I
           want *yours*, my own gracious Elizabeth
           talk to me, let me explain – as you let him
           put his malicious story

ELIZABETH   Go ahead
           Deny your crime. Perjure yourself. Go on.

LEICESTER Let your officious watchman leave the room
           before we speak – Burleigh, get out –
           My Queen and I do not require a witness.

ELIZABETH He stays. By my command.

LEICESTER   Elizabeth
           when have we ever needed anyone else?
           This is between the two of us – send him out.
           I have the right to talk to you alone –

ELIZABETH Do you indeed?

LEICESTER   You made me what I am
           lifted me up – and trusted me – and *more* –
           your heart gave me whatever honour I have
           I will defend that honour with my life
           Two minutes. Send him out. And hear me speak.

ELIZABETH No silky words will talk you out of this.

LEICESTER I only want to speak straight to your heart
           explain my actions – what I've done and why
           how I relied on our relationship
           to take the risks I've taken: my defence
           is only to be judged by your own heart
           and not by any of Lord Burleigh's courts

ELIZABETH Shameless.
           Lord Burleigh, please. Show him the letter.

           BURLEIGH hands the letter over. LEICESTER skim-reads it. His face
           doesn't change at all – not a single flicker of surprise.

LEICESTER   It's Mary Stuart's writing.

ELIZABETH   Read it *silently*.

          LEICESTER finishes reading it.

LEICESTER   I know that this looks bad, but there is more
             than simply how things look

ELIZABETH   Can you deny
             that you've had secret contact with the Stuart
             and Catholic networks plotting her escape?

LEICESTER   If I *were* guilty, I'd claim this was fake,
             my enemies at Court had set me up
             but – my conscience is *clear* – and what she writes
             is true

ELIZABETH   That isn't good, is it?

BURLEIGH   He's just
             pronounced his death sentence himself

ELIZABETH   Enough. Escort Lord Leicester to the Tower.

LEICESTER   I was working for *you* – I got it wrong
             I should have told you everything – but still
             I won her confidence only so we'd know
             the details and could *sabotage* her plan

ELIZABETH   This is absurd

BURLEIGH   Sir, do you *really* think / that

LEICESTER   Yes – I've played a dangerous game. I know.
             And no one else at court would have presumed
             to risk so much – but God, I love my Queen
             I *knew* her faith in me would guarantee
             this high-risk strategy – which was worth the risk
             because, in fact, it has now saved her life.
             They'd tried to kill the Queen three times – and look,
             the honours I've received from her, my rank
             they don't suggest much motive to defect
             and you – and you – and all the world has heard
             how deep my hatred is for Mary Stuart –

BURLEIGH	So if your plan's so great, why keep it secret?
LEICESTER	My lord, you love to talk before you act ringing the bell before you get things done That's your way. This is mine: *talk afterwards.*
BURLEIGH	You're talking now to save your skin.
LEICESTER	And you have come in here to boast that you, again, have done a great fantastic brilliant deed uncovered plots, rescued Her Majesty exposed the treachery to all. *Ironically* you think that you see everything, that you don't miss a trick – but, sad to say, you *do* because – despite your boasting – Mary Stuart would now be free, had I not been alert.
BURLEIGH	Are you really claiming – ?
LEICESTER	*Yes.* Let me explain. Lord Burleigh, I know much more than you think. I know the Queen had trusted Mortimer, revealed her private wishes, ordered him to murder Mary Stuart in her cell – a task which horrified his uncle Paulet who had refused to do it
BURLEIGH	Who told you that?
LEICESTER	It *is* the truth, correct me if I'm wrong? Exactly. Other people do see things. Not you, though, Burleigh – you managed to miss the hundred clues that Mortimer was *false* and Catholic and a murderous radical fighting in secret on the Stuart's *side*, determined – yes – to kill the Queen, but not the Scottish one – *Elizabeth!*
ELIZABETH	Lord Mortimer!
LEICESTER	He was the one who brought the Stuart's letters. That's how I came to know him first. He said

minutes ago – they planned to break her out
tonight – by force – to take her from her cell –
I broke my cover and revealed myself
and called the guards – put him under arrest
but knowing he was trapped with no way out,
without a warning, he has killed himself –

ELIZABETH is hit hard by this new bad news.

ELIZABETH   Betrayed again. The seeds were poisoned too
            and so we reap this poisoned harvest now –

BURLEIGH   This happened now? After I'd left the room?

LEICESTER   I wish he wasn't dead – not least because
            his testimony would prove my innocence.
            That's why I broke my cover when I did.

BURLEIGH   He killed himself, you say? It wasn't you?

LEICESTER   That question isn't worthy of you. Go ask Kent
            he will corroborate everything I've said

ELIZABETH   Oh this is hell

LEICESTER   So who has saved the Queen?
            Was it Lord Burleigh? Did he know the danger
            converging round your Majesty today?
            Where was *his* plan? Which of us served you best?
            Who was the faithful angel to his Queen?

BURLEIGH   Mortimer's death came right on time for you

ELIZABETH   I don't know what to say – I believe you
            and I don't – You're guilty – and you're not.
            And the mother of this hell is Mary Stuart
            I say 'we are the Queen' – '*we* are': *we are*
            'we are the Queen' – the *two of us* are queen:
            I wear the crown, but she holds all the cards
            for years her secret influence – seeps in
            like woodworm hollowing out our government
            and leaving us a husk of what we are
            her prison cell's the centre of the state
            and tension settles thick round us, like snow

LEICESTER   She has to die. I ask for it myself.
             Remember what I said in council – that
             the blade falls when the uprising begins?
             The uprising's begun. The blade should fall.

BURLEIGH   Lord Leicester, you're the one –

LEICESTER   Please let's be clear:
             the safety of her Majesty is paramount
             today has proved they want to end her life
             let's not wait for their next attempt. Extreme
             measures are called for. Execute the sentence.

                    ,

BURLEIGH   So confident – so serious, and so honest
             surely Lord Leicester is the perfect man
             to bear the burden of this crucial act?
             perhaps assign the doing of this to him?

LEICESTER   To me?

BURLEIGH   To you. How better to destroy
             all the suspicion buzzing around your name?
             No one will dare suggest you were in love
             when you're the man that has her put to death.

ELIZABETH fixes her eyes on LEICESTER.

ELIZABETH   That's shrewd advice. So ordered.

LEICESTER   Elizabeth
             my standing in the court makes me unfit
             for such a gory office. Surely it's best
             that Burleigh is responsible – he's not
             so close to you – to the public, then, it's not
             the crown, but the judicial system, which
             takes Mary's life. But if you wish me to,
             I'll prove my love, I'll waive my privileges
             and show my loyalty – I'll accept the task.

ELIZABETH   You're right.
             Burleigh can share responsibility

with you. You're equals now. So get it done.
I want the warrant here *immediately.*

BURLEIGH exits.

ELIZABETH and LEICESTER alone.

Then KENT enters, a bit shaken.

KENT   Your Majesty there's crowds outside the palace.
They want to see your face.

ELIZABETH   What's going on?

KENT   Panic has spread – the rumour that you've died
has travelled fast – but even then they won't
they don't trust what we're telling them
they know the Catholics move against your life
and that they'll strike to break the Stuart free
the crowds are furious and terrified

ELIZABETH   Is there suggestion they'll turn violent?
What do they want?

KENT   They want the Stuart's head.
They won't leave till the death warrant is signed.

BURLEIGH re-enters with DAVISON, who has the warrant in his hands.

ELIZABETH   Are you aware my people are outside?

BURLEIGH   We are.

DAVISON puts down the death warrant. The sheer size of what it represents is overwhelming. Everyone looks at it. ELIZABETH hesitates – fighting with herself.

ELIZABETH   Oh God

BURLEIGH   Your Majesty, obey the people's voice. It is
the voice of God

BURLEIGH takes the lid off a pen, offers it to her.

,

320

Pressure beats in ELIZABETH's ears – she's a trapped animal.

ELIZABETH   And which man here will guarantee me *now*
I hear the voice of all my people, *all*
who stand on England's soil – *no*, on the world?
Is this decision *really* what they want?
'Cause I'm afraid that, once I sign this thing
once I obey the people's lust for death –
then we'll all hear a different, darker voice
and everyone who now wants this thing done
will turn against me as a murderer

Enter TALBOT, as KENT runs back outside.

TALBOT   Don't let them rush you into this, Your Majesty,
take time – stand firm

He sees the death warrant.

                        Has it already happened?
Get that disgusting piece of paper out
of here – Your Majesty, tear it up –

ELIZABETH   What can I do? They're forcing me

TALBOT   Who is?
No man can force the Queen of England's hand.
You're Queen. Command your people to *shut up*.
How dare they threaten you? They're blind and scared
and you're still reeling – you have been attacked
today! You're only human. Suspend judgement.

BURLEIGH   It's already been *judged* – sentence was passed
in court: the *execution* of the sentence
is all that's left.

KENT re-enters. New news. Tenser and tenser.

KENT   It's getting worse out there. The uproar swells
we're told it's getting hard to hold it down

ELIZABETH   They're pushing me and pushing me

TALBOT   Push back

Postpone the thing – tell them you want to *wait*
You sign that paper – that's your legacy
your life, your peace, your happiness – the lot.
You've been debating this for *years* – this storm
is not the place to make a snap decision.
Ask for a pause. Collect your thoughts. And breathe.

BURLEIGH *(Violently.)* Yes, breathe, while London crackles into flames
take your time while the enemy regroups
four times now you've survived assassination
today's one by the fraction of a hair
perhaps you think these miracles are endless
to me, Your Majesty, it's tempting fate

TALBOT It's a miracle God had this old man wrestle
the blade from your assassin's hands – you *are*
not going to die – your duty is to *God*
he won't forgive you if you murder her
against his will – and you can't wind it back

BURLEIGH We've heard your case for her defence before

TALBOT I'm not talking about justice – or the court
those arguments are out of place today
and in this turmoil – but listen to me
you're trembling now – and Mary Stuart *lives*
cut off her head, then everything gets worse
she's just a *problem* now: but when she's dead
her ghost, her story will chase you like a *wolf*
infecting hearts and minds – that hate her now
but once she's dead they'll rise up for revenge
the people in that crowd out there will *turn*
against you and your throne – they'll pity her
she won't be Catholic or their enemy then –
but just the victim of a tyrant Queen
a martyr – and you'll see how fast things change
travel through London when she's lost her head
wait for the jubilant crowds to greet you then
I know Lord Burleigh thirsts for Mary's blood
I know the crowds outside demand her death

322

and in your heart, there's part of *you* desires
to sign that paper, bring this to an end,
but Majesty, here's something else I know:
your people will desert you if you do
you'll push things past the limit: no one's head
is safe if Mary Stuart loses hers.

ELIZABETH   Talbot, you saved my life today. You know,
I wish you'd let me die. All this would *end.*
The blame, doubt, fear, morality – would stop
I would be lying, softening into earth.
Let's bring this to a head – and make it mine.
I'm tired of being Queen. I'm tired of life.
If how it has to be is: lose one queen
so one can live – and that's the only course
then – *please* – let me give in, collapse and grant
the crowds their wish, hand them the crown – oh God,
God is my witness: I have *only* lived
to serve the English people – but Mary Stuart
she offers them the hope of happier days
a younger queen – a better life – they can *have* her.
I'll leave the throne – live out in solitude
look up and see my England's soft green woods
as I did when I was young, and where I found
you see – now, I remember that – I found
the sort of deeper greatness in myself
that doesn't need a crown. I was not born
to be a queen – I'm not *not royal*
I have a heart – I'm soft – and and I have
I have ruled happily in happy times
but now? the first hard test: I'm powerless
weak

,

BURLEIGH   For *God's sake* – these unroyal words
I cannot tolerate them from your mouth
You say you love your people. Act for them.
If you don't serve them now, their lives are lost
Without you to protect them, what comes next?

The Catholic faith restored across your land
raping your subjects' souls – this is no time
for weakness or self pity: Majesty
England's immortal soul is in your hand
each one of them depends on your resolve
everything hangs on what you choose to do
Lord Talbot saved your life – now you save theirs

ELIZABETH   Give me some time alone. No more advice
no counsel on the earth can help me now
I'll ask the higher monarch for his guidance.
Leave.

(To DAVISON.)   You – wait outside.

They all leave.

*As TALBOT exits, he looks pointedly at her – and then goes. ELIZABETH
is on her own. MARY is there too, but in ELIZABETH's thought.*

To serve the people is to be a slave.
I'm tired of flattering them, when – honestly –
I hate them. Really hate them. I have to respect
their unrefined opinions, their approval
and satisfy a fickle population:
the crown is just a prison cell with jewels.
There's only one way you can be a king:
it's having freedom to follow *your* will
without needing permission from the world.
I just want to be free and not tied up
You strive for justice, fairness, seeking balance
rejecting tyranny at every turn
then you look down – you've handcuffed your own wrists
But *have* I ruled like that from my free will?
even my virtues aren't really my *choice*:
they're things you have to be when you're a king.
Surrounded here by rings of enemies
public approval is the only thing
that keeps me on the throne – it's gone, I'm weak
and all the crowds have Mary in their hearts
while I'm reviled abroad – cursed by the Pope

the victim of this French false wedding trick
while Spain, sharpening its swords to slit my throat,
takes to the seas – meanwhile Queen Mary Stuart
sits in her cell, sits *smilingly*
sits waiting for history to hand her my crown
while I stand here alone – pulling my robes around me
to hide the shame that my claim to my throne
was stained by my own father – and my blood
my *birth* was shamefully laid bare as – as – *worth less*
and not fit for a queen. But *Mary Stuart*
my enemies claim her claim is sacrosanct
and so I am a woman on my own
naked against the world.
How can I ever truly wear the crown?

,

No – no – it *stops* – this terror has to end.
Your head will fall. This poison that infects
my life, my joy, my hope, my happiness
snatching my lovers – and my marriage plans
and beating through my reign, my time, my sleep –
and every single evil in my life –
has one hard, hated name: Mary Stuart
and once she is a corpse, I will be free
free and pure and clear as mountain air –

,

The way she looked at me. Like I was [nothing] –
There is a better weapon in my hand.
I use it and you die. You are no more.

ELIZABETH signs her name on the death warrant.

You worthless whore, you said I was a bastard?
I'll stop being a bastard when you're dead
and any doubt about my claim is gone
it's split in two as easily as your neck,
and blotted out as your head rolls in blood.
With no pretender left, I will be royal

by blood, by birth – and born to majesty

,

Davison –

DAVISON enters.

Where are the rest of them?

DAVISON   They've gone
to calm the crowds. Lord Talbot went out first:
they screamed and cheered that he had saved your life.

ELIZABETH   They change their mind with every breeze that blows,
it's fatal to depend on them.

As if that was all she wanted, she dismisses DAVISON.

Dismissed.
And take this paper with you –

DAVISON looks at the paper – is visibly shocked – this is huge. He's hesitant, young, it's difficult for him to speak to the Queen without a massive amount of anxiety.

DAVISON   This is [signed] – your Majesty,
You have decided?

ELIZABETH   They told me to sign,
I signed. A piece of paper can't *decide.*
A name can't kill.

DAVISON   Your name, your Majesty
upon this piece of paper, *does* decide
and kill – this is an execution warrant
if you've signed this, then Mary Stuart dies
your men will go to Fotheringay at once
they will behead her now – before the dawn
her life is over once this leaves the room

ELIZABETH   God has placed something crucial in your hands
make sure you hear His wisdom. Do your duty.

She is about to leave the room.

DAVISON   No – your Majesty – don't leave – I'm sorry –
          I'm not sure what you're asking me to do
          can I be clear – you put this in my hands
          in order that its process will begin?

ELIZABETH I'm sure you're wise enough to work that out

          DAVISON talks quickly – he's terrified.

DAVISON   I'm not – no – please don't put this on my wisdom
          God forbid! I serve you – and obey your will
          and if I make a small mistake, she dies
          that's regicide – a huge catastrophe
          I'm just your instrument in this great cause
          just give me your instruction – in two words –
          what should I do with this death warrant?

ELIZABETH Its name makes that quite clear –

DAVISON   So you want execution carried out?

ELIZABETH My flesh crawls at that thought – I didn't say that

DAVISON   So I should just hold onto it?

ELIZABETH   If you do
          you'll face the consequences

DAVISON   I – ? For God's sake!
          Just give me your instruction – what do you want?

ELIZABETH I want to be alone. And I don't want
          to discuss this matter any more with you
          I want this finished now.

DAVISON   *Please* – one word
          tell me *exactly* what to do with this

ELIZABETH I've told you that already. You're dismissed.

DAVISON   You haven't told me anything? You've said
          nothing – Your Majesty, remember that –

ELIZABETH This is insufferable

DAVISON   Have pity on me
                I'm new to this, I – I don't understand
                the words or ways of court – I beg you, please
                take back this paper! Take it from my hands!
                It's white-hot flame – I do not wish to serve
                your Majesty in this –

ELIZABETH   Just do your duty.

ELIZABETH leaves. DAVISON tearful, perhaps.

DAVISON   I don't know what that is.

BURLEIGH re-enters. DAVISON is terrified of him anyway.

                        I'm sorry, sir, I must
                resign my office – I'm not cut out for this

BURLEIGH   I thought the Queen had summoned you inside?

DAVISON   She's angry – and she left

BURLEIGH   Where is the warrant?

DAVISON   It's here – she signed it – but she wouldn't / say –

BURLEIGH   It's signed? – then hand it over

DAVISON   No – I can't

BURLEIGH   What?

DAVISON   I have not had the order from the Queen

BURLEIGH   She signed it. That's an order. Give me it

DAVISON   I am to execute it – but hold onto it – and
                not execute it – I don't know what to do
                My life is [over] – *this decision can't be mine*

BURLEIGH   We execute it. Now. There isn't time.

BURLEIGH snatches the warrant from DAVISON's hands and exits.

ACT FIVE

The same room as ACT ONE. We've come full circle. The quiet atmosphere of a funeral – hanging in time. Death is present.

MELVIL enters: elderly, reliable, Scottish.

MELVIL	Ah, Hanna Kennedy, we meet again
KENNEDY	Are you – Melvil! I don't believe you're here after this long, long, painful separation
MELVIL	Our reunion is a pretty painful one –
KENNEDY	Oh – then, you've come –
MELVIL	to say goodbye.
KENNEDY	And only now, the day they take her life, they grant permission she can see her friends. So much has happened, Melvil – but we two can share our stories on another day I didn't want to live this long –
MELVIL	*(Gently.)* Let's not [make this worse] How is the Queen?
KENNEDY	Composed. And beautiful. She doesn't seem to mourn her life at all.
MELVIL	She is at peace with what is happening?
KENNEDY	You don't let go of living gradually it's one split-second change: it's sudden. Then the mortal world's behind you, and the rest is all eternal. She gave herself to God. And not a word of fear has passed her lips. She only wept when she heard Mortimer had lost his life (and fighting for her cause) she saw his uncle's tears, and wept herself.
MELVIL	Where is she now?

329

KENNEDY   She prayed most of the night
              sat quietly alone, drew up her will
              and she wrote letters – now she's fast asleep.

Gradually more women arrive, and sit waiting.

MELVIL   Is someone with her?

KENNEDY   Margaret is in there –
              more people have arrived throughout the night.
              It's said they'll set her secretaries free
              the moment she is [dead] –
              And every thing they took – every last jewel
              they've brought them back intact.

MELVIL   Oh these days, these days

Enter MARGARET.

KENNEDY   How is the Queen? Is she awake?

MARGARET   She's dressed.
              She's coming in a moment. Just to say
              she hasn't eaten anything.

KENNEDY nods – sees ALIX about to enter –

MELVIL   She's bringing me the wine.

ALIX, another girl, enters with a single cup of wine, but is weeping –

KENNEDY   Alix? What's wrong?

ALIX   They've built the stage
              I saw it – I was walking past the hall –
              black cloth is thickly hanging down the walls
              a huge dark platform rising from the floor
              a hard block in the centre and a cushion
              and a glinting pearl-grey axe – it's full, the hall
              there's people pushing all around the stage
              waiting –

MELVIL   Shh-shh – she's coming

330

*MARY enters. She is magnificently dressed. She makes an impression
on everyone as she arrives among them – things fall quiet. This is star
quality, pure and simple – and someone who is about to die.*

MARY   Why are we crying? We should all rejoice
                rejoice because our grief is at an end
                my chains all come apart, the prison gates
                lift up – and my pure, joyous soul soars free
                for ever, this time. There's no need to weep.
                We could have wept when under lock and key
                and made to suffer what no queen should suffer
                but now Death is a friend, holds out his hand
                covers my shame with inky wings and offers
                peace. I feel the crown, back on my head.
                The final moment lifts a human up
                no matter who they are or what they've done.
                Is that you, Melvil? Don't kneel down – stand up!
                I'm so happy to see you here – to know
                that you will tell my story once I'm gone,
                a Catholic to witness my last hour.
                But tell me first – what's happened to you all
                since they decided I should be alone?

MELVIL   No – nothing bad has happened – just my rage
                at being so powerless to help your Majesty.

MARY   And how is Didier, my dear old chamberlain?
                He cannot still be with us –

MELVIL   He's alive –
                he's still [alive] –

                '

MARY   If only I could hold my family
                embrace them one last time, instead
                I'll die with strangers – circling crowds
                and only your tears shed for me. Melvil,
                I bless my Catholic family abroad
                I've written to them all, and to the Pope
                and to the King of France – all in my will

and every gift I give to them is filled
a thousandfold with thanks – however poor.
The King of France will keep you in his care
but please – for my sake – don't stay here in England
don't let them gloat and sing over you all
because you once served me – pack up your things
and quickly leave – today. I want you all to swear –

MELVIL   I swear it – on behalf of everyone

*People murmur assent, say 'yes'. The atmosphere is very teary – loving
but could break out into sobs at any moment.*

MARY   The few possessions I have left, I've shared
among you, if the Queen honours my will –
to my girls – my Alix, Gertrude, Margaret, Rosalind
I leave my pearls – and all my clothes
you're young, you will enjoy them. So, so young.
the clothes I'm wearing now are yours as well.
And Hanna, my faithful, beautiful Hanna
I know you don't want jewels or gold or anything
our memories are our jewels. But still –

MARY has a cloth.

I made you this. Made it for you myself.
My tears are in the stitches. And when it's time
you'll blindfold me with this – fold me into dark
your final service in a history
of matchless duty.

KENNEDY   I don't think I can bear it

MELVIL   Give me a final moment with the Queen

Everyone but MELVIL leaves.

MARY   I stand at the edge of eternity
all my affairs on earth are set in order
You know, I never understood the Protestant faith
setting our own belief above the world
as if the things we see are not God's work.

332

Humanity is a visible sign itself
we're God's celestial architecture – *here* [on Earth]
The russet of the autumn, and the rise
of some great shimmering butter-yellow tree
laughter in sharp blue eyes – a dragonfly:
all palaces, all signs, written by his hand.
I bid them – and this heavy earth – farewell
I know I go before the Highest Judge
I only wish my God had granted me
a final Catholic service, my last rites.
I'll die without the peace of my own Church.

MELVIL   God can create an altar anywhere –
and in this prison.

MELVIL looks at the cup of wine.

MARY   Do you mean – ? Yes – Melvil, yes you do
There is no priest here – but as our Lord said
when two of you are gathered in my name
there am I in the midst of you – Melvil!
what *makes* a priest? It is something *inside,*
and with that thing within, you are my priest
as I am still your queen, despite a world
that counts us merely as two mortal souls.
I'll make my last confession now – to you.

MELVIL   You say there's not a priest here – or a church
but God brings you another miracle.

MELVIL produces a Host [communion wafer] in a gold case.

I have received my holy orders – I am a priest
inside and outside. I bring this for you
from Rome – and blessed by the Holy Father,
Communion.

MARY   And once you were my servant. Now you are
the servant of a greater judge – and throne.
As you once knelt to me, I kneel to you
in gratitude. You've brought me happiness.
Thank you.

MARY kneels.

MELVIL   In the name of the Father, the Son
                 and the Holy Spirit. Amen.

MARY   Bless me Father, for I have sinned.

MELVIL   What sins weigh on your soul since the last time
                 you made confession to the God of truth?

MARY   My heart was full of jealous, vengeful hate.
                 I've prayed to God that He forgives my sins
                 when I could not forgive my enemy.

MELVIL   Do you repent this sin?

MARY   I do repent.

MELVIL   I'm listening, Mary –

MARY   It wasn't only hate
                 but love – impulsive, sinful love – my heart –
                 my heart was always drawn to poisonous men

MELVIL   Do you repent this sin?

MARY   I do repent
                 it was the hardest fight for me
                 to let that go. But now the knot's undone.

                 ,

                 I caused a murder once. My husband's death.
                 I gave myself in marriage to his murderer.
                 And though I did the penance for the sin
                 the guilt's still swarming over me – even here,
                 my last few minutes.

MELVIL   Do you have more to say?

MARY   That's everything. There's nothing else.

MELVIL   Take care
                 be sure that your confession is complete
                 leave *nothing* out, offer up every sin
                 you're near to God now. Seek forgiveness.

MARY	There's nothing I've concealed.

MELVIL   Mary, there is.
           The plots against the English Queen – inciting
           Babington and Parry to their deaths:
           you've not confessed the crimes you're dying for.

MARY   There's nothing I've concealed

MELVIL   So they were lies?
           Your secretaries lied on oath?

MARY   Their judge is God
           I've told the truth. Those crimes were not my crimes.
           I'm ready for eternity – the hand of the clock
           cuts swiftly through my final minutes – and
           I have made my full confession.

MELVIL   You're going to the scaffold innocent?

MARY   This is my penance for my early life.
           My early death redeems my early life.
           God's granting me atonement.

MELVIL   Then may God
           the King, the Father of Mercies,
           who through the death of Jesus Christ Our Lord
           grant you forgiveness – that your frailty
           may not pursue your soul as it finds rest.
           May He pardon your sins.

MARY   Amen. Amen.

MELVIL sees BURLEIGH standing at the door.

The ritual – which would have come to full communion – is interrupted: the cup of wine and the host wait, vulnerable, to one side.

PAULET enters. HANNA and the GIRLS come in, slightly stricken – it's happening now, it seems. The grief, the horror of what is about to happen is unbearable.

BURLEIGH   Lady Stuart, I have come here to confirm
           your last commands.

MARY	Lord Burleigh, thank you. My will contains my wishes – Lord Paulet you have the document. Please follow it.
PAULET	I will. I swear to you.
MARY	I ask the Queen to let my people leave England unharmed. And grant me here my last communion.
BURLEIGH	The Queen will grant you both of these requests.
MARY	And will the Queen allow me burial on consecrated ground?
BURLEIGH	That cannot be.
MARY	Then let my Hanna take my heart with her, and bury it, where it has always been – in France.
BURLEIGH	It shall be done.
MARY	Paulet – come here give me your hand. I'm sorry for your grief whatever part I played – unknowingly in your poor nephew's death, forgive me. They couldn't break your goodness. Please: I beg don't hate the memory of me.
PAULET	My lady, God be with you. Go in peace.

One by one, MARY hugs her girls and kisses them –

MARY	My girls, it's time. Come here. Our last goodbyes. Margaret, your lips are warm! Be kind. Farewell. Gertrude, goodbye. Don't work too hard, my love. There's time. For all of you – there's so much time. My Alix – trust that brain, and trust yourself. And Rosalind, sweet heart, you'll find the man the husband that you're dreaming of – you're going to be loved. I know that's true. My girls, look up! Material things – on earth

they're traps. Your Queen fell into them. Beware.
No more, now. Girls – *look up!*
They can write that I was hated, but I know
I can call myself loved. I was loved.

LEICESTER has entered, too. Perhaps ELIZABETH too – though she's not literally in the room with everyone else.

BURLEIGH   Do you have / any other –

MARY looks at ELIZABETH.

MARY   Lord Burleigh, tell the Queen I offered my love,
that I was sorry for my violence yesterday
and loved her as a sister – and my heart
in every tiny fibre of its beat
forgave her.
May her reign be a long and happy one.
I wish her luck. In the end, we were the same.

MELVIL has picked up the wine and the host, perhaps.

BURLEIGH   The Dean of our religion waits outside
if you'll allow, he'll bring your soul to God.

MARY   We must be that we are.

A sense now of things coming through their final motions before the finish. History in the making. MARY and HANNA and the WOMEN receive communion from MELVIL, who delivers the service in Latin (if text is needed). MARY is dressed in a simple, clean garment, blessed, and stands barefoot.

MARY   It's come: the time to go. Hanna, my love
walk with me as I take my final steps

BURLEIGH   That's not been authorised

MARY   Would you refuse?
My sister would not let the hands of men
be on my body as I die –

BURLEIGH   The women will *cry*

337

MARY   These women will not cry. I promise, sir,
              you underestimate the female sex.
              I *guarantee* you Hanna will not cry.
              Do not divide me from my own true nurse
              she held me as I came into the world
              you'll let her hold me as I leave it

PAULET   My lord, allow it

BURLEIGH   Very well

MARY   Now
              I have nothing more in the world. My God,
              as you opened your arms upon the cross
              open them to me

*It's at this moment that she and LEICESTER catch sight of each other.
As she takes those final steps, perhaps there is a sudden, queasy moment
of panic in MARY, she falters, perhaps almost faints and LEICESTER
instinctively catches her. And now the two of them are together.*

MARY looks at LEICESTER.

              You kept your word. You said you'd get me out
              I'm leaving now.

He stands as though annihilated. She speaks in a mild tone.

              It wasn't just my freedom that I wished
              to give to you – I wished you'd make it *worth*
              the years of misery – held up by your love
              I thought we might create a whole new life.
              And now, as the earth falls away from me
              and in the brightening air, I am a spirit,
              now I can tell you – without any shame,
              you conquered me. You really conquered me.
              Leicester. Goodbye. Live happy, if you can.
              You made love to two queens. You made your choice
              you chose the proud heart, not the loving one.
              Kneel down before Elizabeth. I hope
              the loss of me transforms into a profit
              and not a greater loss. For me, on earth
              there's nothing more.

LEICESTER struggles to control himself. He can't speak. The other men look at him: MARY has just confirmed him as part of a plot against ELIZABETH. She's left him no choice but to disappear. Perhaps we hear the noise of the crowds.

MARY walks on, hand in hand with KENNEDY, to her execution.

ELIZABETH is alone. Perhaps a clock ticks somewhere.

,

ELIZABETH   Still no one here. No message. Is it day?
Does the sun still carve its circle in the sky?
This waiting is a prison. Is it *done*?
The day is just a flash inside the night.
The arrow has been shot – it curves in flight
it hits the target soon – already – now
and nothing brings it back.

Enter KENT.

Send Davison in. You're dismissed.

Exit KENT.

I feel such terror I can hardly breathe.
But who can say I did it?
I want to cry for her. I won't know how
to stop –

Enter TALBOT, with urgency.

TALBOT   My Queen, I'm sorry to be here so late
but there's important news –

ELIZABETH   Go on, my lord

TALBOT   I've had an anxious heart tonight, your Majesty
so worried for your reputation
given the Stuart case – and so I went
to see again the witnesses in the Tower
the secretaries that testified against
the Queen, I'm sorry, against Mary Stuart.
I got there – and my God – they're terrified:

they'd heard the rumour Mary was to die
and fearing heaven's justice more than ours
confessed to me their testimony was *false*.
Those letters were not dictated by the Stuart
the central evidence in Mary's trial
was wrong.

ELIZABETH   They're mad – can they be *trusted*?

TALBOT   Do nothing hastily. We re-open it
examine them again, give her the trial
she should have had before – by English law.

ELIZABETH   We will take your advice. Re-open it.
Though more for your own peace of mind
than fearing reckless judgement from my lords.
There is still time. We must remove all doubt.

Enter DAVISON. KENT waits by the door.

Where is the warrant I left in your hands?

DAVISON   The warrant?

ELIZABETH   The one I gave you yesterday to keep

DAVISON   To keep?

ELIZABETH   I already have a voice. I don't need two.
The people called for me to sign the thing
I did, gave it to you to buy some time
but you know this – and now I want it back.

TALBOT   Davison, we can't lose any time
the legal process has to be re-opened

DAVISON   Re-open?

ELIZABETH   Come *on*. Where is the warrant?

DAVISON   I'm dead.

ELIZABETH   *(Fast.)* Don't tell me that / you –

DAVISON   I don't have it.

340

ELIZABETH How is that [possible]? What?

TALBOT   Christ in Heaven!

DAVISON   It is in Burleigh's hands – since yesterday.

ELIZABETH I ordered you to keep it

DAVISON   You did *not* / order me to

ELIZABETH Am I a liar, then? So when did I
                    tell you to give the death warrant to Burleigh?

DAVISON   Not in so many words, Your Majesty, but –

ELIZABETH *'BUT'?* How dare you interpret my words.
                    Lord Talbot, do you see how my royal name
                    has been abused

TALBOT   Your Majesty, if he has
                    without your knowledge, killed a royal queen
                    he must face formal judgement – if it's done,
                    your legacy, your history – are mud.

            Enter BURLEIGH.

BURLEIGH   Long live the Queen – and may your enemies
                    all perish as your enemy has today.
                    The Queen of Scots is dead.

                    ʼ

ELIZABETH And did I authorise Queen Mary's death?

BURLEIGH   I had the death warrant from Davison

ELIZABETH Did he give you the warrant in *my* name?

BURLEIGH   No, he didn't.

ELIZABETH   But you thought that you would
                    without an order, execute a queen?
                    Of course, she had been sentenced, and the world
                    cannot claim that her death was not decreed
                    but *we know* it was not decreed *by me.*

We have no choice – Burleigh, we banish you
from court – and from our sight. Make no reply.
Dismissed.

BURLEIGH exits. She addresses DAVISON.

Your sentence must be equal to your crime.
You were my secretary. You broke my trust.
For grossly overstepping your authority
you lose your life. They will take you to the Tower.

DAVISON exits. Pale.

,

I should have listened to you from the start,
Lord Talbot, you're the only man I trust
I need you now: my councillor – my friend –

TALBOT   I'm not sure that you'll like my council: it's
'don't banish your best friends'. Honestly, they tried
to serve Your Majesty – as I have, for twelve years
but now you have to set me free – I'm old
too old to bend to these new policies.
Your Majesty, I must resign my office –

ELIZABETH   You cannot leave me now. You saved my life –

TALBOT   Not where it counts. I have saved very little,
I didn't save your better part, my love.
Live long, live happily. Your enemy is dead.
There's nothing more to be afraid of, now.

Exit TALBOT. The room seems huge, empty.

KENT enters.

ELIZABETH   Send in the Earl of Leicester

KENT   Your Majesty
the Earl of Leicester begs to be excused,
he's on a ship to France.

,

342

ELIZABETH overcomes herself. Calm. Composed.

She has never felt more profoundly terrified.

The play ends.

THE WILD DUCK

I can take any empty space and call it a bare stage. A man walks across this empty space whilst someone else is watching him, and this is all that is needed for an act of theatre to be engaged.

Peter Brook, *The Empty Space*

Each partner strives to find in the other, or induces the other to become, the very embodiment of the other whose co-operation is required as a complement of the particular identity he feels compelled to sustain.

R.D. Laing, *The Self and Others*

Acknowledgements

My greatest debt is to the actors and creative team of the original production, whose ideas, instincts and input quite literally make the show, and to all of whom I am genuinely grateful.

This sort of work would scarcely be possible without the support and backing of its originating theatre – on multiple levels, I'm thankful to my whole team at the Almeida, who, five years in, are really my Almeida family – and on this one, as on so many before, I owe big thanks to Rupert Goold, Lucy Pattison, Denise Wood, Emma Pritchard, Rebecca Frecknall and Stephanie Bain.

And on top of that, thanks to everyone else who read the play or watched a performance and gave suggestions or support – significantly: Rachel Taylor, Helena Clark, Stephen Grosz, David Hare, Helen Lewis, Josh Higgott, Jon Sedmak, Laura Marling, Andrew Scott, Ben Naylor, Ilinca Radulian, Denzel Wesley-Sanderson and Zara Tempest-Walters.

RI, October 2018

This adaptation was commissed by and originally produced at the Almeida, where it had its first performance on 15th October, 2018.

Cast (in alphabetical order)

Charles Woods	Nicholas Day
Hedwig Ekdal	Grace Doherty
Francis Ekdal	Nicholas Farrell
Anna Sowerby	Andrea Hall
Gregory Woods	Kevin Harvey
James Ekdal	Edward Hogg
Gina Ekdal	Lyndsey Marshal
Hedwig Ekdal	Clara Read
John Relling	Rick Warden

Creative Team

Direction	Robert Icke
Design	Bunny Christie
Light	Elliot Griggs
Sound	Tom Gibbons
Casting	Julia Horan CDG
Costume Supervision	Claire Wardroper
Fight Direction	Kevin McCurdy
Assistant Direction	Denzel Westley-Sanderson
Design Assistant	Verity Sadler
Photography	Manuel Harlan
Company Stage Manager	Claire Sibley
Deputy Stage Manager	Adam Cox
Assistant Stage Manager	Beth Cotton

Characters

GREGORY WOODS

CHARLES WOODS, father of GREGORY

GINA EKDAL

HEDWIG EKDAL, her daughter, nearly 13

JAMES EKDAL, husband of GINA

FRANCIS EKDAL, father of JAMES

ANNA SOWERBY

JOHN RELLING

A note on the text

A forward slash (/) marks the point of interruption of overlapping dialogue.

A comma on a separate line (,) indicates a pause, a rest, a silence, an upbeat or a lift. Length and intensity are context dependent.

Square brackets [like this] indicates words which are part of the intention of the line but which are not spoken aloud. They are also used to indicate information that will need to be update to reflect the time of the present performance.

This text went to press before the production opened and so may differ slightly from what was performed. But let's not worry too much about that.

[ACT ONE]

Bare stage. Emptiness.

As the evening progresses, the stage will move, piece by piece, towards a kind of naturalism – a subtle and unobtrusive progression towards the final image of the Ekdals' home. Think of it like a photograph developing. The actors start in what feel like rehearsal clothes, and move slowly – item by item – into costume.

The lights are bright. As the evening progresses they will get darker and darker.

The actor playing GREGORY comes out and waits for the audience to fall silent. When they do, he switches on a handheld microphone (or just speaks to them directly if you prefer: the aim is the difference between this mode of speech and normal dialogue). When characters are speaking into a mic, their name is followed by (m) – and they are speaking to the audience. Ideally, the microphones seem objective, like 'the truth'. To start with at least.

GREGORY (m)   The devices – this is just a reminder [to turn them off]. Even if you think you've already done it, that feeling certain – that feeling could be wrong. We don't need intrusions; the world can wait for a few hours. Anyway, it's all lies.

The play has started.

Hello.

In 1884, Henrik Ibsen wrote *The Wild Duck*. People say they want to see the real version, true to Ibsen, but that version is in Norwegian – actually, a sort of out-dated Danish-Norwegian, so even if we could do it, you very likely wouldn't understand it. We would say words you couldn't understand and ones we can't mean. And saying things you don't mean – well, there's a word for that, and it's 'lying'. I mean, to tell the story like that would be a sort of lie. Going through the motions. The real thing buried somewhere underneath.

In the beginning one person would have stood before you and told the story. Told the truth, I suppose – it's funny, we *tell* the truth, don't we, we don't say it, we *tell* it, it's a tale, it has to be – carefully packaged.

And then – we started to pretend. Tell you we aren't who we are and the stage is a sky or a battlefield or a funfair. We started to lie. And the illusion bit in, the edges blurred and you forgot about truths and instead you only wanted to make your time go by, take a break from thinking about how disappointing everything is these days, how it's all lies. But even if you heap lies on top of truth, it waits underneath.

So this is a true story

In 1884, Henrik Ibsen wrote *The Wild Duck*. He was a white man. He was fifty-six years old. He was Norwegian. He had a strict routine that he stuck to until he died. He's dead now. As a much younger man, he had fathered an illegitimate child on a young girl. When he was a child, his father was declared bankrupt. He had a sister called Hedvig. There are more facts, but we'd be here all night, and anyway, probably none of them are relevant –

Anyway. My character, Gregory Woods, on his first day home – where he was brought up, I mean, not [home] – he's decided to come back. It's the first time he's been back for several years. And, as the afternoon is deep and the light is starting to turn creamy, he pauses outside a familiar house, an imposing, detached townhouse, buttons his top button, puts on a white bow tie, slides the familiar, heavy gate aside, and in his jet-black shoes, crunches his way up the drive –

This story starts in the entrance hall of a dinner party.

JAMES   Gregers? My god, you look exactly the same –

JAMES takes the microphone from GREGORY

JAMES (m)   This is a lie.

GREGORY   And you look *incredible* –

(m)   James Ekdal and Gregory Woods – my character – were friends at school but now, this evening is the first time they have set eyes on each other for over fifteen years.

JAMES addresses a member of the audience.

JAMES (m)   I'm sorry to bother you, but I couldn't just borrow your jacket, could I? I won't damage it, you'll get it back – they're insured here (I hope). Thank you.

JAMES borrows a coat or a jacket from the audience.

Imagine this jacket is a deep, bottle green. It's clean, it's well-made, but its appearance this evening, right now, worn by my character, James Ekdal, seems – *eccentric.*

The invitation said 'white tie'. James had thought that white tie meant any suit worn with a white tie. His father had – his father had told him – sorry – he'd borrowed his father's dress suit. As the other guests arrived in black suits, white shirts – in white tie – James could only see one colour. Green.

GREGORY   You really do look incredible.

Is there something homoerotic about GREGORY's gaze on JAMES? Maybe.

JAMES   Don't. I'm embarrassed, actually – I hadn't realised

He gestures around him.

GREGORY   What?

JAMES   This place: it's like a royal palace.

GREGORY   But you've been here before?

JAMES   No – [why would I have been?]

GREGORY   But – *sorry* –

               given the – your relationship with my father
               –

JAMES   Are you sure he invited me tonight?

GREGORY   [Yes] – You're on the seating plan – but –
               hang on

               Sorry

	I've not *spoken* to him much, or at all, really, but he *writes* to me, usually when there's something with the company, but he implied he'd been supporting you –
JAMES	Oh, he *has*, he absolutely has, he's been so generous – since, what happened to my father – you know [about that]
GREGORY	*(Quickly.)* Yes – of course

,

JAMES (m)	Francis Ekdal – my father – had been a partner in Woods and Son and it was his signature on the company's financial accounts when around the world, the bubbles burst and the markets sank. And to tell you the briefest version of the story, it turned out that key investments hadn't been registered – and so didn't officially exist. The company's stock dropped two thirds of its value. People lost their savings. And Francis Ekdal was tried, found guilty, served with a fine he would never live long enough to pay, and a ten-year, minimum security prison term for investment fraud.
GREGORY	How is he, your dad? Do you see much of him?
JAMES	Lives with us, now. And he's all right. He's – all right.
(m)	He's never been the same.
	But let's not talk about him, anyway, it's – it's not, the [best topic of conversation]

	How are *you*? Where have you been all this time?
GREGORY	Oh, you know, here and there. Seeking higher ground. Thinking, mainly.
JAMES	And you've been happy?
GREGORY	Lonely. I've been lonely. You know, I thought I saw him before – your father –
JAMES	Here? No.
GREGORY	I'm *sure* it was
JAMES	No, it must have been someone else, it couldn't have been him
GREGORY	We should go in.

JAMES a bit jumpy, suddenly –

JAMES	Go in?
GREGORY	For dinner? I know it's early but for some reason they want to eat while it's light –
JAMES	Yes. You know, actually I had a list of names. Of the guests. To have them fresh in the mind. There's only twelve, well, you and your father are both Woods, and then me, so there's only nine, but I've gone and left it in the bathroom, I'll just be a minute – back in one minute –

JAMES exits.

As GREGORY picks up the mic to talk to the audience – enter FRANCIS. He's an elderly man, kindly but absent. He might be drunk. He behaves as if he's interrupted the scene – as if the actor has come out at the wrong moment. Terrified by the presence of the audience, he looks straight at them.

FRANCIS   I'm sorry –

                   ,

                   you've started, haven't you?

GREGORY is horrified – open-mouthed – to see FRANCIS.

GREGORY   The party? Yes – they've just gone in for
                   dinner –

FRANCIS   I had the wrong sheets. I had the wrong
                   pages. I pick them up here – it's easier – but
                   I wanted to get them before it started and
                   get back home. I really didn't want to be
                   here when all the people were here.

GREGORY is shocked to see FRANCIS like this.

GREGORY   Francis? Don't worry – I want to help you

FRANCIS   No, my friend, but thank you –

GREGORY   I'm Gregory. Charles' son.

                   You don't remember me.

FRANCIS looks at GREGORY. Nothing.

FRANCIS   I don't at all.

                   ,

GREGORY   Never mind.

FRANCIS   Never mind, never mind –

JAMES comes back on – sees FRANCIS, suddenly there's a scene –

359

JAMES	No no *NO* – what the fuck are you doing here? We *had* this conversation. Can you just *go home* – it's *humiliating* –
FRANCIS	Yes – ah – very sorry –

FRANCIS heads for the exit.

GREGORY	He can stay for / dinner if you like –
FRANCIS	No – can't be seen to / do that
JAMES	Can YOU JUST GO HOME –

FRANCIS has gone.

Sorry.

GREGORY	I knew it was him.
JAMES	Can we just take a breather out here for a minute before we go in?

'

I hate seeing him like this.

You don't mind if I smoke, do you?

GREGORY	I'm not sure you can in here – and anyway, it's bad for you –
JAMES	Well, they *say* that –
GREGORY	You're upset.
JAMES	Am I?

Not with you. With you, honestly, I'm just relieved there's no hard feelings –

GREGORY	Hard feelings? About what?

JAMES	No, I totally understand – when what happened happened, I had to stand up for my dad, and you had to stand up for yours –
GREGORY	But why would I hold that against you?
JAMES	It's okay – he *told* me not to contact you: I wanted to write and apologise – for what dad had done, to try and make amends, but Mr Woods – I mean, your dad said there would be no point-- which I understood.
GREGORY	Ah.

He may have been right.

I'm still [surprised] – you've never been here before. So does he come to your place? |
JAMES	No. You're very interested (!) in [all of this] – no – Anna does sometimes. His [what's the word?] *friend*. She's a good woman, I think.
GREGORY	So he supports you but – there's a distance –
JAMES	There's a mutual respect, I think. I go to the office. You know, let him know how the business is coming along.
GREGORY	Photography, right?
JAMES	Exactly. Specialists in photographic film.
GREGORY	Film?
JAMES	Your dad said it: find a unique angle. Everyone's carrying a camera these days – but they do digital, and we do film. The dying part of the living art. I mean, we do digital as well –

GREGORY   I didn't even realise you could – that you
were a photographer –

JAMES   Well, I wasn't –

GREGORY   I thought you were going to study / at least,
my [memory was...]

JAMES   I dropped out – when everything happened,
I dropped out to have time to work on Dad's
case, but there was never any way we were
going to stand against the tide, all the lawyers,
the press and everything, totally foregone
conclusion – *anyway*. We know what the
outcome of that was. And I wasn't in a good
way.

GREGORY   But my dad helped you set up – your
business –

JAMES   Yes. He's our principal investor. Of course,
we'll pay him back, as soon as we get it to
the next level, but he's – well, we couldn't
have done it without him.

GREGORY   Who's we?

JAMES   Oh – god – yes, I'm married now – of
course [you wouldn't know that] – and
actually, your father sorted that out too!
Gave us a gift of some money which allowed
us to actually do it. Our fairy godfather.

GREGORY   Wow.

But why?

Sorry – why would he do that?

JAMES   He'd only buried your mother the year
before. So I think he understood what it was

to be – wounded. We really do respect each other, him and me. And he knew Gina, of course, so he was doubly invested. I wanted you to be there, to be part of the wedding, I mean, but the case, and – well, he said / you were [out of contact] –

GREGORY   Gina –

JAMES   My wife –

JAMES enjoys GREGORY remembering this – waits for him to figure it out –

GREGORY   Gina. The same Gina who worked here – when my mum was ill?

JAMES   Exactly the same Gina.

                      ,

GREGORY   That's – amazing

JAMES   He's been generous, above and beyond the call of duty. He didn't forget the son of his old friend, when he knew our family was on the ropes.

GREGORY   I didn't think he had it in him.

GREGORY is almost disturbed by this view of his father. In his head, something's not right about it but he can't put his finger on what.

JAMES (m)   And then the sound of a dinner gong.

GREGORY   Well, given everything you've been through, you really do look wonderful –

JAMES   Do I? Thank god you can't see inside. But we keep going – and I have my eye on the future.

Then with a different kind of intimacy –

>Sometimes when I'm lying awake in the morning, staring up at the beams, I see them pushing his head down to take him out of the court. Pushing him down. But not forever.

GREGORY (m)   And scene –

The scene ends.

>Gregory Woods had been in the house for thirty minutes, and had had exactly one conversation – but everything was spinning. He put his head against the wall and tried to breathe.

JAMES (m)   Until the end of it, James Ekdal had barely noticed that the conversation was happening. He felt *out of place.* He felt unwelcome, he felt scared of being exposed – a feeling that's got its roots deep in class or wealth – and when you feel like that, it gets harder to focus, hard to see – because of the bell ringing behind your eyes.

GREGORY (m)   As course after course passed through, Gregory had the thought that the people at the table weren't enjoying themselves, but going through the motions of enjoying themselves. Their laughter flashed and faded quickly; their compliments fell flat.

>We go through the motions, don't we?
>We like being rocked because it simulates how we were in the womb. We're *not* in the womb. But it feels like it. That's how it works, we go through the motions, we

	pretend in our own lives, we spin around our memories, repeating and repeating our traumas. It's not real. Until one day we stop – we break the pattern.
JAMES (m)	Later – in the library, after dessert, a very large man with a very loud voice was trying to persuade James to do his party trick, 'recite a poem' or 'why don't you take our photograph?' He was smiling, but James felt small.
GREGORY (m)	Charles Woods, the father of Gregory Woods, laid out some rare bottles of wine on the table, dusty from the cellar, and looked straight at James. 1885, he said, or '89? The room fell quiet.
JAMES	Let's have the third one – the '89. Let's go strong. I've never actually had, uh, chamber tin –

And suddenly CHARLES WOODS is there, and we're into a scene:

CHARLES	*Chambertin.*
JAMES	I'm sorry?
CHARLES	The wine. Chamber tin. *Chambertin.* It's French.
JAMES	Sorry, yes, chamber tin – of course – well, the strongest of the three Chambertin-s it is. 18, 85 or 89, you said – so '89. Go for the top. I think. No?

A pause. Another faux pas. CHARLES isn't cruel here.

| CHARLES | 1889. They're vintages, those numbers: 1889 is the year the grapes were grown and |

harvested. The taste is really the difference
in time between the day it was bottled and
now; so the moment you choose to drink
it – to uncork it and let it meet the air – is
everything

JAMES (m)   And scene –

A few minutes later, James excused himself
and went to the bathroom and vomited.
After the bathroom, he let himself out and
walked the three miles home. Nobody
noticed that he'd gone.

GREGORY (m)   The stories we tell tell us. Who we are. And
old stories tell us truths about where we
came from. And – how we can change.

Gregory Woods stared at his father. He
seemed older, his face was harder – like a
leather map of cruelties past. The guests
had started to leave, the staff were clearing
glasses and closing curtains

The scene clicks into beginning.

CHARLES   Gregory, I wish you hadn't insisted on
having the Ekdal boy here tonight.

GREGORY   Why not?

CHARLES   Can't you count? Thirteen at the table.

GREGORY   So you don't believe in morals but you do
believe in *that*. And Francis Ekdal, your
colleague, your best man, wandering around
half-destitute and half demented – *you* were
his friend –

CHARLES	Yes. And I've paid the price for that friendship.
GREGORY	Your reputation took a knock: he went to prison.
CHARLES	Oh god – it went to trial. The evidence was clear, and so was the verdict.
GREGORY	That's the story, that's the illusion –
CHARLES	An acquittal means not guilty.
GREGORY	People in the street spat at him. He lost everything. He lost who he was. And who benefitted from that? The person who now had a majority share – *convenient*, that, somehow –
CHARLES	Gregory, you were *there*, then, you saw all the papers before / it went to court
GREGORY	Mum was ill. I couldn't think – I couldn't *see* that you were already spinning your webs –
CHARLES	I'm not sure how you think I could have influenced anything, if / that's –
GREGORY	The usual way. Your sort code and your account number.
CHARLES	I don't know why you're being so abrupt –
GREGORY	I am being *honest*. For the first time, perhaps. Honest.
CHARLES	Right. Are we done?
GREGORY (m)	It took a lot for Gregory Woods to resist his father. He'd known a confrontation would come, but now, here, he could only see how

imposing Charles was – how he felt like a man who was *right*.

You don't feel guilty, then?

CHARLES   When Francis Ekdal came out of prison, he was a broken man. I've arranged some work for him, I pay him a blasted sight more than it's worth, and, while trying to safeguard the reputation of the company, I do my bit for him –

GREGORY *(sarc)* Right –

CHARLES   It isn't cheap, you know?

GREGORY   And how much is setting up a photography studio?

CHARLES   I'm sorry?

GREGORY   How much did it cost to set up their business?

CHARLES   I don't understand why something I did out of kindness is interrogated as if it's a *crime*

GREGORY   Because it isn't kindness. Not really. It never is with you.

CHARLES   Okay. Everything's so simple, isn't it?

GREGORY   No. But some things are.

CHARLES   You've been happy enough to take my money. The company's money. You could have set something up on your own –

GREGORY   And what space is there left, Dad, what space did you leave for young people to come along and do something different, do something for themselves, without being son of Charles Woods, the 'son' of 'Woods & Son' – but let's keep on the scent – more than a decade ago, you wrote to me, on your headed paper, short letter, as usual, needing me to return some documents, my shareholding or something, I can't remember, but what I *do* remember is the casual, casual postscript: that 'the Ekdal son' was getting married.

CHARLES   I was trying to make a connection with you –

GREGORY   What you didn't see fit to mention was that he was marrying someone who worked for us, in this house, when Mum was alive –

'

CHARLES   Gina had long since left by then – and I didn't think she was your type, Greg, I didn't know you'd taken such an interest –

GREGORY   I hadn't. But someone had.

CHARLES   I don't follow –

GREGORY   *You.*

CHARLES   I'm not sure which particular rumours you're / focussing on

GREGORY   Dad. You can stop the lies because *my mother told me* before she passed away. Told me *everything*.

'

369

	You want to know why I went, you can think about / that –
CHARLES	And you're happy to accept her view of things? Her view of me?
GREGORY	Yes. Because she told me the trauma she suffered –
CHARLES	I'm sorry to burst your bubble but she didn't suffer – at least, no more than could be helped with her condition. And I can tell you, she had the very best available / care
GREGORY	Sort code. Account number. Same reason you married her.
CHARLES	And if you really wanted to talk to me about this, you could have done it *then*, rather than run for the hills when her body was still warm in the grave – and then file your complaint sixteen years later.
GREGORY	I didn't run for the hills – my mother died –
CHARLES	Greg, I don't want to argue. You up and vanish, not so much as a birthday card most years, and then, when the prodigal son returns, you want to dig up fights that finished years ago. Well I don't.
GREGORY	You in*sisted* I come back –
CHARLES	Well, you could have said no –
GREGORY	I thought you might be ill –
CHARLES	I am ill –

GREGORY doesn't believe this –

GREGORY   Are you? What do you really want? Why
            am I here?

CHARLES   You're here because I wanted to say to you
            that, if you were willing, I would hand over
            the company to you. It's already got your
            name on it.

GREGORY   Why would I take on something corrupt?

CHARLES   To remake it. To make it better. I can't do it
            in the same way anymore – it's time for new
            energy. I'm too old and my eyes are getting
            weak –

GREGORY   They always were weak

            ,

CHARLES   I know there's a lot of – mess – between us.
            History. I do know that. But I'm your father
            and I do / love you

GREGORY   What do you *want?*

CHARLES   I'm old, Gregory. I'm lonely – have been all
            my life. It'd be nice to have you around and
            involved. Nice to have a conversation. Nice
            to hand my son the thing I've spent my life
            creating.

GREGORY   You've got Anna.

CHARLES   I have. She's a wonder, quite frankly.

GREGORY   Then strap her down. Marry her.

CHARLES lowers his head. GREGORY has hit on the truth.

CHARLES   Would you be opposed to that?

GREGORY   Why would I care?

CHARLES   Because since we buried your mother /
             there's

GREGORY   I'm not a romantic.

CHARLES   Well. Thank you, whatever you are.

*A penny drops in GREGORY's mind. And it makes him angry, angry
enough to set events in motion –*

GREGORY   And that's it. That's why I'm here, isn't it?
             That's why the party. The estranged son
             returns, forgives the father, implicitly blesses
             the wedding – which is already planned?
             Of course it is. This was just a – *photo
             opportunity*. Happy families. And all those
             stories about Charles Woods – the ones
             about how the vicious bully hammered his
             first wife into her grave – well, they can't be
             true if the son's come back and giving it all
             his blessing.

CHARLES   God, the way you hate me –

GREGORY   I'm the only one who sees you.

CHARLES   But with your mother's eyes – and she didn't
             see things clearly.

GREGORY   So she made up the other women, did she?
             That was her fault, that you went whirling
             off with whoever caught your eye, big grin
             on your face – and then writing a cheque for
             the consequences –

CHARLES   Word for word. It's like hearing her speak.

GREGORY   So what my mother told me was a lie?

372

CHARLES	I don't need to be spoken to like this –
GREGORY	God, what you've *done* to people, Dad – [I don't know] how you sleep! So many lives you've shattered and pushed under the carpet – like chicken bones under your feet – and you think the whole thing's buried so far down that nothing can ever come back –
CHARLES	I don't know how to talk to you, Gregory –
GREGORY	I agree. You don't.
	,
CHARLES	I do have regrets. I do.
	But I think, if you're in my house, to treat me with respect / is hardly
GREGORY	I was thinking the same thing: I'm going to go.
CHARLES	Go?
GREGORY	Leave.
CHARLES	It's getting dark, Greg – you don't have to leave.
GREGORY	And yet – I'm leaving.
CHARLES	Don't end up lonely, Gregory.
GREGORY (m)	And *scene* –
	Seeing the truth can be a gradual process. But then there's the moment. The moment when you really *hear,* really understand, the lyrics of an old song; the moment when your eyes adjust to the darkness, or an old

story suddenly exposes its real meaning.
When the floor of an old system gives way.
In 1884, Henrik Ibsen wrote *The Wild Duck*.

[ACT TWO]

… but in fact, there are no breaks between the acts, they're just here to help organise rehearsals.

HEDWIG enters. She's twelve but she seems younger. GINA enters, starts to prepare. A black curtain starts to descend, lowering the height of the stage picture. GREGORY explains to us:

The top floor of a nineteenth-century house, converted into flats by someone long forgotten. It's three miles away from the house of Charles Woods, in one of those areas where people with aspirations pretend it's in a different, nearby, area when actually – it's in this one.

It isn't a palace, but it is a home. The ceiling hangs low. A bulb dangles from the roof, where once-white paint is cracking and stained – a wooden floor, an old sofa, a battered brown armchair, a record player, a work table – that have all seen better days.

GINA (m)   The Ekdals used to own the whole house, but a few years earlier, they sold it. The ground floor flat was privately rented, but they'd kept a lifetime lease on the first and second floors. But times got harder, the money from the sale ran out – and so the Ekdals had recently taken a practical decision – to move their lives up into the second floor, into their photography studio, and rent out their bedroom on the floor below.

> Gina Ekdal – my character – is staring at an old calculator and a series of receipts trying to make sense of where all the money went *this week.*

GINA   Heddy.

            Heddy.

            Are you reading?

HEDWIG   No. Yes.

GINA   Come on. Not this late. Do you remember how much we paid for Dad's butter?

HEDWIG   Three pounds twenty-nine.

GINA   Did we? The amount of butter we get through. Is there any left?

HEDWIG opens a butter dish. It's empty.

HEDWIG   Not much.

GINA   And sausages and beer and cheese. That comes to …

She does the calculation.

            A lot of money.

HEDWIG   But we've saved some by us not having dinner this evening because we weren't hungry.

GINA   That's true. And those photographs sold.

HEDWIG   Yes that really is good isn't it?

GINA   Mmmhmm

            ,

HEDWIG	I wonder what Daddy's doing now.
GINA	Mmmhmm
HEDWIG	Talking probably. Or maybe he's eating. No, I think he's talking.
GINA	Mmmhmm
HEDWIG	He'll be talking to Mr Woods.

GINA, not obviously, looks up.

| GINA | Maybe |

FRANCIS comes in.

	You're late back.
FRANCIS	They'd shut the back door, the buggers, but nevertheless, I got in and picked up another big batch of receipts. At least a week's worth.
GINA	I could just go to the office and pick them up for you –
FRANCIS	No, no, good to get out – Corporal Ekdal, reporting for inspection, lieutenant.
HEDWIG	Very good, corporal – all in order.
FRANCIS	Do I need to patrol the forest, sir?
HEDWIG	Everyone asleep up there, corporal
FRANCIS	Very good, lieutenant. Permission to retire for the night?
HEDWIG	Permission granted. Stand down, corporal.
FRANCIS	Permission to kiss the lieutenant on the head?
HEDWIG	Permission granted.

They salute. As he heads off to bed –

GINA   There's a bottle in your pocket, corporal.

              ,

FRANCIS   Is there?

              Deal with that problem later, I will, colonel.

There isn't a bottle – at least, not that we can see. Off he goes.

HEDWIG   Does Granddad get paid for his work?

GINA   Yes, he does, but – don't tell your dad.

HEDWIG   What do you think Daddy's doing *now*?

GINA   I don't know, sweetheart –

HEDWIG   Do you think he's eating delicious food?
              Like a – pie. Or cheese. Or chocolate
              mousse.

GINA   Maybe he is. Are you hungry?

HEDWIG   No.

GINA   Really?

HEDWIG   No –

              Anyway Daddy promised he'd bring a treat
              back for me.

GINA   You can still eat something –

HEDWIG   But I don't want to be full because we don't
              know what the treat *is*. Do you think he'll be
              in a good mood?

GINA   Maybe. Though I wish someone had asked
              about the room.

HEDWIG	Mm.
	This is worrying.
	,
	But – he'll be in a good mood tonight anyway because he's had that dinner and because Grandad's happy so that's two things – and even if we had got someone to rent the bedroom it'd be a waste of good news on a night when he'll already be in a good mood so it's better as it is. I think.

FRANCIS comes back in.

GINA	Where's he going?
HEDWIG	Sink.
GINA (m)	When the Ekdals had moved into the photography studio on the top floor they couldn't afford to put in a kitchen. So a small work sink had to suffice – but if you needed the kitchen, or indeed the bathroom, it was a trip down a flight of stairs to the floor they used to live on.

FRANCIS is caught, slightly shamefaced – with a whisky glass.

FRANCIS	Had to get this –

He waves a pair of glasses as he scarpers.

GINA	Where do you think he gets the money from?
HEDWIG	For his drink? Isn't it from his work?
GINA	No, they send that straight to me –

HEDWIG	I dunno. Maybe someone gives him it.
GINA (m)	And scene. This evening wasn't an unusual evening. This is how it was.

Enter JAMES, still in the jacket.

JAMES	Helloo-oo
GINA	You're back early –
HEDWIG	Daddy!

HEDWIG races to her father and greets him.

	How was it? What did you eat? Who was there?
JAMES	Lots of people were there.
HEDWIG	And did you talk to all of them?
JAMES	I did, but Gregers monopolised me, somewhat –
GINA	God, Gregory Woods. Is he still the same?
JAMES	He is indeed still the same
HEDWIG	Who was there? What did you eat?
JAMES	Shoes!

HEDWIG pulls his shoes off for him

	Is the old man not back yet?
HEDWIG	He's in his room –
JAMES	Is he alright?
HEDWIG	He's fine
GINA	Why wouldn't he be?

JAMES	No, there's no [reason] – I'll nip in and see him before he puts his head down
GINA	I wouldn't –
JAMES	Oh he's – D-R-I-N-K-I-N-G?
GINA	He is.
JAMES	Poor old thing – let him have his pleasure –

Enter FRANCIS. Does he remember the moment at the Woods' House?

FRANCIS	I thought I heard your voice. You're back early.
JAMES	Just this minute in –
FRANCIS	I was there as well.
GINA	Were you?
FRANCIS	You didn't see me, did you?
JAMES	Did I?
	,
	No – no, I didn't see you. You didn't see me?
FRANCIS	No, my boy, didn't see *you* at all. Who was in attendance?
JAMES	Oh the Browns, Mr Kasperson, Lord Lewis, you know – I don't remember all the names –
FRANCIS	All the same people as it always was – only now they're high society –
JAMES	Well –

GINA	It's all very grand up there, these days
JAMES	It is –
HEDWIG	Did you play any games?

HEDWIG might react to swearing in the below speech, causing JAMES to emphasise it more.

JAMES	Well, we'd finished our meal, and were having a drink in the library, and they tried to get me to recite some poetry or take their photo but I thought, actually, why should I provide the bloody entertainment on one of the few nights in my life when I'm out for my own enjoyment? They're the ones with the money, all they ever do is trot from house to house stuffing their fat faces: if they want a poem, they can – hire a bloody poet. And if they want their photo taken, that'll be chargeable at the usual rate, thank you very much –
HEDWIG *(wow)*	Did you say that?
JAMES	I gave them a piece of my mind. I said – I hadn't realised I was here, dressed as the entertainment?
GINA	You didn't!
FRANCIS	You said that to their faces!

JAMES implies 'yes I did' without quite saying it.

JAMES	And then there was a whole thing about Chambertin after dinner –
FRANCIS	Chambertin – God, I remember that stuff, Burgundy, isn't it?

JAMES *(no idea)*   It's wine

FRANCIS   Very fine wine indeed –

JAMES   It *can* be a fine wine – but there's a bit of
difference between the vintages. Depends
on how much sunshine the grapes have had.

GINA   I don't know where you pick this stuff up!

HEDWIG   Did you say that to them as well?

JAMES   It's not a bad lesson for them to learn.
However much is written on it, the label
isn't all there is to know.

FRANCIS   The idea of you in that place telling them what
for. All these years later, my boy is in there.
After all that's happened with that crowd.

,

GINA   Did you really say it to their faces?

JAMES   Yes, but let's not keep talking about it, it was
all friendly, they're not terrible people. Why
hurt their feelings?

HEDWIG is ingratiating, thoughts of her promised gift.

HEDWIG   I like that jacket, Daddy –

JAMES   Do you? And it's the perfect fit – almost like
it was made for me – little tight under here,
actually, tell you what, let's take it off –

*They help him – it really doesn't fit – he notices something. There's
no carpet visible to the audience at this point.*

Carpet didn't come then – or is it an
invisible carpet?

GINA   Tomorrow.

JAMES   *That'll* be nice, won't it, Hedwiggicus – your
                clever old mummy getting us a bargain
                carpet at the perfect size arriving in time for
                your birthday – are you excited? I'm excited
                –

HEDWIG   Dad-dy? –

JAMES   Hed-wig –

She looks at him – as if to say 'Come on' –

                What?

HEDWIG   You know what.

JAMES   Do I?

                I don't think I do –

HEDWIG   Stop teasing me! You haven't forgotten, I
                know you haven't –

He has forgotten.

JAMES   Forgotten what?

HEDWIG   You promised you'd bring me a treat back.

                Is it in your jacket?

JAMES   No – it's not. But – wait – something even
                better *is* in my jacket and it's there just for you.

*HEDWIG is jumping around. JAMES finds the audience member's
jacket and from the pocket, a menu card – properly designed, on
thick card.*

HEDWIG   Yes – yes – yes!

GINA   Give him a minute!

JAMES   Here it is.

He gives HEDWIG the card.

HEDWIG   It's a piece of paper.

JAMES   No – *wrong* –

HEDWIG   It is –

JAMES   That is the complete menu that lists every
               single dish served tonight.

HEDWIG   Haven't you brought anything?

JAMES   I forgot – but it's not really much of a treat
               having to eat all of these rich foods. You sit
               down and read what it says on the card and
               I'll tell you what each of the courses tasted
               like. Okay?

HEDWIG   Okay.

               I'm not supposed to read at night-time,
               though, am I?

*HEDWIG is tearful but tries to hide it. GINA signals to her not to
make a fuss, but JAMES notices.*

JAMES   For god's sake, it isn't *easy*, having to be at
               these places for the good of the business and
               the good of the name of this household, and
               hold a thousand things in your head at once
               – you forget one little thing and you come
               home to abject misery.

               '

FRANCIS   Good news from the forest, my boy –

JAMES   What?

FRANCIS	She has gone into the basket.
JAMES	Has she?
FRANCIS	She has indeed. Must be getting used to it. But there's a few things to be done, couple of little adjustments we might make. We'll get on with that tomorrow, eh?
JAMES	Absolutely.
GINA	You can't.
JAMES	Why not?
GINA	You've got things to do. You need to sort those family pictures out, the what-were-they-called?, that family with all the children, get the light balanced properly. And there's two of them need combining together – the baby's eyes are red.
JAMES	Are they?
GINA	*Yes,* baby, it won't take long but we promised them a week ago.
JAMES	I said I would do it tomorrow, didn't I? And it will be done tomorrow. Any new orders today?
GINA	No. There are those two sittings here tomorrow but that's all.
JAMES	Am I the only person trying to keep this business going?
GINA	What do you want me to do? I'm putting as many adverts in the paper as we can afford –

JAMES	Has anyone come to view the room downstairs?
GINA	Nope.
JAMES	Well, what can we expect when nobody takes any bloody initiative.
	,
	I'm sorry, Dad, working tomorrow is absolutely what I'll be doing. Day and night. As usual. Working 'til I drop into my grave.
GINA	I didn't mean it like that, and you know it.
HEDWIG	Daddy, do you want a beer?
JAMES	No. No pleasures for me.
HEDWIG	A record on?
JAMES	No.
HEDWIG	Something to / eat?
JAMES	Hang on, wait, did you say a *beer?*
HEDWIG	Yes
JAMES	Is it cold?
HEDWIG	Ice and cold
JAMES	You mean 'ice cold' –
GINA	Go on, go and get it – it'll cheer us up a bit.

HEDWIG heads off for the door. And then suddenly, JAMES gets up from where he's sitting and scoops her up in his arms and kisses her and the two of them end up on the floor.

JAMES	Oh little Hedwig, little Hedwig, I'm sorry – I'm sorry my little duckling, I've been sitting there,

stuffing my face at the rich man's table, and I couldn't even – couldn't even bring myself to think

JAMES is tearful.

GINA   Stop it –

JAMES   It's the truth. But don't you think forgetting means I love you any less. Because it doesn't. It really does not.

HEDWIG   And we love you, Daddy, the most [that's] possible –

JAMES   And I'm sorry I'm grumpy sometimes, I don't want you to be – I don't want you to have even a speck of negativity in your little life –

              Forget the beer. Shall we … summon the orchestra?

HEDWIG   Yes!

JAMES   Go on then. Well, times are hard, but we are all here together, aren't we, we three? And Grandad. Aren't we, wifey? Whatever anyone else says, better days are coming –

HEDWIG puts a record on and the family dance together. It's interrupted by GINA picking up the microphone:

GINA (m)   And then, a noise downstairs –

              ,

HEDWIG   Who's that?

JAMES   I – don't know –

GINA (m)	It was Gregory Woods, unexpected and uninvited. Carrying a bag.

GREGORY, same clothes as before, but with an outdoor coat on. No bag.

GREGORY	Sorry – I did ring – the front door was open –
GINA	We don't hear the bell from up here –
JAMES	Have you left the party?
GREGORY	And my father's house. I'm not sure you recognise me, Mrs Ekdal –
GINA	I do. Of course I do.
GREGORY	I look like my mum – of course – you remember her?
GINA	Do I? Yes, of course – come in.
JAMES	Come in – come in – sorry, you've left the house?
GREGORY	I'll go to a hotel tonight – so *this* is the place –
JAMES	This is the place. This is the studio – this is where the magic happens: where we make memories you can hold in your hot little hand –
GREGORY	The mission command of Ekdal Photography
JAMES *(fast)*	No – City Photography. More neutral, less – foreign-sounding. And anyway, there's a room to rent on the first floor and there's

a doctor living by the front door. Now
somebody mentioned a beer –

HEDWIG has been standing staring at GREGORY.

HEDWIG   I'll go – I'll go

GREGORY   Hello. I'm Gregory.

HEDWIG   I'm Hedwig.

GINA   Leave that menu here. Read it in the
                morning, it'll strain your eyes at this time.
                And put the stairwell light on for yourself.

HEDWIG heads off downstairs.

GREGORY   So that's Heddy. Is she an only child?

GINA   Yes. Spoilt. Like they always are.

GREGORY   She's pretty.

JAMES   She is. The reason she has to have the light
                on is she's got a condition, her eyes – god, I
                can hardly get the words out –

GINA   It's muscular degeneration, but Gregory
                won't [want to know this]

GREGORY   Muscular?

JAMES might find this frustrating.

JAMES   Macular. Macular degeneration. Her
                retinas. She'll go blind – eventually – I
                mean, now, she's only showing the first
                signs, so here's hoping we have a long
                time before that, but the consultant thinks
                it's inevitable.

GREGORY   How old is she?

GINA	Thirteen in a day's time –
GREGORY	My god, that's so *young*
JAMES	It's hereditary, probably – that's what they think, now –
GINA	James' mother had it as well –
JAMES	Yes, that's what Dad says – I actually can't remember it at all! But then I was even younger than Hedwig.
GREGORY	The poor thing. Does it frighten her?
JAMES	Oh, she doesn't know.
GREGORY	She [doesn't know]?
JAMES	She's so *happy,* the little songbird, and she's dancing into a life of darkness, endless night. It absolutely breaks my heart – you know, why would you tell her something like that?
GINA	So if you could [keep it under your hat] –

HEDWIG re-enters.

HEDWIG	What? Do you want a sandwich or something, Daddy?
JAMES	That entirely depends what sort of sandwich it is you're offering, Hedwig?
HEDWIG	It's a special sandwich
JAMES	Gregers, will you join me in a special sandwich?
GREGORY	No.

Oddly final, that was.

	I mean, we had that meal, so I'm – I don't need food, thank you.
JAMES	Not too many, waitress. Sit down –

HEDWIG beams and leaves the room. GREGORY sits.

GREGORY	Why is it special?
GINA	It's got no filling – well, it's filled with butter. A lot of butter.
GREGORY	Seeing children always makes me feel old. How long have you two been married now?
JAMES	Twelve years last year.
GREGORY	God – is it?

GINA is suddenly attentive.

GINA	Yes.
JAMES	That's right, isn't it?
GINA	Yes!
JAMES	And that whole time you've been – where did you say you went?
GREGORY	Away. I spent most of it living – on my own – at the top of a mountain.
JAMES	Must have felt like a long time to you?
GREGORY	At the time, it did. Looking back, it feels like it passed in a second.

Enter FRANCIS, drunk.

FRANCIS	I wanted to wake, wanted to make a plan for tomorrow, for the birthday tomorrow, so I thought –

JAMES	Dad – this is Gregory. You might remember him. Gregory Woods.

The name panics FRANCIS.

FRANCIS	Woods? Is that the son? What does he want with me?
JAMES	He's here to see me, it's okay –
FRANCIS	So nothing wrong?
JAMES	Nothing wrong –
FRANCIS	Not that it would be, of course –

GREGORY goes to him.

GREGORY	Hello, Mr Ekdal.
	We were in a shooting party together once – in the summer season, nearly twenty years ago. You were a great shot. You helped me, I don't know if you remember?
FRANCIS	Army-trained, sah –
GREGORY	Of course. And I used to visit you – at your city house – number 115.
FRANCIS	Beautiful house, that was. Stag's head over the door. Shot him myself.
GREGORY	Yes. You must miss it.
FRANCIS	The house?
GREGORY	The hunting. The great outdoors. Sorry –

GREGORY, aware that he's caused some discomfort, tries to make it better and makes it worse

	All I mean is how can someone like you *cope* being locked up / here like this – when
FRANCIS	locked up

FRANCIS goes cold. This is awkward.

GREGORY	when when when you're used to the countryside, I mean. The wild. Sorry, you know what I mean.

JAMES steps in.

JAMES	Well, Gregers, there's actually a better way of answering that question than words. See that ladder? Have a look.
GREGORY (m)	Gregory Woods noticed a large ladder, heading up into the attic. He climbed up, put his head through the hatch and peered through it into the loft.

GREGORY stands on a chair with his head behind the lowered black curtain –

GREGORY	It smells like Christmas. Are these – trees?
JAMES	Yes –
FRANCIS	They're cutting down half the trees now, laying cables in the land. The forests are angry. The forests are angry.
JAMES	Can you see anything?
GREGORY	There's moonlight, so –

GREGORY suddenly jumps – maybe we hear wings flapping.

	God – there are pigeons nesting up here! And is that a rabbit hutch!

FRANCIS	It is. Five of them now. Breeding like rabbits.
GREGORY	And there's a bird – in a basket
FRANCIS	Aha! A bird?
GREGORY	Isn't it a duck?
FRANCIS	Is it a duck?
HEDWIG	It's a duck it's a duck it's a duck! But it's not just any old duck –
FRANCIS	Mr Woods, the floor is yours. Please. Say what you see.
GREGORY	It's … brown, I think. It's quite fat.
FRANCIS	But what kind of duck is it?
GREGORY	I don't know.
FRANCIS	That, my boy, is a wild duck.
	,
GREGORY	But – it's *here* (?) [i.e. it's not wild]
FRANCIS	It's wild.
HEDWIG	It's my wild duck.
GREGORY	But it lives here?
JAMES	It does. Fresh water every other day for it to swim in, regular gourmet meals courtesy of the Duck-Keeper General here and it's happy as a pig in, uh, a pig-sty.
HEDWIG	It's not a *pig* –

GINA	I think we've maybe had enough nature-watch for one night. It's freezing in here when that thing is open.
GREGORY	Where did a wild duck come from in the middle of a town?
(m)	And scene. In 1884, Henrik Ibsen wrote *The Wild Duck*. His father was a huntsman, so it might be that he had real experience of wild ducks. But the answer to Gregory Woods' question – the origin story of this wild duck was Francis Ekdal's to tell, and had been since it arrived at the Ekdal house some months earlier –
	Sorry, this really is the last time, but we couldn't just borrow that bag – we won't look in it, it's just to be the – you'll see.

GREGORY puts the bag unceremoniously into a big cardboard box that's been onstage since the beginning.

	This was six months ago – when Hedwig came up here to find her grandfather sitting in his battered, red-leather armchair with his outdoor coat still on.

A scene begins. FRANCIS' memory and speech are noticeably more fluent here. It could be that he's simply not drunk in this sequence – or it could be something more worrying.

HEDWIG	Grandad –
FRANCIS	Shhh shh shh – where's your mum?
HEDWIG	She's in the kitchen having a coffee and working on those photographs. The problem is that there are too many lines on Mrs Fisher's face and Mr Fisher's eyes are

very red so she's re-changing them so they look more like they look.

FRANCIS   Very good, lieutenant. *Now* then.

HEDWIG   What's the box?

FRANCIS   Wait. Look.

,

HEDWIG   It's moving. The box is moving!

FRANCIS   Is it?

HEDWIG   Did you catch a rabbit?

FRANCIS   Nope. I didn't catch anything.

HEDWIG   Tell me – tell me!

FRANCIS   But are you ready for a story?

HEDWIG   Yes!

FRANCIS   Very good. Once upon a time, humans were out in the wild. And there, we'd have to hunt our own food, track it down and kill it and eat it – and a hunter is a man who feels a deep connection to these ways of old. He roams the fields with a gun in his hand, and his friends by his side, and he *listens* – to the land and the trees, and he follows a scent – the smallest scent – to lead him to his prey. So, this morning, a hunter was out in the deep green countryside, stalking the woods – and he waits and he waits – and then suddenly a fluttering – and quick as a jack-rabbit he whips his shotgun up onto his shoulder and he takes his aim and BANG

,

he hits her, hit her in flight – a wild duck –

and she falls from the sky

but the hunter's eyes aren't twenty twenty:
he hasn't hit her in the breast, not *here,*
which is where you want to hit to kill the
critter instantly – he hit her *on the wing.* She's
wounded. And here's the thing –

HEDWIG   Was she bleeding?

FRANCIS   Ducks don't bleed, my little peppermint.
                 [But here's the thing] – the hunter runs up to
                 where she's fallen, to get a hold of her and
                 she's ahead of him. She's scuttled fifty feet
                 to the nearby *lake,* and it's a deep one that
                 lake, salt-water lake, I remember it well, and
                 into the water she *dives* –

                 plunging right down deep to the very, very
                 bottom. The blue goes green down there,
                 and then huge, dark, leathery weeds swirling,
                 mud rising in plumes from the bed of the
                 lake.

HEDWIG   Why? Why has she gone down there?

FRANCIS   This is what a wild duck does when it
                 knows the game's up. Bottom of the lake,
                 she gets a beak-full of weeds, hangs on
                 tight and she waits. She won't ever come
                 up to the surface again. She's waiting for
                 the air to run out.

HEDWIG   But she'll die.

FRANCIS   She will.

HEDWIG	Why?
FRANCIS	She was very badly hurt. She knew her life wasn't worth living any more. She took a decision. Sometimes it's the bravest choice you have.

,

He's speaking from his experience. HEDWIG is awe-struck by this.

> But that's not the end of the story – what animal does a hunter take with him?

Maybe HEDWIG doesn't know so FRANCIS barks for a clue.

HEDWIG	A dog?
FRANCIS	A *dog!* And this hunter has a very clever dog indeed, one that's trained to get after the fallen bird and bring it back to the hunter, so the dog gets on the scent, dives in, swims to the bottom, and he pulls the duck back up.
HEDWIG	Alive?
FRANCIS	Alive. And the hunter takes it back to the house but it doesn't do so well there, only there's a man who works for the hunter who knew me a little bit in another lifetime and I bump into him – and, well, here we are.

He gestures to the box. HEDWIG lifts the box – and screams with delight to see the bag – holds it, cradles it, walks around with it –

GREGORY (m)	And scene.
	It might be that Henrik Ibsen knew, in 1884, that hunters – even today – think that wild ducks have an instinct for suicide, to dive

	to the bottom and stay there. But now, this evening, when Francis Ekdal re-told a version of exactly the same story, Gregory Woods started to see another story underneath it, waiting to be brought to the surface –
	The hunter's my father, isn't he?
FRANCIS	Spot on! What makes you say that?
GREGORY	He was always keen on it –
FRANCIS	I got him into it, my boy, before the – before.
GINA	That duck was shot by Charles Woods? You didn't tell me that.
FRANCIS	You didn't ask me.
	,
GREGORY	But it's thriving now, is it, the duck?
HEDWIG	Yes!
JAMES	She's got a bit fat, as you said, but honestly I think she's forgotten what life in the wild was like, and she's happy up there with the rest of us. Though Hedwig lately has been conspiring with the duck to put her back in her box, which must be against some kind of law –
HEDWIG	She likes it in there! All safe and warm –
GINA	The duck does seem to sit in there for hours, sometimes – must be the closed-in-ness, it's like a cuck-oo –
GREGORY	A cuckoo?

JAMES	She means cocoon. You mean cocoon, don't you, Gina?
GINA	Sorry. Yes. Cocoon.
JAMES	Cuckoo! – cocoon! – cuckold! – my wife, and the perils of language!

GINA is embarrassed and deflects the attention –

GINA	Can we have the duck to bed please, Hedwig, and Hedwig to bed too?
FRANCIS	I might have a drink before I turn in, if anyone wants to join?
GINA	You've had a drink
FRANCIS	Have I?

There's a moment of panic before certainty.

I haven't. Not *tonight*, Gina, love. Permission to retire for the night, lieutenant?

HEDWIG is quite happy to do this routine again.

HEDWIG	Permission granted. Stand down, corporal.
FRANCIS	Permission to kiss the lieutenant on the head?
HEDWIG	Permission granted.

FRANCIS goes out.

FRANCIS	Goodnight, my friend –
GREGORY	Goodnight, Mr Ekdal
GINA	I'm worried about his memory. It's getting worse. And *fast.*
JAMES	He's all right.

GINA   Is he?

It feels like the scene is over. It isn't.

GREGORY   Sorry – you said before you had a room to
                   let –

GINA   The room downstairs, yes, we're advertising it –

GREGORY   Can I have it?

JAMES   You?

GREGORY   Yes. I could move in tomorrow –

GINA   For how long?

GREGORY   Uh, a month, to begin with?

GINA   I mean, it's a small room and it doesn't get
                   any natural light at all –

JAMES   It's a good size room and it gets lots of light
                   from the hall –

GINA   And then there's him downstairs.

GREGORY   Who?

GINA   Relling. Doctor. Out very late, comes back
                   very drunk. And not quietly.

GREGORY   I could get used to that, I'm sure!

GINA   Sleep on it and we'll show you the room
                   tomorrow.

GREGORY   It feels as if you're not keen on me being
                   here, Gina –

GINA (m)   This is true –

GINA   Does it? No, I'm fine –

JAMES	You are being a bit odd. If the man wants to rent the room, the man can rent the room. It's a free country, last time I checked. For the next month, that room is in the name of Gregory Woods.
GREGORY	Don't –
JAMES	What?
GREGORY	I don't like hearing my name – out loud –
GINA	Who does?
JAMES	Oh I don't mind mine – though I suppose, it's *his* really –
GREGORY	But saying it out loud. I'm [Gregory Woods] – I mean, can you imagine having to go through life being called Gregory Woods?

HEDWIG's interest is aroused and this last question to her, half in play.

	Can you imagine walking around having to be Gregory Woods?
HEDWIG	So what would you be if you could be anything in the universe?
GREGORY	That is a good question. I think I'd be a dog.
HEDWIG	What?
GINA	Hedwig – bedtime –
GREGORY	I'd be a brilliantly trained, incredibly clever dog that could plunge in after a wild duck that's dived down to the sea-bed – and drag it back out into the air.

,

This is weird. JAMES, gleeful at renting the room, breaks the tension.

JAMES   Lives in a dream world! Always did. I have
                 to say, Gregers, my old friend, I have no
                 idea at all what you're saying with that –

GREGORY   Me neither, really. We'll sort out the details
                 in the morning – I'll come back with my
                 stuff and – move in. Good night, Gina –
                 Heddy –

GINA   Good night

HEDWIG   Night night

JAMES   I'll show you out – can get a bit dark on
                 those stairs –

JAMES and GREGORY go out.

GINA   Wants to be a dog. Course he does.

HEDWIG   I think he meant something else.

GINA   Like what?

HEDWIG   I don't know. But all the time it was like there
                 was what he was saying [*she holds up one hand*]
                 and then [*the other hand, away from it*] what
                 he really meant.

GINA   He's always been a strange one. No wonder,
                 with those parents.

JAMES comes back in

JAMES   You see – bit of initiative!

GINA   What do you mean?

JAMES   Gregers letting the room –

GINA   I don't even know where to *start*

HEDWIG	It's good news – it'll be good for us
GINA	I wish it was someone else. What do you think Charles Woods will say?
JAMES	He'll say 'what good news!'
GINA	He won't. It's a funny relationship, the two of them. It doesn't look good, him moving out of the family mansion and coming here. Might upset his father. And you don't want Charles Woods upset and blaming you.
JAMES	No – God knows he's done enough for us over the years. But: rent is money and money at a time when we need money. But we won't need money for long, Hedwig, will we?
HEDWIG	No!
JAMES	Because soon your father will redeem the name of his father and elevate this family, lift us out of the – [*can't think of it*] – Lake of Despondency –
GINA	It was bedtime some time ago, little lady –
HEDWIG	Can I have a story?
GINA	Do thirteen year olds get stories?
HEDWIG	But I'm not thirteen for… twenty-seven hours.
JAMES	If you're in bed by the time I get there, then maybe –
HEDWIG	Your bed?
GINA	Go on –

HEDWIG kisses her father and goes skidding off to bed. GINA might be about to be annoyed.

JAMES   I want it all for her you know –

GINA   I know

JAMES   Let her be proud to be an Ekdal. Putting right where Dad went wrong.

She kisses him.

GINA   But before that, let's get her to bed.

                 Are you asleep?

He is well on the way to being asleep.

JAMES   Am I – ?

GINA (m)   And scene –

The scene dissolves.

[ACT THREE]

GINA (m)   The next morning Gregory Woods moved in. First he set a bath running, but then while moving his things in, locked himself out. Then he tried his other keys, then he comes upstairs to get us to find the spare and let him in – by which time the bath had overflowed. Gregory Woods then, for some reason, tried to put floor cleaner onto the water. He said he thought it would make it easier to clean up. What it did was make a sort of – swamp of foaming water, which dripped through the light fittings onto the floor below.

JAMES is shifting a sofa into position –

The reason I moved that out of the way is
because the carpet is coming later and it
can't go down through the furniture, can it?

JAMES   When's it coming?

GINA   Afternoon.

JAMES   It will be back in place by then.

            Oh – and Gregers is coming for lunch.

GINA   Today?

JAMES   Yup. Only polite, we can't *not,* can we? I'm
            sure we've got something in

GINA   Well, we have to have something in, now.
            Are you going to do those photos?

JAMES   Oh, and Relling's coming too –

GINA   Relling?

JAMES   He came out of his door when I was talking
            to Gregers on the stairs. What difference
            does it make, it's *two more people?*

GINA not impressed.

            Oh, and Gi-na –

GINA   Ye-es

JAMES   I am trying to stick to the diet –

GINA   The weight loss one?

JAMES   The *weight maintenance* one. It's on the piece
            of paper.

GINA   Sweetheart, I was just [asking] –

FRANCIS appears.

FRANCIS   You busy, son?

JAMES   I am WORKING – if I ever get any peace
                 to be able to get some done!

FRANCIS   Very sorry, very sorry – I'm busy as well,
                 we're all busy

*FRANCIS storms off; JAMES, exasperated, does too. GINA looks at
the audience.*

GINA (m)   Gina Ekdal had always loved photography.
                 You could look at a person through a
                 viewfinder and somehow they wouldn't be
                 there – you couldn't see them – but then,
                 by little adjustments, you suddenly, at a
                 certain angle, *had* them – saw them – like a
                 bird shooting out of the sky – and that was
                 your moment. You were committing to this
                 shot – and this shot alone. With the press
                 of a button, a million possible pictures fell
                 away – and one was held fast in memory.
                 She loved that – loved that you could
                 leave things out. When she was in town,
                 sometimes people would say 'Are you taking
                 a photo of me?', and she'd say, 'No, I'm
                 leaving you out of it'.

                 What she really loved was film and
                 developing the pictures by hand – and
                 though technology had moved on, Gina still
                 loved the old way. The dark room – a little
                 haven that moves at its own … [slow speed]

JAMES reappears with a piece of paper.

                 What's this?

JAMES	That's my diet, just so it's to hand. And can we get the nice bread?
GINA	Are you busy on the family pictures?
JAMES	I'm *doing it now* –
GINA	Great. Get it out of the way and then later you can *(She quacks.)*

JAMES pulls a face at her. GINA pulls a face back. GINA leaves.

JAMES starts to re-touch some photographs. He produces and then turns on a laptop. It powers up, making a little sound. He opens the photographs. He clicks at it, inexpertly. Looks at the photograph. Little pause. Then from the laptop, he plays some music. Clicks back at the photographs. He really doesn't want to do the photographs.

He switches the music off. He thinks about doing the photographs again. He really doesn't want to do the photographs.

JAMES	Da-ad
FRANCIS	I'm busy.

JAMES makes a sign at his dad through the wall. Eventually FRANCIS comes back in.

	I'm not really that busy, in fact.
JAMES	Do you want to go up? Shall I put the ladders up for you?
FRANCIS	Appreciated, appreciated.

JAMES pulls a ladder on castors into place; like library steps. The top of the ladder extends out upwards, out of sight, behind the black curtain. The steps bolt into the floor.

	Got to all be ready for tomorrow. It is tomorrow, the birthday, isn't it?

JAMES   Yes indeed it is. And there you are.

FRANCIS climbs up the ladders. From above:

FRANCIS   Not coming?

JAMES   Well –

GINA re-enters, heading out to pick up the food for lunch.

               no, no, so much to do. Got to do these
               photographs.

GINA   You haven't forgotten that that couple are
               coming this afternoon for their portrait shoot –

JAMES   Oh, those two –

GINA   I thought you could sleep after lunch and I'll
               shoot them –

JAMES   Make sure you clean up afterwards. What?
               I'm working – I'm sitting here doing it now,
               I am making these photographs better.

GINA goes. Slight pause. Then, from above:

FRANCIS   I'm just saying –

JAMES   Yes

FRANCIS   I think we will have to move her water-
               trough

JAMES   I did say that yesterday

FRANCIS   Righteo.

*JAMES carries on working but he's plainly finding the computer hard
to use. HEDWIG comes in. Puts her hands over his eyes from behind.*

HEDWIG   Guess who it is

JAMES pulls her hands over his shoulders, maybe lifts her over onto his knee.

JAMES   You haven't been sent to spy on me, have
                 you?

HEDWIG   No!

JAMES   What's mum doing?

HEDWIG   Gone for food. Can I help you?

JAMES   No, no, must keep dragging the rocks up the
                 hill. Have to keep on working, working till
                 my body bursts like an old paper bag

HEDWIG *(forcefully)* Don't say that. It's not *nice*.

JAMES manages to get the computer to make an error sound. Annoyed, he tries to fix it and it makes the error sound again.

JAMES   I must sit in my seat and play my role as the
                 breadwinner of the household.

He makes it make the error sound again.

HEDWIG   Let me do it.

JAMES   It's not good for your eyes, sweetheart –

HEDWIG   It doesn't hurt them. I promise. I'll do it in
                 no time.

JAMES   But you don't know what I'm trying to do

HEDWIG   You're trying to put *that* on *there*, and then
                 smooth over *that* like *that*, so the whole
                 thing looks nicer

JAMES   Okay.

                 But you take responsibility for your own
                 eyes. If it hurts your eyes, you have to say,

	you have to take responsibility yourself. Yes?
HEDWIG	Ye-es
JAMES	You are the most brilliant, beautiful, intelligent child in the known universe. I'll just be a few minutes.

JAMES goes up to the loft. As HEDWIG works, there's knocking, from above. More knocking. And then GREGORY opens the door, stands in the doorway. HEDWIG's manner of speaking is factual in the way that children often are – she thinks of herself as an adult, but there is an innocence about her lack of irony.

HEDWIG	Hi
GREGORY	Hello.
HEDWIG	You can come in.
GREGORY	Where is everyone?
HEDWIG	Mum's gone to get food and Dad and Grandad are working in the attic.

HEDWIG stops working.

GREGORY	No, don't let me disturb you
	,
	How did the wild duck sleep? Last night?
HEDWIG	Very well, I think. Thank you.
	,
GREGORY	Do you like being in there?
HEDWIG	I do, but to be honest, it's only when I can, because I'm busy.

GREGORY	Because [you have to go to] school?
HEDWIG	Well I used to but then they took me out. Well, my dad did. My mum wanted me to stay but he was worried about my eyes and I had to go and get tested a lot, at the hospital – and then we have money troubles and the teachers at my school weren't good teachers – and Dad said I wasn't going back and he'd teach me at home instead and read with me.
GREGORY	So he reads with you?
HEDWIG	Well, he hasn't yet but he's busy.
	,
GREGORY	Tell me about what's up there. With the wild duck.
HEDWIG	There are trees. Old trees. And there's a clock which is called a grandfather clock but it's stopped. And there's quite a lot of books, actually there's one book it's in a different language and – it's got a picture on the front of death so I don't really like to look at it.
GREGORY	Death?
HEDWIG	Yes but he's like a tall skull wrapped up in a big dark shadowy curtain, and he's got an hourglass and a little girl.
GREGORY	And what's going to happen to you? When you're grown up – in the real world?
HEDWIG	This is the real world.
GREGORY	Well, sometimes. But don't you want to see the world out there?

412

HEDWIG	Probably not. Probably I'll just stay here. I have to look after the wild duck.
GREGORY	Does it not have a name?
HEDWIG	No. It's a *wild* duck. Don't you know what wild means?
GREGORY	I –
HEDWIG	We used to have chickens in there who would have all been family or at least known each other and the rabbits in there are different because probably they do [know each other], but nobody knows the wild duck or knows where she came from or anything.
GREGORY	But it's yours?
HEDWIG	It's mine. Daddy and Grandad can borrow her whenever they want but mainly they just build things for her. I feel sad for her because she's been separated from everyone she knows.
GREGORY	And she's been to the very limits. To the deep of the green salt sea.
HEDWIG	Why do you say that?
GREGORY	Well, if you imagine the sea, you imagine the surface. It just looks flat. Like a carpet. Or there – like that piece of paper.

GREGORY lays out a piece of paper, perhaps a photograph.

	But there's more underneath – it goes down and down as far as the sky hangs up.

HEDWIG	I think that's how you speak. Things under the surface.
GREGORY	Do I?
HEDWIG	That's what I think.
GREGORY	Doesn't everything have a meaning kept under the surface? If we're honest. Deeper reasons.
HEDWIG	Like what?
GREGORY	Like why your grandad drinks.
HEDWIG	Why?
GREGORY	You know why. We both do. There's a meaning deep under the surface. The ripples are what you see, but if you dive down… he drinks / because
HEDWIG	Because he went to prison.
GREGORY	Exactly. There it is. Something else under the surface. The deep of the green salt sea.
	What's funny?
HEDWIG	You could just say 'the sea bed'.
GREGORY	Why can't I say 'the deep of the green, salt sea'?
HEDWIG	No, it's just

HEDWIG smiles again.

It sounds odd to me when other people say that because in my own head I always think of there – up there [the attic] – as 'the deep'. That's what I call it, to myself.

<table>
<tr><td></td><td>It's stupid –</td></tr>
<tr><td>GREGORY</td><td>It isn't stupid.</td></tr>
<tr><td>HEDWIG</td><td>It is because it's just an attic.</td></tr>
<tr><td>GREGORY</td><td>How do you know?</td></tr>
<tr><td>HEDWIG</td><td>What?</td></tr>
<tr><td>GREGORY</td><td>How do you know it's just an attic?</td></tr>
<tr><td></td><td>,</td></tr>
<tr><td>HEDWIG</td><td>It's a fact</td></tr>
<tr><td>GREGORY</td><td>Is it the truth? Every room is a pocket – it's a little catch of space. A way of shutting things out. Rooms aren't real. What is a room – what *is* a room – what is this room?</td></tr>
<tr><td>HEDWIG</td><td>A space</td></tr>
<tr><td>GREGORY</td><td>A space, right, but space is *space* – space is nothing. Walls holding in nothing. What does it mean? Really? What's the truth?</td></tr>
</table>

HEDWIG stares at him. She goes to speak – and then GINA comes in with a tablecloth.

GINA	You're early –
GREGORY	Apologies –
GINA	No, you have to be somewhere. Table, please, Hedwig –
	,

GREGORY is unsure what to do here – unusual atmosphere.

GREGORY	Are you taking photographs today?

GINA	Why? Want yours done?
GREGORY	No, thank you. I never quite trusted cameras.
GINA	Because?
GREGORY	I don't know – appearances rather than – reality. Maybe.
GINA	It must be difficult, being you.
GREGORY	It is.
	Is it you who does most of the photography?
GINA	We do it together. Anyway it's not really a job for someone like James, taking pictures of people all day, is it?
GREGORY	No – I suppose not
GINA	He's not any old photographer, you know. I'm probably going to start doing some classes – people seem to want to learn how to do the darkroom, the old ways, you know –

A shot is fired from above.

GREGORY	What's that?
GINA	Hunting.
GREGORY	Hunting? How / could it be?
HEDWIG	They hunt in the loft. Daddy and Grandad but mainly Grandad.

This is said with such normality that GREGORY doesn't know how to respond. JAMES comes back down the stairs.

JAMES	Hello! Welcome –

The fire alarm starts.

GINA   Don't worry – it's them firing that gun – sets the alarm off –

GINA runs to the back to turn it off. GREGORY continues.

GREGORY   Good hunting?

JAMES is embarrassed.

JAMES   Oh it's just for Dad, just rabbits –

GREGORY   Rabbits? You *shoot rabbits* up there? With a gun?

JAMES   Yes, of course with a gun – what else would we use?

GREGORY   A shotgun?

JAMES   A handgun.

GREGORY   Have you got a licence?

JAMES   Dad does. Did, anyway. But we're at the top of the house, so no one hears him firing it. He hardly ever fires it.

GINA   Men have to have something to abstract themselves with –

GREGORY   What?

JAMES   *Dis*tract themselves with

GINA   That's what I said –

JAMES   Abstract, though, means something different

GINA   Everyone has their own meanings

GREGORY   How's the duck?

JAMES	For someone who's been filled full of shot and dragged around in a dog's mouth, she is in remarkable form
GREGORY	And been down for so long in the deep of the green salt sea –

HEDWIG smiles –

HEDWIG	Yes!
GINA	Come and help me with lunch, Hedwig.
GREGORY	I might go and have a look at her in the daylight –

GINA and HEDWIG leave for the kitchen.

JAMES	I wouldn't watch father when he's in there – not least as he's got that gun. He gets a bit jumpy.
GREGORY	Right
JAMES	I'll show you it later. We've done quite a lot up there. It's a regular little forest for Dad to roam around in. I used to let him have them in here but Gina didn't like it.
GREGORY	Does she do a lot of the business work?
JAMES	I let her do the more routine things, keeps me little slices of time free for strategy and to work on other things
GREGORY	Like what?
JAMES	Have I not told you about the invention?
GREGORY	The invention? No –

JAMES	That's the main project these days. We started the business for financial reasons, but I knew for *me* taking pictures would never be enough, not in the long run –
GREGORY	Gina was just saying –
JAMES	So if I was going to dedicate myself to photography, how could I make it an *art?* And that led to the idea for my invention –
GREGORY	Which is?
JAMES	It takes time to explain. But it'll be ready soon – it's not a vanity project, it's a real thing, and I can see what I have to do: these days, it's funny, my life's work is really pretty clear.
GREGORY	Go on –
JAMES	Him up there. Dad, I mean, not God. I can try and repair his self-respect by putting the name Ekdal on a real idea. 'Patent pending name of Ekdal'. Let him see that there's a golden future ahead for us lot when, God forbid, he's no longer here.
	What happened to him was – unthinkable, really. And that gun up there – don't say this to him – but that handgun he's got up there has played its own part in the Tragedy of the House of Ekdal. The morning he was sentenced, we were in our old house, his house, you remember, I couldn't find him, it was time to leave for the sentencing, middle of winter, engine was started – and then I hear him: he was in the downstairs bathroom, I had to open the lock with a knife

419

– and he's sitting in there sobbing with that gun in his hand. In my darkest moments I think: maybe he should have just done it. Spared himself. But he didn't dare – already broken then by the publicity, the trial, you know, they really dragged him through the mud.

GREGORY   Yes.

JAMES   The shame. And then that evening, I came back home – alone, he was in custody – alone for the first time in that big house. Knowing it'd be years before he came back.

JAMES stands up – looks around as if looking up in a huge house, on his own.

I'd see people outside in the sunlight, you know, laughing, talking about nothing – it didn't seem real any more. It didn't make any sense. I thought the whole grand parade of life should have *stopped* – stood completely deadly still.

GREGORY   I felt like that – when Mum died. Everything lost its taste. Everything was simulated.

JAMES   Really it was me that was simulated. Inside. I closed all the curtains, pulled down the blinds. For weeks. I walked around that house, walking up and down the stairs, touching every door handle, nowhere to go, no one to live for. And one evening I open the door of the downstairs bathroom and that pistol is still sitting there on the sink –

no one else has touched it. Come on, it was saying. Why would you *not?*

,

GREGORY	You didn't [shoot]?
JAMES	No.
	No, I won a significant victory over myself. I kept going. And thank god I did: I met Gina, and then Hedwig and now my invention … But that choice takes some courage when life is like that.
GREGORY	I guess. It depends how you look at it.
JAMES	You try it. It takes courage.
GREGORY	But it's coming along well? The invention?
JAMES	It's coming along very well.
GREGORY	And the attic isn't a distraction [from your work]?
JAMES	No – on the contrary, I need to rest, sometimes. Often it's when you're relaxing that inspiration strikes – your brain's working away the whole time on how to put the jigsaw together. All the things your eyes see when you don't even realise you're seeing them –
GREGORY (m)	And then I realised something. I realised that on some level, James needed me to help him see.
JAMES	Sorry?
GREGORY	Who is the wild duck?

,

JAMES   Who is it? Well, funny you ask that, I'd
               always thought that the reason Dad had
               been so keen to keep it is that he felt a sort
               of identification with it. Wounded, very
               nearly killed –

GREGORY   It's you. You don't even see it, but he's hit
               you. And you dropped to the bottom of the
               lake and you're holding on. You'll die in the
               dark, green water – it's poisonous.

JAMES   I have no idea what you're talking about –

GREGORY (m)   And scene.

JAMES   Leave *me* out of it, Gregers. If you ever have
               a family and have to provide for them, you
               don't have time for – speculation. You have
               to act.

GREGORY (m)   It was becoming clearer and clearer what
               had to happen.

*GINA and HEDWIG put the lunch down. Another notch up here
in naturalism.*

RELLING   What a luncheon. A luncheon of kings.
               Actually, where is the reigning monarch of
               the house?

JAMES   In the loft. He'll have his later.

RELLING   In which case, let's drink to him – the
               master hunter – to Lord Francis Ekdal!

JAMES   May his latter days be his happiest days –
               and welcome, Gregers!

RELLING	So when did the junior Mr Woods descend from on high?
GREGORY	I moved in this morning, if that's what you're asking.
RELLING	I remember you. Very right on, if memory serves. Or should I say, very left[-wing] on. You worked for your dad, didn't you?
GREGORY	Yes
RELLING	In the warehouse, walking among the people. Work your way up from the bottom. And most of his free time was spent trying to sign his father's workers up to the revolution. Not entirely successfully.
GREGORY	Not at all successfully
RELLING	Growing up is the process of adding water to the wine of your dreams.
GREGORY	Not if you're pouring for someone with a true palate –
	,
RELLING	Too much wine and even the sommelier gets drunk.
GREGORY	Meaning?
RELLING	In all things, moderation. Add water.
GINA	You were in late last night again, speaking of moderation –
JAMES	Can I have the butter?

HEDWIG gets the butter for him. It's a butter dish – he opens it: no butter.

RELLING   I was hoping you'd hear me – it was all an act, designed to get your attention, Gina

GINA   If this is supposed to be flirting

RELLING   You're a lucky man, James Ekdal. All the butter you can eat. A forest above your head with its own noble old custodian. A beautiful wife beside you, holding the fort, while you make ready to unleash your glorious invention on an unexpectant world –

GINA   And Hedwig –

RELLING   And Hedwig!

HEDWIG   And the wild duck!

RELLING   I come up those stairs and I am wracked with envy – if I had been him [James], the things I would have done – the luckiest / man in the world

GREGORY   Oh come on – if my dad hadn't thrown his dad under the bus, we'd be eating this meal in a mansion.

JAMES   Gregers, I won't to hear a word against your dad. He's been good to me.

GREGORY   And you're not even the people worst off – there are people he's sacked from the bottom rungs of the company who are a feather away from the street – taking hand outs to even have food on their table –

RELLING	I don't actually understand what you're preaching –
GREGORY	That the water is rising. That there's going to be a change. A major change which will force us to open our eyes.
RELLING	God, this again –
GREGORY	Ideals, you mean? Integrity?
RELLING	That's not what I would call it –
GREGORY	I think we had this conversation years ago
RELLING	I think we did too. And I'll ask you now what I asked you then. When you've demolished the corrupt, patriarchal, capitalist system, what are you going to do? What happens next? Start a new world order in innocence and the spirit of human nobility like the Garden of bloody Eden? People will still be people.
GREGORY	And people like my father will still have people like us under his thumb.
RELLING	And people like you never have a fucking clue – pardon my language – never have a *clue* about how to actually get anything *done* in the real world, with real, ordinary people who don't have the luxury of living in ideals.
GREGORY	And you do?
RELLING	Accredited thorassic surgeon. If your illness was in your chest and not in your head, I could crack your ribs open and cut it out for you.

GREGORY	But – you no longer practice?
RELLING	No need for practise when you're really, really good. Salt, please.

Down comes FRANCIS with a dead rabbit and a real gun.

FRANCIS	Good afternoon, all, very successful morning's hunting – bagged a biggun – Gina, I'm going to pop it in the kitchen and I'll skin it later on –

Out he goes.

GINA	Put it in the sink – Francis, please! It's a tiny kitchen, and he wrecks it with those things. Destroys it. Blood all over the place. Put it in the sink!
GREGORY	That's not ideal –
RELLING	Is anything?
JAMES	Not in the Ekdal family. Not so far, at least. But we must keep on working, ey, Hedwig?
HEDWIG	Yes!

GINA has spotted the cardboard box, sitting conspicuously.

GINA	Heddy, is there a duck in that box?
HEDWIG	She *likes* it in there –
GINA	Can she *please* stay upstairs, James –
JAMES	Hedwiddikins, I want a solemn promise that the duck will be back in her basket before the afternoon's over –
HEDWIG	I promise.
JAMES	Promise promise?

HEDWIG	Promise promise.
JAMES	Doesn't miss a thing, this one – come here!
RELLING	You still working for the company?
GREGORY	Not really.
RELLING	And Woods & Son will one day all be yours.
GREGORY	Hopefully not.
RELLING	Someone wouldn't drink his daddy's Kool-Aid
GREGORY	I don't drink poison. For you or for him.
JAMES	God, not this again –
RELLING	Alcohol's a poison. When will I die? Who knows. Am I *happy?* As much as I can be, given circumstances.
JAMES	Right, Gregers, here's a story you'll like. My dad had to have an operation a year or so ago, nothing major, but at one point he needed a blood transfusion. Unexpectedly. And I actually have quite a rare blood type – must be from my mother – so I couldn't, or obviously I would have done it, but Hedwig here is a direct match. Anyway – she agrees to give blood to Grandpa, so she says goodbye to her mum, big hug, we go into the room and they wash her arm and then she's sitting there with the doctor, with the thing coming out of her arm, giving blood to her granddad. Solemn little face. 'You're being very brave', the doctor says. 'I know but when you love someone, what can you do?', she says. Doctor's a bit taken aback by

that. Then Hedwig looks at me, vulnerable –
'Dad', she says, 'am I going to die tonight or
tomorrow?'

,

And my heart just

He mimes his heart exploding.

GREGORY   That is beautiful.

HEDWIG   You're teasing me – *again* –

GREGORY   It really / is beautiful, Hedwig –

JAMES   No, I am *celebrating* you because you are
            a pure, gorgeous little goddess – and I am
            practising celebrating you because what day
            is it tomorrow?

HEDWIG   Stop it –

JAMES   But I tell you what, you deserve a million
            times more than I can give you. A small
            party in the loft. A meagre little party in a
            loft. I mean –

The mood could drop here – HEDWIG knows how to buck him up.

HEDWIG   I'm excited!

She puts her arms round his neck.

RELLING   You just wait for this invention. You just
            wait, Heddy. The things you'll have then.

JAMES   Oh you shall want for *nothing* – you'll have
            [he can't think of it] – *anything* you want –
            and that will be my reward for years of toil
            and trouble and toil

HEDWIG	I love you

HEDWIG squeezes him. There's a little pause. RELLING addresses GREGORY.

RELLING	I like your daddy. Sir Charles. Good man.
GREGORY	He's not a sir. And he's not a good man.
RELLING	And that's your contribution to this lovely family atmosphere!
GREGORY	It's a poisoned atmosphere.

,

GINA	What is? The windows have been open all morning –
RELLING	The only poison round here comes out of your mouth –
JAMES	Gentlemen, gentlemen –
GREGORY (m)	And scene –
	A few minutes later / the

As the others make to leave, RELLING breaks the convention, grabs hold of GREGORY.

RELLING	Don't try it on them. Oy. Listen. Don't. Try. It. Here.
GREGORY	Try what?
RELLING	Smashing the reality of the mind into the reality of the world.
GREGORY	What if I do?
RELLING	Then I will kick you down all three flights of stairs and out of the fucking door.

,

           I see you. And I see how you look at the girl

GREGORY is winded by this

GREGORY   I would never lay a finger / on Hedwig –

RELLING   It's the idea, though, no?

RELLING goes

,

GREGORY (m)   A few minutes later, the bell rings. It's my
                  father. He wants to speak to me, my room's
                  still full of water – so we have to speak in
                  here.

CHARLES and GREGORY alone.

CHARLES   You said some things last evening. And your
                  moving in here suggests to me that you're
                  fixating on something I did – or said. I was
                  worried.

GREGORY   I'm here because I don't want to stay in
                  your house. Well, actually this *is* your house,
                  isn't it, it's been a sort of doll's house little-
                  theatre for you to play your games, hasn't it,
                  but I have something I need to do here

CHARLES   Which is?

GREGORY   Which is *open their eyes*

CHARLES   And so why the aggression to me? It's
                  not because of me their eyes / are closed
                  [whatever you mean by that].

GREGORY	I feel guilty *all the time*. And that is because of you. I have your name written on me – written *through* me like a stick of rock –
CHARLES	Why do you feel guilty?
GREGORY	I should have stood up to you then. I should have warned Francis Ekdal. I shouldn't have let it happen, I should have told him to mount his own case – and not let a sweet man go to jail. He is *broken*.
CHARLES	Perhaps you should. Why didn't you?
GREGORY	Because I was frightened of you. Terrified.
	'
CHARLES	Well, it seems that fear has passed –
GREGORY	[But] too late for me to put things right. With the father. He's too far gone. But I can put things right for his son. I can show him the invisible lies that tie his hands together so that he can get himself free –
CHARLES	Greg. Please. Honestly – really honestly – do you think that will do any good?
GREGORY	It will (!) – OF COURSE IT WILL
CHARLES	If I hadn't helped them, they'd have been in dire straits –
GREGORY	And maybe they'd have found their *own* way. I know what you've done here, Dad. I know what you've done.

CHARLES	You really think James Ekdal is the kind of person who's going to thank you for doing this to him?
GREGORY	He is *exactly* that kind of person, yes –
CHARLES	I disagree –
GREGORY	I would rather shoot myself in the head than do nothing and have to live with feeling like this –
CHARLES	You've always felt like this, you've *always* felt like this
GREGORY	Have I?
CHARLES	Yes – this is who you've always been. And it's not your *fault*, Gregory, it's not your fault – you had a parent with a serious mental illness –
GREGORY	That is absolutely true –
CHARLES	I meant / your mother, as you know perfectly well –
GREGORY	And I meant *you*.
CHARLES	And paranoid, over-heated conversations like this one are your inheritance from her – one thing she did leave you –
GREGORY	He's still bitter about the life insurance! Sixteen years later! Married her for the money and the dead bitch didn't pay out –

CHARLES loses it momentarily, a real flash of rage, grabs his son by the throat – GREGORY is frightened of him, doesn't respond –

CHARLES	*I am not going to justify myself to you, Gregory.* I will not do it.
	I hope, I really hope you never have to understand what it was like, when the person you love gets ill – that you never have to watch the person you love slowly fall into total confusion.
GREGORY	So you think you *loved* her?
CHARLES	Shall we keep to the point in hand? You seem certain of your course of action here.
GREGORY	I am.
CHARLES	Then I shouldn't have bothered coming. You'll always have a home at / my house
GREGORY	I'm not coming back.
CHARLES	And as for the business, [I presume]
GREGORY	It's a no from me.
	And you can take me off the payroll. Dismantle my stockholding. I don't want anything to do with it. It's a sack of bricks. I don't want any of it.
CHARLES	You don't / want any – ?
GREGORY	No.
CHARLES	How are you going to live?
GREGORY	I have savings.
CHARLES	And how long are they going to last?
GREGORY	Long enough. They'll last me out.

,

CHARLES   What do you mean by that?

GREGORY   No more questions. Go home.

GREGORY picks up the microphone, momentum building –
CHARLES exits –

(m)   In 1884, Henrik Ib –

                 I'm just going to speak for myself.

                 There are times when there are rights and
                 there are times when there are wrongs, and
                 we pretend that it's all grey area, all in the
                 middle. And why? Because we tell ourselves
                 the lies and we tell ourselves the lies and
                 we say the things that we're supposed to
                 say – we let the toxic people, the cancerous
                 personalities continue, continue spooning
                 the poison into our water, we turn a blind
                 eye – no, our eyes *are* blind to it: we look
                 without seeing, deny that it even *happens,*
                 saying 'but it's their business', 'not to do
                 with me', and then at a certain point, on
                 some afternoon in the middle of a mouthful
                 of a dinner, we WAKE THE FUCK UP
                 – and we SEE that this isn't *good,* this isn't
                 right, that it's nothing to do with politeness,
                 we see how injustices invisibly persist, and
                 we *see* that a lie can just *grow* like a tumour –
                 and then we are the doctors and it becomes
                 our mission, to do what it takes, to *risk*
                 ourselves, to gamble our social standing,
                 to cut free, to change the story, forget what
                 people might think – and say: *stop*

He takes a breath –

                 James!

JAMES enters – hurriedly – GINA and HEDWIG and RELLING after him – GREGORY slams the mic down (or into RELLING's hand) grabs JAMES's jacket and throws it to him –

We need to go for a walk. The two of us. Now.

JAMES What's happened? What did your dad want?

GREGORY Here – come on

GREGORY sweeps out of the front door –

RELLING He's off his head –

GINA James, his mother was the same – I said to / you

JAMES I'm his *friend* – okay? I'm his friend.

JAMES goes after him.

RELLING Dogs that sick should be put down.

GINA Do you really think he's ill? Gregers?

RELLING It's more serious than physical illness –

GINA What do you think it is?

RELLING Severely inflamed sense of victimhood leading to uncontrollable presentations of how virtuous he is. He's a sick puppy.

GINA He's always been strange. When I first met that family, he was strange.

GINA heads back into the kitchen. RELLING stands alone onstage. Picks up the bottle of wine left on the lunch table. RELLING surveys the audience.

RELLING (m) Time for a drink.

RELLING puts the microphone down. The house lights rise. As the audience start to applaud, and RELLING leaves, HEDWIG enters, hurriedly –

HEDWIG   WAIT WAIT WAIT – hang on – wait –

If I said I would, then I have to, otherwise that's lying –

Hello duck – I'm going to open the box now, okay?

HEDWIG opens the box. In it, like magic, a real duck.

How are you?

HEDWIG picks the duck up.

Yes, you *look* well –

My eyes are a little bit sore today but otherwise I'm fine.

Exit HEDWIG, carrying duck –

[INTERVAL]

In the interval, the space stays live. A carpet is delivered and laid. GINA hoovers it, and then sets about developing, by hand, a series of photographs, which are hung on a line at the very back.

[ACT FOUR]

As the interval ends, GINA finishes a job and picks up a microphone. HEDWIG sits at the table, waiting – and very slowly, the house lights go down –

GINA (m)   He was never late for dinner. Only today, he was. An hour after the normal time, the table was ready, the bread was cut and he –

JAMES enters. (This section fast).

HEDWIG	DADDY! We waited for you and waited – where have you been?
GINA	You've been a long time, James.
JAMES	Have I?
GINA	Did you have dinner with Gregers?
JAMES	No.

JAMES hangs up his coat. GINA to HEDWIG:

GINA	Right, sweetheart, let's get this show on the road –
JAMES	I don't need food. I don't want food.
HEDWIG	Are you ill?
JAMES	I'm fine. I had a punishing walk, that's all.
GINA	You should be careful, Jamesy, don't do too much –
JAMES	Any new orders while I was out?
GINA	Not today, no –
HEDWIG	There will be tomorrow, Daddy, wait and see – there will be
JAMES	Tomorrow's when the work really starts for me.
HEDWIG	Not tomorrow – remember what tomorrow is –
JAMES	Well, the day after tomorrow. Because then, I am going to manage my business myself, hands on, just me, on my own.

,

GINA   But you have to work on your invention /
              and

JAMES   Don't talk to me about that –

HEDWIG   But Daddy, you have to help me look after
              the wild duck –

JAMES bangs the table or something

JAMES   I don't want to ever see the wild duck again.

HEDWIG   She *needs* you –

JAMES   Hedwig, *enough*

HEDWIG   And we're having my *party* tomorrow –
              you'll *have* to see her –

JAMES   I will go into that loft and I will take the wild
              duck and I will wring her fucking neck.

,

*It's now clear that something is seriously wrong. HEDWIG looks to
GINA who is looking at JAMES.*

HEDWIG   But it's *my* wild duck –

,

JAMES   And that is the only reason I will spare its
              life. Because I should take anything – *anything*
              from this house that has been in *his* hands
              and I should *burn it* –

GINA   James, what is going on?

JAMES	There are certain things – certain – certain principles, certain ideas that are – *necessary* for someone to feel worth *anything,* for a marriage to – to be a marriage there are certain ideas, that are essential, that cannot be *broken.*
HEDWIG	But Daddy, the poor wild duck –
JAMES	I won't touch a hair on its head. Okay? I said that. Now – you're going to be a good little duckling and go into your bedroom for a minute so I can talk to your mum.
	,
	Have you put your [eye] drops in?
HEDWIG	No.
JAMES	Right then.
HEDWIG	You won't go up there and hurt her when I'm gone –
JAMES	I promise I won't.
HEDWIG	Promise promise
JAMES	Promise promise

HEDWIG goes, but then turns – and rushes back at her dad – and hugs him. He gives into it. Then:

Go on.

HEDWIG goes.

GINA	James, what's / wrong?
JAMES	From tomorrow I'll be doing the accounts myself. Here, in the house.

GINA	What is this about? *Why* would you / want to –
JAMES	Because I want to know where the money is coming from.
GINA	Well, that won't take long. There's hardly any of it.
JAMES	I want to see how so little money can stretch so strangely far –
GINA	Hedwig and I don't need very much –
JAMES	Would you say it was true that my father is paid – and generously paid – by Charles Woods for the accounts work or stocks or whatever it is he's doing?
	,
GINA	I wouldn't say it was generous but he's paid.
JAMES	And is it true that you know that I didn't know that –
GINA	It pays his way and very little more –
JAMES	It pays his way – but you *knew* that I took pride in being able to look after my dad – you do *know* that, because I have *said* that –
GINA	I don't know why you're getting so upset –
JAMES	Because Woods's money is secretly leaking into my family and my wife is keeping his secrets –
GINA	Don't shout at me.
	We don't know if Woods even *knows* about your Dad's money, it could just be that

	secretary, whatever his name was, his people, someone else who knew your dad back in the day – I don't understand why it matters –
JAMES	Your voice has gone funny. I'd like to put a light on.

GINA puts a lamp on.

GINA	I didn't get your dad his job; if you really want to know, it was Anna. Her suggestion. I knew it made you happy to look after him and I didn't want to spoil your happiness for nothing. So you can stop being angry with me.
JAMES	I think your hands are shaking.
GINA	Are they?
(firm)	Okay, what has he said about me?
JAMES	Who?
GINA	Gregory. Mad Gregory. Seriously. Spit it out. Tell the truth.
JAMES	Could it be true – could it be true that you and Mr Woods conducted some sort of relationship, in the period when you were his employee?

This is huge. GINA's reaction is not explosive – at all – and lasts only the smallest fraction of a second before she plays it down.

GINA	Oh – that.
	No. No, James, that isn't true.
JAMES	No?

GINA	No. I told you. You know this story. His wife thought there was something going on and there was a whole thing, calling me at night, one time she turned up at the flat, screaming and screaming, pulled out a clump of my hair, actually – but, really what that was, was that she was crazy. Medically crazy. Like her son. This was years ago, I was still in my twenties. But that whole thing is one of the reasons I put my resignation in.
JAMES	And that's it?
GINA	Yes.
	No
	He came to see me afterwards at home. To apologise for his wife. He brought me flowers. And – one thing led to another – it was inevitable, really, I mean, we'd –
JAMES	What?
GINA	When someone else says that it's already *happened* between two people, it creates a – I don't know, a *charge,* when people think – it's what people think – there's an idea of it now. And he came to the house and his wife had gone into the hospital by then, and he was lonely and he wanted me and I didn't know how to say no.
JAMES	So he forced you?
GINA	It wasn't – no, he didn't – but we weren't thinking.
JAMES	And we were together then. You and me.

442

,

GINA	Yes. It didn't *mean* anything, we weren't thinking –
JAMES	And that was the only time the two of you –
GINA	No.
JAMES	How many times?
	How many times?
GINA	Three.

GINA picks up the microphone.

(m)	More than three.

GINA leaves and heads somewhere else in the room.

Do you want a drink?

,

JAMES	Of course you realise what you've done. It's – my own home, my own life is just completely poisoned. Has been for years. For years and years.
GINA	And what exactly would have happened to you? What would you *do* if you didn't have me?
JAMES	What does that mean?
GINA	The rages. The drinking. The moods. When I met you, you were totally off the rails: half-child, half-wild, your father in prison – and look at you now: you're a parent, a married man, a *different man*,

	you've become who I always knew you *were* –
JAMES	Well, I'm sorry you don't know what it's like to feel sad –
GINA	I know what it's like – I KNOW WHAT IT'S LIKE.

,

Are you not going to eat?

JAMES lifts up the butter dish. There's real butter in it. He looks at it, almost tearful.

(m)	And scene –

JAMES snatches the microphone from GINA's hands and destroys it.

JAMES	NO.

No. We *have* the conversation. We have the fucking conversation. We made vows to each other. I am entitled to know the truth about my own life. You owe me the truth. Why? Why did you do that to me?

,

GINA	I don't know –
JAMES	I wasn't enough.
GINA	*No* –
JAMES	Well?

,

GINA	I don't know –

Slight feeling that GINA doesn't know what to say here, as if we've run out of script and JAMES is pushing us into new territory.

JAMES   So, to be absolutely clear, the truth is: when we were – first – when we first – when we first were *with each other*, you were also – with him?

GINA   No – it wasn't like that –

JAMES   How was it?

GINA   James –

JAMES   No, *please,* tell me how it was

GINA   I came back. I chose you. You won –

JAMES   I can't tell you how happy that makes me –

GINA   I missed you. I missed the excitement of each new day – with you. I thought about it and the idea that I wouldn't get to do the next things with you and choose furniture and *carpets* and make a home and have a child – I couldn't bear that, I couldn't bear that all that time we'd put behind us together would all just crack apart. I didn't want that. That wasn't what I wanted.

GINA might wish she had a microphone at this point. But there isn't one.

JAMES   You should have told me.

GINA   You're right.

JAMES   So – WHY?

GINA   Because –

                 I thought you'd leave me. I couldn't throw my life away.

JAMES	God all of it – everything – my home – all of it I owe to that gnarled, old, rutting, rapist – it's all *HIS,* I could rip his eyes out – god what have you *done* to me?

JAMES sends a chair flying.

GINA	James, this is crazy, this is ancient history. You can't regret the time we've had together –
JAMES	I've lived for fifteen years, every day, every single second, in a web of lies and secrecy and eaten my dinner without realising that there are little bodies buried in every fucking inch of my home. If you want to talk about regrets, surely – *surely* – we are talking about *you.*
GINA	I –
	I'd forgotten. I'd made myself forget it ever happened.
JAMES	Keep your eyes down. Hope it goes away. Who else knows?
GINA	Nobody – I didn't think about it – I don't think about it –
JAMES	Like an animal that's got used to the poison.
GINA	Stop it James, just – you're not a child. I know it was wrong. I know it was wrong, and it wasn't fair, but I have given you a *lot* – I hold this house together. I keep this whole thing going, I keep the whole thing going. I give you the space for your work, I support your invention – I am a good wife and a good businesswoman and a good

mother. A really, really good mother –
better than yours and better than mine and
better than Gregory Woods's

,

I'm sorry. About –

I didn't ever want to make you unhappy.

GREGORY enters.

GREGORY I know this is hard. But – the truth will set
you free. And Hedwig will be free from
lies. You can start again. In truth. With
everything brought out into light.

GINA takes a shade off a light.

GINA That better?

GREGORY Gina, I didn't mean to –

GINA Those old stories were *gone*. And you have
brought them here. So now might be a great
time to shut the fuck up.

JAMES This is the worst day of my life.

GREGORY But there is another way of understanding
this, James – of starting anew

GINA Gregers –

RELLING Thought as much.

RELLING's come in. To the implied 'what?'

The wild ducks are flying around again.

JAMES The victims of Mr Woods.

RELLING Who are?

JAMES	Some of us have been for a long time, Relling, but we only found out today.

RELLING looks at GREGORY. He realises what's happened.

RELLING	What are you trying to do?
GREGORY	I'm sorry?
RELLING	What are you trying to do?
GREGORY	I'm trying to allow them to have a real marriage. An honest marriage.
GINA	It's our marriage –
RELLING	Not good enough for you as it was?
JAMES	Relling, I'm not sure you understand –
RELLING	How many real, honest marriages have you come across in your life, Mr Woods?
GREGORY	I'm not sure I've ever encountered one.
RELLING	Me neither. Funny that.
JAMES	You wouldn't know, Relling, because it's morality, it's a moral foundation, it's basic right and wrong, truth and lies. It's not some abstract thing: it's the ideals by which we stay alive. It's the world underneath your feet. He's [GREGORY] done me a favour.
RELLING	I'm sure. I'm not going to stay for this. And you two can do whatever you like with your marriage. End of the day, no one else cares. But I'll tell you this for free: Hedwig is *thirteen*. And she is as much a part of your marriage as the two of you – and a damn sight more than he [GREGORY] is. She's soft mud, she's open

to any impression. She's innocent here. Be
gentle with her. She'll be easy harmed.

GINA   She's twelve. Hedwig. She's / twelve

ANNA   I'm sorry, I rang the bell but no one –

ANNA comes in. She's older, wiser. She's younger than CHARLES,
maybe the right age to have been GREGORY's mum. An immediate
charge between her and RELLING.

              Is this a bad moment?

GINA   – no, no, it's fine

ANNA   Oh, I like the carpet –

GINA   Yes! We're very happy with it. Came this
              afternoon.

ANNA   Well, we're pleased you're pleased with it. It
              looks right here: I told you it would.

JAMES looks at GINA. The carpet story was a lie.

GINA *(quick)* What can we do for you, Anna?

ANNA   Well, I wanted to bring Heddy's present
              over for tomorrow – Charles is away now,
              until [next week] – but it's from both of us –

GINA   You're always so generous –

JAMES *(mocking)* From both of you?

GREGORY   They're getting married.

No one sure of whether GREGORY is joking – this is new news.

ANNA   Yes. Yes we are.

449

GINA	Oh that is such good news, Anna – at *last* – congratulations, really. I'm so happy for you – for you *both* –

ANNA is looking at RELLING.

ANNA	Me too.
RELLING	Are you telling the truth?
ANNA	I am.
RELLING	So you want to get married again?
ANNA	That's what I said
RELLING	Working for Charles all these years, you'll know exactly how plush a wedding he can afford –
ANNA	Nothing big, nothing fancy.
RELLING	Well it has to be better than your first try. *(To GREGORY.)* Your dad's not a big drinker, is he? And as far as I've heard, he doesn't go around beating his wives up. So already a significant improvement on Anna's dear departed first husband.
ANNA	My first husband had his better parts too, John.
RELLING	I'm sure.
ANNA	And he didn't let his go to waste.

,

RELLING struggles to find a response to this. When he can't: self-destruct.

RELLING	James – I'm going to hit the town tonight. Hard. I'm going to drink until I go temporarily blind and I'm sick in my own mouth. Fancy coming?
ANNA	Oh, don't do that, John. Please don't – / let's just
RELLING	Well – what else is there?

RELLING goes, slamming the door. No one really knows what to make of that.

ANNA	Yes, there is a history there. There was a time when –
GREGORY	Which I'm sure your future husband knows all about –
ANNA	Of course he does. We tell each other everything. Anything that anyone could say about me – any true thing, at least – I've told him. And he's done the same for me.

ANNA looks at GINA, no malice at all.

GINA	That's – wonderful.
ANNA	It really is. It's a bit of a – relief. We're like a pair of kids together, embarrassingly honest and open and *happy*. And that's a first for both of us.
GREGORY	A first?
ANNA	He's a good man, your father, whatever you think of him. He's worked a long life, and spent too many years being the target of someone else's rage – his father's [rage] when he was a boy, and your mother's most of his adult life. And from what I can see, his crimes have very

	often been committed only in someone else's imagination. I'm not criticising her, Greg, she was ill and she couldn't help it – but at the same time, it doesn't mean it's the life *he* deserved.
GREGORY	'In sickness and in health' was the vow he swore, I think. You've got that coming. Though I presume you're more focussed on the 'death do us part' section ... spousal inheritance being / what it is –
ANNA	You can disapprove as much as you like. But if you want to talk about sickness, I don't notice his son coming in to calm his fears and care for him, the outlook being as it is –
GINA	What outlook?
GREGORY	It doesn't matter –
ANNA	There's no point trying to hide it. He's going blind.
JAMES	Going [blind]? Your father? Gregers, you didn't say [anything] –
GREGORY	I didn't know –
ANNA	He's been diagnosed now: it's a specific condition –
JAMES	Macular degeneration
ANNA	Yes – that's it –

,

A silence roars. Things suddenly become clear.

| GINA | It happens to lots of people |

ANNA	But my eyes will have to do for the both of us. Anyway. I'll do what I came to do, and I'll put this here for Heddy, in the morning.
GINA	Thank you

She puts a present down, which is better wrapped than the others. And an envelope.

ANNA	And this, too. This is the more important thing. Don't let her rip it open in excitement. Right. We were sorry not to see you to say goodbye the other night, James. I'm sorry about Charles' friends. Pompous sacks of self-regard, the lot of them.
JAMES	Tell your husband that I will come to see him to discuss the payment of my debts. That the key thing sustaining me as I work on my invention is the hope that one day I will be able to give back every last penny and stand on my own two feet.
ANNA	I'm not sure what's happening here, but I'm going to go. Give Heddy my love.

She goes. A long silence.

Then, genuinely dangerous, JAMES moves to the letter ANNA has just put down

GINA	James, what are you doing?

JAMES has opened the letter addressed to HEDWIG. And reads it. There's a few different pieces of paper inside.

That's *her* birthday present –

JAMES	I know exactly what it is, thank you, I do not need you to paint me a picture.

453

JAMES reads. A pause. Then:

Do you know what this says?

GINA   How could I?

JAMES   Do you *know* what this *says*?

GINA   NO

JAMES   It is documentation that a trust has been set up, from which the sum of one thousand pounds will be paid to Hedwig Ekdal on a fortnightly basis for the rest of her life, including a pretty fucking huge lump sum on her eighteenth birthday –

,

GREGORY   This is a trap, James –

JAMES shuts GREGORY down.

JAMES   I don't need help, thanks, Greg, I am fully, *fully* aware of what is going on here. I can – in fact – *see*. And however little you both think of me, I'm not a man who can be bought.

JAMES rips the piece of paper neatly in two. GREGORY didn't predict this next development – didn't see it himself.

So much for that. But we haven't had the truth yet, have we, Gina? It's not the first time your father has put money into this household – Gregers, as you've already told me, he's pouring money into my father's pocket.

GINA   James –

454

JAMES	He is *paying* my dad. Overpaying him. Maybe paying him *for nothing*. Has done for years. My dad is living off *his* money. That's true –
GINA	Yes.
JAMES	And – another generous gift – he put up almost all of the money for our wedding –
GINA	Yes.
JAMES	So – wait – if you and he were together just as we were getting engaged, why would he – why would he pay for you to get married? Why would he want to do that?
GINA	Honestly?
	I think he thought he could come and – *have* me whenever he wanted.

JAMES momentarily shocked –

JAMES	And is that / what's been – ?
GINA	No – no, I haven't, please god I wouldn't do that to you – nothing has happened since then. There hasn't been any physical contact at all, James, I promise, nothing has happened since the day we were married.
JAMES	I don't think that's why he paid for the wedding. I think that the truth of it is that he was worried about something else.
GINA	I don't understand –
JAMES	She doesn't need *this* [the letter] because Hedwig's already got her inheritance from

	him, hasn't she? *Here. (He violently gestures at his eyes.)*
GINA	James, I don't understand –
JAMES	Does your child have the right to live in this home? In *my* home?
GINA	Oh *Jesus Christ* –
JAMES	Is Hedwig mine?

GINA smacks JAMES hard across the face.

| GINA | How dare you ask me that – |
| JAMES | Is. Hedwig. Mine? |

,

GINA is unhysterical. Almost hard.

| GINA | I don't know. |

,

| JAMES | You don't know. But there are tests / and |
| GINA | I didn't – I haven't done that – and I don't know. |

,

| JAMES | Right. |
| | Then I have to get out of here. There's no way I can stay in this house. |

JAMES heads over to get his overcoat and puts it on. A sudden whirl of activity –

456

GREGORY	James, the three of you have to stay *together* now – you have to *forgive her*
JAMES	No I don't – and no I don't – for fuck's *sake*, you heard what she said –
GINA	Please don't do this
GREGORY	*James* –
JAMES	I don't have a daughter – I *don't have* a daughter –
HEDWIG	Daddy?

'

Everyone realises a tearful HEDWIG's in the room. And she heard that. JAMES is distraught, can't face her, moves first for the door – she runs to grab hold of him, he fights her off, it's pretty ugly and probably requires quite a bit of ad-lib –

JAMES	I can't, Hedwig, I can't – don't look at me – get off, get off me, get off me, I can't bear it, I can't bear it, I can't bear it – I have to get out –
GINA	James, look at her – look at her –
HEDWIG	Daddy – daddy – daddy – please

…until JAMES is gone.

HEDWIG is in tears, GINA is hugging her.

	He's never coming back –
GINA	No, sweetheart, he'll come back. He'll come back, I promise. Nothing to cry about.

GREGORY   It's important to me that – it's important –
                 Gina, look, do you believe that I only ever
                 wanted the best for you?

GINA looks at GREGORY, as if she's seeing him for the first time.

GINA   You know, I do. But God help you.

GREGORY   Thank you. The best can still prevail. There's
                 a happy ending here, Gina, I promise, it's
                 going to be better than it's ever been –

HEDWIG   I'm never going to see him again –

GREGORY   Just a minute –

GINA   Don't you dare tell her to be quiet. Don't
                 you dare.

                 ,

                 Okay Heddy – I'm going after him – but
                 you have to promise me you're going to
                 stop these tears. Come on.

HEDWIG   Okay –

GINA   I'll be back.

She shouts down the stairs.

                 Francis! Francis! Hedwig, find your grandad
                 –

*GINA leaves. GREGORY sees the microphone, which has reappeared.
He might be puzzled that it's reappeared.*

GREGORY (m)   There's more to say. There's – there's –
                 more to say –

                 Ibsen. Ibsen – Ibsen fathered an illegitimate
                 child on a serving girl. And the law forced

him to pay for that child until the end of its
thirteenth year – and thereafter, Ibsen had
no contact *at all* with the child or its mother.
And so *The Wild Duck* – *The Wild Duck* is his
story is – a *lie* – a lie with something to prove,
sold to audiences night after night after night
– a lie that covers up what sort of father he
is: and a lie that warns you to stay quiet, tells
you that truth is destructive and corruption is
better off *buried* – *The Wild Duck* is a lie.

HEDWIG   Why doesn't my daddy want to look at me
           any more?

GREGORY   It doesn't matter.

HEDWIG   It's because I'm not his child.

           ,

GREGORY   How could that be true?

HEDWIG thinks.

HEDWIG   There was a story once where there was
           a baby left in the water in a basket in the
           reeds and they found it and kept it. Maybe
           I'm like that. Maybe Mummy found me and
           now Daddy's found out.

GREGORY   But –

HEDWIG   But even then, he could still love me.
           Maybe even love me *more*. I mean, the wild
           duck came to us by surprise and we're not
           its family but I still love it.

GREGORY   You love the wild duck. You really do –

HEDWIG   Yes

GREGORY	And it isn't yours. It is. But not in nature.
HEDWIG	I don't understand.
GREGORY	What *is* love?
HEDWIG	What do you mean?
GREGORY	How do you – show it?
HEDWIG	… you feel it, you don't show it.
GREGORY	So. It's a meaning kept under the surface.

HEDWIG smiles

We can make the world a better place if we trust our – our deepest sense of what is *right*. What is *true*. But those feelings get hidden, get buried –

HEDWIG   I didn't like it when he said he would hurt the wild duck. I say a prayer for her every single night. Because when she first came she was wounded, only now she's nearly healed, and I think that might be because she knows how much we love her.

GREGORY   So. What could you do to prove to your daddy how much you love him? There's nothing you wouldn't give up for him?

,

What's the thing you love most in the world? Apart from him and your mum.

HEDWIG points up to the loft. GREGORY nods.

HEDWIG   But he wanted to kill it.

GREGORY	He only wanted to end the lies. What if you sacrificed the wild duck?
HEDWIG	The wild duck?
GREGORY	If you gave up the thing that was most important to you –
	,
	to show to your dad what you feel?
HEDWIG	Kill it?
GREGORY	Sacrifice it.
HEDWIG	Why?
GREGORY	Because even if you're not his child, even if they found you in a basket, there's a deeper meaning: you still love your daddy as much as you possibly could, don't you?
HEDWIG	Yes
GREGORY	Even if you came from – the ends of the earth –
HEDWIG	from the deep of the green, salt sea.
	Do you think Daddy would understand it? That it had a meaning?
GREGORY	Yes.
HEDWIG	And love me even if I'm not / his child?
GREGORY	Yes.
HEDWIG	That would be beautiful –
GREGORY	Things are beautiful when we live honestly. I really believe that.

HEDWIG	Are you crying?
GREGORY	Am I [crying]?
HEDWIG	Would you like a hug? It's a sad night for everyone.

HEDWIG hugs GREGORY. A pause.

> I think I should ask Granddad to do it. Tomorrow morning.

GREGORY	Okay. But not a word to your mother.
HEDWIG	Why?
GREGORY	She doesn't understand us.

GINA comes back in.

GINA	He's not in the house, but they saw him with Relling.
GREGORY	He'll come back tonight. Don't worry. You'll see him before you go to bed. He'll come back.

GINA takes the microphone from GREGORY.

GINA (m)	He didn't come back.

GREGORY and HEDWIG leave the stage. GINA stands there, aware of the audience looking at her. Still on the microphone:

> Please don't look at me like that.

> James didn't come home that night. He and Relling hit the bottle, withdrawing the little money left in his – in *our* current account, and drinking it. I think he slept at Relling's, I'm not sure.

The next day – went by with no sign of him
– until now. It's almost night.

[ACT FIVE]

It's now the next day, HEDWIG's birthday. She starts to clear up the room.

There is nothing. Blankness. There are a
million things that you can *change,* later – to
rebalance the negative, to alter the end result
– temperature, time but really it comes down
to two simple things: an exposure – and a
blank sheet on which it will be written. A
moment and its future impression. There
is nothing at all. Blankness. And then as it
blossoms into colour, as its shadows drop and
its highlights hold firm – the image creeps
into life. Out of the air, out of thin air, depth
falls into a flat page – a cathedral, a hot air
balloon, your sweetheart's face, his smile, his
glass of drink, his head. Caught there forever.
Held against time. This is what magic is. We
are the writers of the eyes, and our ink is
light

CHARLES   I'm / sorry

GINA   Oh my god I didn't see you there – I didn't
             see you –

CHARLES   Who were you talking to?

GINA is surprised – and then taken aback –

GINA   Myself. I didn't see you, I sometimes
             imagine – sorry, oh god it's stupid, really, I
             sometimes pretend I'm giving, like a lecture,

463

a talk, the truth of [photography], if I'm
having a bad day – it *doesn't matter*, sorry –
sorry – what are you doing here?

GINA catches her breath, adjusts her appearance. She puts the microphone down.

CHARLES   I was looking for my son –

GINA   His room's downstairs.

            ,

CHARLES   Ah, sorry. To interrupt. It sounded / good

GINA   Please don't.

CHARLES   Are you having a bad day?

GINA   She said you'd gone away – your wife

CHARLES   I told her to say that. And she's not my wife.

GINA   Not *yet.*

There's a lot of conversation here, but very little in the lines.

CHARLES   No.

            ,

GINA   Your birthday present to Hedwig was
            incredibly generous.

CHARLES   Ah, yes?

            I try and give it away, try and share the luck.

            Look, you're not – we're not –

            Full disclosure: I actually came to see you.

464

	I feel I should say that I didn't want to, with everything going on these days, I don't want you to feel like you were in any way [abused] –
GINA	I don't feel that
CHARLES	Or that you were pressured –
GINA	I wasn't. I really wasn't, Charles
	I'm actually – it's actually – nice to see you. Again.
CHARLES	Ah – I'm glad –
GINA	I didn't ever mean to hurt you.
CHARLES	No, I know – you didn't *mean* to hurt anyone.
GINA	It doesn't mean I *didn't* hurt you, I realise that but –
CHARLES	No, I was heartbroken, actually – but it's a long time ago, now.
GINA	Doesn't *feel* it, though, does it? It sort of stands still in a strange way, like you can try and drive away from it, you can *drive,* if you want, but it's still on your windscreen. It's still there. Here. Sorry.
	God, I could never talk when you're around –
CHARLES	You could. You did.
GINA	Sometimes.
CHARLES	Sometimes – with your camera in your hand. Do you still have the one I / bought you?

GINA   Of course – yes, of course I do, that's the
                one we use for the business, it's actually how
                we make most of the money, two thirds of
                the orders are people wanting photographic
                film, for whatever reason – nostalgia,
                probably, desperately wanting to pretend it's
                the past (!)

CHARLES   I can sympathise with that.

They smile.

                Is she having a good birthday?

                ,

*GINA opens her mouth. She lowers her head and then she speaks in
a way that really is honest.*

GINA   I think about you all the time. And there
                are times when I don't know whether that
                decision – whether it's him or [you]–

A whole other world becomes open and possible in this pause.

                this is ridiculous, you need to turn round
                and walk out of my home. Please.

CHARLES   Okay.

                But do we need to talk? To have a
                conversation?

GINA   No, we don't. We don't.

CHARLES   I see an old man in the mirror these days,
                Gina, and in that respect alone I have no
                doubt that you made the right decision for
                yourself in all kinds of ways I don't or can't
                or won't understand.

But from where I'm standing, I know this much: I'll lie in the dark on my deathbed and I'll think of the one mother and the one father I had, and the one son – and I'll wonder whether I also had one [true love] – that is, whether a life with you, whether a life with you – if there was *anything* I could have done

That probably isn't true, is it? I don't think I'll wonder at all. I can barely see now, but on that bed, on that last day – I'll be seeing *your face*

GREGORY appears at the door.

GREGORY   He won't see me, won't listen [to a word I say].

GREGORY sees CHARLES.

GINA   I'm going to change, you two can stay in here if you want –

GINA goes.

CHARLES   I've met a lot of people in my life, Gregory, and

GREGORY   I'm not *interested* in hearing your memoirs

,

CHARLES   and not one of those people thinks the way you do. I'm not sure what we did, what I did, that made you the way you are, I'm not even sure it's a bad thing, entirely, but – it's like: you're the protagonist of this construct called reality, and it's your job to force the rest of us to pull up our socks and sort the whole thing out.

	I can't say I'm proud of everything I did. Nobody can, I expect.
GREGORY	Right –
CHARLES	But I don't love to focus on the worst things in people. It doesn't give me any pleasure. I don't consider every person I meet to be simply the worst part of themselves; I don't think someone's failings always wipe out their many thousand other things. And I don't think true integrity is something you have to perform.

RELLING appears.

> Good evening, John.

And then to GREGORY:

> I would appreciate it if you might give some *real* thought to the company. I won't waste your evening.

CHARLES goes.

RELLING	James is in the shower. Then he's coming up to get his things.
GREGORY	How is he?
RELLING	Hungover. You know how he grew up?
GREGORY	James? With his aunties, wasn't it –
RELLING	It was. The hero of the household. The best, most handsomest boy in the whole world. That's his problem.
GREGORY	He's an idealist, yes

RELLING   He's an idiot. And he's an idiot who's been told he's a genius.

GREGORY   That you think that reflects only on you.

RELLING   Enlighten me –

GREGORY   Because you're clearly disappointed with your life, you've forgotten who you were before – before you gave in. When you had hope that the broken old things would change – rather than just *shrug* and open a bottle and put up with it – and all you can do is mock the people who could change things. Who will.

             But there is a real truth, a purer human truth – which has become corralled, compromised and imprisoned and beaten down by corrupt people and corrupt systems and the weight of years of rotten history leaking down into it. And releasing it begins with telling the truth.

RELLING   And what's the collateral damage of that?

GREGORY   Truth is hard. People get hurt along the way. Like in any revolution.

RELLING   Truth is hard for James. A man incapable of surviving without the secret support of everyone around him – and whose ego would just crumble if he realised that was true –

GREGORY   I disagree.

RELLING   Because – on this subject – you're blind.

GREGORY   I think I see this situation pretty clearly –

RELLING	You're walking wounded. Carrying real damage. Here.
GREGORY	I know. I know.
	,
RELLING	Always worshipping someone, fixated on some super-hero. Probably your dad, then when the scales fell from your eyes, your mum, and she's dead, she can't ruin the holy image, and now it's James Ekdal, and that's a bit beyond worship, but I bet there's been a few other innocents worshipped in between. Though he himself is the most pathetic.
GREGORY	If that's what you think of him, why live in his house?
RELLING	It's not.
GREGORY	What?
RELLING	He doesn't own this house. Your father does.
	,
GREGORY	He bought their house?
RELLING	He did.
	And I live here because whatever you might think of me, I try and help him. Help them.
GREGORY	And what's your prescription? Whisky?
RELLING	The same one everyone else is on. The life lie.
GREGORY	The what?

RELLING	The life lie. It's a universal stimulant. The stories I tell them are the ones they tell themselves, and stories are *lies*. Even true stories. His dad didn't even need help: he self-medicates. The great military man, the noble hunter climbing up into the attic with a battered old handgun to chase around six rabbits, a handful of pigeons and an obese, domesticated duck.
GREGORY	I don't understand –
RELLING	He's *happy* – to him, those old Christmas trees held up with wires are towering forests, the pigeons are the wild game, sitting pert at the tops of the thousand-foot pines. It's a lie. But he's *happy*.
GREGORY	He's deluded
RELLING	So you'd – what? – tell him the truth? The thing you don't understand: is that telling the truth about things isn't the same as getting them to change. Pointing out the problem, getting angry about it, even, is not getting ideas to become real, *in the real world*. He's *happy*.
GREGORY	He's abandoned the ideals he had when he was young. / And that's *sad*.
RELLING	'Ideals' is a word from a foreign language. The word you're after is 'lies'.
GREGORY	They're not the same thing
RELLING	Oh, they really are. We hand out the same poison, me and you, only difference is the

labels on the bottles. And my patients are
happier.

GREGORY might be tearful.

GREGORY   That isn't what I'm doing – that isn't [what
            I'm doing] – if you want to talk about lies,
            my father, my *father* has – I was at school
            with James, and he was exceptional – a
            young *prince*, blessed with vision, he was
            going to *be someone who could do things* – and
            then my father flipped his dad onto his back,
            got to him, into him, wormed through the
            fabric of his life like a virus – he bought this
            house – he *bought* their fucking house

RELLING   I know

GREGORY   This carpet, this business, the photography
            studio, this piece of bread, the old man,
            Hedwig, every last thing you see has *him* in
            it like a virus – and he is *venom* –

RELLING   And you?

GREGORY   I'm nothing like him. I am nothing like him.

RELLING   People who don't feel liked tend to try to be
            right. Or make things right. Or sometimes
            pick up megaphones to scream their
            rightness at the world. But it's not rightness.
            Not really. It's pain.

            ,

GREGORY   I want James to break free from my father's
            lies. And I still believe he will.

RELLING   Then I feel sorry for him. Take away
            someone's life lie and you take their

472

happiness with it. There's nothing left to live for.

HEDWIG comes in.

Hey, mother of the wild duck, it's time for me to go and see where your daddy is.

RELLING goes out. GREGORY and HEDWIG look at each other.

GREGORY   I can tell you didn't do it.

HEDWIG   When I woke up it seemed like a strange idea. Not like it did yesterday.

GREGORY   You gave me real hope last night.

            Tell me. If the dog hadn't dived in, dived down, what would have happened to the duck?

FRANCIS comes in, coat on, wet –

FRANCIS   Not interrupting, I hope. It's horrible out there.

HEDWIG   Are you going hunting?

FRANCIS   It's cats and dogs. Bad hunting weather, my darling. Overcast. Can't hardly see your hand in front of your face.

GREGORY looks at HEDWIG and leaves.

HEDWIG   Grandad?

FRANCIS   Yes?

HEDWIG   Does it hurt the birds? Or the rabbits? Does it hurt the creatures who are hunted?

FRANCIS   What?

HEDWIG	The gun
FRANCIS	No, sweetheart – you stop their hearts. One bullet in the right place and they don't feel a thing. Like a light going out.
HEDWIG	Okay

GINA comes in.

FRANCIS	But we don't worry about that. I've got a present for you for dinnertime that you're going to absolutely love.
HEDWIG	Grandad –
FRANCIS	Yes –
HEDWIG	Why did you go to prison?

,

FRANCIS	Because, my darling, I wasn't brave enough to do the right thing.

He kisses her on the head.

I'll get out of these wet things, smarten up –

He goes out.

GINA	Has he been for his walk?

As HEDWIG opens her mouth to answer, JAMES comes in, in a coat which is stained, badly, and perhaps ripped.

JAMES	I've come but I am going.
GINA	Yes – god, James, look at your coat.
JAMES	What?
GINA	Your good winter coat.

HEDWIG	Hello Daddy.
JAMES	Hello.

,

Could you go into your – Gina, could she go into the bedroom, please?

GINA	Give me a minute, Hedwig.

Tears in HEDWIG's eyes.

It seems for a moment as if HEDWIG isn't going to leave – but then, she does. GINA does too after a moment.

JAMES	I need my books. I'm going to need to take the books with me.

He opens – perhaps unlocks – drawers in the tables and takes out books and papers – that weren't there before. Real props now, to the very end.

The gun is taken out too.

I'm going to need them – for my invention, there's technical things – they're in there, actually in the cupboard, there's papers which –

GINA	They're here.

GINA has come back in with them. Suddenly the table seems full of things.

So you're really going to leave us?

,

JAMES	Do I have any choice?

	How can I *possibly* live like *this* – knowing what I know, everything I look / at reminding me –
GINA	Okay, I understand.
	What about Granddad?
JAMES	I know whose responsibility he is, Gina. My father will come with me.
GINA	Right.
JAMES	Are my glasses around here somewhere?
GINA	I – don't know. You had them / last night
JAMES	I had them last night but I can't find them this morning.
GINA	What did you *do* with them, James?
JAMES	It's not really your concern, is it?

GINA goes out. JAMES bangs around drawers, looking for things.

Fucking Relling. Someone should push him down the bloody stairs.

The two halves of the letter he tore up stare back at him from the table. He looks at them. He picks them up. Then GINA comes back in, with a tray. He puts them down, fast.

GINA	There's a coffee there for you. And there's bread and butter and some other bits and pieces.
JAMES	I can't eat here, Gina. I haven't eaten for – since yesterday – but it doesn't matter, I just need to get my things and get out.
	I'm missing a notebook – which I left in …

He opens the door and HEDWIG *is right behind it –*

Oh GOD everywhere I LOOK.

He doesn't mean to be cruel, the frustration is from real pain and sadness –

GINA   She has to be somewhere.

JAMES   Can you *please* go into your *bedroom –*

HEDWIG   I'm sorry daddy – I'm really sorry for
                  everything.

JAMES *(at once)* Gina, can you please get her to –
GINA *(at once)*   It's not your fault, sweetheart, there's
                  nothing to be sorry for

HEDWIG   *Please* don't go away from us –

JAMES goes off into the kitchen, away from her.

GINA   Please, Hedwig, give us a minute. Go downstairs.

GINA follows him out.

*HEDWIG, alone on stage. She looks at what's on the table. Her eyes
are hurting. She picks up the gun from the table and exits as, from
off, we hear the below: as the door re-opens and JAMES re-enters
with a bag, mid-conversation.*

JAMES   That bag will in no way be big enough to
                  take everything I have to take, and we do
                  have a bigger one, I swear we have a – we
                  had a –

JAMES slumps in a chair –

                  I'm finding this hard and exhausting to have
                  to pack, while –

He gestures to where HEDWIG *was. He puts his head in his hands.*

,

GINA   Take a shirt and some underwear and get
              the rest later. Your coffee's getting cold.

He takes a sip of his coffee.

              I don't know if you've thought about – the
              animals – if you're going to take them too.

JAMES   How can I take them?

GINA   I don't know how Granddad will feel
              without / them

JAMES   He'll have to learn. There won't be the
              space, with what I can afford, for him to
              have his forest – I'm having to give up more
              than that, so he –

*JAMES thinks about how much he's going to have to lose if he leaves.
His resolve slightly slackens.*

GINA   Do you want to take the record player?

JAMES   Yes. No. No record player. But I should
              [take the gun] – where's the gun?

GINA   It was sitting there. He must have taken it up
              with him.

JAMES   Is he up in the attic?

GINA   Where else would he be?

Tiny smile – tiny thawing – he's looking at the bread and butter.

JAMES   It's sleet and rain out there.

He takes a piece of bread. He's looking for something on the table.

GINA   What are you looking for?

JAMES	Butter?
GINA	Coming up
JAMES	No, you don't have to – it doesn't matter –

She gives him the butter, in the butter dish. He butters his bread. A sense of completion here, a sense that some part of the final picture is clear.

GINA	James. Is this the end?
	,
	I mean, are we going to – get divorced?
	Is this it?
	,
JAMES	I don't know. I don't know what I feel. I don't know what you feel.
GINA	It doesn't feel like the end. And I don't – I don't want not to be there for when you're ill and when you're old and when your invention is finished. I don't want Hedwig to have two sets of presents at Christmas. I don't want that life for her when she could have this one – has had –
	I have been so scared of this. I don't *know* if I love you. I don't – but it's my best guess that I do because I don't know what other people mean when they say those words. I don't know if I match up. I have this fear, that really the whole time I've understood something completely different, and one day they'll look into my head and be like –

>*what? No.* And say, no, your whole life was
>like an optical conclusion.

A crack in his armour – this is funny – he can't let it go by,
somehow –

JAMES   Illusion. Optical illusion.

GINA   I'm sorry, yes. I mean: to be in love. In
                   love. Inside love. It's the world you live in,
                   not a thing that happens to you.

                   I know that this is reaping what I sowed – I
                   do know that, I know I had this coming to
                   me, but I don't know, Jamesy, I do wonder
                   if this is the thing that's going to bring us
                   closer together and give us a new start, and
                   if stupid crazy Gregers might actually have
                   had a point and it might – maybe it – now
                   the worst has happened and we're still
                   here, we're still alive and we still love each
                   other. I hope.

                        ,

                   But if you can listen to this music and look
                   me in the face in this room, in this little
                   nest at the top of the house, that we made,
                   away from the noise, and the world, then –
                   then then really this is the end of the story

JAMES   Gina –

She puts a record on. It hisses for a while, and then a song plays.
FRANCIS enters, talking into the microphone.

FRANCIS (m)   The record player was bought some years
                   earlier at an auction and had been sold to
                   James as a rarity: an art deco turntable and

matching speakers made by Decca in 1969. That the Decca logo didn't appear on it anywhere suggested that in fact its history might be a fiction. But that's so often the way it goes.

The introduction plays. JAMES holds out his hands to GINA, like a baby. She lifts him into her arms, and JAMES sobs into GINA's shoulder. She strokes his hair and comforts him. She tells him, again and again, that she's sorry. The two of them start to dance. They're a bit silly with each other, both trying to stop his tears. She holds his face and says again that she's sorry. He says he's sorry too.

I don't know where they first heard it – but this song was the kids' choice for the first dance at their wedding reception: and as it played, as evening fell, twenty tables, entangled in strings of lights, one by one, went dark, until the couple, wound together, wrapped in lines of light, were the only thing visible – dancing, alone against the darkcloth of the night.

The couple dance.

Of course, I missed the wedding. And now, tonight, I didn't even remember that story – but when, sitting in my bedroom, I heard that song, the rootless, unpindownable feeling of happiness it triggered flowed through my body like rain.

I didn't know that, only two weeks later, a blood vessel would explode in my head as I was slowly ascending the stairs from the bathroom, and that my body would lie there until morning before it was found.

You see, I hadn't opened the letter, my
results, because I didn't want to know. Or
because somewhere I did know, and I didn't
want to see. But we're all just walking, ticking
time bombs, aren't we? Who needs the truth?

*The music plays. HEDWIG enters. She sees her parents dancing
together. They don't see her.*

*The loft is revealed, exactly as we have imagined it. It completes
the picture of the Ekdal family home. HEDWIG looks up at the loft.*

She smiles. She climbs the ladder and disappears into its darkness.

*The song finishes, or maybe the song skips. It shouldn't end. The
turntable hisses.*

JAMES	I don't know
	I know it's –
	I don't know.
GINA	You don't know what?
JAMES	I don't know what this means, now.
	I don't know what happens next.
	I don't really know who you *are* any more.

GREGORY comes in.

GREGORY	Should I go?
GINA	You're a part of what's happened. As much as anyone. I'm telling James that we can start again. You can work on your / invention –
JAMES	Oh *come on* that's not a real thing.

,

482

Relling started me off on it, it made me happy to think I might actually achieve something – but it was when Hedwig started to believe in it, I mean, I let myself think that she did –

I loved that child. It was the greatest part of my day every day to come back to this house and see her little face and now I don't know any more. I don't know.

GREGORY   You don't know what?

,

JAMES   Did she ever love me?

GREGORY   You can't be seriously doubting *that*

JAMES   I am. Because if she isn't mine, and it's – the eyes, you know, it's *likely* she isn't mine

GINA   She's yours in every way that matters

JAMES   Then why this letter?

He picks up the two halves of the letter.

Her father's calling to her. Anna loves her, you know that, they'd love to have her. And here it is, handsfull of gold and they're offering her a life

GINA   And what do you think she'll say?

Commotion in the loft – rustling, the duck quacks.

JAMES   She's not old enough to know yet. She'd have to be an adult. Have to understand what was being offered. Because she would have to give up a whole *life*. Her life, which

483

is hers by rights, hers by birth, she would
have to give it up – and why would she?
Why would she want to stay – for a man
who isn't her father, isn't her blood, with
no money, no education, in a rented flat
with her alcoholic grandad? Why would
she give up her life for some dead-dog
photographer lounging around useless with
nowhere to go?

A real pistol shot is heard from the attic. It's loud.

GINA   What's he doing, hunting on his own? I
              thought we said –

GREGORY   You don't know what that means

GINA   Sorry?

GREGORY   She did it. He did it, but she asked him to –
              he's shot the wild duck.

              ,

JAMES   Shot the wild duck?

GINA   Why?

GREGORY   She wanted to sacrifice the thing that was
              most precious to her in the world. For you.
              She wanted you to love her again.

*JAMES is moved – this feels like it could be a happy ending – GINA
also tearful.*

JAMES   Hedwig?

GREGORY   Yes

JAMES   Oh little Hedwig –

GINA   You see, James? You see?

GREGORY smiles, moved too –

GREGORY   She wanted her dad. She couldn't live
                    without him.

JAMES   Where is she?

The fire alarm starts.

GINA   She's in her bedroom –

JAMES   Hedwig – HEDWIG!

He runs into her bedroom. No HEDWIG –

                    is she in the kitchen?

GINA moves to check –

GINA   Heddy?

FRANCIS appears in his military uniform, green jacket and all.

FRANCIS   Where is she?

JAMES   I thought you were up there?

FRANCIS   Are we ready?

He's got a birthday cake for HEDWIG, in the shape of a duck.

GINA   Did you fire the gun?

FRANCIS   When?

GINA   Now – just now

*JAMES has instinctively climbed the ladder, fast. Perhaps he switches
on a light which reveals the loft as less magical than we thought –
more real. Or if you like, more fake.*

FRANCIS   Me?

GREGORY   She's killed the wild duck.

JAMES has found HEDWIG

JAMES   Hedwig? What are you doing down there?

Sudden desperation sets in –

Help – *help* – the gun's warm – oh god, she's
on the floor – Gregers, help me, help me get
her down

*JAMES, in the loft, picks up HEDWIG and he and GREGORY get
HEDWIG down out of the loft, as GINA runs to the door and screams
out of it.*

GINA   Relling – Relling – call an ambulance – call
an ambulance – it's the gun, it's HEDDY,
it's the gun – oh god, be gentle with her –
careful, careful, Hedwig, it's your mum, I'm
here, sweetheart, I'm right here –

FRANCIS   The forest has had its revenge.

*JAMES sends the contents of the table – butter, bread, the lot – flying
to make room for HEDWIG's little body.*

GINA   We can't put her on a hard table – she's
bleeding – oh god, she's bleeding –

*Blood everywhere. GREGORY's trying to blanche the wound with
white kitchen roll and blood is getting all over it.*

JAMES   She's coming round – she's going to come
round –

GINA   Get out of the way – get out of the way I
can't find where she's / shot herself –

JAMES	It isn't serious, Gina, it's not a serious thing, she's going to be all right, she's going to be all right – she's going to be all right –

RELLING enters on the phone, adrenalin pulsing through his body – he's visible, slurringly, embarrassingly drunk.

GREGORY and JAMES may well need to ad lib a bit – but there shouldn't be silence until the realisation starts to drop.

RELLING	It's a bullet wound –
GINA	HELP HER
JAMES	Hedwig, Hedwig, you have to keep breathing, we have to keep breathing, Hedwig – / we're all here with you Hedwig, we're all here, can you see us, Heddy, can you see any of us, any sign you can give us –
RELLING	How old is she? Gina, how old is she?
GINA	She's thirteen – for fuck's sake hurry – she isn't breathing –
RELLING	Thirteen – yes / yes – sorry, someone is on their way?

Maybe RELLING opens a first-aid kit, drunkenly and the contents go everywhere.

GINA	She isn't breathing – she isn't breathing –
RELLING	I don't think she's conscious, no –

RELLING tries to find a pulse –

JAMES	And scene – and *scene* –
	HEDWIG STOP THIS AND STAND UP, this isn't funny – oh god, Hedwig, this isn't funny – and *SCENE* –

,

Nothing happens.

RELLING   I do apologise, I'm a little drunk so it night
       might have been, be difficult – could you
       send somebody *immediately*?

GINA grabs the phone from RELLING

GINA   It's her mum – no, no – no no she's not,
       she's not – she's not – she's not –

*As FRANCIS moves to GINA, the truth is in his eyes. GINA drops
the phone and slumps into FRANCIS' arms. And then, primal,
maternal, screams and batters a cushion and feathers go everywhere.
It looks as if a duck has died. And bled. Ducks bleed. After that
storm exhausts itself, she says to JAMES.*

       She's yours now, as much as mine.

JAMES   Take her downstairs – for when they get here
       –

*As JAMES carries her out, RELLING opening the door for him,
GINA helps him lift the body. Only GREGORY and RELLING left.
Stunned. RELLING hands the microphone to GREGERS.*

GREGORY (m) Hedwig Ekdal committed suicide on her
       thirteenth birthday. But for James and
       Gina Ekdal, it was a new beginning. They
       were changed. James Ekdal was a different
       man. RELLING (m) For a year. Most
       people feel noble in the presence of death.
       And then: it fades.

GREGORY (m) The truth is –

       The truth of the story

       It can't be that this *justifies* his his

RELLING (m)   A year later the memory of Hedwig Ekdal
                became just another self-aggrandising, self-
                pitying anecdote. With what had happened,
                James Ekdal crafted a story to suit him –
                because reality was simply too painful.

GREGORY   If you're right about that, then – if that's
                what this means, then

                why do any of us stay alive?

                ,

RELLING looks at GREGERS.

RELLING (m)   Gregory Woods hanged himself. Good
                riddance.

GREGORY (m)   But something

                something of what he stood for survived. It
                is with us. It lives on.

With real contempt, RELLING shakes his head – and laughs.

And spits on the floor at GREGORY's feet.

And then goes out of the front door, perhaps laughing.

GREGORY stands in the middle of the stage, just as at the beginning.

He clicks the mic on.

Clicks it off.

He looks like he's about to say something. Draws breath.

And then the rest of the cast enter to join him for the curtain call.

THE DOCTOR

The purpose of poetry is to remind us
how difficult it is to remain just one person,
for our house is open, there are no keys in the doors,
and invisible guests come in and out at will.
(from *Ars Poetica?* by Czeslaw Milosz)

Acknowledgements

My greatest debt is to the actors and creative team of the original production, whose ideas, instincts and input quite literally create the show, and to all of whom I am genuinely grateful. For many of them, their involvement precedes this script – and theirs is the first thank you and the biggest.

Another team of actors read a draft of the play and offered their thoughts and encouragement at an early stage of development – to them, much thanks, and a heartfelt thank you to the exceptional Julia Horan, whose role in creating a production before it even knows itself cannot be underestimated.

Many other people kindly spoke to me, answered my questions, shared their expertise, and offered thoughts and notes on the script in its various drafts – including Helen Lewis, Rachel Taylor, Helena Clark, Stephen Grosz, Ben Naylor, Ilinca Radulian, Branden Jacobs-Jenkins, Anne Washburn, Chris Campbell, Adam Crossley, Adam Kay, Daniel Sokol, Jonathan Freedland, Josh Higgott, Rupert Goold, Lucy Pattison, Emma Pritchard, Rebecca Frecknall, Stephanie Bain, Alexander Scott, Judith Beniston, Emily Vaughan-Barratt, Anastasia Bruce-Jones, Ingoh Brux, Duncan Macmillan and Zara Tempest-Walters. Thank you all and apologies, and thanks, to anyone I've forgotten.

RI, August 2019

Characters

at home
RUTH WOLFF
CHARLIE, her 'partner'
SAMI

at the Elizabeth Institute
BRIAN CYPRIAN
ROGER HARDIMAN
PAUL MURPHY
MICHAEL COPLEY
REBECCA ROBERTS
a JUNIOR doctor, whose name we never learn

FATHER Jacob Rice, a Catholic priest
the FATHER of Emily Ronan
and JEMIMA FLINT, Minister for Health

and a HOST and five PANELLISTS on the TV
programme *Take the Debate*

This play was originally produced at the Almeida Theatre, where it had its first performance on 10th August, 2019.

Cast (in alphabetical order)
Oliver Alvin-Wilson
Nathalie Armin
Paul Higgins
Mariah Louca
Pamela Nomvete
Daniel Rabin
Joy Richardson
Kirsty Rider
Juliet Stevenson
Naomi Wirthner
Ria Zmitrowicz

Creative Team	
Direction	Robert Icke
Design	Hildegard Bechtler
Light	Natasha Chivers
Sound and Composition	Tom Gibbons
Associate Costume Design	Deborah Andrews
Additional Composition	Hannah Ledwidge
Casting	Julia Horan CDG
Resident Director	TD Moyo
Costume Supervision	Megan Doyle
Photography	Manuel Harlan
Company Stage Manager	Claire Sibley
Deputy Stage Manager	Bethan McKnight
Assistant Stage Manager	Beth Cotton
Bioethics Consultant	Daniel Sokol

The production (eventually) transferred to the Duke of York's Theatre, London, where it played its first performance on 29th September, 2022.

Cast (in alphabetical order)
Christopher Osikanlu Colquhoun
Doña Croll
Juliet Garricks
Mark Hammersley
Preeya Kalidas
Takiyah Kamaria
Hannah Ledwidge
Mariah Louca
John Mackay
Celia Nelson
Daniel Rabin
Juliet Stevenson
Diana Thomas
Matilda Tucker
Naomi Wirthner
Sabrina Wu

A note on the text

A forward slash (/) marks the point of interruption of overlapping dialogue.

A comma on a separate line

,

indicates a pause, a rest, a silence, an upbeat or a lift. Length and intensity are context dependent.

Square brackets [like this] indicates words which are part of the intention of the line but which are not spoken aloud.

A * on a separate line denotes a change of scene or a time-jump. They should feel like the change of (or the loss of) a train of thought for RUTH but mostly the dialogue should continue uninterrupted.

A note on the casting

Actors' identities should be carefully considered in the casting of the play. In all sections except for *Take the Debate*, each actor's identity should be directly dissonant with their character's in at least one way. Sometimes these dissonances are specifically designated in the text, sometimes it's up to the production – but the acting should hold the mystery until the play reveals it. The idea is that the audience are made to re-consider characters (and events) as they learn more about who the characters are.

This text went to press before the production opened and so may differ slightly from what was performed. But let's not worry too much about that.

RUTH on the phone

RUTH which

which is it

Hello, yes, sorry – my name is Ruth Wolff, double-f

which is it (god, you'd think I'd know this)

which is it I need if someone's died? a body, yes –

no, not urgent – I'm sure. yes. Yes. I'm crystal clear.

I'm a doctor

*

CHARLIE speaks: THE FIRST DAY

CHARLIE is about the same age as RUTH. It's important that the audience are never told explicitly whether the character is male or female.

A room in the Elizabeth Institute. MURPHY and HARDIMAN come in to a room where JUNIOR waits.

MURPHY	We were playing as a team – I mean, we played better than we've been playing –
JUNIOR	do you know where Professor Hardiman is?
MURPHY	. . . that's him
HARDIMAN	You're the new junior
JUNIOR	Yes –
HARDIMAN	Roger Hardiman, senior consultant, deputy director – [without stopping]
JUNIOR	Oh – I'm / my name's
HARDIMAN	there's supposed to be a report, autopsy, three days ago, male mid-70s
JUNIOR	It's here, it's just come in –

JUNIOR passes it, HARDIMAN takes it and reads

HARDIMAN	It was his liver. She was right.

HARDIMAN goes, furious, leaving the report behind

MURPHY	Which means: I'm now owed money.
JUNIOR	You bet on patients?
MURPHY	Absolutely not. Patient was Hardiman's, very sick, we can't work out whether it's his liver or his kidneys and patient's too weak

for us to treat both – he calls the BB in for an opinion – the BB has her Jedi perception. Professor, says the BB, I have nothing but my intuition, it is not my name above the bed, but I am crystal clear that the patient's kidneys are not the problem. Hardiman disagrees, treats the kidneys, patient dies. That's a fish, isn't it, your tattoo –

JUNIOR   is that a title? The BB?

MURPHY   It's a person. Sort of. Professor Wolff. BB = Big Bad

JUNIOR   Professor Wolff is my consultant

HARDIMAN   Good luck. Woman in name only.

JUNIOR   What does that mean?

HARDIMAN   It's a joke.

    COPLEY comes in

COPLEY   Is Ruth here?

MURPHY   She's on her round, I think –

COPLEY   ok. They need her downstairs.

    COPLEY goes out again

HARDIMAN   Do you go to pharmacology lectures?

JUNIOR   It's not Professor Creswell at the moment –

HARDIMAN   I know that.

JUNIOR   He's off on sick, so Doctor Feinman is filling in.

HARDIMAN   I *know* that. But have you been to them?

JUNIOR	Yes –
HARDIMAN	And how are they?
JUNIOR	How are they?
HARDIMAN	Yes
JUNIOR	Good.

HARDIMAN looks at JUNIOR as if to say 'Say more'

She gets a bit excited.

HARDIMAN	I quite agree

As MURPHY makes to go

MURPHY	BB will need to see that report. And Copley is looking for her –
JUNIOR	For who?

RUTH enters, overhearing

RUTH	For whom.

For whom is Doctor Copley looking? In the case that you care about language at all. Either way, I believe I am the answer.

JUNIOR doesn't really know how to respond, HARDIMAN saves

HARDIMAN	Report's in. It was his liver. You were right.
RUTH	No, *we* were wrong. We are one institution, Roger, not a balkanised set of opinions – and here, we got it wrong. Could I have that report, please?
JUNIOR	This one?

RUTH	That one. In my hand. Thank you.
	,
	I wouldn't join the boys' club just yet. You may have better options.
JUNIOR	Actually I'm with your firm again today, Professor
RUTH	I do not run a 'firm'. Coming through the doors of this institute, we might have cleaning firms, or firms of engineers – solicitors' firms, occasionally, but I run a medical *team*.
JUNIOR	Sure
RUTH	Good. There's a patient in room one, female, fourteen years old, sepsis, antibiotics aren't achieving source control. There's a nurse in there who needs relieving. The parents are on their way here, but someone should be with her at all times. Could you take over?
MURPHY	Why have we got a dying fourteen year old / in an Alzheimer's institute
RUTH	Because I was in A+E when she was brought in and sometimes, Paul, though try not to let this astonish you, doctors treat patients. *(Seamlessly to J.)* She's maximal analgesia, GCS is 9, so she's only half-conscious. Notes are up to date. Bleep me if anything changes. Yes? Go.

JUNIOR goes. RUTH glances over the report

HARDIMAN	You been here all night?

RUTH   Yes, with that patient, trying to get
              antibiotics to work.

HARDIMAN   I can take over if you need to get some rest?

MURPHY   It's basically over

RUTH   It is over when there is a body and not a
              single second before. Doctor Murphy, have
              we cured dementia? Is there nowhere for
              you to be?

MURPHY   Speaking of bodies, I think we're about to be
              looking for a new head of pharmacology –

RUTH   Yes. I visited Professor Creswell this
              weekend. He isn't going to be coming back.
              In either sense.

MURPHY   Ah. Shame. I think we might be able to
              persuade Bob Munro.

RUTH   I'm sure we could. But why would we want
              to?

*MURPHY goes. HARDIMAN refers to the report, which RUTH is
reading.*

HARDIMAN   I should have listened to you, Ruth, you
              called it absolutely / right

RUTH   One of us had to be right and you followed
              your instincts. Nothing to be ashamed of
              there. Patients do die.

COPLEY enters

COPLEY   Someone here to see your sepsis patient –

RUTH   No visitors

COPLEY   I think [he's immediate family]

RUTH	No visitors. Patient's only half with us.
COPLEY	He's making quite a fuss – I think he's immediate family
RUTH	He can't be, they're out of the country.
COPLEY	Okay

COPLEY goes. RUTH carries on reading the report.

,

HARDIMAN	I really do apologise, Ruth, about / the
RUTH	I'm not reading this to humiliate you, Roger. I'm reading it because I need to have read it.
JUNIOR	Professor –
RUTH *(chorus)*	Yes?
HARDIMAN *(chorus)*	Yes?
JUNIOR	Wolff, sorry – Professor – she's saying her boyfriend's coming – the patient is / saying
RUTH	He isn't. He isn't here, he never was. She's been saying that all night.
HARDIMAN	If you want me to take over, Ruth, see her through to the end –
JUNIOR	She's – going to die?
RUTH	It's not over 'til there's a body. You know what – I'm going to come back down.

*

RUTH and JUNIOR have happened upon COPLEY and the FATHER. The FATHER is played by a white actor.

RUTH	Why are we all standing outside my patient's door?
COPLEY	I'm sorry, Professor – I didn't want to call security but this gentleman is insistent he sees your patient –
RUTH	You are not wearing a lanyard. A *badge*, I mean
FATHER	no – (?)
RUTH	I take your point, it's a flawed system, it's a naïve sort of logic, really, that says a rogue gunman might be made conspicuous because he's the only person in the hospital *not* to be wearing ID – could I take your name, Mr –
FATHER	Father –

A beat

RUTH	Forgive me: I was told Emily's parents were on a plane and / wouldn't be here for a couple / of hours [at least]
FATHER	No it's Father – Father Jacob. I'm a priest.
RUTH	I'm afraid Emily isn't up to visitors.
COPLEY	I've told him that, Professor –
FATHER	They said she is conscious
RUTH	She is –
FATHER	Which is surely a good sign
COPLEY	I think we're beyond signs.

RUTH	Thank you, Michael – could you check on the patient, please?
FATHER	She is going to die?
RUTH	As are we all.

RUTH makes to move on. The FATHER puts on a dog collar.

FATHER	Her parents asked me – Emily's parents – suggested she might need me to be here. They phoned me from the airport.
RUTH	Well, they didn't phone me.
FATHER	With respect, Doctor, that's not my problem.
	,
RUTH	Emily's blood pressure is extremely low. That means a real chance of a cardiac event which means we can't risk interventions. Our focus of care at this moment is comfort.
FATHER	Mine too
RUTH	I'm sorry, I don't understand
FATHER	Let me make it clearer. Emily is gravely ill. Emily's parents asked me to be here and to attend to her. Is that not obvious?
RUTH	It's obvious when the patient has requested religious assistance, because it's written on her medical notes. In this instance, there's nothing of the sort.
FATHER	So –
RUTH	So no visitors.

FATHER	I'm not a visitor
RUTH	Then who are you?
FATHER	Doctor, Emily's parents are Catholic, her parents are members of my congregation and they / asked me to be here –
COPLEY	Ruth, do you want me to call / the parents?
RUTH	They're on a plane. And it isn't their decision. So Emily is religious?
FATHER	Yes

He's not 100% certain, somehow

RUTH	And she attends your church?
FATHER	Her parents do.
RUTH	Not her?
FATHER	She has done, yes

,

RUTH	I'm sorry, sir, but I have / no
FATHER	[sir] Father
RUTH	I have no way of knowing whether she last attended church in a Christening gown. The only thing of relevance is what she herself believes – and I don't know. I don't know if you've ever met her.

The FATHER's eyes are blazing but he doesn't raise his voice.

| FATHER | I'm a liar, then |

,

	Shall we go in and ask Emily?
RUTH	No. She isn't expecting your visit, she hasn't asked for your visit, and she's delirious. She's dreaming. She only half knows she's here, in a hospital – but she thinks she's going to be fine. And I am crystal clear that if we snap her out of that state, we cause significant distress. You let her know she's dying, then she panics, that means physiological stress, more demand on her circulation and a number of other things she simply isn't able to cope with.
FATHER	What are you saying?
RUTH	I'm saying you walk in there like the grim reaper and there is no way that she, in her current condition, can die without panic and / distress
FATHER	I wonder what it is about me that you think I'm so incompetent / that

MURPHY arrives to the scene

MURPHY	Professor, can / I borrow you –
RUTH	One minute, Paul –
FATHER	I'm sorry: is there any chance she might be cured?
COPLEY	No.
RUTH	There's always a chance
FATHER	Do you know the cause of her condition?
RUTH	Yes, I do

FATHER	And?
RUTH	*And* I'd need her consent to reveal it to you. And I'd rather not have this conversation out here in front of an audience – Doctor Copley, could you find an empty / room
FATHER	So she could die within the hour. She can't be cured. But you're telling me she can't receive the last rites?
RUTH	It's my name above her bed. And it is my duty to protect my patient –
FATHER	From what?
RUTH	and act in her best interests
FATHER	Protect her from what?
RUTH	From an unpeaceful death
	,
FATHER	But she has the right to make her own choice
RUTH	I'm going to leave this now, and go back in

Quietly, JUNIOR leaves to the patient – this starts to really escalate. CYPRIAN comes in.

FATHER	I thought you couldn't help her –
RUTH	We don't only attend the patients we can help – and I don't have to justify myself to you
FATHER	If she can see you, she can see me –
RUTH	Not here. Not how it works.

CYPRIAN	Professor, is everything all right here?
RUTH	It's fine
FATHER	Sorry, are you her supervisor?
CYPRIAN	what?
FATHER	I want to speak to her supervisor
RUTH	I hate to burst your bubble but I'm the Founding Director of this Institute, so my supervisor is either the board or the General Medical Council and you don't have that kind of time –
COPLEY	Professor, I think we need to calm / down
RUTH	I'm calm. We're finished here.
FATHER	I'm not finished here. What happens if I walk calmly through that door?
RUTH	Then my colleagues here will call security –
CYPRIAN	We would have to / call security
FATHER	Listen, mate, keep out of this. Are you forbidding me / from entering this room?
RUTH	What are you doing?

The FATHER has started a recording device, he speaks into it

FATHER	I'm recording what's left of our conversation
RUTH	In which case I'm going to terminate it.
FATHER	I'm now going to walk calmly into Emily's room, Doctor – I'm sorry, can you get out of my way –

RUTH	You have *zero* authority here. I don't know who the hell you are. You want to get uppity with me, then fine. But you're wasting your time because there is really no way I'm going to let you near that child
MURPHY	Professor, I think / we should
FATHER	I'm now going to walk into the room –
RUTH	There is a child in there, father, about to die a peaceful death and she needs my full attention as a matter of urgency to keep that death peaceful –

As the FATHER moves to the door, RUTH touches him. The FATHER throws her hand off. Probably this shouldn't be naturalistically dramatized: that is, we shouldn't be shown exactly what happens.

FATHER	Get your hands off me – don't you dare TOUCH me, don't you DARE.
JUNIOR	*(From within.)* Doctor Wolff – hello? Can you come in here, please? Quick

The kettle starts to boil. A repeating ding-dong alarm noise perhaps sounds too, as if a machine is reporting a patient in distress. JUNIOR re-enters.

	Doctor – she's panicking – heart-rate's skyrocketing
RUTH	Why?
JUNIOR	She says she doesn't want to die
FATHER	I thought she didn't know – (!)
RUTH	She didn't know. She didn't.

*

CHARLIE	You touched him. The priest
RUTH	Yes –
CHARLIE	How did you touch him?
RUTH	I put my hand on his shoulder
CHARLIE	Was it a touch or a shove? Or a push? Did it have force?
RUTH	I – no. It was a touch. I mean, as if the word itself is material to / the
CHARLIE	If I were your lawyer and not your partner, these are the questions I'd ask you in the first ten minutes –
RUTH	I hate the word partner. It sounds like we're – accountants.

*

The doctors re-enter the corridor where the FATHER waits.

FATHER	Can I go in there now? I need to see Emily / before
JUNIOR	I'm afraid it's too late –
RUTH	*Time*, please
JUNIOR	Time of death eleven minutes past eight.
RUTH	Thank you – everyone

The doctors are aware of the FATHER, not moving – perhaps emotional

COPLEY	[is] cause of death – sepsis arising from complications of termination of pregnancy?

RUTH   [just put] Sepsis.

The FATHER turns around. He looks at RUTH.

MURPHY   I'm sorry things got so heated before, Father –

FATHER   You idiots

                  you don't get to grant absolution. What's
                  happened here is is is a very serious thing

COPLEY   Ok – ok –

FATHER   I trust you won't have a problem if I attend
                  to Emily now, Ms Wolff.

RUTH   Professor Wolff

The FATHER storms out.

MURPHY   You're out of line. You should have let him
                  in.

RUTH   To remind you of the basic rule, you get to
                  call the shots, Doctor Murphy, when the
                  nurse writes your name above the patient's
                  bed. Are you having trouble with your
                  reading?

MURPHY   We'll see. We'll see.

MURPHY exits

*

The kettle clicks off, boiled. We're in RUTH's house.

CHARLIE   And you watched the girl die

RUTH   Yes. Screaming for her parents and
                  scratching the nurse and I don't want to die
                  I don't want to die – five minutes before

514

	she's floating hazy in a dream and she dies trying to tear through a nightmare
CHARLIE	Not the first one you've lost, Ruthie
RUTH	No
CHARLIE	Tea?
RUTH	No thank you
	She was fourteen.
	Is someone in the house?
CHARLIE	Your friend's upstairs.
RUTH	Oh?
CHARLIE	You gave her keys, remember. What did the girl die of?
RUTH	Self-administered abortion. She'd hoped she wasn't pregnant for four months. Parents went away for the week, she'd got the pills online, took them probably two days ago, it's an incomplete abortion, bleeding, she ignores it, tries to stem the bleed with pads, didn't work, falls unconscious, hours pass, her friend's mum finds her, gets her into us, but by that point she's already far gone with sepsis.
	And none of this story is clear until after she's dead.
(Deep: if only.)	If they'd let her have a civilised abortion in a medical setting, she'd be eating ice-cream and surfing the internet.
CHARLIE	who's they?

RUTH	Catholic parents.

*

SAMI	Your cat is quite weird. It has like a proper attitude problem. Last ten times I've been here it's nowhere to be seen and then today it's like sitting on the landing and it's like staring at me, like 'hi'. It looks at you like it knows your secrets.
RUTH	perhaps it does
SAMI	is it a he-cat or a she-cat?
RUTH	it's a cat-cat
SAMI	But it's got a name – (?)
RUTH	Astonishingly, in nine years it's never introduced itself in English –
SAMI	It doesn't have a name – (!)
RUTH	Oh it'll happily ignore a whole variety of names.
SAMI	I am like – appalled –
RUTH	Having spent all day with an abortion patient, I'm *like* philosophical about the things people choose to humanise
SAMI	I thought it was all like Alzheimer's at your institute –
RUTH	It is. But I saw the girl come in and sometimes, something else takes over and I was taking her up to the Institute before I'd even – you know what, this doesn't matter.
SAMI	Your kettle is always boiled.

RUTH	It reminds me I'm alive. You want tea?
SAMI	I don't do tea. Or coffee.
RUTH	You don't *do* them?
SAMI	You are literally doing my head in, language police.

Perhaps CHARLIE makes RUTH a cup of tea

RUTH	Tea was the currency of love in our house, growing up. The transmission of affection in a chipped mug. And a biscuit, if you were really in favour.
SAMI	How long have you lived here?
RUTH	For ever.
	,
SAMI	When I was a kid, people used to call this house the witch's cottage.

SAMI senses potential hurt in RUTH and saves it

	Because it's near the wood. And it's old.
RUTH	And there's a black cat.
	,
	Is that school work you're doing?
SAMI	*(Sarc)* No, I look at circle theorems to, like, relax
RUTH	To *like* relax
SAMI	What would you say?

RUTH	It's the 'likes', everything is – comparative. Nothing contained. No thought *finished.*
SAMI	Don't you like that? Don't you *like* that?
RUTH	Open-ended isn't great in medicine. Usually means someone's about to enter the past tense.

,

I don't look like a witch

SAMI	You look sad.
RUTH	I suppose, in one way, I am *like* a witch. The process of looking at someone, at something about them. Extrapolating evidence. Guessing what will happen to them next. That's fortune telling. Or as we have it, diagnostic medicine.
SAMI	You're not a witch
RUTH	We still give you poison for cancer and chalk for your stomach and the bark of a willow tree for headaches. Only we write different things on the bottles. In a hundred years – two hundred years, they'll look back at us and they'll know the cure. It'll seem so obvious, they'll think we were so stupid not to know. Doctors – are witches in white.
	'Take this potion, my pretty one, uncork the bottle and drink, once at dawn, once at dusk and your back will straighten, your eyes will brighten and your dreams – will set themselves upright for years to come.'
SAMI	OK, witch-doctor, what if I don't?

RUTH	Then you die
SAMI	We're all going to die, though. Like – a sell-by-date for your soul. It's a 'when' not an 'if'. Could be tomorrow. Or tonight. In here.
	now
	now
RUTH	It's over when there's a body. I should find us some food. Your mum knows you're here
SAMI	If she didn't, she wouldn't care –
	Are you okay?
RUTH	oh I don't know. A girl died today. At work.

CHARLIE speaks: THE SECOND DAY

ROBERTS   The important thing is that we don't panic

CYPRIAN   She called me and she wanted to know what
                 we were doing about the situation and I
                 said, what situation, and then she tells me
                 what situation and I said well, there wasn't
                 much we could do about the situation, the
                 situation had happened and she said well
                 people really aren't very happy about it and
                 she slams the phone down

COPLEY   So what?

CYPRIAN   So she has a lot of money and she has a
                 husband who is on our board, and she also,
                 as things currently stand, has promised quite
                 a lot of her money to our new building

COPLEY   She's the one who thought we should have
                 a ball. Big red woman. Met her touring the
                 research centre last year. I mean, a hospital
                 ball.

ROBERTS   Right –

          RUTH enters

COPLEY   She says 'does the hospital ever host events
                 for its donors? I think donors means organ
                 donors, and then she says 'We could
                 organize a ball' and I thought – well, good
                 luck finding a bloke to donate that –

CYPRIAN   Shall we not air our grievances to a junior
                 doctor? That woman is a development asset –

MURPHY   I spoke to development – and development
                 think it's a problem.

CYPRIAN	Ruth, I've got a donor who's very unhappy about our priest situation –
RUTH	and I've got three questions: One, why are we spending time on this? Two, when did we start to use the word 'development' to mean 'us asking people for money'? Three, Doctor Murphy, why are you involved?
CYPRIAN	This is important, Ruth, she's unhappy. So what are we going to do?
RUTH	Cure unhappiness. And Rebecca is here – because – (?)
MURPHY	Because Rebecca is responsible for public relations.
RUTH	And her advice is?
ROBERTS	We shouldn't make a public response –
RUTH	Good. Let's move on.
ROBERTS	– but how does your donor know?

A pause. They look at each other.

MURPHY	I would assume it's either the parents or the priest. Roger Hardiman spoke to the parents when they arrived late last night and they were obviously / very upset
CYPRIAN	They'll sue
JUNIOR	For wrongful death?
ROBERTS *(chorus)*	Probably
CYPRIAN *(chorus)*	Yes – who are you?
JUNIOR	I'm / [goes to say his name but]

COPLEY	They'll lose on wrongful death. Death was inevitable.
MURPHY	Was it, though?
ROBERTS	Medically, did Ruth do anything wrong? What are the actual rules?
COPLEY	If the patient's a child, then it's up to the doctor. There was nothing on the notes about religion. No parents available to contact. No time to consult more widely. There's really nothing else Ruth could have done.
ROBERTS	[but] could she have let the priest give the girl the last rites?
MURPHY	Exactly
COPLEY	He was a man coming in off the street –
MURPHY	wearing a dog collar
COPLEY	which would be impossible to fake, you're quite right
MURPHY	He was a man of God and she basically called him a liar, I mean, why are we pretending we weren't convinced he was a priest?
RUTH	I really don't think any of us are
ROBERTS	What does the Hippocratic oath say?
	,
	I'm asking because other people will.
MURPHY	Brian?

CYPRIAN	No-one swears the Hippocratic oath. Not any more. It's ancient and it's therefore in the bin. The guidelines are still to 'do no harm' – but the thing that really counts is patient choice.
MURPHY	The patient wasn't told she had a choice
RUTH	The patient wasn't conscious
MURPHY	That's not what it says in the notes
RUTH	And why are you reading the notes?
CYPRIAN	OK – we need a report that confirms whether the girl would have died anyway.
RUTH	I asked for it last night. It'll be here this morning. It'll say: yes, she would have [died anyway]. Now let's move onto something important. We need to make a decision about departmental structure / in the new building –
MURPHY	Sorry, Ruth – if the parents are already going to complain, they'll say that if the girl's prognosis was hopeless, the priest should have been allowed in.
ROBERTS	And will the priest have the backing of the church?
COPLEY	Does the pope shit in the woods?
CYPRIAN	Michael, tone, please
COPLEY	Brian, I am merely pointing out that they have a habit of protecting their own
MURPHY	Like doctors, then

JUNIOR	There's a petition online
	,
RUTH	What?
MURPHY	About this? Are you on it now?
CYPRIAN	Read it. Read out what it says
JUNIOR	'The incident that took place at the Elizabeth Institute on – et cetera et cetera, Father Jacob Rice was summoned to the death-bed of Emily Ronan by her parents to give her the last rites. The consultant in charge, who is not a Christian, refused to admit the Father to the girl's bedside, on the grounds that his ministry might be damaging to the dying girl's health.'
COPLEY	But that / isn't
CYPRIAN	Let him read
JUNIOR	'The girl was dying as a result of complications after the termination of her pregnancy. The Elizabeth Institute is a private part of the hospital largely funded by a club of anonymous donors. When the Father tried to enter Emily's room, the consultant in charge used physical force and shoved him out of / the way'
COPLEY	What?
RUTH	That didn't happen –
MURPHY	Well [that definitely did happen]
CYPRIAN	There are witnesses

RUTH	There are not witnesses that / saw me
CYPRIAN	I'm saying there are witnesses, so that's not going to be a *problem*
MURPHY	Brian [I saw her push him]

CYPRIAN crushes the opposition with firm entitlement

CYPRIAN	*That is not going to be a problem.* Continue. Read.
JUNIOR	'During this fight, Emily died without receiving the last rites. We, the undersigned, are horrified at this doctor's treatment of a religious man and call for action to be taken in investigating this incident and to urgently raise the issue that Christian patients need Christian doctors.'
MURPHY	This is a mess.
RUTH	Even at the level of grammar, if that petition's anything to go by –
ROBERTS	We shouldn't respond. It's obviously political, and I don't think people will listen –
COPLEY	Spotting a spotlight and trying to leap into it – though the anti-semitic undertones…
CYPRIAN	What?
COPLEY	'A club of shady anonymous donors'
MURPHY	I disagree
COPLEY	And soon someone's going to be saying 'This is a Christian country'
MURPHY	This is a Christian country

COPLEY	Ignore it and it'll die down.
MURPHY	I disagree – our funding rests on our reputation and our reputation is about to get punched –
CYPRIAN	The timing is unfortunate, given the new building
MURPHY	so then we need to make a statement
ROBERTS	I really don't think / that's
COPLEY	It's the Catholic Church! They're not a moral arbiter!

HARDIMAN enters

HARDIMAN	Ruth, can I borrow you for a minute?
RUTH	How many signatures does it have? That petition
	,
JUNIOR	twenty-seven.
CYPRIAN	Twenty-seven? Then what the hell are you doing bringing it up? Why the hell should anyone care?
JUNIOR	I thought / it might be
RUTH	Now can we please talk about something important
CYPRIAN	This is important
RUTH	Sixty-one year old man, you really are in the danger window for a heart attack, so it really would be best if you kept calm. And stayed

hydrated. Could we please get some water for Brian?

CYPRIAN   Look. No-one knows it's Ruth. There's no way they find out. We deal with the parents internally and we put out a neutral statement that says hospital procedures were followed

ROBERTS *(chorus)*   No –
RUTH *(chorus)*   No

MURPHY   Were they followed?

RUTH   Yes.

HARDIMAN   But if the parents / disagree

RUTH   Patient was a child, so it's for the doctor, not the parents / to decide

COPLEY   Exactly

HARDIMAN   A neutral statement isn't going to cut it. This is already bigger than that. The press love a medical ethics story, we're a wealthy institution, fair-game for punching up – science versus faith. They love all the stuff about the Jehovah's Witnesses who won't accept transfused blood

COPLEY   Exactly, people who'd rather die than accept technological progress– people frightened of a new idea, to which I say, 'Fine, you die if you want to but my kids are having vaccinations'

CYPRIAN   Can we please try and speak in a professional / manner

COPLEY   I'm saying this is not serious

CYPRIAN	This is serious
RUTH	This is the healing power of religious faith squaring up against proven, empirical, scientific medicine. The sound you're hearing is the sound you hear when an old tradition dies. When an elderly man picks a fight to prove that he still can, we smile, we walk away, we don't respond.
HARDIMAN	A tradition dying. You're really comfortable talking about religion like that?
RUTH	I really am, yes. I am not asking anyone to do anything differently. I'm not asking to be involved with their lives or for them to live according to my rules. I am asking them to let us get on with our work. So can we please get on with our work?
HARDIMAN	Religion is people's lives – for these people, their whole identity –
RUTH	Exactly. And progress beats identity every single time. Now can we please move on?
HARDIMAN	I'm a Catholic. Do you want to say that again – and to me?
RUTH	I will happily say that to you, Roger, at the point when you try to stop me having access to a patient, over whom you have no authority, and who I am trying to treat. Until then, I shall live and let live. Let's move on.
CYPRIAN	Yes, but if the press pick this up –
RUTH	Then we will cross that bridge, and if I have to, I will say my piece –

ROBERTS   I don't think we need to worry about press
                 at this point –

RUTH   And you're [ROBERTS] in charge of press
                 and that's good enough for me – so lets /
                 move on

MURPHY   But not for me – I'm sorry, Ruth / but we
                 cannot take this lightly

COPLEY   Oh take the fucking advice –

CYPRIAN   MICHAEL

HARDIMAN   Okay, we need to calm / this down

CYPRIAN *(uncalm)* I am the CLINICAL DIRECTOR of this
                 INSTITUTE and I have spent three bloody
                 miserable years working us to the point of
                 exhausting to raise the funding for this new
                 building and I don't think it's funny that we
                 might be jeopardised [over so little] – we
                 have a meeting, well she has a meeting this
                 week with the Health Secretary –

RUTH   Today, in / fact –

CYPRIAN   TODAY. So of all the hills in all the world,
                 why choose to die on this one? We break
                 ground on our own bespoke building in six
                 months' time which gives us the best tools
                 to have the best chance of being the people
                 who cure dementia. And that could mean a
                 Nobel Prize for her.

RUTH   *(Fast in.)* for all of us, because we are a
                 team. Were you coming to a point, Professor
                 Cyprian?

CYPRIAN   We cannot allow this to become a thing.

HARDIMAN	Too late. It's the morning after and there's already the board, the petition and the pro-life group –
ROBERTS	What?
RUTH	What's happened on the board?
HARDIMAN	Murmurs
ROBERTS	And the pro-life group?
HARDIMAN	E-mails from the anti-abortion people demanding a statement. It's fine, for now. But why not get ahead? Prepare a statement – perhaps only internally, that can be circulated to the board, offered perhaps to the parents, if needs be.
RUTH	A statement saying what?
CYPRIAN	'I'm sorry if any offence was caused'
ROBERTS	You can't say 'sorry if'
MURPHY	'Sorry if' is no different to 'go and fuck yourself'
ROBERTS	Also you can't be sorry for them being offended, you have to be sorry for what you did
RUTH	I think the lack of my having done something makes that really quite difficult
HARDIMAN	'I got it wrong. I'm sorry.'
	,
	I was being her
RUTH	I didn't get it wrong

MURPHY	Wait. You think this autopsy report will say the girl would have died regardless.
RUTH	Yes. I'm crystal clear.
MURPHY	Then she *could* have had the last rites and nothing would have changed.
RUTH	Except a deeply distressing final few minutes alive –
HARDIMAN	which *is* what actually happened.
COPLEY	Can the autopsy tell us whether she was a Christian?
JUNIOR	I don't think that's funny
COPLEY	And I don't think I'm going to take censure from a junior fucking doctor. Can you go and do your rounds please?
HARDIMAN	Ruth, could I – sorr/y

The JUNIOR goes

ROBERTS	Was she a Christian?

MURPHY *(chorus)*	Yes
COPLEY *(chorus)*	No
HARDIMAN *(chorus)*	Well –

MURPHY	She was wearing a crucifix
COPLEY	That's a generational thing, loads of young / people
MURPHY	when she died, she was wearing / a crucifix
RUTH	Exactly. We don't know. We will now never know. Her parents were Catholics
HARDIMAN	are Catholics

COPLEY	But the point is a single case cannot be blown up into a symbolic campaign / against religion
HARDIMAN	Yes it can. Yes it can.

CYPRIAN suddenly has an idea

CYPRIAN	Hang on but you're religious [Ruth]
RUTH	I'm not
CYPRIAN	I thought you were Jewish
COPLEY	Not religiously Jewish
RUTH	that's right, not Jewish. My parents were Jewish. They were religious people: I am not.
CYPRIAN	right.
	,
MURPHY	But you would have been thought of as Jewish – in the 1940s.
COPLEY	*(!)* Jesus Christ
MURPHY	What? That's the truth, isn't it?
RUTH	It is Paul, yes, but I think Michael's point is that maybe there might be more sensitive ways to reflect on the Jewish identity than the ones pioneered by the Nazis. *(COPLEY is ready to interrupt.)* Thank you, Michael, yes, you and I lost grandparents in that war, and they had stars sewn onto their lapels, but their legacy is this: we now get to choose what defines us – so can we please get on with our lives.

CYPRIAN has been thinking about the statement

CYPRIAN   How about 'The Elizabeth Institute takes
                 seriously any complaint, and in this instance
                 we find / no cause'

ROBERTS   Not 'we'

COPLEY   What's wrong with we?

ROBERTS   Every 'we' implies a 'they'. It's like tacitly
                 – you lot are making a huge fuss about
                 nothing and we in here think it's hilarious –

HARDIMAN   Ruth, could I [borrow you]?

*

HARDIMAN   Sorry to pull you out of there, Ruth –

RUTH   It's not a problem

HARDIMAN   Good. I'm a bit worried that people could
                 interpret this as you trying to make your
                 point. With the priest.

RUTH   My point?

HARDIMAN   Putting faith in its place, below medicine.
                 Religion is ancient, medicine is modern.

RUTH   Candles versus electricity, you mean?

HARDIMAN   I think candles might still exist, Ruth

RUTH   Not lighting many homes, though, are they,
                 now: more sort of decorative knick-knacks

HARDIMAN   You know as well as I do, it's not ideal
                 timing for a controversy.

RUTH   I do know that, yes

HARDIMAN	And the board are / wobbling –
RUTH	We'll have to see how it plays out
HARDIMAN	We could do that. But it is the whole institute that's involved, here, Ruth, not only you –
RUTH	I am aware of that, Roger
HARDIMAN	So the best thing would be to calm things down before they begin –
RUTH	Which is almost by definition difficult to do
HARDIMAN	But not here. All we need is for people to know that you had no intention of beginning some sort of anti-religious crusade –
RUTH	And you really think people have to be told that?
HARDIMAN	No. Shown.
	,
	The executive meets this week. And now, given Creswell's health, we're going to have to appoint a new head of pharmacology.
RUTH	Ah
HARDIMAN	And there are two serious contenders.
RUTH	One of whom is an excellent doctor
	,
HARDIMAN	I didn't know pharmacology was your specialism, Professor –

RUTH	I know you love playing charades, Roger, but I've read the materials, same as you – so can we be direct? Doctor Feinman's articles are exceptional where Doctor Munro simply lists case histories one after the other until this reader grinds her teeth. Doctor Feinman is a current employee, she knows us, knows the department: the advantage of institutional knowledge.
HARDIMAN	Some people think his case histories are excellent – and that her articles, though bursting with ideas, are over-excited and well – under-controlled. And personality-wise, for a head of department, a steadier hand / might
RUTH	It's not up to us, though, is it – the appointment is voted for by the exec
HARDIMAN	Which will split fifty-fifty, I think
RUTH	We'll see
HARDIMAN	And if it does, it's your deciding vote.
RUTH	I really am fully conversant with the procedures of this institute, Professor
HARDIMAN	Let's not get emotional, Ruth. Creswell said he would endorse Munro as his successor, said it'd be good to have a black man in that job.
RUTH	Well yes, he's a man, he doesn't want her to be promoted and prove a better HOD than him – which is exactly what will happen.
HARDIMAN	'He's a man'. It's a bit tedious, Ruth, after a while

RUTH	And so is Creswell's carping especially when one considers that the majority of what he's published in the last five years has been largely Janet Feinman's work.
HARDIMAN	And you'll say that to his face, will you?
RUTH	I don't have an issue with honesty. Shall we be straight with each other, Professor? Whether or not it's to calm the flames, you want to appoint Munro because he's a Christian.
	,
HARDIMAN	And it looks *good* to hire a *black man* in that job. I think it's our best move, Ruth.
RUTH	Right.
HARDIMAN	I could just as well say you want to appoint Feinman because she's *not* a Christian.
RUTH	But I appointed you. And Creswell. Both subscribers to the Christian religion.
HARDIMAN	'Believers', Ruth, it's not a magazine. And we are the exception, in this Institute, Professor, not the rule.
RUTH	There's not a rule
HARDIMAN	We're seen as a closed shop, Ruth.
RUTH	However we're seen, that's not what we are.
HARDIMAN	Thought experiment. We announce we're appointing Munro, we make it clear that he is a Christian and in our current crisis, subtly but definitely things calm / down

RUTH	The appointment is subject to a vote of the executive committee
HARDIMAN	I'm not asking you to vote for a fool. I think he's the better doctor.
RUTH	And I'm sure he'll be devastated it's not your deciding vote –
HARDIMAN	OK, Ruth. This is becoming a serious thing. I am being asked questions. From significant people. About this incident. And I'm very confident that those people will take the news of Munro's appointment as a clear suggestion that there's nothing here to find.

,

Think about it. We'll talk it through again before tomorrow –

RUTH	No need
HARDIMAN	Don't let pride get in the way, Ruth, please. And it goes without saying, all this is between us.
RUTH	No need. Tell whomever you like. Start with your noteworthy whoevers – and tell them this from me: I don't make deals.

ROBERTS enters

No wedding ring. Strange you're not married, isn't it? You live with her, don't you, but you're not married – not very Catholic.

ROBERTS	Sorry – the petition's at a touch under a hundred signatures now. Brian asked me to / tell you
RUTH	Thank you, I'm coming back, need to get on with the day. We're finished in here. Roger? Thought experiment: if I were a man, do you think you'd be dealing with this differently?
HARDIMAN	In what way differently?
RUTH	If it were a male doctor who'd handled the priest as I did.
HARDIMAN	You're suggesting that, as a man, my Y chromosome might be causing early-onset blindness and making me unconsciously deal with this crisis through a fog of misogyny? No, Ruth, I don't think I am. We are all entitled to our opinion. Aren't we? All of us. I'll keep in touch today.

HARDIMAN goes

ROBERTS	Can I speak freely?
RUTH	Go on
ROBERTS	He's an anti-Semitic prick.
RUTH	oh that's simplistic –
ROBERTS	I mean it –
RUTH	I know – but there's really a huge plurality of ways in which Roger Hardiman is a patronising moron, so I'm saying let's not just focus on the anti-Semitism with so many other irons in the fire. You're Jewish, aren't you?

ROBERTS	Yes indeed. Can I speak freely again?
RUTH	You can.
ROBERTS	Why is he still working here?
RUTH	Because he is a good doctor and if someone had to cut into my brain, I'd want him.
ROBERTS	Even though / he
RUTH	Yep. If someone has to cut open my brain, I want the best. and he is a deplorable human being, but he is also the best. There you have it. Life's complicated.
REBECCA	Are you holding up?
RUTH	It takes years to build an institution from nothing. We have nearly five hundred members of staff. To most of them, it's always been here. It's a fixture. I can only ever think of it as vulnerable.

*

CHARLIE	Not like you to be home
RUTH	Home for lunch
CHARLIE	And yet – no food
RUTH	I needed space.

,

CHARLIE	It might be the moment to bring me up.
RUTH	At work? They don't get my life. They don't get to be involved.
CHARLIE	– they don't get to know about me.

RUTH   what?

CHARLIE   you know

RUTH   and why would I not talk about you?

CHARLIE   because you are ashamed of the way it
                makes you seem.

RUTH   I'm afraid I have to dissent –

CHARLIE   I do not have a place in the story you tell
                the world about Ruth Wolff, and nor have I
                ever had one.

RUTH   I'm proud of you.

CHARLIE   I know that:

CHARLIE *(chorus)* they don't.
RUTH *(chorus)*   they don't.

RUTH   I go in tomorrow and start talking about
                you, now, it's going to seem like – like I'm
                asking for my 'I'm a human too' badge –
                some get me off the hook scheme. No. Not
                doing it.

        CHARLIE looks at her

*

                Hello?

        RUTH on the phone

ROBERTS   I'm sorry to phone again but they're trying
                to draw you out – well, someone's put out
                a challenge for you to step forward and
                defend yourself in a debate. 'The dead girl
                can't speak but the doctor responsible / can'

RUTH	I don't need to hear it –
ROBERTS	Okay. And this politics programme – you won't have watched it – debate on a hot topic, panellists interrogating the guest, they want us to send someone on. And social media is starting to heat up
RUTH	I don't need to hear what's on social media.
ROBERTS	No

We still think the best route is silence, Ruth. This is going to blow over.

*

CYPRIAN and FLINT meet RUTH

CYPRIAN	You were a great girl then and you're a great girl now. And I'm very hopeful, we're all very hopeful, you're going to come out and fight for this old place when we need you. Funding – I mean, in terms of funding. Aren't we, Ruth? Hopeful?
RUTH	We are, Brian.
CYPRIAN	Always a pleasure to see you, my darling. I'll leave you ladies to it.

CYPRIAN goes. They look at each other.

RUTH	Minister
FLINT	Professor. It has been a while.
RUTH	I was there for your BMA speech –– which I admired.

FLINT	Then it's been a while for me. And anyway, the woman who gives the speeches is an entirely different person from the one you taught –
RUTH	well, they're both the most senior woman in the country now

FLINT smiles

FLINT	It's not the job, it's what you do with it. And God there's such a lot to do. Leaky roofs and nursing numbers, sure – but then, there's monuments to build. Not merely curing patients but curing the diseases.
RUTH	I liked that line the first time too. When the woman who gives the speeches said it.
FLINT	I mean it. And I'm going to do it.
RUTH	You were always determined.
FLINT	It sounds double-edged, when you say it like that –
RUTH	I look back now and I remember things. There was one patient, you were a junior, I was a registrar perhaps, observing your consultant, anyway you're standing there with the suction pump – and you whisper to me, the treatment's wrong. We're treating the wrong thing. Anyone got anything to add?, the consultant says, he's heard your voice, he's looking straight at you. You knew. You'd told me the answer. And I looked at you – and you said nothing. And an hour later, the patient dies on the table. Because – you were right.

FLINT	That's fifteen (?) years ago –
RUTH	That's a life saved. Or not, in that instance.
FLINT	I didn't want the doctor in charge to be upstaged – I didn't want to embarrass him. Not in front of you. And it was that consultant
RUTH *(chorus)* FLINT *(chorus)*	Henley, wasn't it? Henley, exactly – who would write me the recommendation that would lead to my being the first woman in that hospital to get a chair, first professorship – before even your eminent self – so it could be / that…
RUTH	You think that one decision might have damaged your relationship with Henley –
FLINT	You never know. People are petty.
RUTH	You didn't put that in the manifesto
FLINT	Oh really? It was on every single page. Right there between the lines. , Ruth. I understand I disappointed you. By changing course. People would rather their kids became perverts than professional politicians. I get it. But when I walk through the door of my office, there are things I can get done for medicine, more than – researching proteins or curing patients.
RUTH	We get things done here too, Jemima –
FLINT	And you're an incredible success story. Exceptional results. Though there is a sense

543

that the Elizabeth isn't on board with the wider, how to put this, dynamics of the field. Not joining in. Elite class. Very you. And yet, year after year, you do the best research and produce the best results. And you're a woman. So there's a little envy operating. Among other things, a desire to bring you down to earth. Not that that's what this is, but that's the weather system we're standing under.

RUTH   I'm sorry, did Brian tell you about [the incident] – ?

FLINT *(obvious)*   My office briefed me this morning

RUTH *(what?)*   How did they know?

FLINT   Roger Hardiman's an ambitious little man.

RUTH   And a very good surgeon – but surely he's not [ringing round]

FLINT   his brother's now the PM's chief of staff. Came in same time I did. Phone calls are being made. And then there's the petition and so on, but for my money your real enemies live in your own house. I assume the apology's coming –

RUTH   No. It's a storm in a teacup.

FLINT   Then why take it so seriously? Pick up the teacup [and] put it in the bin. You can just close the gap between their story and yours: surf with the tide: apologise, move on. Show your staff you know how to listen –

RUTH   It's not leadership, really, though, that, is it, so much as followership

FLINT   What do you call a leader with no followers?

RUTH   If she's a real leader, she won't care what
             you call her.

FLINT   I like that. Might borrow it. People don't like
             you, Professor, but god do they admire you
             – a woman of integrity. I say that because
             no-one admires me. But I'm not sentimental
             – and, Ruth, this – self-ness, all the little
             pieces for the jigsaw – 'that doesn't fit who I
             am', 'that's not me'– that sort of integrity is
             a tiny, private quality. Out here – the world
             – it doesn't do much good. I'm saying why
             lose sight of the higher idea for the sake of
             the bits and pieces?

             Let me take off the ministerial hat. I want
             the government to pay for your new
             building. Whatever funding you've got, fine,
             but you're a way off and what if we make up
             the deficit – absorb the Elizabeth Institute as
             a public asset, bankroll its new premises and
             then use it as a shining example of what this
             country can do.

RUTH   And how long might that take to achieve?

FLINT   I'll have the confirmation in a month.
             And when we announce that we're curing
             dementia, I want to talk about you – and me
             – and I want to talk about women. Though
             given we're both white, I'm not sure we're
             necessarily going to [get the reaction we
             hope for] – though, actually, a woman still
             counts, I think – what?

RUTH   No, I – hadn't expected –

FLINT	I told you one day I'd come good. But look – did you push him? This priest?
RUTH	Push him? No –
FLINT	But you were brusque
RUTH	I was firm
FLINT	It's politics –
RUTH	It's Darwin. And politics isn't my problem
FLINT	Politics is all of our problem. So make this go away. It'd be good if you could out yourself. As a vulnerable person as well.
RUTH	And say what? Woman in a man's world?
FLINT	I meant make it about religious tolerance, you know, acceptance of each other – the doctor, she's religious too –
RUTH	She isn't
FLINT	Oh. I thought you did the candles thing on Fridays
RUTH	That was a long time ago – and my parents were alive, and my Jewishness is cultural if it's anything at all: it's not about believing anything
FLINT	Shame. Good time to talk about Jews.
RUTH	But a bad time to talk about doctors?
FLINT	It might be the right time to talk about doctors. If only you were gay. Forgive me, I don't actually know where you'd put / yourself
RUTH	I don't go in for badges, Jemima

FLINT	No, quite. It must be a tough thing to go through, this.
RUTH	Nothing compared to what the girl went through.
FLINT	No, quite. Look. You and I are going to be working together. We're on the same team once again. You deal with these problems internally and I'll step in on the external stuff. If it blows up, I mean.
RUTH	Do you think it will?
FLINT	These days, who can tell? But if it does, we can separate faith and medicine, I can say it's strange it's so often a senior woman that has abuse rained down on her –
RUTH	I wouldn't want you to risk your job, Jemima.
FLINT	I mean, I'm not declaring war on the Catholic church. Tempting as it is – but look at Martin Luther, he tried it in 1519, and here we are and he's long dead and the fucking thing's still here. Though the price of a cabinet post can't be more than
RUTH	Than me?
FLINT	Than the truth. How better to die than in a just cause.
RUTH	How best to die is – well, the whole point, really –
FLINT	If this gets bad, Ruth, I'll be there. I owe you that.

*

SAMI	Why is your whole kitchen labelled? CUTLERY. BRAN FLAKES. Like did you worry that by sight alone you wouldn't know the rice was rice?
RUTH	That's funny.
SAMI	Tell your face. Am I being like more annoying than normal?
RUTH	I have absolutely no idea
SAMI	Bad day?
RUTH	Don't ever become the boss of anything. Or become really good at anything. I don't know. We evolve to fantasise about our enemies. It's evolution, the idea that the predators are coming. The rustle in the bush that might make this meal our last meal. It's a special place in our imagination. They who long to harm us. So killing them brings special kinds of joy. David screamed with delight over the corpse of Goliath. Talk to me. About something else. Your day. Anyone's day except mine.
SAMI	You'll literally never guess what I did at school today
RUTH	I'm – feeling crystal clear that you had sex.
SAMI	How do you do that? You are a witch.
	,
RUTH	where?

SAMI	Changing rooms. There's a weird cupboard at the back as you go through towards the swimming pool and it's like a corridor that joins together the boys' and the girls' blocks and there's a – joint toilet I think, not that it ever gets like used –
RUTH	A disabled toilet?
SAMI	Yeah
RUTH	And you and he – is it a he? – had sex in there –
SAMI	Not the first time. We did other stuff. But it's – sorry I'm embarrassed now
RUTH	It's ok, we don't have to / talk about it
SAMI	Yeah. No. I want to. It's – is it possible that I can control him? Can thoughts like move through the air like – perfume. I felt this [power] – like I had a whip wrapped round his head and it would pull and like sweep him in towards me. Like I'd cast a spell. I saw him, I had the thought and then I went there and I left the door unlocked and I sort of turned this current on in his brain – and my heart was like a – fist punching the inside of my ribcage – and I sat on the bench and – then the door was open and he's there – gripping my shoulders and he was kissing me hard like there was another person literally coming up out of him and they were like hungry like they wanted the salt off my skin and we were locking the door only it didn't lock properly so he was sort of holding it shut and then I had this

strange sense like flexing up on my tiptoes
like I knew what I wanted him to do – and
then he was doing it – like it was like a light
I could turn on in his brain – and it was nice –

and then that was it, I was walking over the
field and that was it. Next time I saw him I
didn't want it. So I didn't switch it on. Time
after that, this is last week, I really wanted
it. So switched it on. Went to the swimming
block in my last lesson and as I was walking
there so was he. Like – it was like I had him
on a magnet and I was just like bending him
towards me. Same today. And today we –

RUTH   Had sex. Yes. [I'm a] Doctor. [and therefore]
                Unshockable.

SAMI   But –

                but I'd brought clothes in. I knew this
                morning. I knew I was going to do it with
                him in there and I knew it was going to be
                at lunchtime and I knew. So I brought stuff.
                A dress. And other stuff. And I felt – unreal.
                And then I switched it on and at lunchtime

RUTH   Have you actually had a conversation with
                this boy?

SAMI   no.

RUTH   But presumably he won't tell / other people

SAMI   no. No way. During it he said he loved me.
                Felt weird that someone was saying that
                about me. Like it's just *me*.

RUTH   Do you love him?

SAMI	I don't know. Don't think so. How do you know? I don't know. During it he said 'I can't even look you in your eyes, I love you so much' –

*

CHARLIE	I'm sorry – I'm sorry but I can't find a knife, anywhere, sweetheart
RUTH	I know the feeling
CHARLIE	I mean it
RUTH	I know, I know –
CHARLIE	I spoke to the woman today about the thing
	I went to speak to her, today –
	I didn't mean to interrupt you.

*

SAMI	Ruth?
RUTH	Yes
SAMI	You're not saying anything. Which is like weird. Sorry. I only told you / because
RUTH	No, I'm – glad, I'm glad you told me – it's part of you
SAMI	Yeah?
RUTH	Yes

CHARLIE speaks: THE THIRD DAY

At the Institute, RUTH comes into a meeting room

RUTH	Ah. You're all here early. I wasn't aware there was a closed session.
CYPRIAN	There wasn't, Professor –
RUTH	I am, as far as I'm aware, still the Director of this Institute, and therefore Chair of the Executive Committee. Yes? / Yes. Yes. Good. Shall we open the meeting?
CYPRIAN	Yes
MURPHY	Are we really going to go through the motions like this?
RUTH	Which motion in particular?
	I propose we follow the agenda. I declare the meeting open. We are quorate, despite the usual apologies, including from Professor Creswell, who is stepping down from his post as Head of Pharmacology directly we appoint his replacement. We had sixteen applications, and our two contenders on the ballot were Doctor Bob Munro and Doctor Janet Feinman. Would anyone like to add anything further to the materials that have been circulated? No. Very good.
MURPHY	Hardiman isn't here
RUTH	No, very good, though I feel confident he will have no desire to change his vote. Would anyone here like to change their vote from the ballot you filled in this morning? In which case. The ballot returned equal

	votes on both sides. Which means the deciding vote is mine and therefore that this committee has voted to appoint Doctor Feinman as head of Pharmacology. I shall propose the motion, will someone second it?
MURPHY	I'm sorry – [but]
RUTH	Apology accepted.
MURPHY	I really don't see how we can continue down that agenda when everyone in this room knows that the future of this institution is in serious question.
RUTH	Is it? Well, the next thing on the agenda is Professor Cyprian and an update from the board, / so once
CYPRIAN	Perhaps we shouldn't minute this –

JUNIOR is taking minutes

MURPHY	Why not?
COPLEY	Try listening and maybe we'll find out
CYPRIAN	The board have formally stated their – I am quoting – 'serious concerns' in a letter, signed by all of them except for three, who have sent a separate letter informing us that they have resigned.
RUTH	Resigned?
CYPRIAN	yes.
RUTH	And *this meeting* is the place to break that news?
MURPHY	I'm sorry, but this can't be a surprise –

CYPRIAN	It's *not* a surprise. I'm *furious* we've let it get to here. I'm disgusted that this whole witch hunt has been allowed to blow up – and I'm disgusted at the way it's being manipulated to achieve other ends. It's politics.
RUTH	Do people have responses to this agenda item?
CYPRIAN	Yes. I'd like to propose a motion, right now at this meeting – no, put this on the minutes – in support of Ruth Wolff and her work for this institute since its founding twenty years ago. And I'd like it passed unanimously.

HARDIMAN comes in as MURPHY is saying

MURPHY	I'm sorry, no – I'm not going to endorse a statement of support because I think the board having resigned is a sign that we're getting something wrong. I think we have to listen. And I think we have to protect this Institute and work out how to persuade the board members to retract before / this all blows up –
HARDIMAN	I'm sorry to be late, everyone, but I've / got
RUTH	It's not a problem – but could we please keep to the agenda? Professor Cyprian has just told us of that some of our board members intend to resign –
HARDIMAN	It's not an intention. They've resigned.
RUTH	Would anyone like to respond to this item on the agenda?

HARDIMAN	Yes, Ruth, I'd like to ask you whether you know the reasons for the resignation, given that they're not stated on the letter –
CYPRIAN	How have you read their letter?
RUTH	I think the better question is whether there's anyone in the room who doesn't know the reasons, but we have a meeting to get on with and diseases to cure. Yes, I'm fully aware of the reasons. It's about the matter which as we all know has been the subject of some discussion,
HARDIMAN	And about which there's a petition with over twenty thousand signatures which is now well past the limit for a government response. Which is why I was late – I have / brought
CYPRIAN	I've spoken to Whitehall and they said: internal issue, nothing to do with government, [and so] they're going nowhere near it –
MURPHY	Let's see how long they can keep saying that for –
HARDIMAN	The reason I was late is / that I have
RUTH	I'm sorry, Professor Hardiman – I am sorry. This is not an anarchy, we do have an agenda and if people want to respond / to the
CYPRIAN	My response to the board's resignation is this. When Professor Wolff refused that priest access to the girl's sickbed, she was

	acting absolutely as a doctor should and we would have all behaved in the same way –
MURPHY	But you've never barred a priest from a patient
COPLEY	And neither has Ruth until this week
CYPRIAN	LOOK. This is a one-off situation. Nobody is trying to deny that people, some people, find comfort in religion, especially when we're talking about the end of life. Nobody has ever denied a priest – or a rabbi or a Muslim teacher –
HARDIMAN	An imam –
CYPRIAN	Nobody has ever denied a religious representative appropriate access to a patient when that access has been requested by the patient. But we bow to the pressure on this, when there was no clear instruction, then we're putting religion above medicine and allowing public opinion to over-ride the decision of a doctor.
MURPHY	That's not the only issue here –
HARDIMAN	The board have made it very clear to us / that
CYPRIAN	I don't want to get embroiled in repercussions and backlashes: the thing that is important here is this: to act as a doctor is to act as Ruth did. This is what it means to be a doctor. There is only one appropriate response to the board's resignation which is – again – to declare our total and unanimous

confidence in our Director – and I want that motion passed with full support.-

HARDIMAN   I'm not sure that we're clear what we're dealing with here. Ruth is a celebrity by the standards of medicine. She is visible. But we as the executive committee are here to protect this Institute. If we're going to move to this new building, we need sponsors, we need funding and support – and through that lens, this whole crisis around Ruth's conduct is a disaster.

CYPRIAN   No-one out there knows that this was Ruth –

HARDIMAN   I'm not suggesting Ruth set out to cause a problem. But this isn't about intention. The board are unhappy. The Christian community are unhappy. The girl's parents are very unhappy indeed. We cannot put out public statements in support of behaviour which has driven our Institute to the cliff-edge – and may yet push us over –

COPLEY   Forgive me, Roger, but bullshit. We ignore this and it goes away.

HARDIMAN   We *did* and it *hasn't*

CYPRIAN   So what do you propose?

HARDIMAN   The same thing I've been saying for two days – that Ruth should put out a statement of apology or go onto that programme and apologise – expressing her regret about the girl's death / and the surrounding situation –

CYPRIAN   You cannot / be serious

COPLEY   Ruth didn't kill the girl –

HARDIMAN   I didn't say she did, but public opinion is
                 not on our side.

COPLEY   Vox populi over there

HARDIMAN   *(To JUNIOR.)* sorry – you, yes, I don't know
                 your name, could you run and ask Rebecca
                 to come up please? She's the person best-
                 placed to speak to that – any objections?
                 Move.

JUNIOR goes to get ROBERTS

                 but the *reason* I was *late* for this meeting, as I
                 have been *trying* to say / for the last…

CYPRIAN   This is not speakers' corner. Ruth's name is
                 not out there in public. We are a team. We
                 are in this together. We do *not* cut people
                 loose. There will not be institutional damage
                 if the institute pulls together and *that woman*
                 is the top of our field. Twenty-five years of
                 sector-leading research can't just be *deleted* –

MURPHY   Yes it can. / It absolutely can – if she was
                 subject to a malpractice suit

CYPRIAN   Over my dead body it can. Over my dead
                 body.

MURPHY   Not an argument, Brian –

ROBERTS enters

HARDIMAN   Thank you for coming, Rebecca. We hoped
                 you might update us with your view of our
                 current situation with the perception of
                 recent events. In public.

CYPRIAN   I'm sorry, who is the chair of this meeting?

RUTH	Continue –
ROBERTS	There's articles running in two of the broadsheets tomorrow. We haven't commented – and nor has the priest. It's all anonymous so I don't think it's going to become a major story –
MURPHY	People don't like it. I don't like it – I'm sorry, Ruth – but I said that to you at the time, on the day – you got it wrong
COPLEY	Everyone knows what you think, Paul
CYPRIAN	Have the parents commented on the story?
ROBERTS	I couldn't get that info out of them
HARDIMAN	which brings me to why I was late
MURPHY	Sorry, Roger, I've been speaking to people and there is a particular sensitivity around the fact that this priest – the priest that Ruth saw fit to *push* around –
RUTH	I didn't *push* the priest
MURPHY	You absolutely did. – but part of the sensitivity, and nobody is saying it, is because he's a black man
	,
HARDIMAN	Yes –
CYPRIAN	*no* no *no no* – this is *total nonsense, I'm* a black man!
	,
MURPHY	Are you?

CYPRIAN	My grandmother was born in Kenya
MURPHY	it's a slightly different story when you look completely white –
RUTH	*Please*, everyone
ROBERTS	I didn't realise that – I didn't realise there was a racial element

RUTH *(chorus)*   There's *not* a racial element
CYPRIAN *(chorus)* There's *not*

MURPHY	OK – but I'm the most senior person here who isn't white – who doesn't *look* white. And I don't think the way I'm addressed here is neutral.
RUTH	Neutral?
MURPHY	Neutral any more than the way you addressed the priest.

HARDIMAN very calmly addresses ROBERTS

HARDIMAN	What do you think, Rebecca?
ROBERTS	I don't know if race is [the issue] – I mean, I don't like the optics – I'm not saying it means anything but I don't like the way it looks.
HARDIMAN	I agree
RUTH	I think this might be the moment to return to the agenda – and / yes I am nonetheless aware that Professor Hardiman has been trying to address the meeting and has been continually interrupted. As heated as this issue has become, we owe ourselves a

standard of debate. For everyone's sake. Professor Hardiman.

HARDIMAN   Professor –

Thank you, Ruth. The reason I was late is because I have brought the father here. I've spoken to him and he's waiting in my office – I wanted him to have a / chance

COPLEY   What?

CYPRIAN   Why the hell have you got him in the building?

HARDIMAN   Because granting him the opportunity to address the executive might defuse the bomb of a screaming row in public –

RUTH   That is completely against protocol

MURPHY   Which is exactly the view someone might take of your conduct

COPLEY   Oh how many times – she didn't do ANYTHING wrong

HARDIMAN   This situation will cost us our funding and our move to our own building unless we can manage it better – and there is nobody who can speak to the girl's perspective better than her parents –

COPLEY   Everyone knows what her parents think!

CYPRIAN   Roger, you've got the father here? Not the priest?

HARDIMAN   I spoke with him myself this afternoon. He's obviously upset about the whole situation, as are we all –

COPLEY	He's asking: is it the girl's father or the holy father?
CYPRIAN	Jesus Christ –
FATHER	Amen

And they realise that the FATHER is at the doorway, played by the same actor who plays the PRIEST. It's OK if it takes the audience some time to work out which FATHER he is.

	Were you praying there? I guess that's what happens here. The name of the Lord is taken in vain because you all think you're above it. You all think you're bigger than God. Don't you?
CYPRIAN	I'm sorry if I, look, there's / not
FATHER	Keeping me sitting down there waiting for you like you're doing something important. Probably I've not got better things to do because I don't wear a white coat when I do a day's work. Fuck him. Stupid little fucking nobody with his God and his dead daughter. I could hear you screaming down the corridor.
ROBERTS	I'm going to call security
RUTH	No – it's okay – Mr Ronan / I
FATHER	You all protect each other, you people. A little fucking cabal. I've seen it on the TV, incompetence and you kill someone and then it all gets covered up. You've murdered my little girl – and I will exact that pound of flesh – there is no way I'm going to let you write this up as some statistic – some tiny error – she was my little girl and she deserved better

	than this – and from all of you, counting your pennies towards your state of the art new building. You don't have a fucking clue how to treat a Catholic family –
RUTH	Mr Ronan, I'm going to stop you there. I understand that you're upset,
FATHER	Do you? Do you understand what it's like to lose your child? You got children, have you, that died?
RUTH	I wasn't saying my experience / is the same as yours
FATHER	Cut off your hand rather than go to hell. That's what Jesus said. Do you understand hell, any of you? Maggots crawling in your flesh and scalding burns and perpetual fucking torment – that is where she is. That is where she is. She died without being forgiven and she was fourteen years old and she died in mortal sin. She died. She died.

,

	I've got nothing to say to this lot, Roger, that I can't say to the press. I've got all the information. And I am going to scream it from the rooftops
RUTH	Mr Ronan, the decision I took as your daughter's physician / was
FATHER	It was you? You're the one who actually [did it] – I thought I knew your voice. What's your name?

Nobody responds

	Someone tell me what her fucking name is, would you please.
RUTH	You have no right to be in here
FATHER	Name
RUTH	My name is Ruth Wolff.
FATHER	Well, Ruth Wolff, I am going to make you your own personal hell on earth. Believe me. I'll dedicate myself to tearing you to fucking pieces – you push people around, now you get pushed around – give you a taste of your own fucking medicine –

The FATHER shoves RUTH, she falls. Total chaos.

Fuck you all – fuck you all –

The FATHER exits

ROBERTS *(chorus)*	Are you alright, Ruth?
COPLEY *(chorus)*	I'm going to call the police

RUTH	we cannot call the police. We cannot call the police in the middle of this situation, and I can't press charges, it'll leak – *(COPLEY tries to interrupt.)* we cannot have a police car parked *outside of this building – and that is that.*

Worried looks.

CYPRIAN	I think we should adjourn this meeting –
RUTH	no no no No No NO. We keep *going.* SIT DOWN.

RUTH stands up.

JUNIOR	You're bleeding, Professor

ROBERTS	Ruth, you're the victim of an assault –
RUTH	I am not the victim of an anything
ROBERTS	His behaviour is something we can use, you're the victim / of
RUTH	I am not a victim and we are not sinking to that –
ROBERTS	Ruth, I can't / let you
RUTH	Sit down, Rebecca, and SHUT UP. SIT DOWN. ALL OF YOU. SIT DOWN.
	,
HARDIMAN	I didn't expect he would behave like that, I apologise for bringing him here – I thought if we listened to what / he has to say
RUTH	I need to be crystal clear. For one moment, let me be crystal clear about procedure – the chair – that is, me – that is, I am the only person here, the only one empowered to put a motion to the committee. There are two motions on the table. One proposed by Professor Cyprian, expressing absolute confidence in me, and one proposed by Professor Hardiman compelling me to make a statement of apology – and I'll put both of those forward to / the executive, but
HARDIMAN	I withdraw my motion – but allow / me to
CYPRIAN	Then put mine to the vote. Put my motion to the vote.
RUTH	Professor, please –

MURPHY	We will make ourselves look like tone-deaf imbeciles if / we don't
CYPRIAN	She founded this fucking institute
COPLEY	Calm down, Brian –
CYPRIAN	*Put the motion to the vote –*
RUTH	We've not yet formally ratified the appointment of Doctor Feinman.
HARDIMAN	When did that happen?
RUTH	Before your late / intervention, Professor.
MURPHY	Rebecca, how do you think it looks, from a PR point of view, for us to appoint *another* Jewish woman –

RUTH *(chorus)*   *another* Jewish woman?
CYPRIAN *(chorus)* I'm sorry?
COPLEY *(chorus)* Fucking hell

MURPHY	a *white* Jewish woman –
CYPRIAN	Can you *put* my *motion* to the *vote*
MURPHY	The reason we are having a problem with Christians is because there are hardly any of us who *work* here
RUTH	that's not why / this happened
MURPHY	and so they don't have a voice in this institute – there are people on the internet from the Christian community saying that *right now*
COPLEY	SHUT UP. SHUT UP. I don't want to hear the opinions of people on the internet. I really do have better things to do. But if

that petition leads to an inquiry, then Ruth will be found innocent – and unlike some of you, I can say that, because I was there when the incident happened. So I say, bring it on. Let's let the procedure do its work and return the verdict we know will be returned.

MURPHY   Trigger an external inquiry ourselves, you mean? Admit it's Ruth, invite the scrutiny?

RUTH   Is that what you mean?

COPLEY   I think you're innocent Ruth, but your name's out there now. Girl's father is going to do his best, you heard him, and this is all very uncomfortable. So we have to be above board and transparent. We have to be.

RUTH   Which means handing me over, does it?

COPLEY   I – well, Ruth, I wouldn't quite put it / [like that]

RUTH   I'm sure you wouldn't

COPLEY   I'm not trying to insult you, Ruth, I'm / trying to solve

HARDIMAN   Can we return to the agenda?

              ,

RUTH   Of course we may.

HARDIMAN   This isn't personal, Ruth, it really isn't personal. But the function of this committee is to protect this institute and the institute is in serious jeopardy. We are getting it wrong. I would like to propose a motion of no confidence in Ruth Wolff.

RUTH	Thank you. Before I put your motion to the executive, Professor, perhaps you might give an outline of the conversation we had in which you attempted to use this situation as a lever to persuade me to vote for Doctor Munro.

,

HARDIMAN	This meeting becomes ever more extraordinary. I'm happy to say now – for the minutes – what I said to you in private. I offered, on the day, to take over that patient. I'm a Catholic. So was she. And this is a real issue – whether certain types of patient need certain types of doctors to attend them – but you refused without a second thought, exactly as you have refused before when this same question has been raised –
RUTH	It's called leadership
HARDIMAN	It's called management – and this has not been managed. We have a petition with – how many signatures?
ROBERTS	Over fifty thousand now
HARDIMAN *(chorus)*	Thank you.
CYPRIAN *(chorus)*	Sorry, what are you trying to imply?
HARDIMAN	I told Professor Wolff that this institute was seen as an exclusive Jewish organisation, which historically has been more the case than it is now – but our history and our director and many of the foundations that fund us create an impression that there are certain types of person allowed in –

COPLEY	And those types of people are Jews?
HARDIMAN	You know exactly what I mean: we are seen as an elite –
COPLEY	I cannot believe these arguments are being made with a straight face
HARDIMAN	So – how many Jews on our board?
RUTH	Now there's a question with a dark history
COPLEY	I'm sorry, I wasn't aware we were a restricted species –
CYPRIAN	Professor, could you come to your point
HARDIMAN	I told Ruth that it would be good for us to appoint a black, Catholic doctor, because it sends the message clear as day that this institute is open to all the types of people she upset –
MURPHY	exactly
COPLEY	and given that the doctor in question is the godparent to your kids –

This angers HARDIMAN and his argument really starts to burn, this now heats up

HARDIMAN	Which has absolutely nothing to do with it. She *dismissed* me out of hand.
RUTH	Because she couldn't see any integrity in your proposal
HARDIMAN	Because Ruth Wolff can't see it doesn't mean it isn't there –
RUTH	You also implied that the petition could be made to disappear if I did so. I told you then

and I *stand by it now*, that I would vote for
the most capable doctor and that is exactly
what I have done –

HARDIMAN   The most capable doctor *in your opinion*

RUTH   I thought it might be clear it was my opinion
            given that it was my words in my voice
            emerging from my body –

HARDIMAN   I offered help and you declined. And now
            look where we are. We have a major crisis
            on our hands and this Institute is about to be
            embarrassingly dragged face down through
            the mud in full view of the medical world.
            Everything exposed. And *why?* Because
            you treated this priest with your trademark
            disdain, a disdain that attends to particular
            groups, and a disdain that is the culture of
            the way this building runs – not so much a
            culture as a cult: a cult of personality –

MURPHY   I second Professor Hardiman's motion of no
            confidence

RUTH   It hasn't been proposed yet

HARDIMAN   Then *propose* it

            ,

RUTH   As Professor Hardiman points out, clearly
            I have not done everything in my power
            to protect the institute from the onslaught
            of spiteful public attention – unwilling as I
            am to sacrifice my integrity on the altar of
            political expediency –

MURPHY   I don't think that is / a reasonable

RUTH *(sharp)*   I don't think I had finished speaking, thank
                you, Doctor.

                I could have done more to protect the
                reputation of this institute among those who
                now are crying outrage. I will therefore take
                the appropriate action myself and, *until*
                this matter can be cleared up, resign as the
                director of the institute

Total uproar, all the below at the same sort of time –

CYPRIAN   What?

MURPHY   It has to be put to the vote –

ROBERTS   No it fucking doesn't, if / she wants to resign
               she can

HARDIMAN   I don't think that – I don't know if

MURPHY   Leaving us to pick up the pieces

COPLEY   Are you sure, Ruth, is that really the way to
               / resolve this

CYPRIAN bangs on the table until they all go quiet

CYPRIAN   Are we to understand, Professor Wolff, that you
               have resigned the directorship of this institute?

               ,

RUTH   Yes

CYPRIAN   In which case, I believe the way it works
               is that the role of Director will be filled on
               an acting basis by the deputy director, the
               responsibilities of which include – in the
               immediate – the chairing of this meeting –

HARDIMAN stands up

HARDIMAN	Thank you, Professor.
	I believe before we move to the bigger, public questions facing us, we should discuss who will manage Professor Wolff's department and research responsibilities until such a time / as
RUTH	I will. I've resigned the directorship, nothing more.
MURPHY	The suspended director of this institute cannot continue to / work at
COPLEY	Who was suspended? She resigned
MURPHY	Not of her own volition
HARDIMAN	Can we please bring this meeting to order
RUTH	I'm going to ask for leave from my department until this case can be resolved if the Acting Director will grant me it –

Micro-beat pause

HARDIMAN	Granted.
RUTH	Then I shall commence my leave
COPLEY	I'm coming with you
ROBERTS	Me too –
RUTH	Let's not give these gentlemen everything they want –
COPLEY	I'm not giving them you, Ruth
RUTH	Thank you, Michael. Good evening, everyone.

COPLEY   No – you don't, you do not – [go through
                that door]

                if we let that woman go through that door,
                we open ourselves up to a poison which
                could warp the nature of this profession
                for years and years to come – and this
                might be the turning point, this might be
                where we choose. We cut her loose and let
                them have her – and have her as white or
                a Jew or godless or a woman – we let her
                be anything other than a doctor, if we let
                them drag in biography, if our identities,
                if doctors' identities are put on the table,
                then let's be clear what that means, because
                it's Jewish doctors for Jewish patients and
                fat doctors for fat patients and 'should
                you perform the surgery if you haven't
                undergone it yourself?', before every minor
                procedure a speech from the consultant, like
                teenage singers on TV talent shows, about
                how 'Today's surgery is dedicated to my
                poor dead grandma who really supported
                my dream to be a doctor, and would be
                so proud of me for operating on today's
                patient' and not one bit of it will do a thing
                to make us better doctors or get better
                results for our patients or in CURING
                THIS FUCKING DISEASE. If we do not
                stem the bleed of this biographical nonsense
                then it will drown us in a flood of blood
                types and birthplaces and the kind of things
                we like to do in bed.

                If we bow to this pressure we WILL NOT
                GET BACK UP.

	She is a DOCTOR. That is all that counts. That is the single qualification and it's handed out by teaching hospitals, not by people sitting in their back bedrooms and screaming into the internet. And if we countenance this, because of the pretended outrage of some pack of sanctimonious non-entities, we delay the work of this institute – and of this first-rate doctor – for a net gain of absolutely nothing. And the patients are the ones who will suffer.
HARDIMAN	Doctor Copley, have we reached the end of your performance? Thank you, Professor Wolff.

RUTH leaves

| COPLEY | You cannot just dump people into piles. And not for nothing but there is really nobody, no human being on this earth that does not defy that sort of simplistic bullshit with their technicolour, thousand-fold complexity. And last time we chopped up the world into identity groups, let's remember where that road led – with tattoos on people's wrists – |

and as a Jew, I get to make that point.

COPLEY leaves.

| CYPRIAN | I don't think we have a quorum any longer, Professor – |
| HARDIMAN | *(To J.)* Let's return to the agenda – and restart the minutes, thank you. Could you close the door, please? |

*

CHARLIE	What are you doing?
RUTH	I am still sitting here, in the car, trying to work out what to do –
CHARLIE	It's been three hours. How's it going?

*

JUNIOR	I need it back.
RUTH	It's got my name on it. It's got my name
JUNIOR	I need it back.
RUTH	I can't give you it back. You didn't give me it. I gave me it – I did found / the institute
JUNIOR	I know. You've resigned.
RUTH	I've resigned from the executive, not from the department –
JUNIOR	No-one thinks you're coming back
RUTH	I am coming back
JUNIOR	Right. Well, until then, I need your pass.
RUTH	I'm going to drive away now. What are you frightened of? That I'm going to break in during the night and illicitly cure people? Doctors having to sit around idle, chatting among the unexpectedly healthy?
JUNIOR	It isn't my decision.
RUTH	It's above your head. Of course. Hardiman? Who you working for?
JUNIOR	It's whom. For whom are you working? In case you care about language at all.

,

RUTH	You told the patient, didn't you, that – the priest had come for her?

,

JUNIOR	I didn't agree with you.
RUTH	Well, it wasn't your decision to make.
JUNIOR	but it should have been Emily's choice.
RUTH	God, men always think they know best – so you decided it was up to you to pick between faith and medicine?
JUNIOR	No – I chose between faith and atheism. He might have been able to comfort her. Keeping him out would not have saved her life – she was always going to die –
RUTH	And so you let her die confused and panicked, entirely without *peace*, slamming her head against her pillow – well, many congratulations, that really must feel good –
JUNIOR	If the priest had got to her earlier, perhaps that would never have happened –
RUTH	She was FOURTEEN years old –
JUNIOR	I disagree with what you did. And how you treat people. And the fact that you haven't said sorry. Can you please just hand me your pass. Thank you.

*

576

There might be an interval here – if there is, it's important that RUTH stays on stage. When the play resumes, SAMI enters. We're at RUTH's house. She has a phone.

SAMI	When I saw it I literally died
RUTH	You didn't literally die
SAMI	What?
RUTH	Literally means literally, not figuratively – in fact the whole point of the word literally is so that we can indicate that we're not speaking figuratively. It's a word to say that a *thing actually happened.* Use literally figuratively and you've successfully destroyed the whole purpose of the word. So when I say that the people I work with are literally fat fucking ignorant pigs wandering around on their hind trotters, you now don't know whether I actually work with medical pigs or whether I'm just speaking figuratively.
	,
SAMI	Who did that to the car?
RUTH	What?
SAMI	There's a swastika. Sprayed on it.
	,
RUTH	Well, it wasn't me testing out a new paint colour, if that's what you mean.
SAMI	Saw the cat out there, but it didn't look guilty. Ruth, what's going on?
RUTH	Nothing

577

SAMI	The phone's unplugged
RUTH	Is it?
SAMI	Who phoned you?
RUTH	If I wanted to talk about it, I'd talk about it.
SAMI	Mum –

And they both hear that word –

	I mean, I didn't – Ruth – sorry, I didn't actually realise that
RUTH	It's fine, it's fine – it was a slip of / the [tongue]
SAMI	Yeah, no, yeah it was
	,
SAMI	Shall I make you some tea?
RUTH	Are you having some? / No, you don't 'do' it
SAMI	No, thank you
	,
	I read the story online. Are you okay?
RUTH	I am trending.

There is something dangerous about her

which as a present participle is both ugly and inelegant.

When the end comes, it shows itself first in the language.

What are they saying?

SAMI   You don't need to hear it

RUTH   The only acceptable response is that I die.
                This is public hanging for the digital age,
                hands-rubbing, a community ready with
                boiling tar and feathers. The crowds are
                assembling and I have to be purged. Joe
                McCarthy caught me with the reds. Goody
                Nurse has seen me with the devil. Fling me
                out beyond the city walls. Because it's only
                by pushing people outside your boundaries
                that you work out where your boundaries
                even are. There were death threats, Rebecca
                told me that. It's *over* when there's a body.
                Maybe that is what's required.

SAMI   Ruth – I don't know if you're joking or not?

RUTH   I'm not. The witch has to die for the story to
                end.

SAMI   You're talking about suicide –

RUTH   If I get there, I'll call the ambulance first,
                there's no danger of you being the one that
                finds me. No, I promise you, if I kill myself,
                I won't leave the clear-up to you.

        Atmosphere is getting dangerous

SAMI   I wasn't asking for that [reason]

        RUTH has taken the phone

RUTH   But these people, these barely-informed
                fucking people – you want to make a
                difference do you? – you want to get a
                reaction? Do something well. Actually
                achieve something and then maybe you can
                put your real names on it

RUTH suddenly destroys the mobile phone and it really shocks SAMI who doesn't know how to react

,

The phone is in little pieces. A calm. SAMI doesn't know what to say.

SAMI   Well, I hope you're insured

RUTH   Insurance to a doctor is like water to a fish

,

SAMI   Maybe – maybe we should put some music on.

       Okay? Okay. I'm going to just press play and whatever's there can play

SAMI puts some music on. It plays for a while. RUTH laughs. And then.

RUTH   This isn't my music, it's Charlie's, and I'm afraid it is filed under the category 'music that makes me want to kill myself'.

The music is still playing

CHARLIE   And what is it about this track that makes you want to kill yourself?

RUTH   it's either the music or the lyrics

CHARLIE   Sarcasm. Thought of as the lowest form of wit.

RUTH   Karaoke is the lowest form of wit

CHARLIE   Don't be so bloody joyless, come on, woman –

with a bit of ad lib – CHARLIE makes RUTH dance – she's not naturally given to it, but she does give in and it's okay – in a gentle,

sweet way they're happy – and the music keeps playing. CHARLIE
singing along with the lyrics hits a certain point and then says

I can't remember them –

I know the words to this – I know I know
the words –

CHARLIE gets quite frustrated

RUTH   It doesn't matter, sweetheart, it's a nonsense
                song anyway

CHARLIE   It was casting its spell – you were letting
                yourself go

RUTH   It's perfectly nice music –

CHARLIE   Nice music for killing yourself

RUTH   Turn it off. I can't [bear to listen to it –]

Music stops

The sound of a smashing window – the two of them suddenly alert.

SAMI   What's that?

VOICE   *(Loud.)* MURDERER

A silence. They're frightened. The sound of more glass breaking.

RUTH   *(Quietly.)* Turn it off. Sit very still. Don't
                move. The door's locked, don't worry –

SAMI nods

The town has to mark the witch.

A bang on the door

We'll talk quietly. We'll ask questions. You
ask one then I ask one. Favourite colour

SAMI	Purple. Favourite animal
RUTH	– koala. Favourite word
SAMI	Pomegranate.

A bang on the door

RUTH	Your turn – come on
SAMI	Favourite person?
RUTH	I –
SAMI	Too slow. And it's still me. How many times have you been in love?
RUTH	Once: one time. Are you happy?
SAMI	Sometimes – are you happy?
RUTH	Sometimes. What's happened to your eye?
SAMI	It doesn't matter –
RUTH	That's not a game question

Another bang on the door. They sit still.

Tell me what happened to your eye.

,

SAMI	That boy I was telling you about. Kind of turned weird. I'm okay. But he like pulled my bag today in front of people and pulled all my stuff out, including, like the dress and stuff that I told you about, make-up and was throwing it and like laughing, being – being a total prick basically. I don't know why but in a second it all just *changed*.

582

	And then he pushed me and I fell and that happened to my eye – I'm okay. He went off and I was looking at all my books and stuff on the floor and I didn't want to pick the dress up really so I just left it there so I think it's gone now
RUTH	He is not worth a single eyelash of you. I think he's probably terrified by what you've made him feel. Because you are a gold-standard human being and I've seen enough of them to know. You will look back on him one day – and he will seem so far below you –

Another bang on the door

	And suddenly I'm crystal clear: you don't apologise for who you are. You don't hide. So it's time that I opened the door.
SAMI	Ruth –
RUTH	*(Loud.)* Silence me, will you? Try it. TRY it. Here I come –

She opens the door, the sound of outdoors

	,
	(Loud.) And there is no-one here at all
SAMI	because you don't see it, doesn't mean it's not there –

She's relieved and breathes out

RUTH	Though I see what you mean about the car. Do you think the swastika is a reference to my Jewish roots or is does it more generally denote my alleged fascism or acc-[use]

She breaks off as she sees it – to SAMI, the silence is worrying –

SAMI	What?
RUTH	*(Gentle.)* Stay where you are. Stay where you are.
SAMI	what? What is it?
RUTH	It's cat

,

and it's dead and they've put its blood onto the front door and – a baby's dummy in its mouth and left it here on the doorstep

There may be blood on her hands

SAMI	We should call the police
RUTH	*(As in 'no'.)* There's nothing they can do for cat, I fear.
SAMI	Are you okay?
RUTH	*(Quietly.)* I'm angry.
SAMI	What are we going to do?

CHARLIE speaks: THE FOURTH DAY

*

A TV Studio.

[in the original production, ONE was the actor playing ROBERTS, TWO the actor playing HARDIMAN, THREE the actor playing MURPHY, FOUR is CYPRIAN and FIVE is JUNIOR. The actor playing FLINT stays the same. The actor playing COPLEY was the host.]

HOST	Good evening. If you've seen the news this week you'll know her name – and, likely, you'll have an opinion. We're joined tonight by Professor Ruth Wolff, Director of the Elizabeth Institute – and our panel, independently convened as experts in their fields. This is Take the Debate.

Music, the panellists enter and sit down

	Thank you for joining us. Tonight: Do groups really matter? And if you're thinking 'no', I'd like to know where you've been for the last century of social history: if you know any women with the vote or gay married couples or see non-white faces on your screens. Wherever you stand on the issues, this is the fact: no human is an island. We don't drive change alone.
	In the studio tonight, the individuals on our panel, representing the groups with a stake in this incident, sit side by side, despite their disagreements. Is tonight's debate religion? Abortion? Is it race? Is it – should it be – simply medical ethics? What matters here is hearing all the points of view – as we take the debate.
ONE	Professor Wolff, I'm a minister and activist on behalf of CreationVoice, which is a non-denominational Christian group who works on political policy. Good evening.
RUTH	Good evening

ONE	In the current system, it's impossible to ensure that the religious beliefs of doctors don't impact on their patients, isn't it?
RUTH	I don't think it is – a doctor with a religious objection to a certain practice would state that themselves up front and recuse themselves / from having to treat it
ONE	But you didn't do that in this instance?
RUTH	No. The key point in this / situation
ONE	Sorry – why not?
RUTH	Because I had no moral objection
ONE	But also you're not Christian?
RUTH	No, I'm not –
ONE	And so you didn't feel the last rites were important. Your religious belief – your belief about religion – had an impact on Emily Ronan.
RUTH	It's nothing to do with important or not – the fact is, there was nothing to instruct the medical team to allow the priest access. The patient's own wishes – not those of her parents – but her own wishes were simply not clear to her medical team, or, of course, we would have followed them to the letter.
ONE	But you knew that her family was Christian.
RUTH	Yes – but not whether Emily was.
ONE	Your argument was that Emily could be seriously distressed by the knowledge of her

	impending death. Hence your decision to deny the priest access.
RUTH	That's right –
ONE	But if she was conscious enough to realise she was dying, why not simply ask her whether she was a Catholic?
RUTH	I –
ONE	Are you an atheist?
RUTH	I'm a doctor. I don't go in for groups –
TWO	I'm a medical ethicist and a lawyer, and among other things I work on behalf of the campaign against abortion. Reports suggest that Emily Ronan died of a botched abortion procedure. Did you perform it?
RUTH	I cannot talk to you about the specifics of a patient's care –
TWO	Can we hear the recording?
HOST	We can hear part of your conversation with Father Jacob Rice, who we did invite on our programme this evening and who declined to make any response. We'll hear part of it now.

We hear, from before:

RUTH	In which case I'm going to terminate it.
FATHER	I'm now going to walk calmly into Emily's room, Doctor – I'm sorry, can you get out of my way –

RUTH	Hey –
FATHER	Get out of my way –
TWO	'In which case I'm going to terminate it'. Those are your words. Was the priest trying to stop you from carrying out an abortion procedure?
RUTH	the conversation. I meant terminate the conversation. He was recording me / and
TWO	But Emily Ronan had an abortion at your institute?
RUTH	I can't give out details of Emily's care and that / was a condition of
TWO	The details are all over the press!
RUTH	That is *not* an indication that it's right for me to discuss them –
ONE	I mean, this is ridiculous – if we asked you if you cut off her hands, you'd still say 'no comment', even if you didn't – surely confidentiality doesn't extend to things that you *didn't* do?
RUTH	OK, I didn't perform the abortion, no.
TWO	Thank you. But you *are* pro-abortion?
RUTH	Yes
FIVE	So you're pro-choice
TWO	So had Emily Ronan had a Catholic doctor, he would have known that an abortion to a Catholic is a mortal sin / and

RUTH	*He* might well have taken the same decisions I did – if *he* understood that, pro-choice or anti-choice, the choice under scrutiny *here* is whether or not to see a priest.
ONE	Emily Ronan didn't get that choice.
RUTH	No, because, as her doctor, I was acting in the patient's best interests and in this instance, the best thing I could give her was a *peaceful death*.
TWO	But that isn't what she got. You were wrong.
	,
ONE	Your institute has about five hundred staff. How do you choose your doctors?
RUTH	By their ability to perform the task in hand
ONE	So someone's religion plays no conscious part in who you employ?
RUTH	It plays no part at all. We're doctors and we hire doctors. We're trying to cure a disease. The only thing that matters is qualified. We don't pry into people's lives.
THREE	I'm a senior reader in Jewish history and a specialist in the study of Jewish culture. Are you Jewish?
RUTH	I was born to Jewish parents. I don't subscribe to a religion.
THREE	… it's not a trick question, Doctor / Wolff. Many of us have noticed the ways in which attacks on you this week employ anti-Semitic tropes. You're a hugely successful, very visible, Jewish woman – and, as you'll

know, there's been support from Jewish groups for your position.

RUTH   I'm not.

              I appreciate the support – but, my identity isn't the issue. I don't go in for groups.

THREE   That confuses me when nearly 65% of the doctors you employ are women.

RUTH   Being a woman doesn't put me in a group –

THREE   But a moment ago you told us your only criteria was quality. Now you believe it's OK to discriminate to have more women?

RUTH   I think most people would agree that, for women / there is a systemic imbalance in our field and that the / opportunities

ONE   I think that's fair

THREE   this week, your Institute voted to employ a doctor in a high-ranking position, and that doctor was a Jewish woman. Her gender is important, but her Judaism isn't. Why? The Jewish people are also a minority – a minority in far smaller numbers than women –

She can't resist correcting the grammar, but almost unnoticeably

RUTH   The Jewish people is a minority, yes – look, we are trying to cure dementia. We pick the best people we can get. And some of them – are women.

THREE   Are you the beneficiary of any positive discrimination? You're born to Jewish parents, so you're Jewish. You're also a

	woman. Why is one characteristic worth more than another?
RUTH	We don't put our doctors in groups.

Other than the pause, this next section: fast

TWO	But – wait a minute – you do when it comes to abortion.
FIVE	I don't think we need to hear more about this [i.e. from TWO]
ONE	I think everyone deserves a chance to speak
TWO	Thank you. You said yourself, you're in favour. A Christian doctor might well be opposed.
RUTH	I'm not in favour. As a doctor, I'm neutral. I'm in favour of patient choice.
TWO	But can you be neutral about abortion if you've had one yourself?
	,
RUTH	*(Fast.)* I can't *believe* you've – OK, my private life was never part of / the deal –
ONE *(chorus)*	Wow
FIVE *(chorus)*	I don't think that's / a fair question
HOST	It's up to you, Professor, which questions / you [answer]
TWO	I asked a hypothetical / question!
RUTH	yes, I had an abortion, yes it was late-term and yes I have regrets but I would make the same call again if I were making it today – and the majority of people have open minds

and *understand* that people get to make their own choices – including me – though let me be clear, it's people like you / that are the root of the problem, grubbing through the bins of my teenage years and then sitting in moral judgment –

TWO   'People like me'

I'm here to try and put / to you people's concern

RUTH   to expose my life in the public domain? That doesn't make you a hero, it makes you a tabloid journalist – with the bloodthirsty morality of the Spanish Inquisition –

TWO   Many people think abortion is a choice made *too easily available* – and in Emily's case / one that should

RUTH   Emily did it at HOME. Went online, did her research, got hold of the drugs, and aborted her baby at *home* – now had we done it, in the hospital, she'd still be with us today – so that's all thanks to the Catholic Church – and the fascist politicians they enable – pouring Luddite hatred on a procedure which, every single day since it began, quite literally saves *women's lives* –

TWO   I'm not going to sit here and listen to this abortion-loving propaganda –

RUTH   Abortion loving? Say that to me again. Say that to any woman who has been through that – *horror*, but let's first acknowledge that the Catholic Church, which is *morally* opposed to abortion, has been openly

	corrupt since the twelfth century and is now most famous for its systemic abuse of children –
TWO	You clearly feel more strongly about abused children than murdered ones –
RUTH	No-one was MURDERED, the girl would have DIED ANYWAY.
TWO *(chorus)*	wait–
ONE *(chorus)*	Then – sorry – why not *let the priest see her?*
	,
FOUR	Professor Wolff, I'm an academic, author and activist specialising in the study of post-colonial social politics. Do you understand why people are angry?
RUTH	Clearly it's fun to ride the bandwagon.
FOUR	Speaking as a black woman, the picture of a privileged white academic using physical force to get a black man out of / a room is
RUTH	I didn't use physical force –
FOUR	I'm interested that you think you can interrupt me. But I'd like to hear the recording – can we?

We hear again

RUTH	Hey –
FATHER	Get out of my way –
RUTH	You have zero authority here. I don't know who the hell you are. You want to get uppity with me, then fine. But

	you're wasting your time because there is really no way I'm going to let you near that child
FATHER	Don't touch me –
FOUR	So you did use physical force?
RUTH	I touched his shoulder
FOUR	I think it sounds more violent than that –
RUTH	I think you weren't there – and so it doesn't matter what you think
FOUR	It doesn't matter what I think?
RUTH	No, no more than it matters what I think about the moon landing: I wasn't there and I don't know. You can all live in your personal realities, but nobody else has to join you there.
FIVE	Let's talk about your personal reality. I'm a researcher and the chair of a nationally recognised campaign group for the understanding of unconscious bias. Had the priest been white, would you have acted the same way?
RUTH	Yes. Of course.
FIVE	You went to a private school, didn't you, Professor?
RUTH	I don't see any relevance / in
FIVE	How would you describe your politics?
RUTH	I'd describe them as none of your business. And this is nothing to do with the incident I

	came here to clarify – in which I am defined one way: as a *doctor*.
FIVE	You're defined one way. As a doctor. You're not part of a group.
RUTH	I've only said that twenty times so far this evening, but I don't think I'm part of a group, no.
FIVE	I wish that was something I was able to say. But people force me to remember the groups I belong to when I walk down the street. Society groups us: *that's the thing it does*. You get to ignore your groups – as a white woman of a certain age, of a certain class – because you're in the elite groups.
ONE	Hang on – I don't think a *woman* is an / elite group!
THREE	Elite groups, I think, need to / be [thought about more in …]
FIVE	I'm saying that the Professor gets to see her groups only when they suit her. But what if you're not white? What if you're religious? What if you're in a group which gets less status – less freedom – less privilege –
RUTH	I have absolutely no idea what you mean
FIVE	You think 'doctor' over-rules every other type of identity. But speaking *now*, in this socio-political moment, from a contemporary perspective, I disagree –
ONE	A 'woke' perspective isn't something any of us need to / hear

FIVE	This is supposed to be a variety of viewpoints, and a 'woke' perspective / might
RUTH	Oh *god*
THREE *(chorus)*	I think if we're going to talk about elite groups, there's a bigger conversation
ONE *(chorus)*	I agree / but it
RUTH	A 'woke' perspective – a 'woke' perspective – the use of language makes one want to *weep* – *woke* means *'awakened'* – from what? *from sleep?* – it sounds like you're a member of a cult, / it's the language of spiritual conversion – when in fact, it's *one view* and if that's your view, that's your view, but it's not intrinsically *better* than any other view – other people's views are not *asleep*
FIVE	Professor – I didn't use that word
	First, I didn't use the word 'woke'. She did. Second, your definition of that word is binary: you're woke or you're not. Mine isn't, my definition of what it means to be 'woke' is much more expansive.
RUTH	Right. Well, for me, a *doctor*, language is *precise* – a diagnosis has to be specific.
FIVE	So – what? you're discounting a whole history, a whole system of ideas, because you don't like the nasty word 'woke'? Woke is an attempt – and an honest attempt – to create a consciousness of people who aren't like you.
RUTH	And *this* is not about me

FIVE	It's so *upsetting* that you won't *understand*, you think you're *above* what we're saying to you. You're a doctor, yes, but you're a human being too.
RUTH	Astonishing
FIVE	Am I wrong?
RUTH	No, you're mixing things together which aren't related – and when you mix up all your colours you only get brown –
FOUR	And brown is bad, is it?
FIVE	Exactly – that's exactly / it –
RUTH	What is your problem
FIVE	My problem is educated white people shoving black people out of the way and then behaving like they have every right to do so. My problem is thousands of years of oppression and its legacies in the world we live in now, in the language you're happy to use. My problem is that you see it as my problem.
RUTH	I'm not sure I'm responsible for my ancestors
FIVE	Then who the fuck is?
HOST	I'll have to intervene here and apologise for that language – and ask you not to swear – we're live with Professor Ruth Wolff and this is *Take the Debate*.
FOUR	Professor, do you like to be addressed as Professor?

RUTH	I don't mind – it's a word like any other
FOUR	It's a word you wear that says you get to speak – isn't it?
RUTH	I didn't get that title for Christmas, it's the result of quite a lot of *work*
FOUR	But Professor, part of the anger here is about who *owns* language, who gets the right to make things mean. Who gets to choose. The guardians of the status quo. The gatekeepers who block the doors and stop us getting through.
RUTH	Us? Who is us? I'm not a gatekeeper –
FOUR	You blocked a man from getting through a door. And that action for many people was symbolic, given that he was a priest and that he was black.
RUTH	What I can't abide is this endless dividing up of people into tribes and smaller tribes of smaller tribes. You cut humanity in half enough times, eventually it ceases to exist.
FIVE	It was people like you who cut the world in half in the first place – we are at the end of a whole history of / this
RUTH	But now we all get to choose who we are –
FIVE	But everyone has bias. And none of us can switch our bias off –
RUTH	I'm – I have a little friend, comes to my house some nights in the week to do her homework, a friend of mine, she was born a boy but now, since I've known her, at this

	point, for her, she's a she, as far as she's concerned, you know, she wears female clothes: it's what you're saying: she gets to choose. And that is fine by me –
FOUR	And I bet you have black friends too – and that isn't what she said –
RUTH	and this idea that I somehow hate black people / – I don't even
FOUR	I'm not accusing you of hatred, we are talking about something deeper and more complicated, it's the air we all breathe, in the language we speak –
RUTH	It really is rather low-risk, isn't it, all these battles fought on the plane of language –
FIVE	Language is step one – because some of us have to push back before we get to choose, select how we are described. You don't do groups, to you it's 'political correctness', but for people who look like me, it's the right to self-determine using language.
RUTH	Words are words –
FOUR	'Words are words'. Can we hear the recording again?

The recording again

FATHER	Get out of my way –
RUTH	You have *zero* authority here. I don't know who the hell you are. You want to get uppity with me, then fine. But you're wasting your time because

	there is really no way I'm going to let you near that child.
FOUR	You called him 'uppity'.
RUTH	Yes. Uppity. Adjective. Above one's station. High-handed. Yes.
FOUR	And you're aware that that word has a specifically racist connotation?
RUTH	No. It's an adjective that means 'above one's station' and 'high-handed'.
FIVE	It's a racist word – it has a history / of racist
RUTH	Well, I didn't know that – and I certainly didn't intend / to be
FOUR	It's not about intention. It's the act. And it seems to me perfectly possible that without intending to, you stepped into a long tradition of dismissing people of colour – of shutting down their voice
RUTH	All because of a word
FOUR	But uppity implies another word. Uppity is followed by a noun. For years, for hundreds of years, my people were referred to using that name, which is too poisonous even to speak aloud on this programme. You know the word / I mean, I think –
RUTH	In the heat of the moment, I / made a decision
FOUR	Would you mind if I continue? As a black woman, it astonishes me that you dismiss the whole idea of labels or titles or names. But I'm talking about a particular word – a

single word that is one hell of a lot more
than a *word*. But if words are words, then say
that word. On this programme. Now. Call
me that word.

,

RUTH	My intention with that patient / was extremely clear
FOUR	I asked you to call me that word
RUTH	No
FOUR	I thought words were words.

,

RUTH	No
FOUR	*(Quiet.)* So you do understand that there are wider sensitivities, that there is a *history* here which carries for me a certain amount of anger and for you a certain amount of guilt. You do understand on some level that there is a context bigger than this single incident.
RUTH	Yes. Of course –
	I'm completely in favour of people getting to –
	,
	and the truth is I'm so tired
FOUR	Me too
RUTH	and the truth is, I don't know
	I didn't mean to – it was about the patient –

FOUR	And so can we expect an apology?
RUTH	For what?
FOUR	For anything you feel might merit an apology

,

The camera pushes in on RUTH. This could be the apology.

RUTH	As a doctor, I did nothing wrong –
HOST	I'm going to go now to Minister for Health, Jemima Flint, who's arrived with us live from Westminster tonight –
FLINT	That's right, very happy to be here –
HOST	What's your take on everything you've heard?
FLINT	Well, full disclosure: I've known Ruth since I was a very junior doctor – and she was always pretty formidable. It's important to me as a senior woman in medicine that we don't victimise a senior woman in medicine – but at the same time, your panel and people in the wider country are taking a keen interest in this case. So it feels appropriate for us to look more closely at Ruth's conduct so that in a neutral and reasonable manner we can take a clear view of what happened on the day of Emily's deeply regrettable death – so that's what we're going to do –
HOST	A formal inquiry?

FLINT draws breath –

| FLINT | Yes. |

*

The broadcast is over, immediately we switch to afterwards – FLINT talking to someone else

	Is it raining yet out there?
RUTH	You turned on me. You turned on me –
FLINT	And what did you expect?
RUTH	That you'd stick to your fucking word
FLINT	I cannot be seen to back someone running round tipping over every sacred cow she comes across –
RUTH	DisLOYAL. DIS. LOYAL.
HOST	Ladies, could you keep your voices down – there's still an audience
FLINT	There are things more important than you. I'll fund that new building –
RUTH	Of course you will –
FLINT	and you won't be there to see it. It's the thing you never understood, Professor. You have to *compromise* to get yourself some power, swallow a few pills because without any power you are *powerless*, ergo you can't DO ANYTHING. And you getting to speak your truth is only worth so much – and it's not as much as hospitals or nurses. That's ego, not integrity. Maybe it always was.

FLINT has slightly lost her cool. So she makes to leave and then turns –

What d'you call a leader with no followers, Ruth?

Just an old lady out for a stroll.

*

A taxi

RUTH   Can we stop? Pull over – stop – I'm getting out –

It pours with rain. RUTH is soaked. Perhaps she screams at the rain. Drums. It rains and rains and rains. As it stops raining. RUTH puts the kettle on.

*

RUTH's house

RUTH   You're here late

                And you've smashed my certificates.

SAMI   'A little friend'. OK so I heard what you said. And my parents didn't know and like it was obvious – and – I defended you, I –

                – and so everyone gets to choose who they are except for when it suits you to *choose who I am* – and actually isn't that exactly what you did to that girl – like decided she wasn't Christian because it suited what *you* thought, and now I'm your next little project – I hope you *fucking literally DIE* –

                And you don't like me using that word, but did you ever think it's maybe not that I'm new and like wrong but that your old way got *old* – that it's like *CHANGE* – but no, you're right Ruth – you are like one hundred percent right – you are *so fucking right* but you are also *alone* – so I hope you're happy

and just so you know, it's not a choice, it's not like options. It's not a set thing, this or this, it's not something you can like crush down into a symptom – it's me –

I didn't think that was like *us* – I thought we were [...] – and yeah I smashed your certificates. Because who even *are* you without them?

You're at home and you're on your own and you *know* [everything] and you're right and I hope that you literally literally die –

RUTH   I'm sorry, Sami – come back – I'm really sorry.

But SAMI is gone.

'Literally die.'

CHARLIE speaks: DAY, and then says:

CHARLIE   I don't know what day it is.

CHARLIE looks at RUTH.

RUTH   Doorbell.

CHARLIE   How long now since you saw her?

RUTH   Days and days. I don't know

CHARLIE   Longest ever?

RUTH   Yes indeed

CHARLIE   Doorbell –

RUTH	I gave her keys, remember
	And again
CHARLIE	Doorbell –

RUTH stands up, expecting SAMI. It isn't SAMI.

| RUTH | Ah. I suppose I had better let you in. |

The FATHER smiles, without meaning to. He has been at the door.

	The irony is not lost on me.
FATHER	Thank you. I didn't stay til the end of the tribunal, so I haven't / heard
RUTH	Struck off. Discrediting my profession. Ten years. By which time I'm too old to practice anyway. So the drawbridge is up and the door slammed shut. Irony. I know.
	,
FATHER	I'm sorry.
RUTH	Shall we have a cup of tea in the garden? There's still some light left.
FATHER	I'd like that
RUTH	It'd be an insult to thank you for telling the truth – not least as you were under oath – but what you said was [generous]
FATHER	the only thing I could have said.
	The more I think about it, the more I think it couldn't have been any different. As a priest, I couldn't have acted differently. As a doctor, nor could you.

RUTH	I did the only thing I could have done?
FATHER	– as a doctor. Yes.
RUTH	I wish you'd seen fit to say that at the tribunal.
FATHER	You and I both are the representative of a set of ideas – of the mission of a much wider group. 'The people like me. The progress of the ideas I believe.' We can't jeopardise that for one person's benefit –
RUTH	My benefit, you mean
FATHER	Or mine. My own egotistical feeling of 'I'd done the right thing'. The ideas that this [collar] stands for are sacred. If I'd said – in public – 'she was right as a doctor to turn me away', my little truth would be a wider lie. It's a million miles from personal. I'm nothing more than a dog collar.
RUTH	And I'm a white coat.
	And there was me, thinking Jesus spoke the difficult truths and let come whatever came –
FATHER	Jesus didn't live in the digital age.
RUTH	We crucify them differently now.
	,
FATHER	Though that death only amplified his life – and his ideas. His suffering only highlighted all the things he'd stood for.
RUTH	Suffering's not a symbol to the person going through it. You've seen people die. It's a solo sport. And it's not very often ethereal

	and calm – it's scratching and struggling and bodily fluids spraying around – and then, very suddenly, silence. For all we try and scoop up our lives into a firm story, the ending is always the same. One person's worth of flesh, going cold in a zip-up bag.
FATHER	But the ending isn't always the same. In faith, the endpoint doesn't mean the end. Death's just a bump in the road.
RUTH	We're so far apart, you and I, aren't we? Body and soul.
FATHER	Every person is a city full of people. We all contain a thousand different selves, and – they can't all be equally important. We choose which selves we want to put in charge. You've got medicine. I've got God. Something – one thing – rises to the top.
RUTH	Medicine is faith. God, I used to say that to my juniors. What's the difference between a criminal assault and a surgical procedure?
FATHER	I don't know –
RUTH	A qualification in medicine.
FATHER	Or – only one of them is an act of love.
	It's a warm night
RUTH	My hands are stone. I haven't spoken to anyone like this for a long time.
	I might smoke a cigarette. Join me, by all means. Only don't be surprised that a doctor smokes.

FATHER	Doctors smoke. God lets bad things happen. We love our parents, but we put them in homes. We love nature, but we will destroy it. 'People' isn't simple.
RUTH	I bet that's not a thing you say on Sundays.
FATHER	not everything's worth saying. Even honesty is a relative good.
RUTH	Oh, tell that to medicine. 'The patient cannot be lied to.' But does the truth fill us with hope? Hope is the silver bullet. One day someone will do a study, use numbers to prove how effective it is and – it will change everything. If a lie means hope, that lie could save your life.
FATHER	In my line of work, we've known that a long time.
RUTH	Well you should have told us
FATHER	Well you should have listened.
RUTH	Yes
FATHER	Difficult to *hear* each other over all the history, crashing around us like waves
RUTH	It's so hard, isn't it? So, so, so hard.
	I want to say I – I didn't see your colour, your race / when
FATHER	It - it isn't what you saw. It's what you didn't see. Or wouldn't see.
RUTH	And *(clicks her fingers)* I'm a racist. Final diagnosis.

The FATHER looks at RUTH. He's gentle but firm.

FATHER　　　　The good news is: it's always been a
　　　　　　　treatable condition. A dose of humility.
　　　　　　　Some learning: learning to see the history
　　　　　　　you're standing on. Learning to be gentle
　　　　　　　when you're handling the bruises. Learning
　　　　　　　to see how much harm has been done.

　　　　　　　'

RUTH　　　　　I have – I mean, I will. I know: it's not just
　　　　　　　black and white

She realises, too late, closes her eyes – he smiles. And then:

FATHER　　　　Except - the times it is.

　　　　　　　'

RUTH　　　　　Here's a question –

FATHER　　　　Yes?

RUTH　　　　　You couldn't have read the last rites over
　　　　　　　her body.

FATHER　　　　No. When you're dead, you're dead. You
　　　　　　　have to be alive. A hundred bishops could
　　　　　　　pour holy oil over the body and chant the
　　　　　　　sacrament in full ceremonial regalia – and
　　　　　　　your sins are still your sins. It's an apology,
　　　　　　　a forgiveness before you leave

RUTH　　　　　an apology before the end –

FATHER　　　　or when you fear it's ending –

RUTH　　　　　Yes.

　　　　　　　'

I feel things are ending. The post-war institutions, the post-war ideals. The public good that blossomed after peace. All the things they fought for. Starting to crack.

FATHER   I like being here at the end of a period. Who wants the golden age?

RUTH   Does it feel like faith is ending?

FATHER   It feels like it's shedding a skin. Finding new forms. It terrifies me sometimes. But then, that's God's gift – the turning world. Forward motion. You keep going to find out the ending, trying to find the beauty in the mystery 'til you do.

RUTH   Only sometimes the mystery is boring. The days all run over and into each other – these days. I garden. People still look at me strangely in the supermarket. I try and read but it's hard.

FATHER   Hard to re-enter the real world?

RUTH   I think it's my first visit. I'm not sure I like it. How could I? I've had a human heart beat like a bird in my hand. I've held a new-born baby we'd already pronounced dead as she clicks her eyes open and cries. I've seen old eyes stretching upwards in their final minutes, breath rattling as life rolls away, one old man's skin blossoming into gooseflesh in the moment of death, halfway through the punch-line of his joke. Smile still on his face. As a doctor, you stare right into human existence. Watching it begin and end, begin and end, begin –

and we end up in those wide, white
corridors, all of us end up there, watching
the ceiling spool over our head, rolled along
a corridor, under the horrendous lighting –
it's waiting for us, the hospital. The starting
line and the end of the story. The final date
on the gravestone. We should build hospitals
as beautifully as churches.

FATHER   says the doctor to the priest.

RUTH   From above we're opposites, but there,
                we're the same. When you're old and lying
                on a ward, it's not mystery you'll want, but
                doctors. You're not the priest then. You're
                the patient. I'm saying, in the end, it's me
                you'll come to when you have your heart
                attack.

FATHER   And it's God you'll pray to when someone
                you love dies.

RUTH   I didn't, actually. Pray. I didn't pray.

                'when someone I loved died'.

                I've spent the last decades of my life fighting
                a brutal, ugly, merciless disease. Alzheimer's
                is [terrible] – well, I'd take cancer anyday.
                Your brain's a tall set of drawers with all
                your memories laid in, the most recent up
                here, ink still wet on the paper, down to
                baby's first ladybird at the bottom – and that
                disease sets a fire burning hot on the top.
                Your short-term memory's the first to go
                to ash, then the flames eat their way down
                through the drawers – and before you know

it, you have really no idea who you are. No memories, no history – no you.

Not that we made it to total oblivion. Charlie, my partner, was still lucid half the time, though not remembering – and I had to put fences up, gates, like for a toddler, all the knives in a room and lock the door sort of thing – I'd come in and the hobs would be turned on, if you can imagine that, the smell of the gas – and it was in a more lucid moment that a decision was apparently made that the way the story ended, where the line was drawn, was going to be a matter of – well – choice.

FATHER   Charlie – it was suicide?

RUTH   You probably aren't familiar with the exit hood.

FATHER   No

RUTH   Thick plastic bag goes over your head. Big elastic band round your neck. You take enough sleeping pills to knock you out. You hold the band tense. You wait – to fall asleep. It chills my blood. A hypoxic death, is the medical [term]. Charlie did some research, met with a woman who knew the routine, read a hundred things online. I had – completely inadvertently – planted the seed: someone had tried the same thing on the ward, I talked about it at home – and then, years later, I come home late and –

            that music is on and the kettle's cold.

	and I remember there was a plastic bag on the kitchen worktop and I suddenly realise that's it gone – and what it was for.
FATHER	You'd talked about it, the two of you?
RUTH	Can you imagine? No. The goodbye would have been impossible. There was a letter. But we knew, I think. I think we knew.

,

FATHER	And you were the one who found
RUTH	the body? No. I heard the music, I felt the kettle. I was crystal clear: I knew. I made the phone call – and I waited for the knock on the door.

It's only when the people arrive that you realise your person is gone. Their little place now vacant. I remember walking out later that morning, 5am or something, I could see them taking croissants into a hotel, all in a little basket.

And Charlie   was   dead.

That plastic bag had sat on there for days. I don't know if I looked at it and didn't recognise what it really was because I didn't want to know. I don't know if the reason I didn't know is genuinely because I didn't know.

FATHER	Charlie didn't want you there – at the end? Present, I mean –
RUTH	I wasn't invited. With my career, too many ways I could have got hold of pills, and

	Charlie chose a method to protect me from blame. It's manslaughter. You have to be alone: you can't be touched, you can't allow anyone in. Better not even to be in the room.
FATHER	you really think they would have come down on you / if?
RUTH	Yes.
FATHER	Because?
RUTH	Against the law. And I'm a doctor.
FATHER	you're a person too
RUTH	I think I'm a doctor more.

*

CHARLIE	You shouldn't say that
RUTH	And you shouldn't have killed yourself
CHARLIE	I couldn't have forgotten us, sweetheart. I couldn't come to that.
RUTH	I wanted to be there at the end
	I wanted to be there
	Every time a memory is accessed it is *eroded*, worn away, and so by remembering you I am forgetting you. At this point you're a virus in my brain – and I don't see the present because I'm chained to the past, the perfect past, the action complete, the thing *gone*. I'm not here.
CHARLIE	Me neither.

RUTH	And I'm not funny any more. You thought I was funny.
CHARLIE	Do you miss me or do you miss you?
RUTH	What's the difference? I miss the way you looked at me. I miss what you saw. I miss having a million dimensions.
CHARLIE	When you did what you did, what might your patient have gained?

RUTH walks to the kettle and switches it on. It starts to boil.

RUTH	A peaceful end

CHARLIE smiles as if 'see?'

CHARLIE	And
RUTH	And hope, I suppose.
	False hope.
CHARLIE	I'm not sure there's such a thing. Hope's hope, isn't it? [If] you feel it then it's there

,

RUTH	Oh Charlie I miss you so much

She, for the first time, sobs.

The kettle clicks off.

She looks up and CHARLIE has gone. She looks at the plastic bag, folded neatly on the table. She touches it.

,

RUTH is on the phone. We shouldn't know whether this scene moves forward in real time, or takes us back round to the beginning.

which

which is it

Hello, yes, sorry – my name is Ruth Wolff, double-f

which is it (god, you'd think I'd know this)

which is it I need if someone's died? a body, yes –

no, not urgent – I'm sure. yes. Yes. I'm crystal clear.

I'm a doctor

It ends

For a complete listing of
Methuen Drama titles, visit:
www.bloomsbury.com/drama

Follow us on Twitter and keep up to date
with our news and publications
@MethuenDrama